Interacting with Saints
in the Late Antique and Medieval Worlds

HAGIOLOGIA

Études sur la sainteté et l'hagiographie – Studies on Sanctity and Hagiography

Volume 20

Comité de Rédaction – Editorial Board

HAGIOLOGIA

Anne-Marie Helvétius Gordon Blennemann Philippe Castagnetti
Stefanos Efthymiadis Stéphane Gioanni

BREPOLS PUBLISHERS

2023

Interacting with Saints in the Late Antique and Medieval Worlds

Edited by
Robert Wiśniewski, Raymond Van Dam and
Bryan Ward-Perkins

BREPOLS

© 2023, Brepols Publishers n. v., Turnhout, Belgium.

All rights reserved. No part of this publication may be reproduced, stored in a retrieval system, or transmitted, in any form or by any means, electronic, mechanical, photocopying, recording, or otherwise without the prior permission of the publisher.

D/2023/0095/124
ISBN 978-2-503-60558-6
E-ISBN 978-2-503-60559-3
DOI 10.1484/M.HAG-EB.5.133151
ISSN 1378-1006
E-ISSN 2565-9553

Printed in the EU on acid-free paper.

Table of Contents

Abbreviations 7

Robert WIŚNIEWSKI, Introduction 9

I
Seeing and Hearing the Saints

Robin M. JENSEN, Icons as Relics, Relics as Icons 17

Maria LIDOVA, Placing Martyrs in the Apse: Visual Strategies for the
Promotion of Saints in Late Antiquity............................. 47

Julia DOROSZEWSKA, Saintly In-betweeners: The Liminal Identity
of Thekla and Artemios in their Late Antique Miracle Collections... 79

Arkadiy AVDOKHIN, Resounding Martyrs: Hymns and the Veneration of Saints in Late Antique Miracle Collections 97

Xavier LEQUEUX, Les saints myroblytes en Orient et en Occident
jusqu'à l'an mil: Prolégomènes à l'histoire d'un phénomène
miraculeux.. 123

II
Local and Cosmopolitan Cults

András HANDL, Reinvented by Julius, Ignored by Damasus:
Dynamics of the Cult of Callixtus in Late Antique Rome.......... 141

Stephanos EFTHYMIADIS, The Cult of Saints in Constantinople
(Sixth-Twelfth Century): Some Observations 161

Anna LAMPADARIDI, The Origins and Later Development of the
First Italo-Greek Hagiographies: The *Dossiers* of the Sicilian
Martyrs Agatha, Lucia, and Euplus.............................. 181

III
Constructing Paradigms

Ian WOOD, The Lives of Episcopal Saints in Gaul: Models for a Time
of Crisis, *c.* 470–550. 213

Michał PIETRANIK, Saints and Sacred Objects in Eastern Roman
Imperial Warfare: The Case of Maurice (582–602). 229

Nikoloz ALEKSIDZE, Martyrs, Hunters and Kings: The 'Political
Theology' of Saints' Relics in Late Antique Caucasia. 249

Abstracts. 269

Index of Saints, Persons, Places, and Subjects 277

Abbreviations

AASS	Acta Sanctorum (Antwerp & Brussels: Société des Bollandistes)
BHG	*Bibliotheca Hagiographica Graeca* (Brussels: Société des Bollandistes, 1895, 1909, 1957); *Bibliothecae Hagiographicae Graecae Actuarium*, ed. by François Halkin (Brussels: Société des Bollandistes, 1961)
BHL	*Bibliotheca Hagiographica Latina* (Brussels: Société des Bollandistes, 1949, 2nd edition); *Bibliothecae Hagiographicae Latinae Novum Supplementum*, ed. by Henryk Fros (Brussels: Société des Bollandistes, 1986)
CCSG	Corpus Christianorum. Series Graeca (Turnhout: Brepols)
CCSL	Corpus Christianorum. Series Latina (Turnhout: Brepols)
CIL	Corpus Inscriptionum Latinarum (Berlin: Reimer)
CSLA	The Cult of Saints in Late Antiquity Database:<http://csla.history.ox.ac.uk>
GCS	Die Griechischen Christlichen Schriftsteller der ersten (drei) Jahrhunderte (Leipzig & Berlin: De Gruyter)
MGH Scr.	Monumenta Germaniae Historica. Scriptores (Berlin: Weidmann)
MGH SRM	Monumenta Germaniae Historica. Scriptores Rerum Merovingicarum (Hannover: Hahn)
PG	Patrologiae Cursus Completus. Series Graeca (Paris: Migne, 1844–55)
PL	Patrologiae Cursus Completus. Series Latina (Paris: Migne, 1841–49)
PLRE	*The Prosopography of the Later Roman Empire*, Vol. 1, AD. 260–395, ed. A. H. M. Jones, J. R. Martindale, and J. Morris; Vol. 3, AD. 527–641, ed. J. R. Martindale (Cambridge: Cambridge University Press, 1971, 1992)
SC	Sources chrétiennes (Paris: Cerf)
SECP	*Synaxarium Ecclesiae Constantinopolitanae e codice sirmondiano nunc berolinensi adjectis synaxariis selectis (Propylaeum ad Acta sanctorum novembris)*, ed. by Hippolyte Delehaye (Brussels: Société des Bollandistes, 1902)

Introduction

Robert Wiśniewski
(University of Warsaw)

The cult of saints is one of the most fascinating religious developments of Late Antiquity and most spectacular aspects of religious life in the Middle Ages. Christians admired martyrs already in the second century and gathered at their tombs to celebrate the anniversary of their martyrdoms, 'both in memory of those who have already finished their course, and for the exercising and preparation of those yet to walk in their steps', as the second-century *Martyrdom of Polycarp* puts it[1]. But for a long time Christians believed that they could call God, whom they addressed as 'Our Father', without any mediators. It is only in Late Antiquity that they began to think that their prayers would be more effective if supported by other people, dead or alive, considered to be efficient intercessors. Symptomatically, when in the sixth century Barsanuphios and John, holy monks and spiritual guides in the region of Gaza, were asked how one should pray to God directly, they gave the following answer: 'You should say: "Master, have mercy on me, for the sake of the holy fathers; forgive my sins, through their intercessions"'[2].

The first glimpses of the new attitude toward saints, perceived now not only as examples to follow but above all as powerful friends of God, able to connect earth and heaven, can be seen in the second half of the third century as attested by the graffiti from the *Memoria apostolorum* in the place known as *Ad Catacumbas* on the via Appia, asking Peter and Paul for their prayers.

---

[1] *Passio Polycarpi* 18.
[2] Barsanuphios and John, *Ep.* 706.

Interacting with Saints in the Late Antique and Medieval Worlds, ed. by Robert Wiśniewski, Raymond Van Dam, and Bryan Ward-Perkins, Hagiologia, 20 (Turnhout, 2023), pp. 9–14.
© BREPOLS ⁂ PUBLISHERS   DOI 10.1484/M.HAG-EB.5.133632

But this practice was not very intensive[3] and the phenomenon gained momentum only in the fourth century, when its new aspects developed: monumental shrines built over the tombs of martyrs, belief in power of their relics, and celebrations of their feasts.

From this point on the cult of saints developed very rapidly, but when developing it constantly changed and adapted to new conditions and demands. Moreover, although it quickly reached almost all regions of Christendom, in some of them it kept or grew very specific features. This evolution concerned many aspects of cult. Some saints, often of obscure origin, quickly gained popularity throughout Christendom, whereas others, despite good literary dossiers from the start, did not attract much cultic attention. Also, types of sanctity changed through time: while the martyrs always attracted cult and were heroes of hagiographical literature, other major models of sanctity, such as monks and bishops, had their ups and downs. The ways in which saints were active varied as well, and their presence was visualised in different ways in different places. New literary genres, presenting the sufferings, the lives, and the miracles of saints developed and at the same time the material side of cult became ever more elaborate. An interesting interplay arose between visual and textual images of saints, which referred and alluded to each other. Finally, the boundary between the role played by visual images and material remains of saints began to blur, as cultic representations appeared alongside the narrative ones.

This volume seeks to capture the dynamic of these processes, showing both those aspects of cult which changed quickly and those which remained stable for a long time. It studies the cults of various regions, from Gaul to Italy to Anatolia to Georgia, with a particular interest in the two greatest centres of the cult of saints: Rome and Constantinople. The book discusses the early third-century beginnings of the cult of saints, the explosion of new cults and practices in the fourth and fifth centuries, and later developments in Merovingian Gaul, the Byzantine empire, and the early medieval Caucasus. It studies changing vectors and patterns of the cult and changing needs and the actors behind them. Of course, this collection of articles, touching upon various features of cult (from sensory aspects to literary history, to interaction with ecclesiastical, lay, and military politics), has no ambition to present the entire field in a systematic way. But it does want to show how various elements of cult evolved in response to changing needs and circumstances, and

---

[3] Antonio E. Felle, 'Late Antique Christian Graffiti: The Case of Rome (Third to Fifth Centuries CE)', in *Cultic Graffiti in the Late Antique Mediterranean and Beyond*, ed. by Antonio E. Felle & Bryan Ward-Perkins (Turnhout: Brepols, 2021), pp. 57–76 (on pp. 60–62).

INTRODUCTION

in constant interaction between the established saints and new generations of believers.

The book is divided into three sections. The first of these studies specific practices, the second particular cults in three regions of Christendom, the third particular patterns of talking about saints and using their power. Section One, entitled *Seeing, Hearing, and Feeling the Saints,* focuses on the sensory experiences of those who visited the martyrial shrines. While our knowledge of what people heard, smelled, and saw (in reality or in a dream) might be mediated by texts, the four chapters in this section collect and study evidence that has been largely overlooked even by those who are familiar with late antique Christian literature. In the opening chapter, Robin JENSEN examines the development of the visual representation of saints. She shows that the phenomenon may have begun much earlier than we usually think. She also draws attention to chronological congruity between the emergence of the cult of images and relics, and draws several parallels between the ways in which these two types of holy objects were perceived, venerated, or criticised. In a corresponding chapter, Maria LIDOVA focuses on representations of saints in late antique churches, and studies the connection between the image, the sacred place, and liturgical action. She also examines how the strategies used to visually promote the cult of specific saints evolved between the fourth and the seventh century. The topic of the representation of saints is continued in the following chapter, which, however, is based on a different type of evidence. Julia DOROSZEWSKA deals with verbal descriptions of two martyrs known from the Greek collections of their miracles: St Thekla, venerated in Seleucia in Isauria, and St Artemios, whose cult fully developed in Constantinople. These texts were written in a similar ritual context, and both saints are pictured in them as liminal beings. However, their images differ greatly. Thekla can be gentle or enraged, but appears always in her own person. Artemios hides his identity and acts like a trickster. When trying to explain these differences Doroszewska studies the connection between the two models and both iconographic and earlier literary traditions. Arkadiy AVDOKHIN, also drawing extensively from collections of miracles, shows the role of liturgical chant in both the festive and daily function of the healing shrines of the Greek East. He emphasises that listening to and singing hymns, usually hardly noticed in scholarship on the cult of saints, was not only a common experience but also a powerful way of coming into ritual contact with the saints. In the last chapter in this part, Xavier LEQUEUX studies yet another way mediated by the senses of coming into contact with saints. He collects, for the first time in modern scholarship, the evidence of the cult of the myroblytes, or the saints whose graves were believed to produce miraculous effluents, generally oil. The literary evidence of this phenomenon, astonishingly rich, can be found throughout late antique and early medieval Christendom.

The second section, *Local and Cosmopolitan Cults*, closely studies the development of specific cults in particular cities and regions, each time over an extended period of several centuries. It opens with a study of the development of one cult in one city. András HANDL shows how the cultic status of Callixtus of Rome changed over time. This contested leader of the Christian community in Rome, remembered mostly by a hostile treatise written by one of his opponents, was an unlikely candidate for a successful cult. And yet, little more than a century after his death, he had fully become one of the famous Roman papal martyrs. This process involved several stages of the monumentalization of his tomb and the construction of a story of his martyrdom which merged topographical information and local traditions. In the second chapter of this section, Stephanos EFTHYMIADIS deals with a city that attracted rather than exported cults. He touches upon the richness and variety that characterized the cult of saints in Constantinople between the inauguration of Hagia Sophia (537) and the Latin conquest of the city (1204). With a very meagre set of local martyrs, hardly reflecting the prestige of the second Rome, Constantinople imported and produced cults on a massive scale. But in spite of its status as the imperial and patriarchal capital, the city did not have a consistent policy in the field of the cults of saints. This largely resulted from the fact that this scene had many actors. The emperors, patriarchs, and aristocrats promoted specific cults for various, often personal reasons, while different groups of immigrants brought saints from a variety of places of origin. The result of this was a rich cultic landscape with a few constant elements and a lot of change. In the last chapter in this part, Anna LAMPADARIDI shows a complex literary history of martyrial cults from one region. She studies the hagiographical dossier of three Sicilian saints, Agatha, Lucia, and Euplus, showing relations between subsequent versions of their stories. These stories evolved and proved to be a powerful instrument, helping to spread their cults beyond the isle, particularly to Constantinople. These three martyrs belonged to a very narrow group of western saints who gained fame and cult in new Rome.

The saints, their relics, and stories about them quite early became instrumental in justifying different practices, customs, and policies. Already in the early fifth century, the hagiographical corpus of Pachomius served to integrate the congregation founded by its hero and strengthen a certain model of monastic life. In the same period discoveries and translations of relics became a powerful weapon in ecclesiastical conflicts. In this early period, however, we

INTRODUCTION

can see only the beginnings of fixed patterns of using the saints' power. Section Three, *Constructing Paradigms*, shows how, in three different regions of Christendom, such patterns developed. Ian WOOD studies the evolution of the hagiographical image of the holy bishops in late antique Gaul, from that of ascetic heroes, which dominated in the late fourth and early fifth century, to more worldly figures in a later period. These *vitae* not only fuelled the veneration of local church leaders but also provided models for the behaviour of bishops in the post-Roman world. Michał PIETRANIK explores the rise of a different pattern, not in the writing about saints, but in interacting with their material remains. He addresses the question of how and why the relics of saints started to be used in military campaigns in the East. His chapter shows that while emperors began to strive for the saints' protection at an early period, during the reign of Maurice we can see not only an intensification of such practices, but also a change in their character: commanders did not pray any more at the tombs of saints before going to war, but took the relics of Christ and the Holy Virgin with them. In the final chapter, Nikoloz ALEKSIDZE studies literary strategies that served to legitimate Georgian and Armenian kingship in the early medieval hagiography of Caucasia. He traces, in particular, the development of literary motifs in which the stories of saints and their cults were combined with old narrative patterns, rooted in Iranian culture, thus creating a new literary model characteristic of the hagiography of this region.

All the chapters in this volume originate from selected papers presented at a conference on *The Cult of Saints in Late Antiquity*, held at the University of Warsaw in 2018. This meeting gathered students of cult and hagiography at different stages of their careers, working on texts, images, and objects related to this phenomenon. It was organised as one of the final acts of an ERC-funded project which aimed to collect and study the textual evidence of the cult of saints from its beginnings up to 700, from all regions of late antique Christendom and written in all its languages[4]. This project, based at the Uni-

---

[4] ERC Advanced Grant *The Cult of Saints: a Christendom-wide study of its origins, spread and development* (340540). The project was directed by Bryan Ward-Perkins, and its Warsaw group by Robert Wiśniewski. The core of the team consisted of Nikoloz Aleksidze (evidence in Georgian and Armenian); Sergey Minov (Syriac); Gesa Schenke (Coptic); Efthymios Rizos, with Julia Doroszewska, Nikolaos Kälviäinen, and Christodoulos Papavarnavas (Greek literary texts); Marta Tycner, Ben Savill, Marta Szada, David Lambert, Philip Polcar, Frances Trzeciak, Matthieu Pignot, Stanisław Adamiak, and Katarzyna Wojtalik (Latin); Paweł Nowakowski, with Małgorzata Krawczyk (Greek and Latin epigraphy); and Marijana Vuković (the *Martyrologium Hieronymianum*). Additional support and advice for the evidence in Syriac, Coptic, and Georgian and Armenian was provided respectively by David Taylor, Arietta Papaconstantinou, and Theo van Lint. The database was designed by Jeremy Worth. Several other people willingly shared their expertise and contributed to specific records.

versity of Oxford with a major offshoot in Warsaw, has already produced two collective volumes and several studies authored by its team members[5]. But, even more importantly, this team has combed as systematically and completely as possible the corpus of literary sources, papyri, and inscriptions in Greek, Latin, Syriac, Coptic, Georgian, and Armenian, assembling the evidence of all aspects of the cult of saints, from constructing their shrines to naming children after them and dancing at their feasts. The identified pieces of evidence have been collected and presented, together with an English translation of the original source and at least a basic contextual commentary, within an electronic database that allows the user to search for attestations of a specific cultic activity in a specific region, time, type of evidence, and language. It makes it possible, for instance, to find all the churches dedicated to St John in Syria, or all the inscriptions commemorating the apostles in the sixth century. The team members and other scholars have found this instrument enormously useful in their research, and we hope that many readers of these words will share this experience. The database is freely accessible[6]. Please, try it out, even as you read this book.

---

[5] *Culte des saints et littérature hagiographique. Accords et désaccords*, ed. by Vincent Déroche, Bryan Ward-Perkins & Robert Wiśniewski, Monographies du Centre de Recherche d'Histoire et Civilisation de Byzance, 55 (Leuven: Peeters, 2020); *Cultic Graffiti in the Late Antique Mediterranean and Beyond*, ed. by Antonio E. Felle & Bryan Ward-Perkins (Turnhout: Brepols, 2021).

[6] http://csla.history.ox.ac.uk.

I

Seeing and Hearing the Saints

Icons as Relics

Relics as Icons

Robin M. Jensen
(University of Notre Dame)

Introduction

The Carolingian document known as the *Opus Caroli Regis* (or *Libri Carolini*) responded to the Seventh Ecumenical Council's definition of the veneration of icons as properly orthodox (787) by clearly distinguishing images from relics. Briefly, the *OCR* states 'They [the Greeks] put almost all the hope of belief in images, while we [venerate] the saints in their bodies, indeed preferably in their relics, or even in their clothing, according to the ancient tradition of the Fathers'[1]. Such a statement not only asserts that images are distinctly different in kind from relics, but also that they have no direct link to the saints they depict. Images, unlike relics, lack actual holy matter or even contact with holy matter and so are not worthy of veneration. Because they are not consecrated by virtue of such proximity, they are not *res sacratae*. Moreover, relics, as parts of saints' bodies, will one day experience resurrection, while images are forever consigned to the earthly realm. Images

---

[1] *Libri Carolini*, 3.16, ed. by Hubertus Bastgen (Hannover and Leizig: Impensis Bibliopolii Hanhiani, 1924), p. 138: 'Illi vero pene omnem suae credulitatis spem in imaginibus conlocent, restat, ut nos sanctos in eorum corporibus vel potius reliquiis corporum, seu etiam vestimentis veneremur, juxta antiquorum patrum traditionem'. The Acts of the Seventh Ecumenical Council (II Nicaea) clearly affirm the veneration of both relics and images as part of the orthodox faith.

Interacting with Saints in the Late Antique and Medieval Worlds, ed. by Robert Wiśniewski, Raymond Van Dam, and Bryan Ward-Perkins, Hagiologia, 20 (Turnhout, 2023), pp. 17–45.
© BREPOLS ❧ PUBLISHERS   DOI 10.1484/M.HAG-EB.5.133631

are merely likenesses that depend upon a human artist's ability and skill in working with base material[2].

Unlike the Carolingian critics of images, the eighth-century Byzantine opponents of holy images made no explicit defence of relics and their sanctity. They maintained that the Eucharist is the true image of Christ and allowed the figure or symbol of the cross (without a corpus), but they apparently took the holiness of relics for granted. As John Wortley has pointed out, no evidence exists to suggest that Byzantine iconoclasts ever attacked relics as such or denied their sacred potential[3].

Nevertheless, Christian theologians in the later Middle Ages and sixteenth-century Protestant reformers both tended to liken relics and images, although espousing quite different opinions. For example, as Jeffrey Hamburger observes, the thirteenth-century Dominican Henry Suso believed that both images and relics functioned as exterior signs that assisted the 'interior fragile human memory'[4]. Suso made little distinction between images and relics and kept images of the saints along with crosses and relics as devotional aids. Suso also maintained that from earliest times 'many saints of the New Testament also made for themselves diverse pictures for the incitement of their devotion; they kept by them certain images or crosses; besides [they kept] near them several relics and other similar things'[5]. Thus, as Hamburger concludes, 'images are classed with relics without a moment's justification'[6].

By contrast, during the Protestant Reformation, both images and relics were condemned as idols, but the opinions of individual reformers varied. Martin Luther, for instance, resolutely condemned the cult of relics but out of his relatively tolerant position on images did not link the two in

---

[2] *Libri Carolini* 3. 24, pp. 153–54. See Thomas Noble, *Images, Iconoclasms, and the Carolingians* (Philadelphia: University of Pennsylvania Press, 2009), p. 200; Celia Chazelle, 'Matter, Image, and the Spirit in the Libri Carolini', *Recherches Augustiniennes*, 21 (1986), 163–84. The author wishes to thank this volume's editors for their excellent suggestions for revision of the earlier draft of this essay, some parts of which have been rephrased and incorporated into her forthcoming book, *From Idols to Icons: The Emergence of Christian Devotional Images in Late Antiquity* (Berkeley: University of California Press, 2022).

[3] John Wortley, 'Images and Relics: A Comparison', *Greek, Roman, and Byzantine Studies*, 43 (2002/3), 161–74.

[4] Jeffrey Hamburger, 'The Use of Images in the Pastoral Care of Nuns: The Case of Heinrich Suso and the Dominicans', *Art Bulletin*, 71 (1989), 20–46 (p. 28). Here Hamburger quotes Suso, *Horologium sapientiae*, ed. by P. Künzle, *Heinrich Seuses Horologium Sapientiae* (Spicilegium Friburgense: Texte zur Geschichte des kirchlichen Lebens, xxiii, Freiburg: Universitätsverlag, 1977), 597. 25–26: 'Ut per exteriora signa interior fragilis humana iuvaretur memoria'.

[5] Hamburger, p. 29 and Suso, 597. 26–30.

[6] Suso, p. 597. 29.

any significant sense[7]. Although some reformers, like Luther, distinguished images from relics, others, like John Calvin tended to equate them. Calvin declares: 'When God is worshipped in images, when fictitious worship is instituted in his name, when supplication is made to the images of saints and divine honours paid to dead men's bones, and other similar things, we call them abominations as they are'[8]. Heinrich Bullinger's treatise, *On the Origin of Error in the Worship of Saints and Images* (1529), was a fulsome condemnation of all the things he found to be idolatrous or heretical. Its thirteenth chapter, in which Bullinger focuses on the cult of relics, argues that the veneration of saints' remains and the expectation that they could provide miracles motivated the development of statues, shrines, and sacred images, which the naïve believed could produce the same effects. He also accuses devotees of considering both relics and images as if they were wonder-working gods[9]. Calvin's and Bullinger's judgments were widely shared insofar as most Protestant reformers condemned images and relics alike, and many sought to destroy them[10].

Although the Carolingians distinguished images from relics, examination of earlier Christian devotional prayer and corporate rituals generally confirms Bullinger's surmise that veneration of sacred images arose out of the cult of relics and remained intrinsically connected to it. The cult of saints' relics emerged during the fourth century when material aids to worship developed in a way that was unprecedented earlier. This was also the time when portrait-type representations of Christ, the Virgin Mary, and the saints also began to appear and even to displace narrative compositions, largely based on biblical or apocryphal stories. Such developments, along with the burgeoning practice of pilgrimage to holy sites, reflected the increasing belief that material objects could facilitate encounters with

---

[7] Luther's position on images changed to a more defensive one after the iconoclastic attack of figures like in Karlstadt. He had a much more consistently negative position on relics, however. For more on this see Sergiusz Michalski, *The Reformation and the Visual Arts* (London: Routledge, 1993), pp. 34–36.

[8] John Calvin, *The Necessity of Reforming the Church*, trans. by J. K. S. Reid, *Calvin Theological Treatises*, Library of Christian Classics, vol. 22 (Philadelphia: Westminster Press, 1954), p. 188.

[9] Heinrich Bullinger, *De origine erroris libri duo* (1539) 59R, accessed through http://dx.doi.org/10.3931/e-rara-2603. See also Carlos M. N. Eire, *War against the Idols: The Reformation of Worship from Erasmus to Calvin* (Cambridge: Cambridge University Press, 1986), pp. 86–88.

[10] See Eamon Duffy, *The Stripping of the Altars: Traditional Religion in England, 1400–1580* (New Haven: Yale University Press, 1992), part III, chapters 11–13 (The Attack on Traditional Religion I–III), pp. 377–477; and Lee Palmer Wandel, *Voracious Idols and Violent Hands: Iconoclasm in Reformation Zurich, Strasbourg, and Basel* (Cambridge: Cambridge University Press), esp. pp. 116–18.

transcendent realities — a belief that would eventually include holy icons as among those objects. From the fifth century onwards, Christian devotional practice as well as corporate liturgy gradually incorporated reverence for both types of material objects: relics and icons, both of which engaged the senses of sight and touch in new modes. While this evolution is well known to historians of late antique and early medieval Christianity, this essay will attend to the stages of that development, arguing that the veneration of relics chronologically preceded the emergence of portraits of Christ and the saints by only a few decades and specify the ways in which relics and icons initially were both similar to and different from one another in this formative period.

The Emergence of Saints' Relics and Holy Portraits

According to Robert Wiśniewski, the earliest dated textual reference to the veneration of a saint's bodily relic comes from a polemical report about a certain Lucilla, an African matron who carried the bone of a martyr with her to church and kissed it before receiving communion[11]. This report comes from Optatus of Milevis, who recounts the incident and regards it as an outrage. Lucilla was unable to bear the archdeacon Caecilian's rebuke and so, with a group of conspirators, fabricated charges against him that led to the so-called Donatist schism at the turn of the fourth century[12]. Dating this event to that time is problematic as Optatus actually composed his treatise against the Donatist bishop Parmenian sometime after 363 and he may have exaggerated or invented his story. Nevertheless, whether true or not, it must have been possible for a late-fourth century reader to believe Optatus's account to be at least plausible[13]. Thus, relic veneration was being practiced by at least some individuals or groups by his time, although perhaps not as early as 300. Although other historians have noted earlier reports of Christians venerating saints' bodily remains (including those of St Polycarp), as Wiśniewski observes, such accounts' dates are disputed and, more importantly, do not

---

[11] Robert Wiśniewski, *The Beginnings of the Cult of Relics* (Oxford: Oxford University Press, 2019), pp. 17–21.

[12] Optatus, *Contra Parmenianum* I. 16–18; for Wiśniewski's argument for dating, see Wiśniewski, pp. 17–18.

[13] Wiśniewski, p. 17, n. 30 cites several historians who accept the Lucilla incident as historically accurate including Peter Brown, *The Cult of Saints. Its Rise and Function in Latin Christianity* (Chicago: University of Chicago Press, 1981), p. 34; and Patricia Cox Miller, 'Differential Networks: Relics and Other Fragments in Late Antiquity', *Journal of Early Christian Studies*, 6 (1998), 113–38.

describe actual fragmentation or dispersal of body parts for the express purpose of their veneration nor any miracles associated with them[14].

By comparison, the earliest saints' portraits also began to appear toward the end of the fourth century, a century and half after the first identifiably Christian pictorial art emerged (around the beginning of the third century). In its earliest phase, Christian art featured symbolic figures like fish, doves, shepherds, and anchors, that were soon followed by scenes drawn from Bible stories (e.g., the temptation of Adam and Eve, Abraham offering Isaac, Jonah emerging from the mouth of the sea monster, the Three Hebrew Youths in the fiery furnace, Daniel with his lions, Moses striking the rock in the wilderness, the baptism of Jesus, Jesus multiplying loaves and fish, and Jesus healing the sick and raising the dead). Most of the extant examples derive from funerary contexts, especially on the walls and vaults of the Roman catacombs and on the fronts, sides, and lids of stone sarcophagi (Fig. 1). Biblical figures also decorated the walls of the mid-third century house church in Syria's Dura Europos house church. While a unique, extant example, the evidence from Dura suggests that third-century Christians elsewhere also may have decorated the walls of their worship spaces with pictorial art.

Even while such works of pictorial art were being painted or sculpted on Christian tombs, early Christian teachers assailed idolatry and particularly ridiculed the cult images of pagan gods. However, these same teachers offer little or no objection to visual depictions of biblical subjects. Presumably, they did not regard these images as idolatrous insofar as they did not invite veneration; they were unlikely to receive the kinds of cultic honours that pagans extended to the statues of their gods. While the standard narrative images were edifying or even inspiring, they would not have prompted a devotee to offer them prayers or sacrifices. Unlike the gods' images, they were not designed to represent — much less mediate the presence of — an otherwise invisible divinity or absent saintly person.

By the mid-fourth century, scenes drawn from biblical stories were augmented by compositions that were not as clearly derived from canonical or extra-canonical stories (e.g., depictions of Jesus giving the law to Peter and Paul). Yet, even while workshops serving Christian clients expanded the catalogue of their subjects, they apparently produced few portrait-type representations of Christ, the Virgin Mary, the apostles, and other saints. Existing depictions of such holy persons, presented frontally and apart from any narrative context, typically as full-figure or bust-type figures gazing directly back at the viewer, are practically unknown before the mid- to late fourth or

---

[14] Wiśniewski, pp. 10–12; cf. *Martyrdom of Polycarp* 18.

Fig. 1: Front frieze of an early Christian sarcophagus with scenes from the Old and New Testaments, Rome. Early fourth century. Now in the Vatican Museo Pio Cristiano.
Photo credit: Vanni Archive/Art Resource, NY.

Fig. 2: Bust image of Christ, Catacomb of Commodilla, Rome. Late fourth or early fifth century.
Photo credit: De Agostini Picture Library/Bridgeman Images.

early fifth century. A survey of the extant evidence reveals that, in general, while Christians did not eschew pictorial art, they avoided actual portraits. Possibly, these may have appeared to cross the line separating didactic images depicting historical/biblical episodes from idolatrous ones that, like the images of the gods, might prompt direct prayers or other veneration.

Documentary sources mention rare exceptions of early Christian portraits and describe them in condemnatory terms that supports making this distinction between narrative and portrait images. For example, Irenaeus of Lyon refers to an image of Christ supposedly made by Pontius Pilate that the sect of Carpocratians set up and venerated alongside images of Plato, Pythagoras, and Aristotle. He specifically accuses the Carpocratians of acting like pagans by crowning and offering various other honours to such objects[15]. Added to this is the apocryphal account of the Ephesian magistrate Lycomedes, who apparently commissioned a likeness of the Apostle John for his personal veneration in a domestic shrine. Contained in the fragmentary *Acts of John*, usually dated to the second or third century, John is described as scolding Lycomedes for treating his (John's) portrait in the manner of a pagan, by setting lit candles before it and draping garlands upon it[16].

As noted above, apart from these controversial instances recorded in documents, the surviving examples of earliest Christian art include hardly any actual portraits of saints or Christ. This lack is striking, considering the ubiquity of these kinds of objects in the surrounding culture. Pagan gods, emperors, heroes, civic benefactors, and ancestors all warranted full-length statues or bust portraits, usually identified by or inscribed with a dedicatory phrase. According to Dio Cassius, the Emperor Claudius resisted having more than one portrait set up for him because all the public buildings in Rome were already stuffed with statues and votives[17]. Early Christian sarcophagi also often feature portrait busts of the deceased (often a married couple), framed or set apart from the surrounding images by a shell or roundel. Sometimes a full-length, relief representation of the dead occupant of the tomb is present. However, these are not images of holy men or women. The near absence of portraits in early Christianity and, in particular, the rarity of free-standing statues suggests that, at least in the third and for most of the fourth century,

---

[15] Irenaeus, *Adversus haereses* I. 25. 6. On Marcellina and with discussion of the Carpocratian's alleged images, see Gregory Snyder, '*She Destroyed Multitudes*: Marcellina's Group in Rome', in *Women and Knowledge in Early Christianity*, ed. by Ulla Tervahauta et al. (Leiden: Brill, 2017), pp. 39–61. Parallel accounts are found in Hippolytus, *Refutatio omnium haeresium* VII. 32. 7 and Epiphanius, *Panarion* XXVII. 6. 10.

[16] *Acts of John* 26–29. The complicated textual history of this document makes it difficult to reliably date the above-cited section, although scholarly consensus usually accepts a date between the mid-second and mid-third century. This section that describes Lycomedes' portrait was, however, given as evidence of the apostle's repudiation of icons at the iconoclastic Council of Hieria in 754 as well as at the Second Council of Nicaea in 787. On the dating and construction of the whole document see Janet E. Spittler, 'Acts of John', in the *Brill Encyclopedia of Early Christianity* on-line and Splitter, 'Is Vienna hist. gr. 63, fol. 51v–55v a 'fragment?', *Ancient Jew Review*, May 6, 2019.

[17] Dio Cassius, *Historia Romana* XL. 5. 4–5.

Christians consciously repudiated these kinds of monuments because of their similarity to pagan 'idols'[18].

Significantly, the dominance of narrative art waned somewhat in the late fourth and early fifth century. This was around the time that the first portraits of saints (e.g. Peter, Paul, and the Virgin Mary) began to appear and, with them, an early bust portrait of Christ (Fig. 2). Within a century, representations of saints and Christ, formally arranged apart from specific narrative settings, numerically surpassed narrative scenes among the catacomb frescoes (Fig. 3) and began to occupy the most prominent places in churches, rendered in glittering glass apse mosaics (Fig. 4). These figures were distinctly different from the narrative scenes they supplanted. No longer representing any particular story, one assumes that they must have invited veneration of some kind. This might have worried those who could remember when Christians mocked their pagan neighbours for praying to inanimate images.

Noting the difference between devotional and narrative imagery is crucially important for understanding the nature and function of Christian iconography. The early narrative-based pictures might have been helpful for meditating on the meaning of sacred stories, but unlike Lycomedes' reported image of the Apostle John, they were not set up on or near altars and did not elicit offerings of crowns, candles, or garlands. Thus, until the later fourth century, most Christians appear to have avoided making or possessing portraits of Christ or a saint, possibly because, like Irenaeus, they regarded them as too similar to the repudiated pagan cult images.

When they eventually appeared in any numbers, the first Christian saints' portraits were relatively modest objects. Almost never life-size statues set up in public places or churches, they were often small images fused into gold glasses, like Agnes in the prayer posture (Fig. 5) or Peter and Paul adorning a child's funerary epitaph (Fig. 6). A set of apostles' busts (Andrew, John, Peter, and Paul) set into round frames adorn a recently opened fourth-century chamber in Rome's Catacomb of St Thekla, which journalists proclaimed

---

[18] Rare examples of Christian statuary do exist (e.g. the so-called statue of Hippolytus in the Vatican, which is likely a reconstruction, or the Christ statuette in the Museo Nazionale Romano and several extant fourth-century statuettes of the Good Shepherd, Jonah, or Peter and Paul). For studies of the exceptional examples of early Christian sculpture, see Heidi J. Hornik, 'Freestanding Sculpture', in *Routledge Handbook of Early Christian Art* (London: Routledge, 2018), pp. 73–85; Katherine Marsengill, 'The Christian Reception of Sculpture in Late Antiquity and the Historical Reception of Late Antique Christian Sculpture', *Journal of the Bible and Its Reception* 1 (2014), 67–101; and Neils Hannestad, 'How Did Rising Christianity Cope with Pagan Sculpture?', in *East and West: Modes of Communication*, ed. by Euangelos Chrysos and Ian Wood (Leiden: Brill, 1999), pp. 173–76.

Fig. 3: Christ with saints, from the Catacomb of Peter and Marcellinus, Rome. J. Wilpert, *Roma sotterranea: le pitture delle catacombe romane*, vol. 2 (Rome: Desclée Lefebvre and C., 1903), taf 252 (p. 258).

to be the oldest existing portraits of these saints[19]. The late fourth-century painted bust of Christ on the ceiling of a cubiculum in the Catacomb of Commodilla (Fig. 2) may be one of the earliest front-facing depictions

---

[19] See, for example, Tom Kington, 'Apostle images from 4th century found under street in Italy', *The Guardian* (US Edition), June 22, 2010: https://www.theguardian.com/science/2010/jun/22/apostles-images-john-andrew-italy.

Fig. 4: Detail from the apse mosaic, from the Basilica of SS. Cosma e Damiano, Rome, first quarter, sixth century.
Photo: Author.

of Jesus, as well as a very early representation of him as mature and darkly bearded instead of youthful and clean-shaven as he appears in earlier Roman iconography (cf. Fig. 1). Throughout the fifth and sixth century portraits of Christ, the Virgin Mary, or saints started to appear on a larger scale in mosaic in church apses, wall paintings, and tapestries (Fig. 7). Soon, haloes appeared to indicate the holy persons' sanctity[20].

Some scholars contend that these early portraits were not actually intended as objects of veneration like later, panel-painted icons. They maintain that the images were merely commemorative or votive gifts, meant to honour the saints or simply to call them to mind. For example, in their monumental history of Byzantine iconoclasm, Leslie Brubaker and John Haldon argue that, prior to the late seventh century, saints' portraits were accorded no special sanctity, much less mediatory power[21]. In this they concur with the historian Paul Speck, who earlier had asserted that no evidence supports

---

[20] See Irene Kabala, 'Halo', in *The Eerdmans Encyclopedia of Early Christian Art and Archaeology*, vol. 1, ed. by Paul Corby Finney (Grand Rapids, MI: Eerdmans, 2017), pp. 627–28.
[21] Leslie Brubaker and John Haldon, *Byzantium in the Iconoclast Era* (Cambridge: Cambridge University Press, 2011), p. 36. Also, Hans Belting, *Likeness and Presence: A History of the Image in the Era before Art*, trans. by E. Jephcott (Chicago: University of Chicago Press,

a Christian cult of images prior to the seventh century[22]. Although the art historian Katherine Marsengill aims to correct this standard position, she acknowledges: 'this has been the narrative, and little has changed in the fundamental assumption that portraits understood as mediating their prototypes did not exist in Christianity before saints' shrines introduced images of the saints into what would become Christian cult space — again not as venerable objects but as adjuncts to relics'[23].

Several surviving documents challenge this scholarly narrative and demonstrate that certain fourth- and fifth-century church authorities were evidently concerned about inappropriate regard being directed to paintings of holy men and women. For example, a brief canon from the Spanish Council of Elvira, dated to the early fourth century, simply states: 'There shall be no pictures in churches, lest what is reverenced and adored be depicted on walls'[24]. While the council's date (probably between 300 and 306), is uncertain, the general consensus is that Canon 36, which deals with images in churches, is genuine, although some scholars think it might be an interpolation and actually dates from the later fourth century[25]. Whether it is from the early or late fourth century, the wording suggests that worshipers were apt to offer inappropriate veneration to images on walls[26]. It is difficult to imagine that the perceived problem lay with biblical narrative scenes, so presumably the prohibition was directed against sacred images that were portraits of God, Christ, or of holy men and women.

1994), pp. 59–63. Here Belting suggests the late sixth or seventh century as the point at which images began to be equated with relics.

[22] Paul Speck, 'Wunderheilige und Bilder. Zur Frage des Beginns der Bilderverehrung', *Poikila Byzantina* 3, Varia 3 (1991), 163–247 (esp. pp. 164 and 227). See also Richard Price, 'Icons before and during Iconoclasm', published on Academia.edu.

[23] Katherine Marsengill, *Portraits and Icons: Between Reality and Spirituality in Byzantine Art* (Turnhout: Brepols, 2013), p. 27. Marsengill goes on to give countering examples, many of them noted below.

[24] Canon 36: *Placuit picturas in ecclesia esse non debere, ne quod colitur et adoratur in parietibus depingatur.* Text and translation in Karl Joseph Hefele, *History of the Christian Councils*, trans. by W. Clark (London: T&T Clark, 1894), p. 151. See also José Vives, *Concilios Visigóticos e Hispano-Romanos, España Cristiana*, Textos 1 (Barcelona: Consejo Superior de Investigaciones Científicas, 1963), p. 78.

[25] Primarily disputed by Maurice Meigne, 'Concile ou collection d'Elvire?', *Revue d'Histoire Ecclésiastique* 70 (1975), 361–87, who sees the canons as a compilation from a later date, allowing the first twenty-one canons to be dated to the turn of the fourth century and the others to later periods. For more on this dispute and a summary of different scholarly views, see the essay by Ste. Croix and appendix of Joseph Streeter, in Geoffrey de Ste. Croix, *Christian Persecution, Martyrdom, and Orthodoxy* (Oxford: Oxford University Press, 2006), pp. 99–105.

[26] Translation variants are discussed by Edwin Bevan, *Holy Images* (London: George Allen & Unwin, 1940), pp. 114–15; and Mary Charles Murray, 'Art and the Early Church', *Journal of Theological Studies*, 28 (1977), 304–45 (esp. p. 317, n. 2).

Fig. 5: Gilded glass with St Agnes. Fourth century, Rome.
Photo credit: Scala/Art Resource, NY.

Fig. 6: Apostles Peter and Paul. Epitaph of the child Asellus. Fourth century.
Now in the Vatican Museo Pio Cristiano.
Photo credit: Erich Lessing/Art Resource, NY.

Fig. 7: Icon of the Virgin and Child, tapestry from Egypt, sixth century, now in the Cleveland Museum of Art.
Photo: Creative Commons License.

The canon from the Elvira council is unparalleled among early conciliar documents but other fourth- and fifth-century textual evidence similarly attests that church officials worried that pious devotees might accord unsuitable veneration to portraits of Christ or the saints. Some even suggest that portraits are simply unacceptable as such. Although historians have questioned some of these sources' authenticity and suspect that they might have been fabricated by adherents of one or another side during the later Byzantine image controversy, others are almost certainly genuine.

Among the disputed documents is a well-known letter attributed to Eusebius of Caesarea and addressed to the Emperor's sister, Constantia, in which he refuses to provide her a portrait of Christ for her personal devotion. He insists that attempting to depict both human and divine natures would be either impossible or heretical. While this letter's authenticity has been challenged, many scholars accept it as genuine[27]. Another group of disputed documents is attributed to Epiphanius of Salamis (d. 403) and includes letters addressed to Bishop John of Jerusalem and the Emperor Theodosius I. In these, the writer decries images of the saints as false, stupid, mute, inanimate, and even dead — terms that earlier Christian apologists had applied to the cult statues of the Roman gods — and condemns those who would venerate them[28].

Doubts about the authenticity of these works of Eusebius and Epiphanius are balanced by two brief testimonies from Augustine of Hippo, one in

---

[27] Eusebius, *Letter to Constantia*, trans. by Cyril Mango, *Art of the Byzantine Empire, 312–1453, Sources and Documents* (Toronto: University of Toronto Press, 1997), pp. 16–18. This was included in the Iconoclasts' *Horos* of 754. The authenticity of the letter has been challenged, though widely (now) accepted as authentic. See Claudia Sode and Paul Speck, 'Ikonoklasmus vor der Zeit? Der Brief des Eusebius von Kaisareia an Kaiserin Konstantia', *Jahrbuch der Österreichischen Byzantinistik*, 54 (2004), 113–34. Among those who question the authenticity of this letter is Murray, pp. 335–36. Murray revised her opinion based on the challenge by Stephen Gero, 'The True Image of Christ: Eusebius' Letter to Constantia Reconsidered', *Journal of Theological Studies*, 32 (1981), 460–70. Another scholar who dismisses the letter's authenticity is Timothy Barnes, *Constantine and Eusebius* (Cambridge, MA: Harvard University Press, 1984), p. 401, n. 82.

[28] Epiphanius's texts include fragments of his letters to the Emperor Theodosius I and Bishop John of Jerusalem: texts and translations in Mango, *Art of the Byzantine Empire*, pp. 41–43. On the question of authenticity see Ernst Kitzinger, 'The Cult of Images in the Age before Iconoclasm', *Dumbarton Oaks Papers*, 8 (1954), 85–150 (esp. p. 93, n. 28); and Murray, pp. 336–38, which outlines the discussion up to the time of her writing. She notes that George Ostrogorsky initially accepted only the *Treatise* (or *Testament*) as authentic but after severe critique allowed that the *Letter to John of Jerusalem* could be authentic as well. See Ostrogorsky, *Studien zur Geschichte des byzantinischen Bilderstreites: Historische Untersuchungen*, vol. 5 (Breslau: Marcus, 1929), pp. 61–113. By contrast Karl Holl, 'Die Schriften des Epiphanius gegen die Bilderverehrung', *Gesammelte Aufsätze zur Kirchengeschichte II, der Osten* (Tübingen: Mohr Siebeck, 1928), accepted them all as genuine.

which he scolds his congregation for acting like pagans for worshipping columns (most likely images upon columns) and another in which he expressly warns them against idolatrously venerating tombs and pictures, presumably martyrs' shrines and their portraits[29]. Additional, albeit much later, examples are two certainly genuine letters from Gregory the Great to Bishop Serenus of Marseilles, written at the turn of the seventh century. In the first of these, written in July of 599, Gregory urges his episcopal colleague to cease destroying images on the walls of his church. While he commends him for warning his flock against idolatrous adoration of pictures, he also gives his famous dictum that images can serve as the Bibles of the illiterate:

> Furthermore, we indicate that it has recently come to our attention that your Fraternity saw some people adoring images, and you smashed those images and threw them out of the churches. And we certainly applauded you for having had the zeal not to allow anything made by human hands to be adored, but we judge that you ought not to have smashed those images. For a picture is provided in churches for the reason that those who are illiterate may at least read by looking at the walls what they cannot read in books[30].

While this text does not specify that the images Serenus destroyed were saints' portraits, Gregory's second letter, written in October of 600, reiterates his points and specifies that Serenus had, in fact, destroyed images of saints (*sanctorum imagines*)[31]. Thus, if bishops like Serenus were concerned about improper adoration of saints' images, something of the sort must have been taking place before the seventh century.

Perhaps the emerging fourth- and fifth-century portrait-type images were not actually intended to be objects of veneration, but the possibility evidently worried some church authorities like Eusebius, Epiphanius, Augustine, and Serenus. Moreover, this significant development in the content of Christian visual art could be viewed as part of the broader material turn in fourth-century Christian practice. The move, from primarily biblical narrative iconography to dominantly portrait images, takes place only a few decades later than the emerging

---

[29] Augustine, *Sermo* 198. 10 (Dolbeau 26.10); and *De moribus ecclesiae catholicae* 1. 34.

[30] Gregory I, *Registrum epistularum* IX. 209, trans. by John R. C. Martyn, *The Letters of Gregory the Great* (Toronto: Pontifical Institute of Medieval studies, 2004), vol. 2, p. 674. 'Praeterea indico dudum ad nos peruenisse quod fraternitas uestra quosdam imaginum adoratores aspiciens easdem ecclesiis imagines confregit atque proiecit. Et quidem zelum uos, ne quid manufactum adorari possit, habuisse laudauimus, sed frangere easdem imagines non debuisse iudicamus. Idcirco enim pictura in ecclesiis adhibetur, ut hi qui litteras nesciunt saltem in parietibus uidendo legant, quae legere in codicibus non ualent', ed. by Dag Norberg, CCSL 140A (1982), p. 768. 8–13.

[31] Gregory I, *Registrum epistularum* XI.10, CCSL 140A (1982), p. 874.

cult of saints along with the veneration of their bodily remains — a practice promoted by bishops like Damasus of Rome or Ambrose of Milan, in their efforts to identify the sites of saints' tombs and promote the cult of the local martyrs.

Undoubtedly, the increasing popularity of the cult of saints fuelled both the cult of relics and the production of holy images. Moreover, it seems that Bullinger's theory, that the cult of relics gave rise to the cult of images, might have been correct. It is also evident that these two, relics and holy portraits, are related in some way, and that one might even think of them as the two sides of the same coin. While one of them came first, the other followed not long afterwards. Like saints' remains, the portrait likenesses of holy men and women soon also became objects for devotion or the focus of prayer. It seems possible that the belief that contact with a relic made the saint more accessible actually fostered the rise and development of holy portraits. Yet, the cult of relics and the practice of venerating saints' portraits had significant differences along with their similarities.

Icons and Relics: Links and Similarities

Many surviving early documents imply direct connections among the cult of saints and the existence of their portrait images. This is evident in John Chrysostom's homily (encomium) on Meletios, sainted bishop of Antioch c. 360–81, delivered at the site of the saint's burial shrine on the day of his feast in 386. After observing how so many of the local members of his flock had given Meletios's name to their children, John went on to describe how popular the man's portrait also was:

> And what you did with the names you also did the same with his image: for many people inscribed that hallowed image on ring-heads, on stamps, on plates, on the walls of rooms, and everywhere, so that it was not only possible to hear that holy name, but also to see everywhere the figure of his body, and have a double means of consolation for his absence[32].

Chrysostom allows that Meletios's likeness carved on peoples' rings or hanging from their walls (presumably as panel paintings) would console those who grieved for their lost shepherd because they might still gaze upon his likeness after his death.

Other texts make connections between verbal and visual recollection of a saint's sufferings, both in vivid narrative form. For example, Gregory of Nyssa's encomium on St Theodore asserts that the impact of a devotee's visit

---

[32] John Chrysostom, *Homilia encomium in Melitium* 3, trans. by Efthymios Rizos, *Cult of Saints in Late Antiquity database*, CSLA E02056.

to the saint's tomb will be heightened by both the beauty of the architecture (the work of mason and carpenter) and the work of the painter who produced an image of the martyr and his brave deeds in vivid colours. Gregory describes the artist spreading out 'the blooms of his art', and 'having erected an image (*en eikoni*)' as 'if it were a book that uttered speech'[33]. Similarly, Asterius of Amasea (*c.* 350–410) describes the shrine of St Euphemia, in which a pious painter 'placed the whole story [of her passion] with vigour on a canvas and placed the painting near to the holy tomb'[34].

The links between verbal narrative, shrine, and visual image are especially evident in the work of the Spanish poet Prudentius (348–413). In his cycle of verses, the *Peristephanon* (*On the Crowns*), Prudentius recounts the gruesome deaths of fourteen martyrs including Peter, Paul, Lawrence, and Cyprian, along with a number of Spanish saints. While these compositions focus on the passions of these figures, they also describe the decoration of their martyria. In one poem, the author presents himself as a pilgrim *en route* to Rome, stopping at the shrine of St Cassian at Imola, close to Ravenna. As he came near the martyr's tomb, he looked up toward heaven and saw Cassian's portrait, painted in vivid colours: 'He bore a thousand wounds, his parts all torn and nicked. It showed his skin with small stabs, punched and pricked'[35]. The caretaker of the shrine then assured Prudentius that the image he saw was an accurate rendering of the saint, and went on to tell him the story of his martyrdom at the hands of wicked schoolboys, concluding with the admonition that he should observe Cassian's glory in full and shining colours.

While these texts imply that the scenes in the tombs were narrative images rather than portraits, what they may actually have been is difficult to ascertain (if they existed at all). Prudentius may have been inspired by existing imagery and expanded on what he saw in order to inspire his readers to make mental pictures of the scenes. In any case, although nothing quite like these extensive and elaborate images has survived, it seems unlikely that the shrines had no pictorial or portrait art. A reliquary, a tomb, or a martyrium would have been enhanced by the portrait of the saint it enshrined;

---

[33] Gregory of Nyssa, *In sancto Theodoro* (PG 46, p. 737), trans. by Mango, *Art of the Byzantine Empire*, 37–38.

[34] Asterius of Amasea, *Passio S. Euphemiae*, ed. by François Halkin, *Euphémie de Chalcédon* (Brussels: Société des Bollandistes, 1965), 4–8; trans. by Johan Leemans et al., *'Let Us Die That We May Live': Greek Homilies on Christian Martyrs from Asia Minor, Palestine and Syria (c. AD 350–AD 450)* (London: Routledge, 2003), p. 175.

[35] Prudentius, *Peristephanon* 9. 11–12, trans. by Len Krisak, *Prudentius's Crown of Martyrs* (London: Routledge, 2019), p. 100.

the image complemented the sacred remnant and was enlivened by recounting (in speech or text) the story of the martyr's trial, torture, and death. Both images and relics were joined to homilies on the saints' heroics or readings of the martyrs' acts, works that became almost as prominent a part of Christian official and popular piety as the proclamation of scripture[36].

Several fourth-century examples from surviving physical evidence may serve as useful, parallel examples. A painting, found in the Catacomb of Domitilla, depicts St Petronilla escorting the matron Veneranda into paradise (Fig. 8). Veneranda's tomb was deliberately selected to be close to Petronilla's remains, a burial *ad sanctos* that was believed to aid the ordinary dead in their attainment of a blessed afterlife. A domestic reliquary shrine below the current Roman basilica of Sts Giovanni and Paolo is set above and next to a set of paintings that presumably depicts saints whose relics it contains, possibly John and Paul, along with their companions Crispus, Crispianus, and Benedicta (Fig. 9)[37]. According to most interpretations of the iconography, representations of Sts John and Paul are to the right and left of the reliquary, while the adjacent walls display scenes of their companions' executions. Immediately below the relic opening is the image of a male saint, standing in the prayer pose. At his feet are two venerating figures, perhaps Pammachius, the owner of the house, and his wife, Paulina[38].

A fifth-century fresco in a chamber of the Catacomb of San Gennaro in Naples displays a bust portrait of St Januarius, standing in the orans posture between two flaming candles (Fig. 10). His halo includes a Christogram with the alpha and omega, and over his head are two tau crosses along with the dedicatory inscription 'Sancto Martyri Ianuario'. Although Januarius's relics were deposited in this Neapolitan catacomb, the bodies actually buried in this particular chamber are those of a child, Nicatiola and a woman, Cominia[39]. As in the case of Veneranda, we may presume that Nicatiola and Cominia were believed to be under the particular patronage of the saint.

---

[36] On the allowance for martyrs' *acta* to be read out in the liturgy on feast days, see the Council of Hippo (393), Can. 5 and the *Breviarium Hipponese*, can. 36D, ed. by Charles Munier, CCSL 149 (1974), p. 21. 43.
[37] See the fifth- or sixth-century *Martyrdom of Gallicanus, Iohannes and Paulus*; the *Notitia ecclesiarum Urbis Romae* (625/38) mentions the basilica, on the Caelian Hill, of Johannes and Paulus, martyrs of Rome under the Emperor Julian.
[38] See Giuseppe [Joseph] Wilpert, 'Le pitture della 'confessio' sotto la basilica dei SS. Giovanni e Paulo', in *Scritti in onore di Bartolomeo Nogara raccolti in occasione del suo LXX anno* (Città del Vaticano: Topografia del Senato, 1973), pp. 517–22. The difficulties of identifying the figures in the paintings are matched by the controversy over the site itself. A helpful summary in Lucy Grig, *Making Martyrs in Antiquity* (London: Duckworth, 2004), pp. 120–27.
[39] See Umberto Fasola, *Le Catacombe di S. Gennaro a Capodimonte* (Rome: Editalia, 1975), pp. 73 and 93; also, Hans Belting, *Likeness and Presence: A History of the Image before the Era of Art*, trans. by E. Jephcott (Chicago: University of Chicago Press, 1994), p. 82.

Fig. 8: Veneranda with St Petronilla, from the Catacomb of Domitilla, Rome. Third century. Wilpert, *Le Pitture*, taf. 213.

Fig. 9: Central fresco (St Pammachius?) from the Confessio in the Case Romane de Celio, basilica of SS Giovanni e Paolo. Photo: Author.

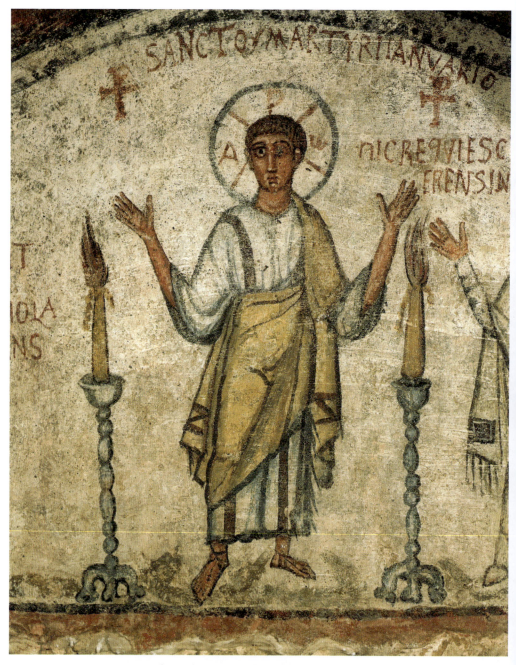

Fig. 10: St Januarius from the Catacomb of San Gennaro, Naples. Fifth century. Photo credit: DeA Picture Library/Art Resource, NY.

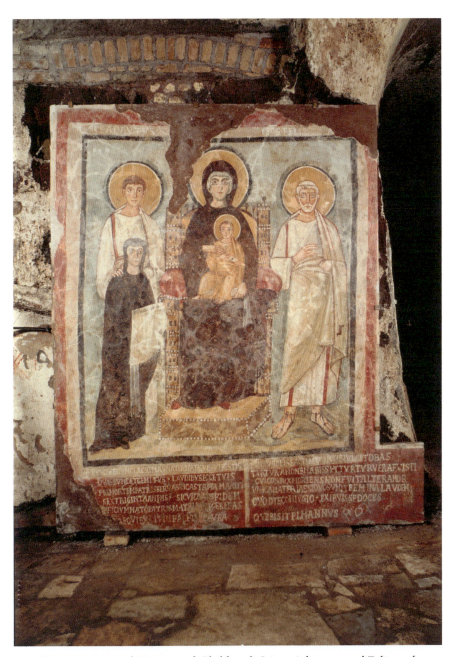

Fig. 11: Fresco with Virgin and Child with Saints Adauctus and Felix and deceased Turtura, from the Catacomb of Commodilla, Rome, ca. 528. Photo credit: Scala/Art Resource, NY.

A later, early sixth-century votive painting from the Catacomb of Commodilla depicts the enthroned Virgin Mary holding the baby Jesus (Fig. 11). Although the Virgin and Child are the immediate objects of the viewer's gaze, two saints, Adauctus and Felix, who were interred nearby, are shown as standing to either side. Adauctus presents a smaller figure on the left of the Virgin. The dedication below identifies her as Turtura and praises her for her faithfulness to her dead husband, likening her to a turtledove, who mates for life.

In each instance, the saint's pictorial representation has some of the qualities of a relic and is often set near to his or her actual bodily remains. In the Domitilla example, the viewer is assured that the saint's proximate remains have some benefit to the deceased Veneranda, even if her image is not itself the medium of aid. The depiction of Turtura displaying her devotion to the Virgin and Child suggests that the Sts Felix and Audauctus can play the role of mediators, presumably because of the physical presence of their buried bodies. Both images convey the idea that the intercession of Sts Petronilla, Januarius, Felix, and Adauctus are more reliable because of the proximity of their relics. In each case the image of the saint and his or her bodily remains are directly connected[40].

The connections between texts, images, and relics are evident, as homilists and poets alike draw their audience's attention to pictorial and portrait iconography. But it is also reasonable to suppose that they could be independent of one another. Not all relics were linked with portraits and not all saints' portraits were set up at shrines or in the proximity of a saint's holy relics. In these situations, one could be regarded as the equivalent of the other or perhaps even its substitute. This raises the question of how saints' relics were like and unlike their portraits and if they served different or similar purposes in devotional practices associated with the cult of saints.

Categorical Comparison of Relics and Images

Distinctions between relics and icons are not always easy to make. Some icons are said to be made by physical contact with the living saint or Christ (e.g. Mandylion of King Abgar); occasionally reliquaries might include a saint's portrait (e.g. the fifth-century Capsella Africana now in the Vatican Museum). These overlaps notwithstanding, icons and relics are similar to one another in at least three particular ways: their function, their treatment, and

---

[40] More examples and discussion of this subject in Robin M. Jensen, *Face to Face: The Portrait of the Divine in Early Christianity* (Minneapolis: Fortress Press, 2005), pp. 173–99.

their replicability or portability. They are different from one another with regard to their composition and material, their visuality, and how they are authenticated.

Function

Relics and icons are both devotional aids. Minimally, they provide a worshiper an object of focus. Depending on the viewer, they also serve as substitutionary recipients of ritual prayer and votive offerings or as instruments that connect devotees on earth with saints in heaven. While both are static objects, they are able to activate encounters. However, while their purposes are similar, they function differently. Whereas relics stimulate the devotee's sense of saintly presence and facilitate miracles from their tangible link to a saint's material body, icons work by representing a saint's corporeal appearance.

Put simply, both icons and relics signify something or someone beyond themselves. Relics, in their corporeal link to a saint's physical body, point beyond the earthly entombed body to the saint who is present in heaven. In a sense they work from the bottom up. Icons, likewise, point beyond themselves, although they are not connected to anything physically and materially contained in a tomb — or even on earth. Nevertheless, both participate in the reality of what they represent, even if they are derived from dynamically different sources. Moreover, relics and icons not only facilitate the presence of the saint, both act as conduits to saints for their intercessory assistance. Relics are more often credited with facilitating answered prayers or miracles. Nevertheless, the faithful can pray to saints and have their prayers answered without the benefit of relics or images, and not all relics necessarily or consistently provide miracles.

The two differ in regard to their facilitation of miracles. The healing power of relics is well-documented from the late fourth century onward. Ambrose authenticated the relics of Sts Gervasius and Protasius from the fact that they performed miracles of healing, and miracles attributed to the relics of St Stephen are prominent in Augustine's *City of God*[41]. By contrast, miracles associated with images are far less numerous in the fourth through sixth centuries, although some reports exist. One of the earliest accounts of an image believed to contain miraculous healing properties concerns a freestanding sculpture group at Paneas (Caesarea Philippi) described by Eusebius of Caesarea in the early fourth century. Apparently local Christians believed the statue depicted Christ healing the hemorrhaging woman. According to

---

[41] Augustine, *De civitate Dei* XXII. 8–10.

Fig. 12: Pilgrim Token of Saint Symeon Stylites. Sixth-seventh century. Photo: Walters Art Museum. Photo: Creative Commons License.

Eusebius, a miracle-producing vine grew up and touched the hem of Jesus's cloak that cured all manner of diseases[42]. Later examples of healing icons include the small tokens made from earth found at the base of the columns of St Symeon Stylites the Elder (d. 459) and St Symeon the Younger (d. 592). These tokens, bearing the image of one of the saints and composed from material permeated with the saint's sacred presence by virtue of its presence to his body, were reported to have performed miraculous cures. Because they were fabricated from sacred soil, they combine the characteristics (and powers) of the relic with the icon (Fig. 12). A passage from the seventh-century document, the *Miracles of Symeon* recounts an instance of this, when the

---

[42] Eusebius, *Historia ecclesiastica* VII. 18. Other ancient references include Sozomen, *Historia ecclesiastica* V. 21; Rufinus, *Historia ecclesiastica* VII. 8. 2 (a rather loose translation of Eusebius); Gregory of Tours, *Liber in gloria martyrum* 20; John Malalas, *Chronica* 10. 12; *Parastaseis Syntomoi Chronikai* 48.

saint tells the father of a son brought for a miraculous healing to depart, but first to take home the token (eulogia) of his dust, stamped with his face[43]. As Charles Barber expresses it, 'On the one hand, there is the material of the object, imbued with the saint's holiness. On the other hand, there is the image itself. Both are granted the priest to fulfil his desire for the presence of the saint'[44]. In even later centuries icons were reported to have effected miracles of various kinds from healing afflictions and defending against enemy invasion to more intimate wonders like speaking or emitting oil, blood, sweat, or tears[45].

Treatment

In practice, devotees may treat icons and relics in similar ways. From the earliest times, saints' portraits were deposited in or on altars, presented with lit tapers and votive gifts, and honoured with burning incense. Initially, these practices caused scandal. Irenaeus had objected to the Carpocratian Marcellina's displaying a portrait of Jesus as if it were an image of a pagan god, crowned and given votive offerings. The Ephesian magistrate Lycomedes supposedly set up the Apostle John's portrait on an altar in his bedroom, draped it with garlands, and set burning lamps before it, earning the rebuke of the saint himself[46]. Yet, the portrait of St Januarius in the Naples Catacomb depicts the saint standing between two tall, burning tapers (Fig. 10), as does the saint on the silver reliquary known at the Capsella Africana (see cover image). Both figures are depicted in the stance of prayer (arms outstretched) and flanked by two monumental candlesticks.

Both relics and icons also received kisses from their devotees, although that practice in regard to relics is clearly documented far earlier than for holy portraits. The Gallican priest Vigilantius, who was appalled by the practice of relic veneration, noted that devotees wrapped up bits of dust in precious

---

[43] Paul van den Ven, *La Vie ancienne de S. Syméon Stylite le Jeune (532–92)*, 2 vols., Subsidia Hagiographia 21 (Brussels: Société des Bollandists, 1962–70), lines 38–41. Text is quoted in Charles Barber, *Figure and Likeness: On the Limits of Representation in Byzantine Iconoclasm* (Princeton: Princeton University Press, 2002), p. 23.

[44] Barber, p. 23; also see Gary Vikan, 'Byzantine Pilgrims' Art' in *Heaven on Earth: Art and the Church in Byzantium*, ed. by Linda Safran (University Park, PA: Penn State University Press, 1998), pp. 229–66.

[45] For some examples see Dimitra Kotoula, 'Experiencing the Miracle: Animated Images and the Senses in the Burial Chapel of the Byzantine Saint', in *The Multi-Sensory Image from Antiquity to the Renaissance*, ed. by Heather Hunter-Crawley and Erica O'Brien (London: Routledge, 2019), pp. 86–106.

[46] *Acts of John* 27.

cloth, kissed them, and carried them ceremoniously into church surrounded by quantities of lit tapers[47]. The story, noted above, of Lucilla's kissing the bone of a relic before receiving the eucharist is another instance of this practice, at least as asserted by Optatus, and may be the earliest surviving documentary reference to the practice of kissing relics[48]. What is possibly the earliest extant textual reference to devotional kissing of icons comes from the transcript of a contentious theological dispute between Maximus the Confessor and Theodosius of Caesarea in 656 that ended happily with each of them kissing icons of Christ and the Virgin Mary[49].

Replicability and Portability

Primary relics are unique and derived from a single source, yet they are also endlessly divisible. The tiniest bit of bone has as much power as the whole body. The most famous instance of this might be the vastly divisible relics of the True Cross, which, according to Paulinus of Nola, cannot be diminished, no matter how much it is split up and disseminated. It seems, he says, to remain whole no matter how small the fragment[50]. They are also replicable. Tertiary relics are produced simply by touching the original with bits of cloth (*brandea*) or passing oil over it into small containers (*eulogia*)[51]. Sometimes merely gathering dust or soil from the area around the saint's tomb suffices. Such objects, though not directly or physically part of the martyr's remains, were credited with nearly equivalent power, even if holding a somewhat lesser status[52].

Icons are similarly replicable, but in a different way. Copies can be infinitely produced without any diminution of their representational capacity, because their validity is based on their following a prescribed pattern.

---

[47] Jerome, *Adversus Vigilantium* 4; on practices and rituals of relic devotion, see Wiśniewski, pp. 122–43.

[48] Optatus, *Contra Parmenianum* I. 16.1, see above. Other early examples are found in Jerome, *Ep.* 46. 8 and 108. 9.

[49] See Apocrisarius, *Disputatio inter Maximum et Theodosium* 4; ed. and trans. in Pauline Allen and Bronwen Neil, *Maximus the Confessor and His Companions: Documents from Exile* (New York: Oxford University Press, 2002), pp. 100–01. John of Damascus cites this reconciliatory kissing of icons in *Apologia* II. 65.

[50] Paulinus of Nola, *Ep.* 31. 6.

[51] On the subject of contact relics see Rebecca Browett, 'Touching the Holy: The Rise of Contact Relics in Medieval England', *Journal of Ecclesiastical History*, 68 (2017), 493–509.

[52] Particularly clear instances of this practice are described in Gregory the Great, *Registrum epistularum* IV. 30, and XIV. 12, when he offers *brandea* to the Empress Constantina in place of bodily relics of St Paul, or pewter ampullae (*eulogia*) containing oil that had been burning near Roman martyrs' shrines to the Lombard Queen Theodolinda.

Novelty is discouraged. Only rare examples are claimed to be originals made from life or by supernatural means (e.g., the Mandylion of King Abgar or the Kamouliana image of Christ) — and even these are reproduced and, in fact, must be, insofar as the originals have been lost. Most of the time, however, the image's likeness to its model was not precisely linked to a single original. Theoretically, they must reproduce their models faithfully, even if — in reality — they inevitably display geographic or chronologically-influenced differences in style, artistic skill, scale, and medium.

Both icons and relics are also portable; they can be moved around, given as gifts, or worn on one's body. They are not restricted to one place or type of space. While some are large or permanently installed in altars or on the walls of churches, many are intimate, personal, and small enough to be carried in the hand or enclosed in a pendant[53].

Composition and Material

The most obvious distinction between relics and icons lies in their composition and basic materiality. Relics are the found or rescued physical remains of saints' bodies or objects that contain sanctity by virtue of contact with them (e.g. fragments of clothing, fragments of the Cross, dust from a shrine, the chains of St Peter). Most icons are acknowledged fabrications of human artisans from materials selected for that purpose (e.g. paint, ivory, metal). Sometimes the icon is also a relic, like the small tokens made from the dirt beneath the stylite saints' columns that also bear his image.

Nevertheless, a fairly basic distinction suggests that relics should be exempted from a common definition of idols, that is, human-made figures, constructed from base materials, to which devotees offer prayers or veneration in place of absent or invisible holy persons or divine beings. Nor can relics imitate or pretend to be something they aren't. However, while relics are not constructed by artisans from stone, wood, paint, or metal, they are just as 'material' in their physical composition. Finally, unlike artistically fabricated images in paint, metal, ivory, or marble, relics ordinarily had no intrinsic value. They are, often as not, merely bits of bone or even dust. As Patrick Geary has noted, a 'bare relic' once separated from its context or outside of its identifying reliquary is 'unintelligible and incomprehensible'[54].

---

[53] An excellent study of this characteristic is in Julia Smith, 'Portable Christianity: Relics in the Medieval West (*c.* 700–1200)', *Proceedings of the British Academy*, 181 (2012), 143–67.
[54] Patrick Geary, *Furta sacra: Theft of Relics in the Central Middle Ages* (Princeton: Princeton University Press, 1978), p. 5.

Visuality

Unlike icons, relics are not *visual* depictions of a saint, nor is seeing the primary way in which they are encountered. Relics are not oriented to sight, but rather to the other senses — especially touch. In fact, they usually aren't visible at all, as they tend to be encased in closed containers (i.e. reliquaries), even though occasionally displayed to the faithful. Those who come to venerate them must trust that they are, indeed, present inside their opulent little boxes or crystal cases. Thus, ironically, although relics are definitively sensible and corporeal, most encounters with them are not; they rely more on spiritual than sensual perception.

Icons, by contrast, are manifestly visible. By definition, they are pointedly the subject of a devotee's gaze. Unlike relics, they actually have eyes that can meet those of the viewer. They also have lips that can be imagined able to speak and ears capable of hearing. Yet, icons are designed to direct the view beyond the visible to the invisible. They are not meant to be mistaken for something they are not. Thus, whereas fragmentary and aniconic relics disclose and confirm the potency of holy bodies, iconic portraits aim at disembodiment — they are stylized and formally flattened so that the physical form is unmistakably rendered as a two-dimensional figure. So again, ironically, the seemingly *visible* icon compositionally and conceptually aims at transparency.

Authentication

The validity of a saint's holy icon is not strictly dependent on an assured physical resemblance between model and image, even though iconophiles typically use the language of 'likeness' or 'similitude'. Their validity depends largely on their conformity to conventional, recognizable features. Furthermore, these traditional features are a basis for recognizing saints who appear in dreams or visions: they conform to those formulaic depictions, undoubtedly initially constructed by a first artist who probably was not working from a living model.

While authenticating icons depends largely on judging whether they are faithful copies of original prototypes, validating relics is a matter of evidence, documentation, and trust. Out of context their identity can be lost or forgotten. Establishing provenance or chain of custody is optimal, and official canonical procedures for guaranteeing relics' validity exist. But even then, believers normally must take them on faith, reassured by testimonies of miracles performed in their presence or by the precious metal and gem studded containers that encase the revered bits. In fact, accusations of false relics are known almost from that first recorded incident: that fourth-century African matron Lucilla, who brazenly carried a (suspected false) martyr's bone with her to mass and kissed it before receiving the consecrated host.

In conclusion, although the cult of relics preceded the emergence of devotional portraits of saints and Christ by some decades, the latter's emergence seems to have been to some degree prompted by the former and both, certainly, emerged out of the developing cult of the saints in Late Antiquity. Moreover, while they exhibit important differences, for example in the fact that images were not initially credited with facilitating miracles, both were tactile and visual instruments for a devotee to express veneration. Finally, a portrait, like a relic, is a point of attachment between devotee and object of veneration, and the story provides the necessary context for giving that point of contact power and meaning.

Placing Martyrs in the Apse

Visual Strategies for the Promotion of Saints in Late Antiquity

Maria Lidova

The cult of martyrs in Late Antiquity has been subject to a long tradition of research. As Kate Cooper notes, 'The rise of the cult of the saints has enjoyed particular historiographical prominence as a medium through which the transformation of Antiquity into the Christian Middle Ages was achieved'[1]. Various attestations to the veneration of martyrs have come down to us preserved in different media, the pre-eminence of which is often debated in scholarship. In his famous sermon given during the unveiling of the image of the Virgin in the apse of Hagia Sophia on 29 March 867, Patriarch Photios makes an interesting distinction between the visual and textual aspects of the veneration of saints:

> The stories of martyrs are contained in books, but paintings offer a much more vivid record. [...] those who see the pictures are more likely to imitate the martyrs than those to whom the stories are simply read[2].

This quotation offers an intriguing view on the role of media in the dissemination of the cult of saints and on the range of senses engaged in the

---

[1] Kate Cooper, 'The Martyr, the *Matrona* and the Bishop: The Matron Lucina and the Politics of Martyr Cult in Fifth- and Sixth-Century Rome', *Early Medieval Europe*, 8 (1999), 297–317 (p. 298).

[2] For discussion of this source and the cultural background of this sermon: Robin Cormack, *Writing in Gold: Byzantine Society and Its Icons* (London: George Philip, 1985), pp. 143–60 (p. 150). See also: *Φωτίου Ομιλίαι. [The Homilies of Photios]*, ed. by Basil Laourdas (Thessaloniki: Hetaireia Makedonikon Spoudon, 1959), no. 17, pp. 170–71; Cyril Mango, *The Homilies of Photius Patriarch of Constantinople* (Cambridge, MA: Harvard University Press, 1958), pp. 279–96 (offering a different translation on p. 294).

Interacting with Saints in the Late Antique and Medieval Worlds, ed. by Robert Wiśniewski, Raymond Van Dam, and Bryan Ward-Perkins, Hagiologia, 20 (Turnhout, 2023), pp. 47–78.
© BREPOLS ❧ PUBLISHERS   DOI 10.1484/M.HAG-EB.5.133621

process of perception. To put it very simply, Photios compares art to hagiography and visual experience to the oral, giving clear preference to the first over the second at a time when iconophiles were celebrating their triumphant victory over iconoclasm[3]. In reality, the two aspects of the cult developed hand in hand, with images not merely appearing as illustrations of existing lives and narratives but, at times, serving as a source of inspiration for textual traditions and accounts of miracles.

At this point in the scholarship, it should be clear that only a comprehensive study of the different media involved in the process of cult dissemination can offer an adequate understanding of the transformations taking place in Late Antiquity. Written sources, hagiography, epigraphy, liturgy, relics, and visual imagery coexisted side by side and were mutually influential in forging the ideas of sainthood in the early Christian church. The recent database compiled for the Cult of Saints project collects many of these testimonies, opening up new perspectives on the study of the expression and contextualization of holiness[4]. Material evidence occupies a special place within this array of sources, since surviving representations found in visual arts not only serve as some of the most vivid indications of the presence or existence of a cult, but also transmit the likeness and the set of ideas which built up around individual saints in Late Antiquity.

It is possible to draw out several distinct visual strategies for the promulgation of saints in early Christian art. This paper focuses on the analysis of a particular tradition in which images of martyrs were placed in the decoration of an apse, thereby turning them into protagonists within the regular worship of the church as well as within special liturgical performances[5]. Since Antiquity,

---

[3] On the sense of vision in Photios's homily: Katerina Ierodiakonou, 'Byzantine Theories of Vision', in *A Companion to Byzantine Science*, ed. by Stavros Lazaris (Leiden: Brill, 2020), pp. 160–76 (pp. 160–61).

[4] http://cultofsaints.history.ox.ac.uk/.

[5] On the importance of liturgy and its relation to visual arts see: Otto von Simson, *Sacred Fortress: Byzantine Art and Statecraft in Ravenna* (Princeton, NJ: Princeton University Press, 1987); Ursula Nilgen, 'Die Bilder über dem Altar: Triumph- und Apsisbogenprogramme in Rom und Mittelitalien und ihr Bezug zur Liturgie', *Kunst und Liturgie im Mittelalter: Akten des internationalen Kongresses der Biblioteca Hertziana und des Nederlands Instituut te Rome*, ed. by Nicolas Bock et al. (Munich: Hirmer, 2000), pp. 75–89; Rainer Warland, 'Strategien der Vergegenwärtigung. Zum Verhältnis von Kunst und Liturgie in frühbyzantinischer Zeit', *Art, cérémonial et liturgie au Moyen Age*, ed. by Nicolas Bock et al. (Rome: Viella, 2002), pp. 277–99; Stefan Heid, *Altar und Kirche. Prinzipien christlicher Liturgie* (Regensburg: Schnell+Steiner, 2019), pp. 353–406. For the significance of saints with regard to the organization of the church space and commemorative practices: Ann Marie Yasin, *Saints and Church Spaces in the Late Antique Mediterranean: Architecture, Cult, and Community* (Cambridge: Cambridge University Press, 2009).

the concave niches and exedras have been used to demarcate the most significant spaces within the official buildings or temple interiors, often being used in such a way as to attract the immediate attention of the beholder[6]. Apses can be interpreted, in some sense, as 'pause elements' within the 'architectural symphony' of late Roman churches, inviting viewers to interrupt their physical motion and the rhythmic exploration which is orchestrated first and foremost by the repetitive forms of columns and arches[7]. Instead, the viewers are invited to concentrate their attention on a moment of stillness as they are drawn into the contemplation of one particular image located in the apse.

When we consider the artistic evidence, it comes as no surprise that the leading role among the saints represented in the apse — aside from Christ, Mary, and the apostles[8] — was usually given to martyrs[9]. In some cases, but

---

[6] On the apse decoration: Christa Ihm, *Die Programme der christlichen Apsismalerei vom 4. Jahrhundert bis zur Mitte des 8. Jahrhunderts* (Wiesbaden: Steiner, 1960; repr. 1992); Maria Andaloro & Serena Romano, 'L'immagine nell'abside', in *Arte e Iconografia a Roma da Constantino a Cola di Rienzo*, ed. by Maria Andaloro & Serena Romano (Milano: Jaca Book, 2000), pp. 93–132; Απόστολος Μαντάς, *Το εικονογραφικό πρόγραμμα του ιερού βήματος των μεσοβυζαντινών ναών της Ελλάδος (843–1204)*, (Athens: Ethniko kai Kapodistriako Panepistemio Athenon, 2001); Beat Brenk, *The Apse, the Image and the Icon. An Historical Perspective of the Apse as a Space for Images* (Wiesbaden: Reichert, 2010). Most recently: Eric Thunø, *The Apse Mosaic in Early Medieval Rome: Time, Network, and Repetition* (New York: Cambridge University Press, 2015).

[7] For similar ideas and 'readings' of the experience of early Christian architectural forms: August Schmarzow, *Grundbegriffe der Kunstwissenschaft: am Übergang vom Altertum zum Mittelalter kritisch erörtert und in systematischem Zusammenhange dargestellt* (Leipzig: Teubner, 1905), pp. 212–28. He writes: "Die Dominante der Basilika ist die liegende Horizontalachse, die von der Giebelfront der Eingangsseite bis zum Triumphbogen der Apsis weiterrückt. Für den eintretenden Menschen, der auf dem Boden entlang geht, liegt diese Bewegungsachse zwischen dem Hauptportal und dem Hochaltar, und erst an der Schwelle des Allerheiligsten steht die Vertikalachse eines Zentralbaues, eben als Höhenlot der Apsis unmittelbar vor ihm, so daß er zu ihr aufblickt" (pp. 218–19).

[8] On images of Christ and apostles: Pasquale Testini, 'Osservazione sull'iconografia del Cristo in trono fra gli apostoli: a proposito dell'affresco di un distrutto oratorio cristiano presso l'Aggere Serviano a Roma', *Rivista dell'Istituto Nazionale d'Archeologia e Storia dell'Arte*, 11–12 (1963), 230–300; Jean-Marie Spieser, 'The Representation of Christ in the Apses of Early Christian Churches', *Gesta*, 37 (1998), 63–73; Fabrizio Bisconti, 'Absidi paleocristiane di Roma: antichi sistemi iconografici e nuove idee figurative', in *Atti del VI Colloquio dell'Associazione Italiana per lo Studio e la Conservazione del Mosaico*, ed. by Federico Guidobaldi & Andrea Paribeni (Ravenna: Edizioni del Girasole, 2000), pp. 451–62; Armin F. Bergmeier, *Visionserwartung: Visualisierung und Präsenzerfahrung des Göttlichen in der Spätantike* (Wiesbaden: Reichert Verlag, 2017). On images of the Mother of God in the apse: Ihm, *Apsismalerei*, pp. 52–68, 100–12; Brenk, pp. 57–82; Brooke L. Shilling, 'Apse Mosaics of the Virgin Mary in Early Byzantine Cyprus' (unpublished doctoral thesis, Johns Hopkins University, 2013); Maria Lidova, 'Virgin Mary and the Adoration of the Magi: From Iconic Space to Icon in Space', in *Icons of Space: Advances in Hierotopy*, ed. by Jelena Bogdanović (Abingdon: Routledge, 2021), pp. 214–38.

[9] For images of martyrs and titular saints in the apse: André Grabar, *Martyrium. Recherches sur le culte des reliques et l'art chrétien antique* (Paris: Collège de France, 1946), II, pp. 105–28

by no means all, the appearance of images of saints in the apse was predetermined by the presence of their corporeal remains and the dedication of the church, by actual tombs located below the sanctuary space, or simply by relics placed within the altar[10]. Therefore, the creation of such representations, as a rule, was part of a more complex programme. They were integrated within the church space, used in liturgical and commemorative services, and sometimes had further connections with a variety of minor objects, altar cloths, and decorative elements complementing the setting of the sanctuary.

Within these late-antique apsidal depictions of martyrs, three main categories can be singled out:
1. Those where martyrs appeared as protagonists within the composition;
2. Those in which martyrs were represented as members of the heavenly court flanking Christ or Mary seated on the throne;
3. Those which portray a pair of martyrs; this category was attested predominantly in lateral apses and separate chapels.

In what follows, I am going to examine each category individually, elaborating the subtle differences that distinguish among them and demonstrating how these various approaches helped to determine the perception of martyrs in Late Antiquity.

Glorifying Martyrs in the Apse

The first category of images is especially interesting since it seems to have been characteristic of the late antique period in particular. The evidence available

---

(pp. 105–17); Ihm, *Apsismalerei*, pp. 113–20. For general discussion on the way saints are grouped in late antique church decoration and how this differed from post iconoclastic tradition: Anna Zakharova, 'Principles of Grouping the Images of Saints in Byzantine Monumental Painting before and after Iconoclasm', *Actual Problems of Theory and History of Art*, 4 (2014), 109–22; Anna Zakharova, 'Images of Saints in Monumental Decoration of Early Christian and Byzantine Churches before the 11th Century', *History Studies. Journal of the History Faculty of Lomonosov Moscow State University*, 2 (2015), 31–62. See also: Rotraut Wisskirchen, 'Christus-Apostelfürsten-Heilige-Stifter. Zur Stellung und Beziehung von Einzelfiguren oder Gruppen in Mosaiken stadtrömischer Kirchen', *Jahrbuch für Antike und Christentum*, 28 (1998), 295–310.
[10] For the tombs located in the sanctuary and apses serving as architectural frames: Francesco Tolotti, 'Le absidi di San Silvestro a Roma e di San Nazaro a Milano', *Mélanges de l'École française de Rome. Antiquité*, 85/2 (1973), 713–54; Francesco Tolotti, 'Il problema dell'altare e della tomba del martire in alcune opere di papa Damaso', *Studien zur spätantiken und byzantinischen Kunst: F. W. Deichmann gewidmet*, ed. by Otto Feld (Bonn: R. Habelt, 1986), pp. 51–71; Thunø, *The Apse Mosaic*, pp. 142–58. See also the classic study by Peter Brown, *The Cult of the Saints: Its Rise and Function in Latin Christianity* (Chicago: Chicago University Press, 1981). On the use and importance of relics in Late Antiquity most recently: Robert Wiśniewski, *The Beginnings of the Cult of Relics* (Oxford: Oxford University Press, 2019).

to us is very scant, but, despite this, it seems clear that in certain contexts an image of the titular saint for a particular ecclesiastical space could take on the role of a protagonist within worship, receiving visual emphasis from the decoration of a conch placed directly above the main altar.

The most famous example of this practice is, of course, the apse of Sant'Apollinare in Classe, near Ravenna[11] (Fig. 1). The mosaic decoration of the sanctuary of this basilica is both unique and symbolically complex, with insertions from later periods serving as complements to the original creation[12]. What interests us here is the central composition, which represents an allegorical or symbolical interpretation of the Transfiguration with an image of God rendered in the form of a cross within a circle. Although the face of Jesus can be seen at the centre of the cross, it is the non-figurative aspect of this image that dominates the scene, which is recognizable by other means thanks to the appearance of Elijah and Moses in the sky while three sheep, most likely alluding to Peter, John, and Jacob, gaze upwards from the ground.

On the central axis, directly beneath the cross, we can see St Apollinaris, who is believed to be the first bishop of Ravenna, buried after death in the port city of Classe[13]. The mosaic decoration would have been completed by 549, the year in which the church was consecrated, and its appearance was

---

[11] Otto von Simson, *Sacred Fortress*, pp. 40–62; Friedrich Wilhelm Deichmann, *Ravenna. Haupstadt des spätantiken Abendlandes* (Wiesbaden: Steiner, 1969/89), I, pp. 257–77; II. 2, pp. 245–80; Deborah Mauskopf Deliyannis, *Ravenna in Late Antiquity* (Cambridge: Cambridge University Press, 2010), pp. 259–74; Alžběta Filipová, 'Santo, vescovo e confessore: l'immagine di Apollinare nei mosaici di Classe', in *L'évêque, l'image et la mort*, ed. by Nicolas Bock, Ivan Foletti & Michele Tomasi (Rome: Viella, 2014), pp. 431–44 (with detailed bibliography cited on p. 431, n. 1).

[12] Cetty Muscolino & Ermano Carbonara, 'Nuovi brani musivi del VI secolo dall'arco trionfale della basilica di Sant'Apollinare in Classe a Ravenna', *Atti del XV Colloquio dell'Associazione Italiana per lo Studio e la Conservazione del Mosaico*, ed. by Claudia Angelelli & Carla Salvetti (Tivoli: Scripta manent, 2010), pp. 161–71; Silvia Pasi, 'Il quadro storico di Sant'Apollinare in Classe. Una lettura attraverso la storia del restauro', *Studi Romagnoli*, 62 (2011), 81–102.

[13] CSLA E02977 and E02088 (both by Matthieu Pignot with a comprehensive and up-to-date bibliography). There is an interesting vagueness regarding Apollinaris's martyr status in earlier sources (see the discussion in Filipová, pp. 431–34). The same view is expressed by Deliyannis, who notes that: 'In the mid-sixth century Apollinaris was revered as Ravenna's founding bishop, and it was only later that he acquired the status of a martyr'. Deliyannis, p. 259. However, this uncertainty may derive from the fact that, according to later accounts, he suffered death several days after having been beaten and not via official execution, which may explain why his martyrdom was not praised in usual terms. In addition, the concept of martyr-bishop was a complex notion not always connected to actual death and physical suffering: Marianne Sághy, 'Martyr-Bishops and the Bishop's Martyrs in Fourth-Century Rome', in *Saintly Bishops and Bishop's Saints*, ed. by John S. Ott & Trpimir Vedriš (Zagreb: Hagiotheca, 2012), pp. 13–30.

predetermined by various political and church agendas of the time in the aftermath of Ravenna's return under Byzantine rule and in an environment of Orthodox faith. Whatever the reasons behind the promotion of St Apollinaris in the sixth century, the visual framework clearly displays the significance of his figure[14]. In a certain sense, Apollinaris takes the place of Christ in this composition, not only as the shepherd of the flock and the leader of the twelve apostles (who are supposedly represented as a row of sheep underneath), but also as a figurative embodiment of the head of the church, who is the only active character in the scene and the only one distinguished by a halo[15]. He is visually glorified in the apse as the first bishop of the city, an idea underlined by his garments and supported by the presence of other bishops placed between the windows in the lower zone of the apse.

A number of political and ecclesiastical issues related to the aspirations of the see of Ravenna that potentially underlie this programme have been widely discussed in the literature[16]. However, earlier scholars, such as André Grabar, Otto von Simson, and Wilhelm Deichmann, in my view correctly emphasized that it was not so much the ecclesiastical status as the martyrdom of the saint, venerated as the first and main martyr of the city, that created the necessary premise and theological justification for his appearance in the central position within the apse decoration[17]. In the words of von Simson, 'the mosaic in Sant'Apollinare in Classe conveys the ancient *ascetical* concept of imitation, i.e., martyrdom. It glorified not only the bishop but also, and above all, the martyr'[18]. This is confirmed by the simple fact that no other bishop appears as the sole or main protagonist in any decoration placed above the altar in Byzantine art[19]. As we will see in the next sections, hierarchs of

---

[14] It has been demonstrated that the initial programme did not include the figure of St Apollinaris and that his image was added later when the original design underwent significant alterations: Davide Longhi, 'The Cosmic Cross as *Logos*' Theophany. First Version of Sant'Apollinare in Classe's Apsidal Mosaic and Jerusalem's Staurophany of AD 351', *IKON*, 6 (2013), 275–86.

[15] On parallelism with Christ: Von Simson, *Sacred Fortress*, pp. 42, 45.

[16] For these aspects and a reading of the whole programme in the light of political agendas, most recently: Filipová, pp. 431–44.

[17] Petrus Chrysologus, *Sermo* 128 (*De natale sancti Apolenaris*), ed. by Alezander Olivar, CCSL 24B (1982), pp. 789–91; Grabar, *Martyrium*, II, pp. 48–49, 66; Deichmann, *Ravenna*, I, pp. 257–77.

[18] Von Simson, *Sacred Fortress*, p. 55.

[19] On representations of bishops and popes and more specifically their appearance in the apse: Jean-Pierre Caillet, 'L'Évêque et le saint en Italie: le témoignage de l'iconographie haut-médiévale et romane', *Les Cahiers de Saint-Michel de Cuxa*, 1 (1998), 29–44; Manuela Gianandrea, 'Il "doppio papa" nelle decorazioni absidali del Medioevo romano', in *Le plaisir de l'art du Moyen Âge*, ed. by Rosa Alcoy & Dominique Allios (Paris: Picard, 2002), pp. 663–69; Christopher Walter, *Art and Ritual of the Byzantine Art and Tradition* (London:

Fig. 1: Apse decoration with St Apollinaris, Sant'Apollinare in Classe, Ravenna, sixth century.
Photo: Author.

Fig. 2: Apse decoration with St Agnes, Sant'Agnese fuori le mura, Rome, first half of the seventh century.
Photo: Author.

the church featured in the apse mosaic predominantly in their role as patrons forming part of the line of saints approaching the figure of Christ or the Virgin Mary who would be located at the centre, or they were portrayed in pairs flanking an image of the cross.

The decoration of Sant'Apollinare church is considered to be a freestanding and isolated case. However, if we analyse it from the perspective of how some saints were depicted within the apse, it can be argued that the Ravenna image exemplifies, to some extent, a more general trend[20]. In fact, another church whose apse is occupied by the figure of the saint is Sant'Agnese fuori le mura in Rome[21]. The original building was constructed in the fourth century (337–51) on top of the catacombs in which, according to tradition, the martyr had been buried[22]. As attested in the *Liber Pontificalis*, the very first fourth-century decoration of St Agnes' church was realized by Pope Liberius (352–66)[23]. Artefacts dated to the fourth century and bearing the image of the saint — such as the marble slab kept today in the catacombs beneath the church and multiple fragments of gold-glass vessels — attest to the spread and importance of Agnes' cult in late antique Rome[24]. Little

---

Variorum, 2003), pp. 166–77; Deborah M. Deliyannis, 'Ecclesius of Ravenna as Donor in Text and Image', in *Envisioning the Bishop: Images and the Episcopacy in the Middle Ages*, ed. by Sigrid Danielson & Evan A. Gatti (Turnhout: Brepols, 2014), pp. 41–62; Thunø, *The Apse Mosaic*, pp. 152–55; Dale Kinney, 'Communication in a Visual Mode: Papal Apse Mosaics', *Journal of Medieval History*, 44 (2018), 311–32; Yasin, *Saints and Church Spaces*, pp. 271–80. On the veneration of bishops in Late Antiquity: Claudia Rapp, *Holy Bishops in Late Antiquity. The Nature of Christian Leadership in an Age of Transition* (Berkeley: University of California Press, 2005); *Saintly Bishops and Bishop's Saints*, ed. by John S. Ott & Trpimir Vedriš (Zagreb: Hagiotheca, 2012). For sources and other publications on the topic, see the various publications and the database of the project the *Presbyters in the Late Antique West* conducted at the University of Warsaw: http://presbytersproject.ihuw.pl/.

[20] For similar views: Grabar, *Martyrium*, pp. 48, 66, 105–06; Von Simson, *Sacred Fortress*, p. 50; Ihm, *Apsismalerei*, pp. 113–20.

[21] Richard Krautheimer, Spencer Corbett & Alfred Knox Frazer, *Corpus basilicarum Christianarum Romae* (Vatican City: Pontificio Istituto di Archeologia Cristiana, 1937), I, pp. 14–39.

[22] On St Agnes most recently: Cécile Lanéry, *Ambroise de Milan hagiographe* (Turnhout: Brepols, 2008), pp. 357–61; Cécile Lanéry, 'La légende de sainte Agnès: quelques réflexions sur la genèse d'un dossier hagiographique (IVᵉ-VIᵉ s.)', *Mélanges de l'École française de Rome — Moyen Âge*, 126/1 (2014), 17–26; Michael Lapidge, *The Roman Martyrs: Introduction, Translations, and Commentary* (Oxford: Oxford University Press, 2017), pp. 348–62. On the church of Sant'Agnese: Hugo Brandenburg, *Ancient Churches of Rome from the Fourth to the Seventh Century. The Dawn of Christian Architecture in the West* (Turnhout: Brepols, 2005), pp. 69–86, 241–47.

[23] *Liber Pontificalis* 37.

[24] Eileen Rubery, 'From Catacomb to Sanctuary: The Orant Figure and the Cults of the Mother of God and S. Agnes in Early Christian Rome, with Special Reference to Gold Glass', *Studia Patristica*, 73 (2014), 169–214.

remains of the original programme, as the basilica underwent significant reconstruction in the seventh century and received a new apse decoration[25] (Fig. 2). The golden spherical curve of the conch is occupied by three figures, with St Agnes placed in the centre and two popes, Honorius I (625–38) and Symmachus (498–514), appearing at her sides[26]. Below Agnes we can see the instruments of her martyrdom — fire and a sword — that reference both her suffering and the tortures known from hagiographical accounts. Above her a segment of sky is visible, with the hand of God holding the crown of martyrdom.

At least three more similar decorations are recorded to have existed in Rome. The first was in the oratory of St Felicitas adjacent to the baths of Trajan on the Oppian Hill[27]. Behind the altar of this small, and probably private, chapel there was a rectangular niche (not an apse in this case) decorated with a painted multi-figured composition representing St Felicitas surrounded by smaller figures depicting her seven sons (Fig. 3). Although the shape and layout do not correspond to the semicircular outline of the exedra typical of an apse, in all likelihood an altar would have been placed in front of the image, which in turn implies that the mural was used in liturgical performance. The decoration does not survive, but it is known thanks to the sketches made in

---

[25] Brandenburg, *Ancient Churches of Rome*, pp. 241–47.

[26] Guglielmo Matthiae, *Mosaici medioevali delle chiese di Roma* (Rome: Istituto Poligrafico dello Stato, 1967), pp. 169–79; Gabriella Delfini Filippi, 'Il mosaico absidale di S. Agnese fuori le Mura: restauri storici e recenti interventi conservativi', in *Mosaici a S. Vitale e altri restauri. Il restauro in situ di mosaici parietali. Atti del Convegno Nazionale sul restauro in situ di mosaici parietali*, ed. by Anna Maria Iannucci & Cesare Fiori (Ravenna: Longo, 1992), pp. 245–49; Beat Brenk, 'Kultgeschichte versus Stilgeschichte: von der 'raison d'être' des Bildes im 7. Jahrhundert in Rom', in *Uomo e spazio nell'Alto Medioevo. Settimane di studio del Centro Italiano di Studi sull'Alto Medioevo* (Spoleto: CISAM, 2003), II, pp. 971–1054, 1034–40; Valentino Pace, 'Immagini sacre a Roma fra VI e VII secolo. In margine al problema 'Roma e Bisanzio', *Acta ad archaeologiam et artium historiam pertinentia*, 18 (2004), 151–54; Antonella Ballardini, '*Habeas corpus*: Agnese nella basilica di via Nomentana', in *'Di Bisanzio dirai ciò che è passato, ciò che passa e che sarà'. Scritti in onore di Alessandra Guiglia*, ed. by Silvia Pedone & Andrea Paribeni (Rome: Bardi edizioni, 2018), I, pp. 253–79; Dennis Trout, 'Pictures with Words: Reading the Apse Mosaic of S. Agnese f. l. m. (Rome)', *Studies in Iconography*, 40 (2019), 1–26 (This paper displays a flat and limited perception of the art historical literature on the topic, but it is nevertheless very useful (although not entirely novel) for its discussion of the relationship between image and word in connection with this mosaic).

[27] Ihm, *Apsismalerei*, p. 147; Alessandra Cerrito, 'Sull'oratorio di S. Felicità presso le terme di Traiano a Roma', in *Donum tuam dilexi. Miscellanea in onore di Aldo Nestori* (Vatican City: Pontificio di Archeologia Cristiana, 1998), pp. 155–84. On St Felicitas: Lapidge, *The Roman Martyrs*, pp. 45–53, CSLA E02494 (Matthieu Pignot). The name Felicitas also appears in a number of epigraphical records tentatively dated to the fourth century: see various records by Paweł Nowakowski linked to CSLA S00525.

Fig. 3: The drawing of the decoration in the oratory of St Felicitas on the Oppio hill in Rome.
Photo from Raffaele Garrucci, *Storia dell'arte cristiana nei primi otto secoli della chiesa* (Prato: G. Guasti, 1873), vol. III, pp. 87–8, Tav. 154.

Fig. 4: The drawing of the decoration in the apse of St Euphemia church in Rome.
Photo from Giovanni Giusto Ciampini, *Vetera monimenta*, pars II, pp. 118–9, Tab. XXXV.

the aftermath of its discovery in 1812[28]. Above St Felicitas there was a half-length image of Christ holding a wreath which was intended as a crown for the saint. This small church was not founded above the place of burial; instead, it complemented an earlier site of worship on the via Salaria where it seems an early Christian basilica once stood in proximity to the catacombs[29]. The chapel discussed above was constructed within the walls of the ancient Roman building, thereby establishing the renewed cult of the saint in the centre of the city. Whether its decoration and arrangement were connected to an earlier site on the via Salaria remains unknown[30].

Sixteenth-century sources attest to the existence of a mosaic decoration once visible in the church of Santa Martina al Foro. The central position was taken by a female figure, most probably the titular saint of the church, Santa Martina, who was represented flanked by two popes tentatively identified as Donus (676–78), holding the model of the church, and Honorius I (625–38)[31]. The described programme seems to replicate the same visual model used for the apse of St Agnes's church several decades earlier.

Another example was found in the church of St Euphemia on the Esquiline hill[32] (Fig. 4). Ciampini, followed by Ihm and many others, believed that the mosaic decoration of the apse in this church had been made at the time of Pope Sergius I (687–701), although some scholars suggested the possibility of an earlier dating to the fifth century[33]. Since the church and its decoration were destroyed, the date cannot be established with certainty, and later

---

[28] Stefano Piale, 'Pitture antiche di S. Felicità e figli', in *Memorie enciclopediche sulle antichità e belle arti di Roma per l'a. 1816*, ed. by Giuseppe Antonio Guattani (Rome: Per Salomoni, 1817), II, pp. 153–60; Raffaele Garrucci, *Storia dell'arte cristiana nei primi otto secoli della chiesa* (Prato: G. Guasti, 1873), III, pp. 87–88, tab. 154.

[29] The principal site of the worship of St Felicitas in the city was connected to her supposed burial with her sons in the cemetery on the via Salaria, which is mentioned in *LP* in the life of Pope Boniface I (418–22): Giovanni Battista de Rossi, 'Scoperta d'una cripta storica nel cimitero di Massimo ad *sanctam Felicitatem* sulla via Salaria Nova', *Bullettino di archeologia cristiana*, 3 (1884–85), 149–84; Geoffrey D. Dunn, 'Life in the Cemetery: Boniface I and the Catacomb of Maximus', *Augustinianum*, 55 (2015), 137–53.

[30] The remains of the mural in the catacombs similar in its design to the iconography in the chapel adjacent to Trajan's baths are generally dated to a later date. De Rossi, 152–57; 166–70 (p. 169).

[31] Gianandrea, 'Il "doppio papa"', pp. 640–41.

[32] Giovanni Giusto Ciampini, *Vetera monimenta: in quibus praecipuè musiva opera sacrarum profanarumque aedium structura, ac nonnulli antique ritus, dissertationibus, iconibusque illustrantur* (Rome: Ex typographia Joannis Jacobi Komarek, 1690), II, pp. 118–19, tab. XXXV; Ihm, *Apsismalerei*, p. 156.

[33] Carlo Cecchelli, 'Mosaici romani del V e VI secolo', *Corsi di cultura sull'arte ravennate e bizantina*, 5 (1958), 37–44 (p. 41); Giuseppe Bovini, *I mosaici paleocristiani di Roma (secoli III–VI)* (Bologna: Pàtron, 1975), pp. 209–11.

reproductions are our only source of information. According to these drawings, the image of the female martyr was placed in the centre of a large mosaic decorating the apse. The saint from Chalcedon was represented with her arms raised in the posture of an orant standing between two snakes, apparently alluding to one of the numerous tortures that the martyr had to endure because of her refusal to venerate the statue of the Roman god Ares. The episode in which the saint is thrown into the pit with snakes, along with her subsequent miraculous salvation, features in some of the hagiographical accounts dedicated to St Euphemia.

Similarly to the apse decoration in Sant'Agnese fuori le mura, the hand of God appeared at the top of the composition offering a crown to the female saint[34]. Visual parallelism between these two programmes is clearly discernible, demonstrating a particular type of representation popular in Rome at the time. It is noteworthy that in all four decorations discussed so far the artists depicted the celestial hierarchy by placing the figures of saints underneath a divine image assuming, variously, the form of a hand, a bust of Christ, or a symbolic representation of the cross. Perhaps this should be seen, among other things, as an allusion to the ascent of the soul to heaven, which was an idea circulating in patristic texts of the time and in poetry dedicated to martyrs[35].

What differentiates the last two sites from previous examples is that they were not built to commemorate the place of a burial, a tomb, or a martyrdom, since St Euphemia is known to have been buried in Chalcedon. Hence, this church in Rome must have acted as a counterpart to the original martyrium in Chalcedon and the churches of the saint in Constantinople. In addition, the cult of the saint was well established in the North of Italy from very early on. Little is known about the original late antique decorations of the churches dedicated to St Euphemia in Asia Minor or in the West. However, an exceptionally interesting description survives recording a series of scenes decorating a painted textile icon, which was placed beside the tomb of the martyr in Chalcedon. This record is found in the account of Asterius, bishop of Amasea (350–410), and seems to indicate a full narrative cycle of Euphemia's various tortures. 'The painter then, demonstrating his own piety by his

---

[34] On the imagery of female saints in Late Antiquity: Maria Lidova, 'Images of Female Martyrs in Early Byzantine Art: The Origins and Forms of Religious Veneration', *Byzantina Xronika*, 104 (2020), pp. 243–60 (with previous bibliography).
[35] Michael Roberts, *Poetry and the Cult of the Martyrs: The Liber Peristephanon of Prudentius* (Ann Arbor, MI: University of Michigan Press, 1993), pp. 69–77. The author also highlights that the word *tribunal* used by Prudentius for the apse of Christian churches alludes to the heavenly realm and creates a parallel between the unjust judgment on earth mentioned in *Vitae* and Christ's supreme judgment of martyrs (pp. 71–72).

art, drew, to the best of his ability, the whole story on a canvas and set it up as a sacred spectacle near the tomb.' A couple of scenes mentioned in this *ekphrasis* are particularly interesting, since they provide a textual counterpart to the way that the saint is represented in the Roman church, and I cite it here using Efthymios Rizos's recent revised translation:

> And while praying, above her head the sign appears to her, which it is the custom for Christians to venerate and inscribe. Next then, the painter has kindled a great fire, blazing up the flame with red colour glowing on its two sides. And he placed her in its midst, stretching her hands up to heaven, yet demonstrating no suffering on her face, for she was moving towards the bodiless and blessed life[36].

André Grabar, in his seminal study on late antique martyria, described a potential trajectory for the evolution of images of martyrs situated in apses.[37] He believed that this format derived from individual portraits created in proximity to the tomb. Later on the images of saints triumphant over death could have been appropriated for more significant church structures, a use which may find attestation in the numerous representations of martyrs depicted standing frontally within sophisticated ciborium–like structures characterized by a semicircular niche[38] (Fig. 5). Finally, such images were employed at the most privileged place in the main apse of the church. Although this development seems probable, it does not fully explain the particular significance of representations of martyrs in later church structures or the role they must have played in liturgical and commemorative services at the altar. In the sixth and seventh centuries the sacred nature of the sanctuary space and, more specifically, of the altar, which would have been dependent on the presence of martyr's relics hidden within, provided the platform and appropriate church setting for renewed attempts at the promulgation of old saints or the promotion of foreign cults.

Hardly any example survives from the East, but the somewhat singular case of the niches at Abu Girgegh indicates that such solutions could be adopted not only in the West, but also in the East, in particular in Egypt[39].

---

[36] CSLA E00477 (E. Rizos).

[37] Grabar, *Martyrium*, pp. 105–17. On the interrelationship between icons and ciboria in Byzantine art, see also: Elena Bogdanović, *The Framing of Sacred Space: The Canopy and the Byzantine Church* (Oxford: Oxford University Press, 2017), pp. 224–29.

[38] For general criticism of Grabar's theory on the evolution of funerary buildings into early Christian shrines: John Bryan Ward-Perkins, 'Memoria, Martyr's Tomb and Martyr's Church', *Journal of Theological Studies*, 17 (1966), 20–37 (on pp. 25–26). The author discusses primarily the architectural forms, but similar concerns may be voiced in relation to the evolution of the imagery offered by Grabar.

[39] Evaristo Breccia, 'Fouilles d'Abou Girgeh', in *Rapport sur la marche du Service du Musée en 1912* (Alexandria: Société de Publications Égyptiennes, 1913), pp. 3–14; Mahmoud Zibawi,

Fig. 5: St Demetrius in front of a ciborium, mosaic decoration in the church of St Demetrius in Thessalonica (fifth-sixth century).
Photo: Author.

Fig. 6: Watercolor copy of a mural representing an orant male saint standing between two ciboria from Abu Girgegh.
Photo from Mahmoud Zibawi, *Images de l'Égypte chrétienne. Iconologie copte* (Paris: Picard, 2003), p. 70, fig. 72.

A two-storey building at Abu Girgegh had apses in the upper and lower church. In both spaces semicircular niches were decorated with painted representations of saints, standing as orants. A slightly better-known image is the young beardless saint standing in the flowery field between two small ciborium-like temple structures (Fig. 6). The identity of the saint is unknown, but the image fits well the approach to depictions of martyrs' figures discussed above and offers an example of how this kind of image could have been used for apses, even if we do not possess a great deal of surviving evidence.

The tradition of portraying martyrs as the main image in apses does not really continue into the later period. Several church decorations of the Middle Byzantine period found in Greece and on Greek islands preserve the memory of this earlier practice by featuring the titular saints, martyrs, and prophets within the sanctuary space, sometimes characterized by not just one but two semi-circular apsidal niches[40]. However, after the eighth century, the images of saints barely ever obtain the dominant position in the apse space above the main altar of a church, which is instead predominantly occupied by the image of Christ or of the Mother of God. Therefore, the images of saints as the visual fulcrum of ecclesiastical space should be considered a feature which developed in connection to early forms of martyr-veneration and gradually disappeared together with early martyria and related decorations from the sixth and seventh century.

Martyrs as Members of the Heavenly Court

Saints tend to appear regularly next to the throne of Christ or Mary. In Rome a traditional scheme of seven figures became established early on[41]. An image of Christ or of Mary with the Christ Child was often placed in the centre of the conch, surrounded by approaching figures (as a rule, three on each side) representing martyrs and the donors (most often the popes) who had paid for the work[42]. In essence, this kind of multi-figured composition reproduced a theme of heavenly reception, often considered as a form of Roman

---

Images de l'Égypte chrétienne. Iconologie copte (Paris: Picard, 2003), pp. 66–71.

[40] Νικόλαος Β. Δρανδάκης, 'Δεόμενοι ἅγιοι ἐπὶ τοῦ τεταρτοσφαρίου ἁψῖδος εἰς ἐκκλησίας τῆς Μέσα Μάνης', in *Μάνη καὶ Λακωνία* (Athens: Εταιρεία Λακωνικών Σπουδών, 2009), pp. 39-47 (reprint of a paper from 1971); Μαντάς, *Το εικονογραφικό πρόγραμμα*, pp. 113–20; 164–69.

[41] Matthiae, *Mosaici medioevali*, pp. 135–42; Ivan Foletti, 'Maranatha: Space, Liturgy, and Image in the Basilica of Saints Cosmas and Damian on the Roman Forum', in *The Fifth Century in Rome*, ed. by Ivan Foletti & Manuela Gianandrea (Rome: Viella, 2017), pp. 161–79.

[42] See note 19.

Theophany[43]. This type of imagery was, in all likelihood, already known in the fifth century, but it became particularly popular from the early sixth century onwards. The solemn scene in which the saints act as members of the entourage of Christ or the Mother of God forms the second category of martyrs' imagery that I would like to discuss in this chapter. In a certain sense, it represents the best-studied and least problematic example of apsidal decorations incorporating the figures of saints.

It is possible that the original decoration in the sanctuary of Santa Maria Maggiore in Rome, belonging to the second quarter of the fifth century, already contained representations of martyrs[44]. This assumption is based on the dedicatory inscription recorded in the description of the basilica by Onofrio Panvinio in the second half of the sixteenth century[45]. In this work the author cites the text of the now lost inscription, most likely executed in mosaic, which he saw on the inner side of the entrance wall:

> Virgo Maria, tibi Xystus nova templa dicavi, / digna salutifero munera ventre tuo. / Tu genitrix ignara viri, te denique feta / visceribus salvis edita nostra salus. / Ecce tui testes uteri tibi praemia portant, / sub pedibusque iacet passio cuique sua: / ferrum, flamma, ferae fluvius saevumque venenum / tot tamen has mortes una corona manet[46].

> Mary Virgin, to thee I, Sixtus, dedicate this new abode: a fitting offering to thy womb, the bearer of salvation. Thou, O Mother, knowing no man yet bearing fruit brought from thy chaste womb the Saviour of us all. Behold, the witnesses of thy fruitfulness bring thee wreaths, at each one's feet the instruments of his passion: sword and fire and water, wild beasts and bitter poison yet one crown awaits these several deaths[47].

---

[43] Ihm, *Apsismalerei*, pp. 24–27; 39–40; Thunø, *The Apse Mosaic*, pp. 13–29. In another paper, Ihm defines these Roman compositions as 'a ceremony staged in heaven': Christa Belting-Ihm, 'Theophanic Images of Divine Majesty in Early Medieval Italian Church Decoration', in *Italian Church Decoration of the Middle Ages and Early Renaissance: Functions, Forms and Regional Traditions*, ed. by William Tronzo (Bologna: Nuova Alfa), pp. 43–50 (p. 49).

[44] Maria Lidova, 'The Imperial *Theotokos*: Revealing the Concept of Early Christian Imagery in Santa Maria Maggiore in Rome', *Convivium*, 2 (2015), 60–81 (pp. 64–65) (with further bibliography).

[45] Onofrio Panvinio, *Le sette chiese principali di Roma* (Roma, 1570), p. 235.

[46] *Initia carminum Latinorum saeculo undecimo antiquiorum. Bibliographisches Repertorium für die lateinische Dichtung der Antike und des früheren Mittelalters*, ed. by Dieter Schaller, Ewald Könsgen & John Tagliabue (Göttingen: Vandenhoeck & Ruprecht, 1977) 17340; *ILCV* 976. Giovanni Battista de Rossi, *Inscriptiones Christianae urbis Romae septimo saeculo antiquiores*, vol. II 1 (Rome: Officina Libraria Pontificia, 1888), pp. 71, 98, 139, 435. Recently on the inscription, see: Carlo Carletti, *Epigrafia dei cristiani in Occidente dal III al VII secolo. Ideologia e prassi* (Bari: Edipuglia, 2008), pp. 253–54.

[47] The translation by Mary F. Hedlund & H. H. Rowley, in Frederik van der Meer & Christine Mohrmann, *Atlas of the Early Christian World* (London: Nelson, 1958), p. 85.

The authenticity of Panvinio's evidence and the ancient origin of the inscription are furthermore confirmed by the fact that it was reproduced in several early medieval *syllogae*, such as the 'Sylloge of Tours' and the 'Fourth Lorsch Sylloge', and it was already cited in the works of the Anglo-Saxon bishop Aldhelm (639–709)[48]. It has been debated whether the location of the inscription by the entrance is original or whether the inscription might have been moved there from the sanctuary, thus potentially referring to the early mosaic decoration in the apse. Neither proposal can be accepted without reservation due to the loss of both the dedicatory text and any direct indication of the original composition inside the apse. However, what the text seems to describe is a representation of Mary and Child being venerated by martyrs, whose role as witnesses of faith, acquired as a result of their individual suffering, is extended so that they become, in addition, witnesses to the mystery of the incarnation. A mutual affirmation seems to be implied by the rhetoric of this passage. The presence of both Mary and the Saviour grants the martyrs a privileged position by making them the beholders of the divine plan, while the depiction of saints in proximity to the Mother of God (*genetrix*) and their reverence towards her, 'sealed' by the act of gift offering, attests to the legitimacy of Mary's role and acts as an acknowledgement of her superior status. The fact that at least four or five martyrs could have been represented within the lost part of the church decoration in S. Maria Maggiore is confirmed by the enumeration of the instruments of martyrdom: a sword, fire, water, wild beasts, poison. One could speculate endlessly on the possible identity of the saints[49]. For example, the sword and/or the fire could easily indicate the Roman martyr Agnes, who is represented with these very attributes in the later sanctuary programme in the church on the via Nomentana discussed in the previous section; however, since the same instruments were characteristic of a number of other saints, this identification cannot be accepted with certitude. Whether a depiction of Pope Sixtus III (432–40), who is mentioned in the text, could also have been part of this composition remains an open question.

---

[48] Michael Lapidge, 'The Career of Aldhelm', *Anglo-Saxon England*, 36 (2007), pp. 15–66 (pp. 52–64).

[49] It has been tentatively suggested that they may have represented the Roman saints Peter, Paul, Sixtus II, Lawrence, and Agnes. Victor Saxer, *Sainte-Marie-Majeure. Une basilique de Rome dans l'histoire de la ville et de son église* (Rome: École française de Rome, 2001), pp. 44–45, n. 33; Carletti, *Epigrafia*, pp. 253–54. For further discussion of the topic and various identifications of saints suggested for this lost decoration: Paolo Liverani, 'The Memory of the Bishop in the Early Christian Basilica', in *Monuments & Memory: Christian Cult Buildings and Constructions of the Past: Essays in Honour of Sible de Blaauw*, ed. by Mariëtte Verhoeven, Lex Bosman & Hanneke van Asperen (Turnhout: Brepols, 2016), pp. 185–97 (pp. 187–88).

The earliest surviving example of apsidal multi-figured compositions that includes a group of saints is to be found in the church of Sts Kosmas and Damian in Rome, which is considered to be the prototype for later apse decorations in the city[50] (Fig. 7). Christ is depicted surrounded by clouds, as if descending from or ascending into heaven. Peter and Paul, the two apostles of particular salience for the church in Rome, appear on either side, standing on the ground. The two apostles are a common feature of church decorations in the city. In the case of this apse, they act as intermediaries assisting the approach of the holy martyrs and physicians Sts Kosmas and Damian, to whom the church is dedicated. The two saints were of oriental origin, and their relics may have been brought to Rome from the East, thereby prompting the consecration and dedication of a new church in their honour[51]. At the edges of this group we can also see the representation of St Theodoros on one side and Pope Felix (526–30) on the other. The latter is believed to be the founder of the church.

This visual formula consisting of an image of Christ in the company of six figures was constantly reproduced in Rome until the ninth century. It is not my task here to examine this development in detail or to analyse the selection of saints chosen in each case; this topic has already been subject to extensive study and has received further attention in a recent monograph by Erik Thunø[52]. What I would like to stress, however, is that, while this formula is often seen as being specifically Roman in nature, an interpretation which Thunø continues to propagate, it may actually have been used abundantly in mosaic and painted decorations across the Empire.

This is attested by the surviving programme in the Euphrasian basilica in Poreč[53] (Fig. 8). In contrast to the majority of the examples at Rome, the central position in this church is taken by the figures of Mary and the Christ

---

[50] Matthiae, *Mosaici medioevali*, pp. 135–42; Beat Brenk, 'Zur Einfürung des Kultes der heiligen Kosmas und Damian in Rom', *Teologische Zeitschrift*, 62 (2006), 303–20; Ivan Foletti, 'Maranatha', pp. 161–79. On iconography of Sts Kosmas and Damian: Angelos Kyriakos, *Η εικονογραφία των Αγίων Αναργύρων Κοσμά και Δαμιανού στην βυζαντινή τέχνη* (Athens: Stamoule, 2018).

[51] Brenk, 'Zur Einfürung des Kultes'; Maya Maskarinec, *City of Saints. Rebuilding Rome in the Early Middle Ages* (Philadelphia: University of Pennsylvania Press, 2018), pp. 89–102.

[52] Thunø, *The Apse Mosaic*, pp. 13–29.

[53] Marina Vicelja Matijašić, *Istra i Bizant* (Rijeka: Izdavaštvo FFRI, 2007), pp. 146–50; Henry Maguire, Ann B. Tierry, *Dynamic Splendor: The Wall Mosaics in the Cathedral of Eufrasius at Poreč* (Pennsylvania: Pennsylvania State University Press, 2007), pp. 72–76; Evan A. Gatti, 'In the Apse or in Between: The Benedictional of Engilmar and Traditions of Episcopal Patronage in the Apse at Poreč', in *Saintly Bishops and Bishop's Saints*, pp. 137–68; Thomas Schweigert, 'San Mauro at Parentium, Saint Sergius at Gaza, Hagia Sophia in Kiev, and the Protoevangelium of James', *Hortus artium medievalium*, 24 (2018), 181–90.

Fig. 7: Apse decoration in the church of SS. Cosma e Damiano, Rome, early sixth century.
Photo: Author.

Fig. 8: Apse decoration, Euphrasian basilica in Poreč, mid-sixth century.
Photo: Author.

Child. Mary is represented seated on a throne, flanked by angels (a feature often omitted in Roman decorations), while groups of male attendants approach her from either side. On the left, we can see a figure who is the titular saint of the church, St Maurus, followed by the founder of the basilica, Bishop Euphrasius. Euphrasius's brother Claudius is represented standing behind him, while a little boy holding candles, Claudius's son and Euphrasius's nephew, is depicted standing at their feet. Together, these three figures form a family portrait of a sort, while their identity is revealed in captions[54]. On the other side of Mary's throne, three saints are represented. The inscriptions which would aid their identification are missing in this case, although the figures are usually associated with Sts Eleutherius, Projectus, and Accolitus[55].

The cultural ties with the city of Ravenna and the similarity with Roman apse decorations have led some scholars to believe that this imagery may have been influenced by visual patterns imported from Italy and, more specifically, from Rome. However, a valuable piece of evidence found in the description of the lost churches of Gaza attests that apses containing multi-figured compositions including martyrs and, more specifically, local martyrs were popular across different centres of the Byzantine Empire.

The apse in the church of St Sergios described by Choricius contained a representation of the Virgin and Child surrounded by approaching figures, foremost of whom is the donor of the church, Stephen, the governor of Palestine, who is introduced to Mary by the titular saint of the church, St Sergios:

> The latter [apse] is adorned with gilded and silver mosaic, and displays in the center the Mother of the Saviour holding on her bosom her newborn Son; on either side stands a pious band. At the extreme right of these [groups] is a person who is in all respects like an emperor, and who is worthy both of being included in the register of God's friends and of bearing the name of the chief of God's deacons of old. [...] He it is who, standing next to the patron of the church, asks him to accept the gift graciously; the latter consents and looks upon the man with a gentle gaze as he lays his right hand on the man's shoulder, being evidently about to present him to the Virgin and her Son, the Saviour[56] (trans. by C. Mango).

Although Choricius, favouring the living patron of the church over and above the range of saints glorified in the apse, does not specify the identity

---

[54] Tierry, Maguire, *Dynamic Splendor*, p. 109.

[55] Tierry, Maguire, *Dynamic Splendor*, pp. 113–16.

[56] Cyril Mango, *The Art of the Byzantine Empire, 312–1453: Sources and Documents* (Englewood Cliffs, NJ: Prentice-Hall, 1972), pp. 60–68 (p. 62). See also: Félix-Marie Abel, 'Gaza au VIᵉ siècle d'après le rhéteur Chorikios', *Revue Biblique*, 40 (1931), 5–31; Glanville Downey, *Gaza in the Sixth Century* (Norman, OK: University of Oklahoma Press, 1963), pp. 127–29.

of other figures, it is highly likely that the two men whom he describes were counterbalanced by other depictions of martyrs on the opposite side of the composition.

Several fragmentary mural decorations surviving in Greece also provide evidence for the use of the same visual pattern featuring Christ or Mary in the centre in a company of saints portrayed at the sides. Most of these wall paintings were either discovered not so long ago or re-dated to the late antique period in recent years. Two saints holding wreaths are still visible in the sanctuary space of the St Kerykos church in Vathy on Kalymnos, recently attributed to the early or mid-sixth century[57]. Slightly better preserved are the wall paintings in a cave church found in Kellia, on the Greek island of Chalki[58]. Only the left side of the original decoration survives, with a youthful Christ represented in the centre of the apse, once flanked by two archangels. Two saints on the left are identified by accompanying inscriptions as St Faustus and St Kerykos. Based on the identification of these saints and study of their cult, it has been recently suggested that the community of monks responsible for the execution of these murals must have come from Egypt some time in the seventh or early eighth century or at least had close ties with Egyptian monasteries[59].

The choice of saints and their positioning as mediators could vary depending on the relics kept within the sanctuary, the dedication of the church, or the aspirations of the donor. Martyrs and their images were evidently used by lay and church patrons for the promotion of political or ecclesiastical goals and for the visual proclamation of their power, as sanctified in heaven. A chain of interactions and mediations would have been triggered as the eyes of the congregation passed from the central figure of God to the saints and martyrs who, in turn, transmitted blessing and divine grace to the living representatives of their power[60]. This type of imagery was equally reflective of

---

[57] Michalis Kappas & Konstantia Kefala, 'Across the Waves. Early Christian Paintings on Kalymnos and Karia', in *Karia and Dodecanese. Cultural Interrelations in the Southeast Aegean II, Early Hellenistic to Early Byzantine*, ed. by Poul Pedersen, John Lund & Birte Poulsen (Oxford: Oxbow Books, 2021), pp. 255–67 (p. 260). I would like to express my profound gratitude to Theodora Konstantellou for bringing these paintings to my attention and for reading this paper at the stage of its preparation.

[58] Maria Sigala, Τα Κελλία της Χάλκης Δωδεκανήσου. Η χρονολόγηση των τοιχογραφίων και η σημασία τους, *Deltion tis Christianikis archeologikis heterias*, 30 (2009), 149–58; Angeliki Katsioti, 'Gazing Beyond Earthly Reality: A Reconsideration of the Wall Paintings at Asketario on the Island of Chalki, Dodecanese', *Deltion tis Christianikis archeologikis heterias*, 42 (2021), 33–56.

[59] Katsioni, 'A Reconsideration', pp. 36–40.

[60] Sághy, 'Martyr-Bishops and the Bishop's Martyrs', p. 29.

the cult of martyrs, as well as of the integration of that cult within the local state and church agendas.

The last aspect that I would like to consider in connection with these compositions is their multi-figured nature. The representation of rows of saints gathered together within the limited space of the conch would have transmitted the idea of a heavenly court. Their placement, attitude, and attire helped to convey the image of an otherworldly kingdom populated by Christian martyrs. In the eyes of worshippers, they would have acted in the apses of the church as members of Christ's spiritual army, witnesses of God's glory, guardians of the Christian faith, and guarantors of both the future life and the eternity of the soul. This multi-figured arrangement was fully in line with contemporary sources that emphasized the notion of an assembly, a choir, or crowds of saints. The life of St Agnes, for example, describes how 'in the middle of the silence of the night they [her parents] saw a host of virgins, who passed by in a great light, all dressed in robes woven with gold'[61]. Similar ideas of saints perceived or acting as a group are found in sermons of Victricius of Rouen and Gaudentius of Brescia[62]. In his recent monograph Robert Wiśniewski considers this evidence in relation to collections of relics circulating in Late Antiquity or gathered within a particular church[63]. It can be argued that this leitmotif in homilies or contemporary hagiographical accounts must have inspired many of the depictions of saints in groups or rows that populate the interior space of late antique churches, not just within the apse but also in the nave or arches.

An early mosaic decoration which once adorned the apse of St Priscus's church in Capua and which can probably be dated to the first half of the fifth century is particularly interesting in this respect[64]. In this programme the figure of Christ was absent. Instead, a large group of sixteen saints, including

---

[61] Hannah Jones, 'Agnes and Constantia: Domesticity and Cult Patronage in the Passion of Agnes', in *Religion, Dynasty, and Patronage in Early Christian Rome, 300–900*, ed. by Kate Cooper & Julia Hillner (Cambridge: Cambridge University Press, 2007), pp. 115–39 (p. 133).
[62] Victricius, *De laude sanctorum* 6; Gaudentius, *Tractatus* 17.37. I am grateful to Robert Wiśniewski for bringing these sources to my attention.
[63] Wiśniewski, *The Beginnings*, p. 89.
[64] Dieter Korol, 'Zum frühchristlichen Apsismosaik der Bischofskirche von "Capua Vetere" (SS. Stefano e Agata) und zu zwei weiteren Apsidenbildern dieser Stadt (S. Pietro in Corpo und S. Maria Maggiore)', in *Bild- und Formensprache der spätantiken Kunst*, ed. by Martina Jordan-Ruwe, Ulrich Real (Berlin: Wasmuth, 1994), pp. 121–48; Chiara Croci, 'Priscus martyr et premier évêque de Capoue? Notes autour de la mosaïque absidale de l'ancienne église de San Prisco', in *L'évêque, l'image et la mort*, ed. by Nicolas Bock, Ivan Foletti & Michele Tomasi (Rome: Viella, 2014), pp. 415–30; Chiara Croci, *Una 'questione campana': La prima arte monumentale Cristiana tra Napoli, Nola e Capua (secc. IV–VI)* (Rome: Viella, 2017), pp. 200–35.

a selection of Roman martyrs and a number of local south Italian saints, were depicted together as a demonstration of their shared aspiration to please God with their gifts[65] (Fig. 9). While the meaning underlying this decoration remains open to interpretation, the emphatic vision of a crowd of martyrs, grouped together, itself conveys a pronounced visual message in which the glory of the Christian church is revealed in the multitude of its members.

Pairs of Saints in Side Chapels

Finally, apses were used to promote individual cults and specific saints, especially when two saints needed to be represented together. The pairing of saints was a characteristic feature of Late Antiquity, and saintly couples were formed in different ways. Some pairs, such as Sts Gervasius and Protasius, were connected by family relationships as siblings, parents and children, or uncles and nephews. Martyrs, such as Sts Nereus and Achilleus, were linked by a spiritual kinship acquired through a shared martyrdom. Others, such as Sts Sergios and Bakchos, were connected by their professional affiliations as doctors, soldiers, or clerics[66].

Local cults generated other pairs of saints, either because of the presence of relics of two prominent saints or because of the proximity of their shrines[67]. These joint cults are well reflected in the dedications of late antique churches, such as the church of Sts Stephen and Agatha in Capua or the Martyrion of Karpos and Papylos in Constantinople[68]. It seems that the development of joint cults and their related visual culture has not yet received the attention it deserves[69]. However, what art tells us is that these saintly couples would often

---

[65] The saints are St Priscus, St Lupulus, St Sinotus, St Rufus, St Marcellus, St Augustine, and St Felicitas on the left, and St Peter, St Lawrence, St Paul, St Cyprian, St Susius, St Timothy, and St Agnes on the right. Two further smaller figures represent Sts Quartus and Quintus.

[66] On soldiers: Christopher Walter, *The Warrior Saints in Byzantine Art and Tradition* (Aldershot: Ashgate, 2003).

[67] An interesting example of pairing within an apse niche has recently been identified in the murals in St Pantaleon church at Lakkomersina on Naxos featuring St Pantaleon and St Isidore of Chios, correctly attributed by Dora Konstantellou to the early Byzantine period: Theodora Konstantellou, 'The Earlier Wall Paintings of the South Apse in the Church of Agios Panteleemon at Lakkomersina, Naxos. A Neglected Example of Early Byzantine Art from the Aegean', *Byzantinische Zeitschrift*, 116/1 (2023), pp. 105-25.

[68] Korol, 'Zum frühchristlichen Apsismosaik der Bischofskirche von "Capua Vetere"', pp. 121–48; Croci, *Una 'questione campana'*, pp. 184–87. On Martyrion of Karpos and Papylos: Wolfgang Müller-Wiener, *Bildlexikon zur Topographie Istanbuls* (Tübingen: Wasmuth, 1977); Mimar Ayça Beygo, *Istanbul Samatya'da Karpos Papylos Martyrion'u* (unpublished MA thesis, Istanbul Teknik Üniversitesi, Fen Bilimleri Enstitüsü, 2005).

[69] It is worth emphasizing that often these pairs did not reflect an existing hagiographical tradition. Some decorations with saints appeared as a result of intentional selection and hence bear precious evidence for local veneration and specific cults introduced by churchmen in a given location.

appear in lateral chapels and side apses so as to create spaces for individual worship complementary to, but apparently quite distinct from, the services performed at the main altar[70].

The most spectacular and best known example is to be found in Santo Stefano Rotondo in Rome[71] (Fig. 10). The niche in the outer ring of walls in the original circular building, which was erected in the fifth century, was used by Pope Theodore (642–49) to create a chapel destined for the burial of his father[72]. According to the *Liber Pontificalis*, Theodore initiated the transportation of relics belonging to the Roman martyr brothers Primus and Felicianus (previously venerated at the place of their burial on the via Nomentana) within the newly created chapel. It is not, therefore, surprising that the decoration of the apse focuses on two martyr saints, depicted face-on, standing, and wearing military costumes. The two brothers appear on either side of a jewelled cross whose upper arm culminates in the image of a bust of Christ within a medallion[73]. The only additional elements that interfere with the golden background of the conch are a segment of the sky, against which is depicted the hand of God holding a diadem above Christ, and a narrow green strip in the lower portion depicting the ground and filled with red flowers. The dimensions of the exedra are so small that Caecilia Davis-Weyer struggles even to call it an apse[74].

Similar compositions depicting a cross flanked by two saints were typical in late antique art from the fourth century onwards and find numerous attestations in the representations found in gold-glass vessels, sarcophagus reliefs, and catacomb paintings (Fig. 11). I will not enter here into the ongoing discussion

---

[70] Beat Brenk, 'Apsismosaiken ohne Altar: Schiffbruch des Funktionalismus?', in *Synergies in Visual Culture — Bildkulturen im Dialog*, ed. by Manuela de Giorgi, Annette Hoffmann & Nicola Suthor (Paderborn: Fink, 2013), pp. 97–109.

[71] Cäcilia Davis-Weyer, 'Das Apsismosaik von S. Stefano Rotondo in Rom', in *Kirchen am Lebensweg*, ed. by Lothar Altmann (München: Schnell & Steiner, 1988), pp. 385–408. Cäcilia Davis-Weyer, 'S. Stefano Rotondo in Rome and the Oratory of Theodore', in *Italian Church Decoration of the Middle Ages and Early Renaissance. Function, Forms and Regional Traditions*, ed. by William Tronzo (Bologna: Nuova Alfa, 1989), pp. 61–80. For restoration and technical analysis see various papers in: *Mosaici a S. Vitale e altri restauri. Atti del Convegno Nazionale sul restauro in situ di mosaici parietali*, ed. by Anna Maria Iannucci & Cesare Fiori (Ravenna: Longo, 1992), pp. 93–110. See also: Gillian Vallance Mackie, *Early Christian Chapels in the West. Decoration, Function, and Patronage* (Toronto: University of Toronto Press, 2003), p. 77.

[72] Krautheimer, Corbett, Frazer, *Corpus basilicarum Christianarum Romae*, IV, pp. 199–240; Brandenburg, *Ancient churches of Rome*, pp. 200–13.

[73] On this iconography: Rainer Warland, 'Das Brustbild Christi. Studien zur spätantiken und frühbyzantinischen Bildgeschichte', *Römische Quartalschrift für christliche Altertumskunde und Kirchengeschichte. Supplementheft*, 41 (1986), 3–288; Helga Tichy, 'Zur Frage der ursprünglichen Funktion von drei Bildnisclipei im christlichen Kultbereich', *Mitteilungen zur Christlichen Archäologie*, 16 (2010), 29–52.

[74] Davis-Weyer, *S. Stefano Rotondo in Rome*, p. 62.

Fig. 9: Engraving of the lost apse decoration of St Priscus church in Capua published by Michele Monaco in *Sanctuarium Capuanum: opus in quo sacrae res Capuae, et per occasionem plura, tam ad diversas civitates regni pertinentia* (Napoli: apud Octauium Beltranum, 1630), insert between pp. 132–3.

Fig. 10: Sts Primus and Felicianus, mosaic decoration in the apse of a side chapel in Santo Stefano Rotondo, Rome, first half of the seventh century.
Photo: Author.

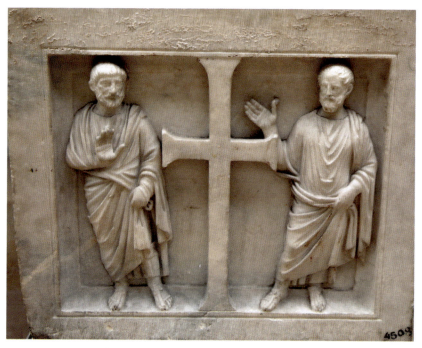

Fig. 11: Two saints (Peter and Paul?) flanking a cross. Lateral side of the marble sarcophagus from Sarigüzel, late fourth or early fifth century, Archaeological Museum, Istanbul.

regarding the possible prototypes for this composition, the potential geographical roots of the iconography, or the wide spectrum of political motivations relating to the events in the Holy Land that could have justified the appearance of such a scene in a commission by Pope Theodore, who himself came from Jerusalem. What I am interested in is the particular mode of visualizing saints within the church space that was used in this case. The programme had to be linked to the altar underneath; it transmitted the idea of paradise as the dwelling place of martyrs, alluded to the theme of salvation which is granted by the cross, and accentuated the all-encompassing glory of Christ alongside the depiction of God's hand granting the victorious crown of salvation.

A comparable example of an early medieval chapel with two paired saints can be found in side apses of the Euphrasian basilica in Poreč[75]. The plan of the church, as has been suggested, may have been based on a Syrian model characterized by three apses. While the main apse contains the complex

---

[75] See note 53.

programme focused on the Mother of God which was briefly discussed above, the two side apses also preserve fragmentary remains of mosaic decorations[76].

The northern niche contains a representation of a youthful beardless Christ towards the top of the apse. Positioned within the clouds, Jesus holds wreaths in both hands above the heads of two standing male figures (Fig. 12). The remains of the inscriptions help us to identify them as Sts Kosmas and Damian. The other apse at the end of the southern aisle was once decorated in a similar manner, with two standing male figures receiving wreaths of victory from Christ, who is placing them directly on their heads (Fig. 13). The fact that, in this case, it is two bishops who are being visually glorified is attested by their ecclesiastical garments, in particular the *pallia* indicating their high rank[77]. A caption placed next to the left shoulder of the man standing on the right reveals his name as Severus, referring most probably to the early Christian bishop of Ravenna. The caption naming the other figure no longer survives, but based on a number of observations and critical deductions, scholars have argued that this figure should most probably be identified as St Hermagoras, the first bishop of Aquileia[78]. If we accept these interpretations, then two bishops who served several decades apart were intentionally brought together in the composition. On the one hand, their appearance together may have been predetermined by political reasons and local ecclesiastical agendas, because the church of Poreč was under the jurisdiction of Aquileia for several centuries. On the other hand, it reflects the commemoration of the bishops of the past as an important part of internal ecclesiastical memory and the veneration of locally important saints[79]. Taken together, the decoration of the two side apses creates a clear parallelism between the martyr-physicians, who demonstrate the spread of imported eastern cults and the locally acclaimed leaders of the church. The lower part of both compositions in the Euphrasian basilica has been destroyed, so no clarity exists as to whether another object or an attribute was depicted between the two figures or whether the cross was placed at the centre, as would have been common in such compositions[80].

A number of decorations, known today exclusively through later descriptions, indicate that apse imagery built around the idea of a pair of saints was

---

[76] On the state of these mosaics and their restoration: Tierry & Maguire, *Dynamic Splendor*, I: pp. 55–56, 117–25.

[77] On the pallium: Bernard Bethod, 'Le pallium, insigne des évêques d'Orient et d'Occident', *Bulletin du CIETA*, 78 (2001), 15–26.

[78] Tierry & Maguire, *Dynamic Splendor*, I, pp. 117–18, 122–23. Other suggestions have included the bishops of Ravenna St Apollinaris or St Ursus.

[79] On veneration of bishops, see notes 19 and 53.

[80] Tierry & Maguire speak of a cross placed above the apses: *Dynamic Splendor*, I, pp. 74, 122; Ihm, *Apsismalerei*, pp. 89–90.

Fig. 12: Apse decoration in the northern chapel with Sts Kosmas and Damian, Euphrasian basilica in Poreč, sixth century.
Photo: Author.

Fig. 13: Apse decoration of the southern chapel with two holy bishops, Euphrasian basilica in Poreč, sixth century.
Photo: Author.

much more widespread and popular than is generally acknowledged. According to some records, for example, an episcopal church in Vercelli dedicated to St Eusebius was renovated between 530 and 542 under Bishop Flavian and received a new mosaic decoration in the apse, which was eventually destroyed during extensive rebuilding in the early 1570s. Based on later testimonies and the fragments of an epitaph, it can be established that the image within the apse contained a representation of a cross flanked by two local saints, the bishops Eusebius (d. in 371) and Limenius (d. in 396). If we accept the scant information available to us as trustworthy, then the sixth-century programme would have been focused on the two ecclesiastics who were venerated as the earliest leaders of the local church. Their role in the church hierarchy, together with the general arrangement of the scene, would echo the representation of two bishops in the southern chapel in the Poreč basilica.

Another record of similar decoration comes from the city of Rimini and an early Christian oratory known as the church of St Gregory[81]. The oratory was demolished in the nineteenth century, but a series of written sources, drawings, and watercolours which were made before the destruction provide sufficient information on its architecture and decoration[82]. The building had a typical cruciform shape with the apse located on the eastern arm of the cross. The modest dimensions of the oratory and its general structure, similar to the so-called mausoleum of Galla Placidia and a number of known early Christian chapels, indicate that it was built in proximity to the larger church, of which it would have formed a part. The architecture fits well with the typology of cruciform *martyria* and other small oratories encountered elsewhere in the Adriatic and beyond[83].

The chapel of St Gregory was decorated with mosaics covering the vaults and cupola, tentatively dated by Iacobini to the end of the fifth century[84]. The apse was decorated with a scene very similar to those already discussed (Fig. 14). Within this scene, the sign of salvation decorated with jewels, the so-called *crux gemmata*, was placed in the centre of the conch[85]. Two male figures were represented standing at the sides, holding crowns and wearing

---

[81] Antonio Iacobini, 'Il sacello di San Gregorio a Rimini e i suoi mosaici. Documenti per un monumento perduto', in *Bisanzio e l'Occidente*, ed. by Claudia Barsanti, Fernanda de Maffei & Mauro della Valle (Rome: Viella, 1996), pp. 345–73.
[82] I would like to thank Prof. Iacobini for providing me with an image of this drawing and reconstruction.
[83] Iacobini, 'Il sacello di San Gregorio', p. 353.
[84] Iacobini, 'Il sacello di San Gregorio', p. 367.
[85] Angelo Lipinsky, 'La 'Crux gemmata' e il culto della Santa Croce nei monumenti superstiti e nelle raffigurazioni monumentali', *Corso di Cultura sull'Arte Ravennate e Bizantina*, 7 (1960), pp. 139–89.

Fig. 14: Reconstruction by G. Fauro of the late antique decoration in
St Gregory's chapel in Rimini based on earlier drawings.
Photo from Antonio Iacobini, 'Il sacello di San Gregorio a Rimini', fig. 18.

robes resembling those of deacons. Two palm trees round off the edges of the composition. In contrast to the depiction in Santo Stefano Rotondo, the two saints were represented not frontally but turned towards the centre, their postures indicating an attitude of offering and reverence towards the Cross[86]. The wreaths in their hands and the presence of palm trees, together with the general environment of the chapel, indicate the likelihood that these depictions represent two martyrs, although the lack of inscriptions and the general silence over their names in later sources do not allow any certitude with regard to their identity.

The Rimini chapel demonstrates that the visual mode under discussion was quite popular in the late antique and early Byzantine period[87]. Whether

---

[86] Such scenes are usually defined as 'aurum coronarium', on which see: Theodor Klauser, 'Aurum Coronarium', *Mitteilungen des Deutschen Archäologischen Instituts*, 59 (1944), 129–53; Roland Delmaire, *Largesses sacrées et res privata. L'aerarium impérial et son administration du IVe au VIe siècle* (Rome: École française de Rome, 1989), pp. 377–400, n. 1.
[87] Grabar, *Martyrium*, II, pp. 68–69. Echoes of this visual tradition can be found in the medieval murals decorating the side chapel in San Giusto church in Trieste: Mario Mirabella Roberti, *San Giusto* (Trieste: Editoriale Libraria, 1970), pp. 33, 330; Iacobini, pp. 365–66.

the iconography and the treatment of the cross needs to be seen as alluding exclusively and predominantly to Jerusalem and the East or whether, based on surviving evidence, this visual formula should be considered primarily a western phenomenon remains an open question. Within the scope of this chapter it is important that images which depict pairs of saints represent a recognisable category within images of martyrs in Late Antiquity. This type of pairing was mainly characteristic of minor spaces reserved for the individual worship of singular saints. Presumably an existing visual formula consisting of two figures arranged beside the cross was initially adopted for the apses of small martyrial shrines, only later taking on a role in the lateral chapels of grander church buildings. The principles of pairing, the significance given to the saints within these compositions, and the message underlying the interaction of the figures both between themselves and with the viewer remain questions for future investigation.

Conclusions

In this chapter I have tried to demonstrate a number of visual strategies that were used for the promotion of saints in Late Antiquity. It is important to single out and analyse individual approaches to the depiction of martyrs, since it can help to formulate a more nuanced understanding of the worship of saints and their role in the Christological universe of the time. The tradition of apsidal martyr representations resonated with a particular historic period and was less popular in the later Middle Ages. Furthermore, it remains an open question whether the issues discussed here need to be restricted to the particular geographical zone of the western and Latin-speaking part of the empire. The scarcity of similar material in the East does not necessarily mean that patterns and iconographic solutions encountered in the West were not practiced there, considering how little evidence survives from that time. Descriptions of the churches of Gaza offer a vivid testimony to a much greater variety of apse decorations once used in the East. Fragmentary remains of early Byzantine church decorations found in Greece and on Greek islands, once studied holistically, can provide precious evidence for the spread and popularity of this tradition. It is evident, however, that after iconoclasm the introduction of cross-in-square churches in Byzantium together with a new system of wall paintings based on liturgical and cosmological interpretations of the space meant that the martyrs would gradually start to take a secondary role in the sacred topography of church architecture and its painted universe, appearing as equal members of the heavenly kingdom but scarcely ever dominating the space from the height of the apse[88]. In the meantime, in the West the medieval examples in which martyrs appear together in the semi-dome above the altar stand primarily as attempts to reproduce late antique decorations, rather than to popularize the cult of saints[89].

The three categories examined in this article both complement each other and bear witness to distinct trends within the popularization of martyrs. From the glorification of individual martyrs, the focus often shifted to the idea of a group of saints and a heavenly reception, in which the figures would share the role of witnesses of faith and jointly act on behalf of living bishops and the congregation gathered in the church. As has been demonstrated, the tradition of pairing saints and creating separate spaces of worship in which two figures would become the focus of particular devotion was also a common practice at the time.

Each type of imagery would have had a distinctive impact on the way in which the saints were perceived by the beholder, although certain aspects are common across the range of images. The *Lives* of saints and hagiography played a relatively small role in the communication of the worshipper with the image of a saint in the conch[90]. Liturgical commemoration, on the other hand, must have been essential in building a connection between the sacrifice and mystery taking place on the altar and the opening of the worship into the heavenly realm populated by saints recreated in the semidome of the apse. The relics of martyrs sanctified the liturgical space, just as liturgical performance would become a tool for the glorification of martyrs and the sanctification of their image. In this two-way interaction the memory of saints would be permanently revived, while their visible images would become the most tangible evidence of their earthly existence, their glorious deaths, and the everlasting peace which they had obtained in heaven.

---

[88] Otto Demus, *Byzantine Mosaic Decoration: Aspects of Monumental Art in Byzantium* (Boston: Boston Book & Art Shop, 1955). On the development and the changes in the church decoration of the Middle Byzantine period, see the classic work by Gordana Babić, 'Les discussions christiologiques et le décor des églises byzantines au XIIᵉ siècle', *Frühmittelalterliche Studien*, 2 (1968), 368–86. See also: Zakharova, 'Principles of Grouping'.

[89] Ernst Kitzinger, 'A Virgin's Face: Antiquarianism in Twelfth-Century Art', *Art Bulletin*, 62 (1980), 6–19; William Tronzo, 'Apse Decoration, the Liturgy and the Perception of Art in Medieval Rome: S. Maria in Trastevere and S. Maria Maggiore', in *Italian Church Decoration of the Middle Ages and Early Renaissance*, ed. by William Tronzo (Bologna: Nuova Alfa ed., 1989), pp. 167–93 (p. 185).

[90] Even if martyrdoms of saints were read during liturgical performances commemorating particular martyrs, and in this way hagiography could complement the image in the apse: Yasin, *Saints and Church*, pp. 240–55; Thunø, *The Apse Mosaic*, 155–56.

Saintly In-betweeners

The Liminal Identity of Thekla and Artemios in their Late Antique Miracle Collections

Julia Doroszewska
(University of Warsaw)

Late antique literature abounds with apparitions of saints, and especially with saintly postmortem epiphanies[1]. This is mirrored in the evidence assembled in the Cult of Saints in Late Antiquity database, which currently displays more than 600 records tagged with 'apparition/vision/dream/revelation' type of miracles, involving about 250 saints[2]. The saints appear to mortals for various reasons that include prophecy, healing, protection, punishment, and many other factors. However, these epiphanies are not always described in detail, and sometimes not at all. Usually the reader simply gets information that a certain saint appeared to an individual, but without any attention paid to the apparition itself. Against this background, one literary genre is particularly important when it comes to studying the saintly epiphanies: late antique collections of miracle stories, known also under their Latin name as *miracula*, which by definition are devoted to manifestations of the saints in this world. The emergence of the genre in the fifth century is inextricably connected to

---

[1] This article results from my research conducted within the framework of the Cult of Saints in Late Antiquity Research Project (ERC Advanced Grant, 340540) and supported by the National Science Centre in Poland project (UMO-2018/31/D/HS3/00870).

[2] See The Cult of Saints in Late Antiquity database. The number of 250 saints includes for the most part single saints or pairs of saints, but also several smaller or bigger groups, such as e.g. the Forty Martyrs of Sebaste.

Interacting with Saints in the Late Antique and Medieval Worlds, ed. by Robert Wiśniewski, Raymond Van Dam, and Bryan Ward-Perkins, Hagiologia, 20 (Turnhout, 2023), pp. 79–95.
© BREPOLS ❧ PUBLISHERS   DOI 10.1484/M.HAG-EB.5.133622

the rise of healing shrines where relics of the saints and martyrs were deposited and where the ritual of incubation usually was practiced[3]. A belief in the supernatural powers of relics brought about a highly developed imagery concerning the afterlife of saints[4]. Collections of miracle stories that are associated with specific cult places are therefore particularly rich sources for the study of the apparitions of saints.

In this chapter I will look closer at some of these texts in order to examine the repertoire of imagery deployed to depict such epiphanies. Drawing from the anthropological concept of liminality, I will point to the representation of the imaginary posthumous existence of the saints as blatantly ambiguous liminal beings ontologically situated between God and ordinary people[5].

---

[3] Stephanos Efthymiadis, 'Collections of Miracles (Fifth–Fifteenth Centuries)', in *The Ashgate Research Companion to Byzantine Hagiography* II: *Genres and Contexts*, ed. by Stephanos Efthymiadis (Farnham, UK and Burlington, VT: Ashgate, 2014), pp. 103–04; Robert Wiśniewski, *The Beginnings of the Cult of Relics* (Oxford: Oxford University Press, 2019), p. 37. On the genre see esp. Ludwig Deubner, *De incubatione capita quattuor* (Lipsiae: Teubner, 1900); Hippolyte Delehaye, 'Les recueils antiques de miracles des saints', *Analecta Bollandiana*, 43 (1925), 5–85; René Aigrain, *L'Hagiographie: ses sources, ses méthodes, son histoire* (Brussels: Société des Bollandistes, 1953); Stephanos Efthymiadis, 'Greek Byzantine Collections of Miracles. A Chronological and Bibliographical Survey', *Symbolae Osloenses*, 74 (1999), 195–211; Stephanos Efthymiadis, 'Collections of Miracles', passim; on Thekla's collection specifically see Scott Johnson, *The Life and Miracles of Thekla: A Literary Study* (Washington, DC: Center for Hellenic Studies, 2006); on the miracle collections in the West see Hippolyte Delehaye, 'Les premiers "libelli miraculorum"', *Analecta Bollandiana*, 29 (1910), 427–34; Yvette Duval, 'Sur la genèse des *libelli miraculorum*', *Revue d'Études Augustiniennes et Patristiques* 52 (2006), 97–112; Raymond Van Dam, *Saints and Their Miracles in Late Antique Gaul* (Princeton, NJ: Princeton University Press, 2011). On incubation, both pagan and Christian, see e.g. Katharina Waldner, 'Les martyrs comme prophètes. Divination et martyre dans le discours chrétien des Ier et IIe siècles', *Revue de l'Histoire des Religions*, 224 (2007), 193–209; Robert Wiśniewski, 'Looking for Dreams and Talking with Martyrs. Internal Roots of Christian Incubation', *Studia Patristica*, 63 (2013), 203–08; Hedvig von Ehrenheim, *Greek Incubation Rituals in Classical and Hellenistic Times* (Liège: Centre interational d'étude de la religion grecque antique, 2015); Stephanos Efthymiadis, 'L'incubation à l'époque mésobyzantine: problèmes de survivance historique et de représentation littéraire (VIIIe-XIIIe siècle)', in *Le saint, le moine et le paysan. Mélanges d'histoire byzantine offerts à Michel Kaplan*, ed. by Olivier Delouis et al. (Paris: Byzantina Sorbonensia, 2016), pp. 155–70; Gil Renberg, *Where Dreams May Come: Incubation Sanctuaries in the Greco-Roman World* (Leiden: Brill, 2017).

[4] On the beginnings of the cult of relics see Wiśniewski, *The Beginnings of the Cult of Relics*, esp. chapter 2.

[5] The conception of liminality was originally minted by the French ethnographer Arnold Van Gennep and presented in his already classic work *Les Rites de passage* (Paris: E. Nourry, 1909). It was then taken up and developed by the anthropologist Victor Turner in the 1960s: Victor Turner, *The Forest of Symbols: Aspects of Ndembu Ritual* (Ithaca, NY: Cornell University Press, 1967); *The Ritual Process: Structure and Anti-Structure* (Chicago: Aldine, 1969); *Dramas, Fields, and Metaphors: Symbolic Action in Human Society*, (Ithaca: Cornell University Press, 1974). Liminality, however, gained independence from the strictly ritual context

An attempt will be made, therefore, to answer the question of how their in-between status is negotiated on the basis of a sample of two collections: an early one, the *Miracles of Thekla*, and a later one, the *Miracles of Artemios*. In this way I aim at pinpointing the dynamics of depicting the saints' 'betwixt and between' position in a diachronic perspective, because despite their undisputable generic affiliation, individual texts display various idiosyncrasies and differences.

Such juxtaposition of the two aforementioned collections seems very promising for several reasons. First, the former text, which dates to the fifth century, is our earliest instance of the genre[6], whereas the latter was composed in the late seventh century, that is, in the period when the *miracula* reached their climax followed by their decline[7]. To use Stephanos Efthymiadis's expression, the *Miracles of Artemios* are pervaded by 'an atmosphere of happy apathy'[8], which was to change shortly. Not long afterward, at the beginning of the eighth century, the Arab conquest brought about radical cultural and political changes that irrevocably altered the religious landscape of the Eastern Roman Empire. Although collections of miracles continued to be produced in the Byzantine Middle Ages, their political, cultural and religious contexts were now vastly different. Furthermore, the character of the texts dating from after the eighth century has also significantly changed, as they usually consist of short and dry stories which describe saintly apparitions much less frequently[9]. The timespan thus defined is therefore an important factor for the present study, as it allows us to grasp the beginning and the end of the cultural and literary phenomenon of late antique miracle collections.

Second, another considerable advantage offered by the juxtaposition of these two texts is the gender differentiation, which provides an insight into how both female and male saints were envisioned in all possible aspects. The differentiation is particularly important, since the *Miracles of Thekla* is the

---

and has been applied to describe various cultural phenomena of a transitional, in-between, bridging, or transformative nature; see e.g. Hein Viljoen & Chris Van der Merwe, *Beyond the Threshold: Explorations of Liminality in Literature* (New York: Peter Lang, 2007); Bjørn Thomassen, *Liminality and the Modern: Living Through the In-Between* (Burlington: Ashgate, 2014). On the liminality of saints see Peter Brown, *The Cult of the Saints: Its Rise and Function in Latin Christianity* (Chicago: University of Chicago Press, 1981).

[6] Along with the miracle collection of Theodore Teron 'the Recruit', which is slightly later (Efthymiadis, 'Greek Byzantine Collections', p. 196; 'Collections of Miracles', pp. 106–07).

[7] Efthymiadis, 'Collections of Miracles', p. 213.

[8] Efthymiadis, 'Collections of Miracles', p. 213.

[9] The elaboration of style and content typical of the late antique collections is observed again in those from the Palaiologian era (thirteenth–fifteenth century) which saw a surge of interest in this genre: Efthymiadis, 'Collections of Miracles', p. 104.

only extant collection devoted to a female saint from the late antique period. Admittedly, while Artemios's specialization is very masculine, since he heals mostly male genitalia, saint Febronia, who was venerated in the same shrine, specializes in healing female genitalia and therefore can be seen as Artemios's counterpart and as a parallel to Thekla[10]. Yet her role, unlike that of Thekla, is rather marginal in the collection.

Third, because both texts are devoted to a single saint, they seem more suitable for such a comparison. The aforementioned Febronia does not work in tandem with Artemios, unlike Cyrus and John or Kosmas and Damian[11].

Finally, in these portrayals both Thekla and Artemios are endowed with a lively and dynamic personality which strongly affects not only their worshippers but also the readers of these miracle collections. As already mentioned, both saints appear as liminal figures, intermediaries between God and mortals, thus bridging the two domains, the earthly and the celestial, the human and the divine. But the means employed in the literary creation of the saints to a large extent vary, as they stress different or even opposing facets of their epiphanies. In this chapter, therefore, I would like to discuss how this blend of domains embodied in the apparitions of saints is depicted in both cases, where the corporeal, human (although not necessarily humane) nature of the saints is combined with supernatural, divine features.

Seeing Thekla

The *Miracles of Thekla*, forty-six in number, were written by an anonymous author[12] around 470 in Seleukeia on the river Kalykadnos, which was the provincial capital of Roman Isauria in southern Asia Minor[13]. In Seleukeia

---

[10] On her role see John Nesbitt, 'Introduction' to *The Miracles of St Artemios: A Collection of Miracle Stories by an Anonymous Author of Seventh Century Byzantium*, ed. by Virgil Crisafulli & John Nesbitt (Leiden: Brill, 1997), p. 13. On this saint see Jean Simon, 'Note sur l'original de la passion de Sainte Fébronie', *Analecta Bollandiana*, 42 (1924), 69–76, and recently Michel Kaplan, 'Une hôtesse importante de l'église Saint-Jean-Baptiste de l'Oxeia à Constantinople: Fébronie', in *Byzantine Religious Culture: Studies in Honor of Alice-Mary Talbot*, ed. by Denis Sullivan et al. (Leiden: Brill, 2011), pp. 31–52. On the cult of Artemios and Febronia in Constantinople see Aude Busine, 'The Dux and the Nun. Hagiography and the Cult of Artemios and Febronia in Constantinople', *Dumbarton Oaks Papers*, 72 (2018), 93–111.

[11] Both of the seventh century: Efthymiadis, 'Collections of Miracles', pp. 197–99.

[12] For a long time spuriously attributed to a fifth-century bishop Basil of Seleukeia (fl. *c.* 448–68); see Gilbert Dagron, 'L'auteur des "Actes" et des "Miracles" de Sainte Thècle', *Analecta Bollandiana*, 92 (1974), 5–11; Alice-Mary Talbot & Scott Johnson, *Miracle Tales from Byzantium* (Cambridge, MA: Harvard University Press, 2012), p. x.

[13] Johnson, *The Life and Miracles of Thekla*, pp. 5–6. The *Miracles* constitute the second part of a work comprising also the *Life* of Thekla, which is an elaborate rewriting of the

there was a site of a flourishing pilgrimage and healing shrine devoted to saint Thekla[14]. With no exaggeration one may claim that after the Virgin Mary, Thekla was the most famous female saint in early Mediterranean Christianity[15]. This may to some extent explain the complex imagery used in the text to present the figure of the martyr.

Let us first focus on Thekla's outward appearance. The *Miracles* provide us with an extensive description of her looks in a scene where she pays a visit to a sick man[16]. The narrator insists that it is a waking vision and not a dream (ὕπαρ οὐκ ὄναρ), which likely derives from the fact that Thekla's apparitions, unlike those of Artemios, essentially do not result from incubation[17]. Moreover, we learn from the passage that the saint appears in her own person and not in the guise of anyone else (αὐτοπροσώπως ἀλλ' οὐ δι' ἑτέρας μορφῆς).

This somewhat puzzling throwaway statement seems to derive from the author's overall conception of the saints when contrasted to pagan divinities. In the Preface to his *Miracles*, he draws a sharp contrast when focusing in particular on the oracular activity of both groups. The latter utter prophecies that are 'deceitful, evil, dishonest, hollow, treacherous, possessing much that is obscure and fraudulent'[18], whereas the former's predictions and healings are 'clear, true, simple, holy, complete, and truly worthy of the God who has granted them'[19]. This paradigmatic model of miracle production is further consequently exemplified by the great martyr Thekla with respect to both her expressions and her actions, which never leave room for any doubt, delusion, or disguise. All the miracles she performs, epiphanies included, are always straightforward and clear, which, as we shall see, significantly distinguishes her from Artemios (and other saints like Cyrus and John or Kosmas and Damian).

---

third-century *Acts of Thekla*: Johnson, *The Life and Miracles of Thekla*, p. 5. For the outline of both parts see Johnson, *The Life and Miracles of Thekla*, p. xix.

[14] Johnson, *The Life and Miracles of Thekla*, pp. 1–3.

[15] Johnson, *The Life and Miracles of Thekla*, pp. 221–26; Davis, *The Cult of Saint Thecla: A Tradition of Women's Piety in Late Antiquity* (Oxford: Oxford University Press, 2001), p. v. See also *Thecla: Paul's disciple and saint in the East and West*, ed. by Jeremy Barrier et al. (Leuven: Peeters, 2017).

[16] *Miracles of Thekla* (henceforward *MTh*) 14; see CSLA E05503.

[17] With an exception of *MTh* 12, where the author claims to be healed by Thekla in a dream in her shrine; see Johnson, *The Life and Miracles of Thekla*, p. 8.

[18] *MTh* Preface, 6: ἀπατηλά, πονηρά, κίβδηλα, ὕπουλα, δολερά, πολὺ τὸ ἀχλυῶδες καὶ διεψευσμένον ἔχοντα. English translation by Alice-Mary Talbot & Scott Johnson, 'Miracle Tales from Byzantium'. All quotations from *MTh* are from this translation.

[19] Ibidem: Σαφῆ, ἀληθῆ, ἁπλᾶ, ἅγια, ὁλόκληρα καὶ τοῦ δεδωκότος θεοῦ ἀληθῶς ἐπάξια. Text: Gilbert Dagron, *Vie et miracles de Sainte Thècle. Texte grec, traduction et commentaire* (Brussels: Société des Bollandistes, 1978).

Thekla is seen as a beautiful yet unassuming girl, with light emanating from her entire body:

> A trim girl and not too tall, fair of face, dignified, steady, graceful, pale with some redness of cheek [...] even more and above all, the beauty of discretion bloomed in her with dignity, with grace, with splendor in her eyes, and splendor in the rest of her body, which sparkled under her somber clothes, and she seemed to gleam like a sun through a thin curtain of purple[20].

The contrast between her modest garment and her splendid gleaming appearance is further emphasized in the following passage:

> In short, she was dressed like a virgin and in a way that is customary for the holy handmaidens of Christ, but she shone with a heavenly and divine light, so that angelic and human natures seemed to be mingled together and, through the two, produced something like a godlike, pure, and living statue[21].

By explicitly pointing out the twofold nature of the saint, human and angelic, the description strongly suggests a liminal nature, which is also highlighted by the clearly paradoxical simile of the living statue.

This liminality is further underscored in the depiction of Thekla's other dwelling in the city of Dalisandos near Seleukeia. The saint is said to have loved this spot more than any other, excepting Seleukeia, and the city is famous for the festival in her honour[22]. The description is clearly modeled on the literary trope of the heavenly garden, paradise, or the *locus amoenus*[23]. The shrine

---

[20] *MTh* 14: εὐσταλής τις καὶ μικρὸν ἀνεστηκυῖα κόρη, εὐπρόσωπος, ἐμβριθής, εὐσταθής, εὔχαρις, ὕπωχρος μετ' ἐρυθήματος [...] πολὺ δὲ ἔτι καὶ παντὸς ἄλλου τὸ τῆς σωφροσύνης ἐπήνθει κάλλος αὐτῇ μετ' αἰδοῦς, μετὰ χαρίτων, μετὰ ὀφθαλμῶν ἀγλαΐας καὶ τῆς τοῦ λοιποῦ σώματος αἴγλης, ὃ τοῖς φαιοῖς μὲν ὑπέστιλβεν ἱματίοις, ἐδόκει δὲ ὥσπερ ἔκ τινος ἁλουργοῦ τε καὶ λεπτοῦ παραπετάσματος ὑπαυγάζειν ἥλιος.

[21] *MTh* 14: καὶ γὰρ ἔσταλτο μὲν παρθενικῶς καὶ ἡ νόμος ταῖς ἱεραῖς τοῦ Χριστοῦ θεραπαινίσιν, οὐράνιον δέ τι καὶ θεῖον ἀπήστραπτε φῶς, ὡς δοκεῖν ἀγγέλου τε ἅμα καὶ ἀνθρώπου φύσιν ἀνακεκρᾶσθαι καὶ δι' ἀμφοῖν ἄγαλμά τι συγκεῖσθαι θεοειδὲς καὶ ἀκήρατον καὶ ἔμπνουν.

[22] *MTh* 26. The city's exact location is unknown; see Dagron, *Vie et miracles de Sainte Thècle*, p. 357 n. 1 for hypotheses. As the author of the *Miracles* admits further in the same passage, Dalisandos has been cast away into obscurity, and its remaining splendour derives only from the cult of Thekla.

[23] *MTh* 26 (CSLA E05643): Τά τε γὰρ ἐν αὐτῇ δένδρα πολλά τε καὶ ὑψηλὰ καὶ ἀμφιλαφῆ καὶ ἀμφιθαλῆ καὶ καλλίκαρπα, αἵ τε αὖ πηγαὶ πολλαί τε καὶ χαριέσταται, καὶ μάλα ψυχροῦ ὕδατος, ἐξ ἑκάστου φυτοῦ τε καὶ πέτρας, ὡς εἰπεῖν, ἑκάστης ἐκθέουσαί τε καὶ διαρρέουσαι καὶ αὐτὸν περιθέουσαι τὸν νεών, τό τε εὔπνουν τοῦ τόπου ὡς πολύ τε καὶ λιγυρὸν καὶ ἀγαπητόν, ἥ τε ὑπὲρ κεφαλῆς ᾠδὴ τῶν ὀρνίθων ὡς μάλα θαυμασία τε καὶ καταθέλξαι ἱκανὴ οὐκ ἀνειμένον μόνον ἤδη καὶ τρυφηλόν, ἀλλὰ γὰρ καὶ κατηφῆ καὶ κατεστεναγμένον ἄνθρωπον, ἥ τε πόα πολλή τε καὶ δαψιλὴς καὶ πολύχρους ἐπικεχυμένη τῇ γῇ, καὶ ἐναναπαύεσθαι παντὶ παρέχουσα, καὶ ἀνδρὶ καὶ γυναικὶ καὶ παιδίοις ἀθύρουσι καὶ βοσκήμασι νεμομένοις, ἔτι μὴν καὶ ἐπιχορεῦσαι βουλομένοις

is represented as a delightful grassy meadow surrounded by numerous trees which abound in blossoms and fruit and traversed by many lovely streams. There is a nice breeze, and the marvellous singing of the birds overhead is able to enchant not only the joyful visitors but also those who are downcast. This setting provides a place for rest, dance, and joy for men, women, children, and animals. Moreover, it is clearly an extension of the martyr's charm and potency, since some sick people are said to have been restored to health only by visiting it. It is therefore a truly liminal space, a heavenly zone in the vale of tears and a piece of heaven warranted by the presence of the martyr. Elsewhere Thekla is also said to frequent a cave — another liminal space — near her church in Seleukeia, which is her favorite place[24].

So much for her appearance and her abode. In her epiphanies, Thekla is also endowed with a lively temperament and does not hesitate to express her emotions, predominantly her wrath. This is seen in several of her epiphanies. In one of them, for instance, Thekla gets angry with Maximos, who was presiding over her shrine in Seleukeia and allowed the burial of a certain Hyperechios inside the shrine. As the grave diggers started their work, the martyr's reaction was immediate: she stood before them, 'looking at them with a more severe and angry gaze, as is typical of those who are extremely irritated' (ἐμβριθέστερον δὲ

καὶ ἐνσκιρτῆσαι φαιδρότατα, θοινήσασθαί τε προθυμουμένοις καὶ ἐμφαγεῖν θυμηρέστατα, ἤδη δὲ καὶ νοσοῦσι πρὸς ὑγίειαν μόνον. On Thekla's shrine see Troels Myrup Kristensen, 'Landscape, Space and Presence in the Cult of Thekla in Meriamlik', *Journal of Early Christian Studies* 24 (2016), 229–63. The Graeco-Roman topos of the *locus amoenus*, an ideal space or landscape, here takes on traits of the biblical paradise; for the classic definition of the *locus amoenus* see Ernst Curtius, *European Literature and the Latin Middle Ages*, trans. by W. R. Trask (Princeton: Princeton University Press, 1953), pp. 196–202; on paradise see Jeffrey Russell, *A History of Heaven: The Singing Silence* (Princeton: Princeton University Press), esp. pp. 12–14.

[24] *MTh* 36 (CSLA E05837): 'This is a cave to the west of her church, lying just opposite it, which is quite delightful and charming and offers a very pleasant spot to walk and spend time, where one can pray in absolute tranquility and obtain from the martyr through prayer whatever one desires. Anyone who comes to pray at the church straightaway also heads to this cave, as if to a bedroom and chamber where the virgin martyr resides. For some say she spends most of her time in this cave, because she loves the quiet and solitude. For this quality is distinctive of the saints, that they enjoy quiet places and spend as much time as possible in them.' Furthermore, in both variant endings of the *MTh* Thekla is said to have settled in a cave and begun accomplishing healings. Either in Myrsineon, i.e. the myrtle grove outside the city of Seleukeia, or on the Mountain Kalameon or Rhodion (see Appendix to Talbot & Johnson, pp. 193–201); on the variant endings see Dagron, *Vie et miracles de Sainte Thècle*, pp. 47–54; Johnson, *The Life and Miracles of Thekla*, pp. 227–31. Caves are usually considered as sites of passage to another world, be it a realm of the dead or that of the divine; on the cave as a liminal place see e.g. Richard Buxton, *Imaginary Greece: The Contexts of Mythology* (Cambridge: Cambridge University Press, 1994), pp. 92–113, esp. pp. 108–09; Margaret Doody, *The True Story of the Novel* (New Brunswick: Rutgers University Press, 1996), chap. 13; Holley Moyes, *Sacred Darkness: A Global Perspective on the Ritual Use of Caves* (Boulder, CO: University Press of Colorado, 2012).

καὶ ὀργιλώτερον εἰς αὐτοὺς ἀπιδοῦσα λοιπόν, καὶ οἷα τῶν ἄγαν χαλεπαινόντων ἐστίν)[25]. She then knocked the breath out of them (ἄπνους αὐτοὺς ἐποίησεν). The emphasis here is on the gaze of the martyr, supposedly endowed with an almost lethal power, as the passage further reads. 'For the martyr is fearsome, not only when she exercises her strength, but also when she gazes directly at those who might be deserving of such a gaze — and she nearly deprived them of their lives'[26]. In this epiphany Thekla's wrath is mediated through her sight.

By contrast, in another passage the saint's fury is represented chiefly through the auditory domain[27]. This time it is roused by the actions of Bishop Dexianos, who dared to remove the decorations from her shrine and, fearing that the treasures would fall prey to plunderers, transferred them to the city. Thekla fills the church with a noise (θόρυβος), disturbance (ταραχή), and shouting (βοή), and the martyr is running back and forth (ἄνω τε καὶ κάτω διαθεούσης), accusing Dexianos of scorning her, as if she were weak. Some virgins who were sleeping inside the church that night *heard* the waking vision of the martyr (παρ' αὐτῆς τῆς μάρτυρος ἀκούσασαι ὕπαρ) and almost lost their minds from fear (μικροῦ μὲν καὶ τῶν φρενῶν ἐξέπεσον ὑπὸ τοῦ δείματος). Other scenes depict Thekla laughing and smiling, sometimes ironically, sometimes with content. In the former case Thekla mocks the idea that a theft would escape her all-seeing and divine eye (εἴπερ οἷόν τε λήσειν αὐτῆς τὸ πανδερκές τε καὶ θεῖον ὄμμα)[28]. Again we are reminded about the powerful gaze of the martyr. Elsewhere we also see her pleased and smiling approvingly when she reads the miracles written down by the author. This passage is particularly interesting, as it describes the author's firsthand experience during which the martyr assists in the very process of the creation of the collection of her miracles:

> The martyr seemed (ἔδοξεν) to appear before my eyes, sitting down beside me in the place where I normally consult my books, and she took from my hand the notebook on which I was transcribing this previous miracle from the writing tablet. Indeed, she seemed to me (ἐδόκει μοι) to read and enjoy it, and to smile and show me by the expression of her eyes that she was pleased with what I had written[29].

---

[25] *MTh* 30 (CSLA E05649).

[26] *MTh* 30 (CSLA E05649): φοβερὰ γὰρ ἡ μάρτυς, οὐ κινοῦσα μόνον τὴν ἰσχύν, ἀλλὰ γὰρ καὶ βλέπουσα ἀτενὲς πρὸς οὓς ἂν καὶ δεηθείη τοιούτου βλέμματος — μικροῦ δ' ἂν καὶ τῆς ζωῆς αὐτοὺς ἀπέρρηξεν. The powerful and dangerous gaze is a distinctive feature of the pagan gods, especially on the grounds of epics, see Helen Lovatt, *The Epic Gaze: Vision, Gender and Narrative in Ancient Epic* (Cambridge: Cambridge University Press, 2013), pp. 29–77.

[27] *MTh* 32 (CSLA E05694).

[28] *MTh* 22 (CSLA E05589). See also *MTh* 34. 5 (CSLA E05711).

[29] *MTh* 31 (CSLA E05693): ἔδοξεν ἡ μάρτυς πλησίον ἐν ὄψει μου παρακαθέζεσθαι, οὗπερ καὶ ἔθος ἦν μοι τὴν πρὸς τὰ βιβλία ποιεῖσθαι συνουσίαν, καὶ ἀφαιρεῖσθαί μου τῆς χειρὸς τὴν

In this scene the apparition is again mediated through the recipient's sight, and again the martyr operates here with her gaze. A striking feature of this epiphany is, however, its ambiguity, which is emphasized by a double repetition of the verb 'to seem' (ἔδοξεν, ἐδόκει μοι).

Even more revealing of Thekla's dual and therefore liminal nature are the accounts of apparitions where she is said to affect objects and people physically. For instance, she is once seen to soak a pregnant woman's forehead to bring her relief in the heat[30]. A particularly instructive example of this interaction is the episode in which she saves two boys on a boat during a severe storm[31]. The martyr appears (φαίνεται) on the boat and literally takes control of it by 'holding the rudder in her hands' (οἰάκων ἁπτομένη), as if she were using her very corporeal body. She 'skilfully swings it to and fro' (κάλως ἀνασείουσα), 'lifts up the sail' (τὸ ἱστίον ἀνατείνουσα), 're-bukes the storm' (τῷ χειμῶνι ἐπιτιμῶσα), and 'does everything fitting for an apostle and a martyr whose power reaches everywhere' (πάντα ποιοῦσα ὅσα πρέπει [...] ἀποστόλῳ καὶ μάρτυρι καὶ πάντοθεν ἐχούσῃ τὸ δύνασθαι)[32]. Apparently, this limitless ability of Thekla is also the reason why she can appear outside of her shrine, in this case on the sea somewhere near the Isaurian shore.

Yet, on the other hand, she is frequently represented as flying away after her epiphany. Καὶ ἡ μὲν εἰρηκυῖα ταῦτα ἀπέπτη ἤΰτε πέλεια — ποιητῶν ἄν τις εἶπεν: 'Having said all of this she flew away like a dove (as one of the poets would say)'[33]. This phenomenon is described with the verb *apopetomai*, which means flying off or away and already in Homer is connected to a dream, that is, something discarnate[34]. This phrase recurs several times throughout the text[35]. Her departure is also once described as sinking down into the earth (καταδῦναι)[36]. We are dealing here with what Patricia Miller calls 'ambiguous corporeality', pointing out the problem faced by ancient hagiographers when they came 'to portray the ongoing liveliness of a sainted, but dead, human

---

τετράδα, ἐν ᾗπερ καὶ ταῦτα ἐκ τῆς δέλτου μετεγραφόμην. Καὶ δὴ καὶ ἀναγινώσκειν ἐδόκει μοι καὶ ἐφήδεσθαι καὶ μειδιᾶν, καὶ ἐνδείκνυσθαί μοι τῷ βλέμματι ὡς ἀρέσκοι τότε τοῖς γραφομένοις. Translation slightly modified.

[30] *MTh* 19 (CSLA E05587).

[31] *MTh* 15 (CSLA E05516).

[32] Translation lightly modified.

[33] *MTh* 11. 3 (CSLA E05495); actually, it is not a quotation from Homer but a use of Homeric language (Talbot & Johnson, p. 419, n. 38).

[34] Homer, *Il.* II. 71 (of a dream); *Od.* XI. 222 (of the soul).

[35] *MTh* 12. 8, 35. 3, 46. 1 (CSLA E05497, E05717, E05837 respectively).

[36] *MTh* 46. 1.

being[37]. She labels this as 'visceral seeing', a phenomenon of peculiar synesthesia, where the traditionally privileged sight is coupled with other senses, especially with touch[38].

The timing of Thekla's epiphanies is also vested with liminal characteristics. Even though she appears on earth both at night and day, there are passages which emphasize a particular moment of transition between these periods. What is particularly revealing in this respect is the author's/narrator's description of his first-hand experience of the saint's apparition:

> I, with fear and weeping, had a dream. It was still night, midway between the decision and the amputation. Having fallen asleep only a little before dawn (at the point when night is coming to an end and the day is beginning, so that both appear mixed together, dark with light, light with dark) [...], I saw the virgin entering the place where I was sleeping[39].

Finally, the distinction between the waking vision (in Greek: ὕπαρ) and the dream (ὄναρ) demands a word of commentary. In several passages[40] the author emphasizes that Thekla appeared in a waking vision and not in a dream, which clearly hints at the existence of a hierarchy of visions, according to which pride of place is given to a waking vision. A waking vision evidently adds to the credibility of the apparition, whereas a dream can be more easily downgraded to a mere phantasy of the dreamer[41].

---

[37] Patricia Cox Miller, *The Corporeal Imagination: Signifying the Holy in Late Ancient Christianity* (Philadelphia: University of Pennsylvania Press, 2009), p. 102.

[38] Miller, *The Corporeal Imagination*, pp. 102–03; the expression of 'visceral seeing' is borrowed from the art historian James Elkins, *Pictures of the Body: Pain and Metamorphosis* (Stanford, CA: Stanford University Center for Hellenic Studies, 1999), p. viii, who defines it as 'a peculiar kind of response to depicted bodies that puts in question the traditional distinction between viewer and viewed'.

[39] *MTh* 12 (CSLA E05497): ἐγὼ δὲ μετὰ δέους καὶ δακρύων ὠνειροπόλουν. Νὺξ δὲ ἦν ἔτι, τὸ μέσον τῆς βουλῆς καὶ τῆς τομῆς. Μικρὸν δὲ ὅσον ἀποκαθευδήσας αὐτὸ τὸ περίορθρον καὶ καθ' ὃν ἀπολήγει μὲν ἔτι καιρὸν ἡ νύξ, ἄρχεται δὲ ἡ ἡμέρα, ὡς καὶ δοκεῖν ἄμφω ἀνακεκρᾶσθαι, φωτὶ μὲν σκότος, σκότει δὲ φῶς [...] ὁρῶ δὲ καὶ τὴν παρθένον ἐπεισελθοῦσαν οὗ ἐκάθευδον.

[40] e.g. *MTh* 14. 3, 18. 1, 19. 1, 29. 5 (CSLA E05503, E05574, E05587, E05648 respectively).

[41] On the terminology of dreams in Antiquity see e.g. George Calofonos, *Byzantine Oneiromancy* (Birmingham: University of Birmingham, 1994), esp. pp. 162–64; Margaret Kenny, 'Distinguishing between Dreams and Visions in Ninth-Century Hagiography', *Gouden Hoorn — Golden Horn* 4 (1996): no page numbers, https://goudenhoorn.com/2011/11/21/distinguishing-between-dreams-and-visions-in-ninth-century-hagiography, accessed on 25 October 2019; Steven Oberhelman, *Dreambooks in Byzantium: Six Oneirocritica in Translation, with Commentary and Introduction* (Farnham: Ashgate, 2008), pp. 23–26; on dreams in general see e.g. Lisa Bitel, '*In Visu Noctis*: Dreams in European Hagiography and Histories, 450–900', *History of Religions*, 31 (1991), 39–59; Calofonos, *Byzantine Oneiromancy*; John Pilch, *Flights of the Soul: Visions, Heavenly Journeys, and Peak Experiences in the Biblical World* (Grand Rapids, MI: Eerdmans Publishing, 2011); Stephen Oberhelman, *Dreams, Healing, and Medicine in Greece: From Antiquity to the Present* (Farnham: Ashgate, 2013);

Artemios the Trickster

Let us now move to the *Miracles of Artemios*. The text was written in the second half of the seventh century, sometime between 658 and 668 by an anonymous author[42]. It is a collection of miracles connected, strangely enough, to the church of John the Forerunner in Constantinople, where the body of the martyr Artemios was deposited[43].

This martyr, although likewise depicted as a liminal figure, significantly differs from his female saintly colleague in many aspects. Unlike Thekla, Artemios, with only few exceptions, appears in dreams received through the practice of incubation. The most common expression denoting this phenomenon is κατ᾿ ὄναρ φαίνεται, such as in the following passage: 'Then one night the holy martyr appeared to him in a dream'[44]. Only in a small number of miracles is his presence real and perceptible; such cases are underscored by the adverb ὀφθαλμοφανῶς, 'apparently to the eye', 'visibly'. For instance: 'One night the saint in full view (ὀφθαλμοφανῶς) approached the man, while many of those awaiting the cure looked on'[45]. Artemios's manifestations in dreams are by default linked to nighttime. The timing is usually explicitly stated in the text, as when we are told that the vision's recipient was sleeping at night[46], or when Artemios appeared to many people[47]. However, some of the scenes are set at a specific time of the 'small hours', which is rendered by the expression ταῖς πολλαῖς[48]. In addition, someone once sees the saint when he fell asleep towards daybreak (τὰ πρὸς τὸν ὄρθρον)[49].

Christine Angelidi and George Calofonos, *Dreaming in Byzantium and Beyond* (Farnham: Ashgate, 2014); Jesse Keskiaho, *Dreams and Visions in the Early Middle Ages. The Reception and Use of Patristic Ideas, 400–900* (Cambridge: Cambridge University Press, 2018).

[42] Nesbitt, 'Introduction', p. 7 and pp. 1–7 on Artemios as a historical figure; see also *PLRE* I:112, s.v. Artemius 2.

[43] Cyril Mango, 'History of the Templon and the Martyrion of St Artemios at Constantinople', *Zograf*, 10 (1979), 40–43.

[44] *Miracles of Artemios* (hereafter *MA*), 1 (CSLA E04228): ἐν μιᾷ οὖν νυκτὶ φαίνεται αὐτῷ κατ᾿ ὄναρ ὁ ἅγιος μάρτυς; text: Athanasios Papadopoulos-Kerameus, *Miracula xlv sancti Artemii*, in *Varia graeca sacra* (St Petersburg: Kirschbaum, 1909), pp. 1–75, reprinted and translated in Crisafulli & Nesbitt, *The Miracles of St Artemios*. All quotations from *MA* are from this translation.

[45] *MA* 6 (CSLA E04231): καὶ δὴ ἔρχεται πρὸς αὐτὸν ὁ ἅγιος ὀφθαλμοφανῶς ἐν μιᾷ νυκτί, θεωρούντων καὶ τῶν πρὸς τὸ ἰαθῆναι παραμενόντων πολλῶν; translation Crisafulli & Nesbitt. See also *MA* 3, 14, 35, 39 (CSLA E04229, E04234, E04251, E07822 respectively).

[46] E.g. *MA* 1: ἐν μιᾷ οὖν νυκτὶ; *MA* 5 (CSLA E07813): ὁρᾷ κατ᾿ ὄναρ τὸν ἅγιον τῇ νυκτὶ ἐκείνῃ; see also *MA* 20 (CSLA E07824): ἐν αὐτῇ οὖν τῇ νυκτὶ ἐφάνη αὐτῷ κατ᾿ ὄναρ ὁ ἅγιος λέγων; *MA* 23 (CSLA E04242): ἐν μιᾷ τῶν νυκτῶν· φαίνεται δὲ αὐτῷ ἐν σχήματι τοῦ νομιζομένου ἰατροῦ; see aso *MA* 24, 27, 36, 42 (CSLA E04243, E07819, E04252, E07823).

[47] *MA* 6 (CSLA E04231), see n. 45.

[48] *MA* 8 and 21 (CSLA E07815 and E04240).

[49] *MA* 2 (CSLA E07812).

JULIA DOROSZEWSKA

Since Artemios is a miracle worker with a specialization, the marvels he performs are less diverse than those of Thekla. Almost all of his healings are diseases of testicles, in particular hernias[50]. The martyr also displays a sense of wicked humour, because sometimes he actually bestows a hernia on those who have sinned against him, for instance by urinating in his church[51]. Furthermore, unlike Thekla, he almost never expresses his emotions. An exception is the passage in which Artemios heals a babbler: 'But this man chattered incessantly. [...] So the saint appeared to him in the small hours saying: When day comes, withdraw from here. If you remain another moment, I will double your hernia. For I hate babblers'[52]. Artemios's corporeality seems to manifest itself quite clearly with interventions in which he physically manipulates the affected body parts. He apparently prefers shock therapy, healing his patients by squeezing their testicles[53], pricking them[54], treading on them[55] or at least touching them[56]; sometimes he even resorts to surgical interventions, such as an incision with a scalpel[57]. However, we should keep in mind that apparitions such as these are nevertheless included in dreams, which by definition renders them elusive and ambiguous.

An even more revealing example of such intervention is found in the passage in which the saint appears as a butcher:

> Now that very night the saint appeared in a dream in the guise of a butcher, holding butchers' tools and a cup, in which there was water; and when he

---

[50] Or other testicle disorders that are described in Greek with technical terms (such as κήλη, 'tumour,' or καταβαρής, 'heavy-laden') that prove difficult for understanding and translation (Crisafulli & Nesbitt, *The Miracles of St Artemios*, p. xvii).

[51] *MA* 17 and 37 (CSLA E04237 and E04253).

[52] *MA* 8 (CSLA E07815): δὲ οὗτος ἦν λαλῶν πολλά [...] φαίνεται οὖν αὐτῷ ταῖς πολλαῖς ὁ ἅγιος λέγων· Ἡνίκα ἡμέρα γένηται, ἀναχώρει τῶν ἔνθεν, ἐπεὶ ἐὰν μείνῃς ἄλλην ῥοπήν, διπλῆν ποιῶ τὴν κήλην σου· ἐγὼ γὰρ μισῶ τοὺς φλυάρους'.

[53] c.g. *MA* 1 and 2 (σφίγγω).

[54] *MA* 13 (νύσσω) (CSLA E07818).

[55] *MA* 14 (πατέω) (CSLA E04234).

[56] *MA* 5 (ἅπτω) (CSLA E07813); 12 (CSLA E04233), 32 (CSLA E04248), 37 (CSLA E04253), 39 (CSLA E07822).

[57] *MA* 3 (CSLA E04229): δέδωκεν αὐτῷ μετὰ ξίφους τομήν, 22 (CSLA E04241): τῇ ἀκμῇ τῆς σμίλης ἥψατο τῆς δορᾶς τοῦ δεξιοῦ διδύμου τοῦ νοσοῦντος; 25 (CSLA E04244): 42 (CSLA E07823): λαβὼν τῇ χειρὶ ἓν τῶν παρακειμένων ἐργαλείων, ὡς ὁρμᾷ ἀπενέγκαι αὐτὸ ἐπὶ τὸν δίδυμον τοῦ παιδός. In all these actions, as Anne Alwis points out (Anne Alwis, 'Men in Pain: Masculinity, Medicine and the Miracles of St Artemios', *Byzantine and Modern Greek Studies*, 36 (2012), 1–19 (p. 8)) he seems to follow the approved medical method explicitly described by the seventh-century medical doctor Paul of Aegina, who for testicular disorders recommends a hands-on examination, see: Paulus Aegineta, *Corpus Medicorum Graecorum* IX. 1 (Heiberg): 3. 54. 1; see *The Medical Works of Paul Aegineta*, trans. F. Adams (London: Welsh, Treuttel, Würtz and Co., 1834), vol. 1, p. 329. See also Alwis, 'Men in Pain', 9–14 for medical explanations of the diseases and treatment found in the *Miracles of Artemios*.

90

observed the suffering man, the butcher pierced him with a knife in his lower abdomen and took out all his intestines. And the sick man saw him folding them up and making sausages, as it were, and said 'O me, I refused to give myself to a doctor and look what you are doing, man. When you have taken everything inside of me, I will no longer be alive!' [...] But the other remained silent, and to all appearances he kept on cleaning his intestines. And arranging them, as it were, in one coil, he put them back again into the sick man's belly[58].

We are dealing here with Artemios's teasing the patient, and that in a rather cruel way, since the man earlier had refused to give himself over to surgery and decided to turn to the martyr's help instead[59].

The dream-like quality of Artemios' interventions, physical on the one hand but elusive on the other, brings out one aspect of his liminality that is shared with Thekla. His presence, like that of the female martyr, is both 'ephemeral and tangible', to refer again to Patricia Miller[60], which results from a certain difficulty and confusion inherent to his ontological status. Another such aspect, already foreshadowed in the account of his apparition in the guise of the butcher/surgeon, is his nature, which is essentially that of a trickster. The martyr likes appearing in various guises, usually in the form of a nobleman, an important person, or even a relative or friend. In fact he appears in disguise in almost half of the miracles[61]. Interestingly, when he appears as himself, we never get a description of his appearance, but simply learn that someone saw the holy martyr in a dream[62]. In contrast, his counterpart Febronia, who appears only four times in the entire collection, is always depicted as a beautiful woman dressed in a monastic garb. Like Thekla, she never impersonates someone else[63].

---

[58] *MA* 25 (CSLA E04244): τῇ οὖν αὐτῇ νυκτὶ φαίνεται αὐτῷ ὁ ἅγιος κατ᾽ ὄναρ ἐν σχήματι μακελλαρίου, κατέχων ἐργαλεῖα μακελλαρικὰ καὶ σκύφιν, ἐν ᾧ ἦν ὕδωρ, καὶ ὅτι ἐσημειώσατο αὐτὸν τὸν πάσχοντα καὶ μετὰ μαχαίρας ἐκέντησεν αὐτὸν κατὰ τοῦ ὑπογαστρίου αὐτοῦ καὶ ἐξήνεγκεν πάντα τὰ ἐντὸς αὐτοῦ· εἶτα καθαρίζει αὐτὰ καὶ ἀποπλύνει καὶ στρέφει μετὰ βεργίου. καὶ ἑώρα αὐτὸν συστέλλοντα αὐτὰ καὶ ποιοῦντα ὡς χορδία, καὶ λέγει ὁ νοσῶν· 'Οὐαί μοι, ἐγὼ ἐμαυτὸν εἰς ἰατρὸν οὐκ ἠνεσχόμην δοῦναι καὶ σὺ τί ποιεῖς, ἄνθρωπε; ἐπὰν τὰ ἐντός μου πάντα ἐξήγαγες, λοιπὸν οὐκέτι ζῶ.' [...] ὁ δὲ ἐσιώπα μέν, τὰ δὲ ἐντὸς αὐτοῦ κατὰ τὸ δοκοῦν ἐκάθαιρεν. καὶ ποιήσας αὐτὰ ὡς ἑνὸς εἰλήματος πάλιν ἐναπέθετο αὐτὰ ἐν τῇ κοιλίᾳ τοῦ νοσοῦντος.

[59] On the inconsistent and ambiguous attitude towards medicine exhibited by the text see John Haldon, 'Supplementary Essay. The Miracles of Artemios and Contemporary Attitudes: Context and significance', in *The Miracles of St Artemios*, ed. by Crisafulli & Nesbitt, 33–73, at pp. 42–56.

[60] Miller, *The Corporeal Imagination*, p. 102.

[61] For the complete lists of his disguises see Virgil Crisafulli, 'Translator's Preface', in *The Miracles of St Artemios*, ed. by Crisafulli & Nesbitt, pp. xiii–xiv.

[62] E.g. *MA* 9: φαίνεται κατ᾽ ὄναρ τῇ γυναικὶ ὁ ἅγιος; see also *MA* 20, 28, 36, etc.

[63] Her description, however, is at best boiled down to just one sentence: ὁρᾷ πάλιν ἡ αὐτὴ τῆς παιδὸς μήτηρ γυναῖκα εὐοπτοτάτην, μοναχικὴν περιβεβλημένην ἀμφίασιν: 'The same mother

Artemios has many disguises. Most frequently he takes on the appearance of a doctor; in one vision he is seen as the chief physician[64]; elsewhere he assumes the garb of the Persian doctor summoned earlier by a patient[65] or of a patient's father, who happened to be chief physician[66]. Sometimes he appears as a man of rank wearing civilian clothes[67], or as an individual's close friend, who was himself a man of distinction[68]. Anne Alwis attributes Artemios' predilection for disguises to his kindness, as he seeks to calm patients by assuming the form of someone the sick recognize and feel the most comfortable with[69]. According to her interpretation, the saint's disguise also serves as a precaution against any sexual associations related to exposing or handling the genitalia; perhaps such an act was also considered less shameful when a friend was involved rather than a stranger[70].

There is an intriguing inconsistency in Artemios' appearances, because the rationale underpinning his choice about whether to assume a disguise or resort to odd behavior remains unclear. This unpredictability shows up in three chapters describing similar cases of healing a sick baby. In one of them we find the wife of a palace official, whose son had a testicular disorder. Artemios appears in a dream disguised as her friend and says to her: 'You were sad that I did not come to visit you during all the time you spent in the church. Since the emperor sent me far from the city on business and I returned, now I have come to see you; what is wrong with your child?'[71] While asleep, she gives an account of her son's illness. Artemios wants to see the child, so the mother fetches him and exposes his testicles. Making the sign of the cross with his finger over his testicles, the saint heals the boy in the name of Jesus Christ. Why does the saint insist on impersonating the woman's friend? As suggested in the narrative, the mother was disappointed, because the friend (otherwise unknown to us) did not come to visit her in the church where she was supplicating the saint. This apparition therefore seems to confirm Alwis's explanation of Artemios's habit of visiting people in disguise of their friends or relatives as a way to comfort them.

---

of the girl once again saw a most attractive woman dressed in monastic garb' (*MA* 24; cf. *MA* 6, 38, 45.

[64] *MA* 22.

[65] *MA* 23, see also *MA* 2, 42, 44.

[66] *MA* 1.

[67] *MA* 18.

[68] *MA* 31.

[69] Alwis, p. 6.

[70] Ibidem.

[71] *MA* 31: Κατεστύγνασας, ὅτι οὐκ ἦλθον εἰς ἐπίσκεψιν ὑμῶν, ὅσον καιρὸν διήγαγες ἐν τῇ ἐκκλησίᾳ. ἐπειδὴ οὖν ὁ βασιλεὺς ἀπέστειλέν με μακρὰν τῆς πόλεως διὰ κεφάλαιον καὶ διέστρεψα, ἦλθον νῦν ἰδεῖν ὑμᾶς· τί δὲ ἔχει τὸ τέκνον σου.

In another episode the saint heals the sick child of a poor widow without any attempt to conceal his identity[72]. He simply appears to her in a dream and places his hand on the boy's testicles. The only misdirection employed by the saint is asking the mother for something in exchange. His request makes allusion to her previous attempts to cure her child with the help of physicians, which had failed because she was too poor to afford their fees. In the end, after she offers to sell her only possessions, the saint, having thus tested her faith, promises to cure the boy if she frequents a night office. This story sits somewhat uncomfortably with Alwis's theory: there is no disguise, but not much kindness on the saint's part either, as toying with a poor mother's feelings and belief can hardly be said to bring her any comfort whatsoever.

An even more radical departure from the image of Artemios as a gentle saint is the story of a woman whose son fell out of bed and severely ruptured his intestines. She goes with the baby to the church and resorts to supplications to the saint along with so many tears that she soaks the floor. The saint appears to her in a dream and says:

> What's wrong? Why do you weep so much?' She reported to him her son's injury and the reason it happened to him. The saint stretched out his hand, grabbed the child by his right foot, and dangled him upside down. When she saw it, she was tormented in her emotions, and like a mother she cried out: 'Oh my! You are killing my child'. The saint shook him gently, but she cried all the more: 'What are you doing? You are murdering my child right in front of me, man. What are you doing?' And he said to her: 'Don't you want me to treat him?'[73]

As one might expect, upon waking up, she found her baby healthy. Not only is there no disguise here; the saint's violent actions are quite explicitly represented as bringing further distress to the child's mother.

We thus see three similar problems, three completely different saintly interventions, but three miraculously positive outcomes. The saint may very well perform miracles using just his power without any spectacular details, but for some mysterious reason he is prone sometimes to complicate the matter. Vincent Déroche, who also was struck by the frequency of what he terms

---

[72] *MA* 36.

[73] *MA* 28: φαίνεται αὐτῇ ὁ ἅγιος καὶ λέγει αὐτῇ καθ' ὕπνους· 'Τί ἔχεις; τί τοσαῦτα κλαίεις'; ἡ δὲ ἀπαγγέλλει αὐτῷ τὴν νόσον τοῦ παιδὸς καὶ τὴν αἰτίαν, πόθεν αὐτῷ συνέβη. ὁ δὲ ἐκτείνας τὴν χεῖρα ἐκράτησεν τὸ παιδίον τοῦ ποδὸς τοῦ δεξιοῦ καὶ ἐκρέμασεν αὐτὸ ἐπὶ κεφαλήν. ἡ δὲ ἑωρακυῖα καὶ τὰ σπλάγχνα ὡς μήτηρ συσχεθεῖσα ἔκραξεν· 'Οὐαί μοι, ἀποκτέννεις τὸ παιδίον μου'. ὁ δὲ ἅγιος ἐτίναξεν αὐτὸ ἠρέμα, ἡ δὲ γυνὴ πλεῖον ἀνέκραξεν. "Τί ποιεῖς; φονεύεις τὸ τέκνον μου ἐπὶ ἐμοῦ, ὦ ἄνθρωπε. τί ποιεῖς";καὶ λέγει αὐτῇ· 'Οὐ θέλεις ἵνα ἰατρεύσω αὐτό'.

l'épiphanie masquée of the Christian saints, points to its paradoxical nature, as it is usually not comprehended as long as it lasts. The saint often plays against type and apparently against expectations, and he behaves in a manner that is far from kind, but in fact he does so with the patients' best interests in mind[74]. Déroche proposes to understand the 'masked epiphany' as a message for future patients not to doubt in the saints' ambiguous behaviour, which is performed only to convert an individual lacking *quelque peu de foi*[75]. All these inconsistencies and paradoxes, he concludes, are ultimately typical of dreams[76].

It is not the aim of this chapter to solve the question of the significance of the saintly disguises and tricks. Technically, however, it is characteristic of liminal beings of various kinds to be able to change their form, not having any stable shape. In the Christian universe the saints share this feature with demonic creatures, which also can transform themselves into animals or beautiful maidens[77]. The last of the three stories quoted above shows Artemios's sense of humour to be somewhat cruel. Other instances of this feature are the already-mentioned stories of his inflicting a hernia instead of curing it[78]. These stories also point to the double nature of someone who both heals and inflicts disease, which is yet another instance of his liminality.

Conclusion

To conclude, I hope to have shown that the epiphanies of Thekla and Artemios are in fact variations on the hybrid construction of sanctity that hint at the dynamics of the development of imagery concerning the afterlife of Christian saints. A wide palette of diverse literary means was used in both

---

[74] Vincent Déroche, '"Tout d'un coup": l'épiphanie masquée dans les recueils de miracles de l'antiquité tardive', in *Dōron Rodopoikilon: Studies in Honour of Jan Olof Rosenqvist*, ed. by Denis Searby et al. (Uppsala: Uppsala Univ., 2012), p. 151.

[75] Déroche, 152.

[76] Ibidem.

[77] As we can observe for instance in the collection of Thekla's miracles, where a demon assumes the form of a beautiful maiden in order to seduce and destroy a man who had fallen in love with her (*MTh* 33). There are very many instances of demons turning into various animals in the Christian literature; see for example Constantius of Lyon, *Life of St Germanus* 2. 10 and Gregory the Great, *Dialogues* III. 4. 1–3. Both examples provide a retelling of a narrative known from earlier pagan sources, such as Plautus' *Mostellaria*, Pliny the Younger's *Letter* VII. 27. 5–11, Lucian's *Philopseudes* 30–31; see Julia Doroszewska, 'The Liminal Space: Suburbs as a Demonic Domain in Classical Literature', *Preternature: Critical and Historical Studies on the Preternatural*, 6 (2017), 7–12; Debbie Felton, *Haunted Greece and Rome: Ghost Stories from Classical Antiquity* (Austin, TX: University of Texas Press, 1999), pp. 81–88.

[78] For other examples of Artemios's sense of humour see Crisafulli and Nesbitt, *The Miracles of Artemios*, p. xv.

collections to represent and bring out the liminal identities of their protagonists and thus to portray their vague ontological status. Both the sensory aspects of their epiphanies and the temper tantrums which not infrequently accompany them clearly show a very human, even physical, side of their otherwise celestial nature. This physicality is most conspicuous in the case of Thekla, whereas the dream-like quality of Artemios's mundane interventions underscores their ambiguity. In addition, the former's outward appearance and dwelling and the latter's trickster nature strongly suggest the liminal character of both saints.

It is noticeable that the portrayal of each saint draws from a different repertory. Thekla's image is far removed from the trickery and theatricality displayed by Artemios. It seems to be shaped by the author's conception of a holiness that expressly refrains from the misleading and teasing that are believed to be typical of demons. Furthermore, the martyr's manner may just lack the peculiarities that are typical of dreams. Her image may also be influenced by her gender. In descriptions of her appearance, it allowed little more than a conventional depiction of a noble and exalted apparition. The very few, and admittedly desultory, accounts of Febronia's epiphanies, representing her in a similar way, seem to support this hypothesis. In addition, Thekla, who was an unquestioned rival of Mary with respect to popularity and an emblem of female piety, might have been considered too monumental and lofty for the sort of playfulness that characterized Artemios, a purebred trickster who shows off his in-betweenness by his role-playing. While the scope of Thekla's miracles is also much wider than that of Artemios, his healing specialization was endowed with more comic potential. It cannot be ruled out, however, that these differences too stem from changes occurring in the tradition of representing saintly epiphanies.

Taking into consideration that our picture is unavoidably patchy, we can nevertheless risk a guess that it may not be an accident that in the earliest collection a saint like Thekla is much more forthright in her acting than the more complex figures of her later colleagues. The collections of Kosmas and Damian and of Cyrus and John, both dated in the period between the collections discussed here, are not deprived of the trickster aspects, yet it is with Artemios that they reached the highest level of sophistication and complexity. Proving this, however, will require a separate, dedicated study that I aim to prepare in the future. In any case, the diverse ways of portraying Thekla and Artemios, although quite distinct, nevertheless serve to locate the two saints conceptually on a boundary, betwixt and between this world and the other world.

Resounding Martyrs

Hymns and the Veneration of Saints in Late Antique Miracle Collections[*]

Arkadiy Avdokhin

(University of Regensburg)

Introduction

At some point in the mid-fifth century, the young and desperate Isaurian Bassiana was kneeling down in the church of saint Thekla, part of the majestic pilgrimage centre at Meriamlik, Seleukeia. Captive, homesick, and vulnerable, Bassiana sought the martyr's assistance in this foreign land. She kept long vigils in the church, and was seen by the crowds of pilgrims both from wider Asia Minor and more-distant lands engaging in the usual practices of a desperate petitioner when they find themselves at the shrine of a saint — praying, singing hymns, and offering propitiation to the saint[1].

---

[*] Results of the project *Models of Representation of the Past in the Middle Ages and Early Modern Period* carried out within the framework of the Basic Research Program at the National Research University Higher School of Economics (HSE) in 2019 are presented in this work.

[1] *Miracles of Thekla* 19: 'She spent her time in the church of the martyr doing the usual things: weeping, singing hymns and psalms, and praying' (ἐνδιέτριβε μὲν τῷ νεῷ τῆς μάρτυρος τὰ συνήθη ποιοῦσα, δακρύουσα, ψάλλουσα, εὐχομένη) — *Vie et miracles de sainte Thècle: texte grec, traduction et commentaire*, ed., trans. and comm. by Gilbert Dagron (Brussels: Société des Bollandistes, 1978), p. 340, lines 10–11 (subsequent reference *MTh*, with miracle number, page and lines).

Interacting with Saints in the Late Antique and Medieval Worlds, ed. by Robert Wiśniewski, Raymond Van Dam, and Bryan Ward-Perkins, Hagiologia, 20 (Turnhout, 2023), pp. 97–122.
© BREPOLS ❧ PUBLISHERS   DOI 10.1484/M.HAG-EB.5.133623

We need not worry excessively about Bassiana, however, as Thekla did not fail to provide assistance. This, in any case, is what the exquisitely refined literary account of the martyr's many miracles composed *c.* AD 467–76 would have its readers, both ancient and modern, believe. For Bassiana, spending time within the space of the church and performing hymns (some, possibly, addressed to Thekla) constituted the core of what it meant to engage with a saint while seeking her (or his) assistance. This engagement was structured around the petitioners' entry into a sacred space and their performance of liturgical acts, rather than other activities such as reading, or writing, devotional texts, or the mediation of relationships of societal power — all of which (amongst others) have formed regular ports of calls in recent academic discussions of the cult of saints in late antiquity that follow the largely dominant model of Peter Brown.

What role did hymn-singing and praying play in how saints were venerated in late antiquity? How central was it in shaping the devotee's experience when seeking the assistance of saints and attempting to ensure their sacred presence? What were the sources, and types, of hymns and prayerful texts — were they single-author compositions, Biblical psalms, or anonymous liturgical texts? How much, ultimately, does hymn-singing and writing feature in modern academic narratives of the early stages of the cult of saints? And in what ways have the fundamental assumptions made and paths trodden in seminal publications contributed to its place in today's scholarly discussions?

In what follows, I will discuss the role that liturgical hymn-singing and prayer played in the cult of saints in Greek-speaking Christian communities, as attested in late antique miracle collections. I will situate my argument amidst earlier studies of late antique hymnody and, crucially, in the academic discussion of the cult of saints as inaugurated and developed in the pathbreaking studies of Peter Brown, as well as in the broader context of late antique studies. As I will argue, the practice of addressing saints and martyrs through liturgical hymns and prayers, although almost overlooked, constituted one of the core elements of the lived experience through which saintly figures would be engaged and appropriated.

(Absent) Hymns as (not) Part of the Cult of Saints

Hymns, as part of the liturgical veneration of saints, are absent from both studies of the late antique cult of saints as pioneered by Peter Brown, and from research on Byzantine hymnody. Spanning two essentially independent academic contexts, this is a remarkable absence, which has to do, as I will suggest, not only with the non-availability of relevant material to discuss but also with particular methodological choices that have been made.

As various scholars have pointed out in their reflections on Brown's methodology and assumptions in his studies — most importantly in 'The Rise and Function of the Holy Man in Late Antiquity' (1971) and *The Cult of Saints: its Rise and Function in Latin Christianity* (1981) — Brown was chiefly interested in functional models adapted from social anthropology, rather than in the phenomenology of experience either on the part of the saintly subjects or on the part of their devotees — to borrow his own phrasing, in '*how* the saints worked'[2]. The Brownian saint and holy man of *The Cult of Saints* has a tantalizing lacuna around questions of *cult* in its original, etymological sense of *cultus*, 'veneration'. Liturgical celebration of saints does not enter the discussion on a serious scale. Indeed, in Brown's main studies, liturgy, hymns, and prayers are, in essence, uncharted territory; he only addresses them in passing, and exclusively within the predominant frame of unpacking liturgical ritual's implications for social relationships and power matrices rather than for the internal logic of the lived experience of their practitioners[3]. Peter Brown is quite aware of this himself; in his substantially later article 'Enjoying the Saints in Late Antiquity' (2001), he briefly turns to liturgical invocations of saints, examining the Visigothic liturgies of the sixth and seventh centuries and thereby offering glimpses into what a different aspect of the cult of saints, as enjoyed by late antique Christians, might have looked like, had it not been massively overlooked in the mainstream scholarship, shaped as it was by Brown's central emphases on the societal implications of the cult[4].

Liturgy, including hymns and prayers, has been substantially underrepresented in the scholarship that has broadly followed Brown's path (as well as in other academic traditions) in discussing the cult of saints, except for the

---

[2] See Peter Brown, 'Enjoying the Saints in Late Antiquity', *Early Medieval Europe*, 9 (2000), 1–24. His key studies where this approach is developed include Peter Brown, 'The Rise and Function of the Holy Man in Late Antiquity', *Journal of Roman Studies*, 61 (1971), 80–101, and *The Cult of the Saints: its Rise and Function in Latin Christianity* (Chicago: University of Chicago Press, 1981). For the chronological dynamic and shifts in Brown's approach to the cult of saints, see the insightful contributions to the volume that set out to take stock of his legacy already more than twenty years ago: James Howard-Johnston, 'Introduction' (pp. 1–26) and Averil Cameron, 'On Defining the Holy Man' (pp. 27–44), in *The Cult of Saints in Late Antiquity and the Middle Ages*, ed. by James Howard-Johnston & Paul A. Hayward (Oxford: Oxford University Press, 1999).

[3] As, for example, in Peter Brown, *Power and Persuasion in Late Antiquity: Towards a Christian Empire* (Madison: University of Wisconsin Press, 1992), pp. 149–50, where liturgical acclamations are discussed as a ritual encoding imperial power and revealing therefore power structures, or in his *Society and the Holy in Late Antiquity* (Berkeley: University of California Press, 1982), p. 183, where parallels between liturgy and the imperial *adventus* briefly come into focus.

[4] See Brown, 'Enjoying the Saints', p. 16 for the distinction between the functional 'how' and the exegetical phenomenology of the 'why'.

predominantly literary studies of hymns by specific Latin authors, most centrally Ambrose and Prudentius[5]. Hippolyte Delehaye's broad-ranging if impressionistic overview of invocation of martyrs (mostly from early epigraphs but also in patristic texts) in his seminal *Les origines du culte des martyrs* (1912) remains mostly neglected[6]. Among the rare exceptions are the studies of Susan A. Harvey, who has looked at how liturgical enactments shaped the very core of the experience for visitors to Symeon the Stylite's pillar[7]. Phil Booth has recently explored and unpacked the 'sacramental saint' as a key figure in important strands of late antique theological and political thought (while taking issue with the concept of the 'liturgification' of power rites and relationships as advanced in many significant studies of Justinian's reign)[8]. The recent work of Lucy Parker (whose doctorate was supervised by Booth) has examined the ways in which liturgical rites contributed to the structuring of the cult of saints in late antiquity[9].

---

[5] Among the now-classic, and more recent studies of the two poets' celebrations of martyrs are, e.g., Jacques Fontaine, 'Le culte des martyrs militaires et son expression poétique au IVe siècle: l'idéal évangélique de la non-violence dans le christianisme théodosien', *Augustinianum*, 20 (1980), 141–71; Rainer Henke, *Studien zum Romanushymnus des Prudentius* (Frankfurt am Main: Peter Lang, 1983); Michael Roberts, *Poetry and the Cult of the Martyrs: The Liber Peristephanon of Prudentius* (Ann Arbor, MI: University of Michigan Press, 1993); Virginia Burrus, 'Reading Agnes: The Rhetoric of Gender in Ambrose and Prudentius', *Journal of Early Christian Studies* 3 (1995), 25–46; Willy Evenepoel, 'Le martyr dans le Liber Peristephanon de Prudence', *Sacris Erudiri* 36 (1996), 5–35; Paul-Augustin Deproost, 'Le martyre chez Prudence: sagesse et tragédie', *Philologus* 143 (1999), 161–80; Brian P. Dunkle, *Enchantment and Creed in the Hymns of Ambrose of Milan* (Oxford: Oxford University Press, 2016).
[6] Hippolyte Delehaye, *Les origines du culte des martyrs* (Brussels: Société de Bollandistes, 1912), Chapter 4 'L'invocation des martyrs', pp. 120–68.
[7] See e.g. Susan A. Harvey, 'The Stylite's Liturgy: Ritual and Religious Identity in Late Antiquity', *Journal of Early Christian Studies* 6 (1998), 523–39, or her recent keynote contribution 'Patristic Worlds', in *Patristic Studies in the Twenty-First Century*, ed. by Brouria Bitton-Ashkelony, Theodore de Bruyn & Carol Harrison (Turnhout: Brepols, 2015), pp. 25–56, where she looks at Syriac homiletics and hymnody.
[8] See Phil Booth's monograph *Crisis of Empire: Doctrine and Dissent at the End of Late Antiquity* (Berkeley, CA: University of California Press, 2014), especially Chapter 1 'Toward the Sacramental Saint'. In Booth's more recent chapter (that builds on his thinking in the *Crisis of Empire*) '"Liturgification" and Dissent in the Crisis of the East Roman Empire (6th–8th centuries)', in *Dynamics of Social Change and Perceptions of Threat*, ed. by Ewald Frie, Thomas Kohl & Mischa Meier (Tübingen: Mohr Siebeck, 2018), pp. 139–56, he critically reconsiders the widely accepted academic narrative of presumably unified 'liturgification' in the sixth and early seventh century and offers a nuanced reading of the diversity of liturgically-grounded modes of doctrinal thinking.
[9] Alongside Lucy Parker's earlier article 'Paradigmatic Piety: Liturgy in the Life of Martha, Mother of Symeon Stylites the Younger', *Journal of Early Christian Studies*, 24 (2016), 99–125, see now her monograph *Symeon Stylites the Younger and Late Antique Antioch: From Hagiography to History* (Oxford: Oxford University Press, 2022) (especially section 'Liturgy

These forays into things liturgical are, however, stranded oddities within the wider field of research on the cult of saints as part of late antique and early Christian studies. This non-engagement on the part of an essentially Brownian English-speaking field of scholarship with a topic that is as promising as it is neglected is somewhat disconcerting, and can seem difficult to explain. Illumination, however, can be gained by examining fundamental disciplinary shifts in the study of Christianity in late antiquity. It has become almost standard to speak of the drift away from the conventional, often confessionally-driven 'patristic (including liturgical) studies' towards a more methodologically innovative 'late antique studies'[10]. To borrow Averil Cameron's apt territorial metaphor, 'The ground that belonged to patristics has therefore been invaded both by early Christian studies and by the field of late antiquity'[11]. From this perspective, the 'invasion' of patristics by late antique scholars, insofar as it affects the territories of liturgy, hymn-singing, and prayer, has been both eager and indecisive. On the one hand, there is definitely a keen and stable interest in hymn-singing and writing, as well as praying, judging by the ever-increasing flow of recent publications[12]. Yet, in methodological terms, scholars have struggled to bridge the gap between text- and author-centred traditional approaches to a very limited number of key personalities (most centrally Romanos the Melodist) on the one hand, and endeavours to find new perspectives on the lived experiences of broader audiences on the other[13]. Derek Krueger's and Andrew Mellas' recent efforts

---

and Ritual Practice' pp. 183–94) that discusses liturgy in late antique Syria in a broader historical context.

[10] See Elizabeth A. Clark, 'From Patristics to Early Christian Studies', in *Oxford Handbook of Early Christian Studies*, ed. by Susan A. Harvey & David G. Hunter (Oxford: Oxford University Press, 2008), pp. 9–41; the various contributions in *Patristic Studies in the Twenty-First Century*, and Averil Cameron, 'Patristics and Late Antiquity: Partners or Rivals?', *Journal of Early Christian Studies*, 28 (2020), 283–302.

[11] Cameron, 'Patristics and Late Antiquity', p. 293.

[12] See e.g. *Jewish and Christian Liturgy and Worship: New Insights into its History and Interaction*, ed. by Albert Gerhards & Clemens Leonhard (Leiden: Brill, 2007), *Literature or Liturgy? Early Christian Hymns and Prayers in Their Literary and Liturgical Context in Antiquity*, ed. by Leonhard Clemens & Hermut Löhr (Tübingen: Mohr Siebeck, 2014); *Early Christian Prayer and Identity Formation*, ed. by Reidar Hvalvik & Karl O. Sandnes (Tübingen: Mohr Siebeck, 2014); *Prayer and Worship in Eastern Christianities, 5th to 11th Centuries*, ed. by Brouria Bitton-Ashkelony & Derek Krueger (Abingdon: Routledge, 2016).

[13] For example, Sarah Gador-Whyte, *Theology and Poetry in Early Byzantium: The Kontakia of Romanos the Melodist* (Cambridge: Cambridge University Press, 2017); Thomas Arentzen, *The Virgin in Song: Mary and the Poetry of Romanos the Melodist* (Philadelphia: University of Pennsylvania Press, 2017); *Hymns, Homilies and Hermeneutics: Experiencing Liturgical Texts in Byzantium*, ed. by Sarah Gador-Whyte & Andrew Mellas (Leiden: Brill, 2021). For an intriguing discussion of the concept of authorship and its implications in late antique

to bring methodologies from the history of emotions to bear on late antique liturgy also belong among the studies that, while striving to be methodologically innovative, are in many significant ways more rooted in conventional scholarship than it may seem at first glance, particularly with regard to their author-centred rather than audience-oriented choice of sources[14]. It would hardly be an overstatement to say that prayer and hymnody has, until now, been a territory that still belongs largely among more conventional approaches centred around texts and authors' personalities, while glimpses into the cultural history of how liturgy worked as an element of the broader picture of late antique Christianities are limited.

This brings me to the other academic context where hymnody as an element of the cult of saints in late antiquity is noteworthy for its absence. When reading (mostly literary) studies of late antique and/or early Christian hymns, the following narrative is typically offered in ways that may not always be explicit, but where it is suggested through the received manner of discussion[15]. Although hymn-singing forms a part of early Christian liturgy and devotion from its earliest stages (New Testament), Greek hymns to saints do not make a systematic appearance before the seventh century at the earliest[16]. Significantly, the *oeuvre* of one of the first (usually seen as the greatest) early Byzantine hymn-writers, Romanos the Melodist (whose *kontakia*

Christian writings in Greek, see Derek Krueger, *Writing and Holiness: The Practice of Authorship in the Early Christian East* (Philadelphia: University of Pennsylvania Press, 2004).

[14] Derek Krueger, *Liturgical Subjects: Christian Ritual, Biblical Narrative, and the Formation of the Self in Byzantium* (Philadelphia: University of Pennsylvania Press, 2014), Andrew Mellas, *Liturgy and the Emotions in Byzantium: Compunction and Hymnody* (Cambridge: Cambridge University Press, 2020). For a critical discussion of the methodological challenges in the quest for new perspectives in recent publications, see Arkadiy Avdokhin, 'Caught in Transition: Liturgical Studies, Grand Narratives, and Methodologies of the Past and the Future: Partial Reflections on the "Liturgical Subjects: Christian Subjects, Biblical Narrative, and the Formation of the Self in Byzantium" by D. Krueger', *Scrinium*, 12 (2016), 329–39, and my review of Arentzen's *The Virgin in Song* in *Byzantinische Zeitschrift*, 113 (2020), 1089–116.

[15] This narrative is found, in a fairly recognizable form, in such standard discussions as e.g. Egon Wellesz, *A History of Byzantine Music and Hymnography* (Oxford: Clarendon Press, 1949); Καριοφύλλης Μητσάκης, *Βυζαντινή υμνογραφία. Από την Καινή Διαθήκη ως την Εικονομαχία* (Θεσσαλονίκη: Πατριαρχικόν Ύδρυμα Πατερικών Μελετών, 1971); José Grosdidier de Matons, 'Romanos le Mélode et les origines de l'hymnographie byzantine' (doctoral thesis, Université Paris IV, 1974) as well as in more recent stock-takings, e.g. John A. McGuckin, 'Poetry and Hymnography (2): The Greek World', in *Oxford Handbook of Early Christian Studies*, pp. 641–56, or Antonia Giannouli, 'Hymn Writing in Byzantium: Forms and Writers', in *A Companion to Byzantine Poetry*, ed. by Wolfram Hörandner, Andreas Rhoby & Nikos Zagklas (Leiden: Brill, 2019), pp. 487–516.

[16] Later Byzantine writers, as e.g. Andrew of Crete († AD 767), Joseph († c. AD 886), and many others did indeed compose hymns — most centrally *kanōnes* and *kontakia* — on specific saints.

are, in practical terms, the only texts of the early period that regularly attract scholarly attention), contains only embryonic engagement with saints[17]. The resulting picture is that in late antique Christianities, the writing and liturgical performance of hymns as an element of the veneration of martyrs and saints is virtually non-existent. This vision does not substantially change even when the pool of sources which are typically neglected — early hymns on papyri — is brought into play, as (Greek) hymns to saints are remarkably rare even there before the seventh century AD[18].

This spectacular absence of hymnody and prayer within predominant strands of Brown-inspired scholarship on the cult of saints and in the studies of hymnody that lie beyond it (and sometimes within more conventional fields of patristics or early Christian literature) may have a common ground. In both cases, primary sources consist of literary texts produced by educated elites, with a pronounced agenda which modern scholars can unpack and fit into their narratives. This, in turn, has led to the tacit assumption that what would count as the proper stuff of history consists of self-consciously styled hymns to saints, that is, texts composed by sufficiently learned poets who dedicate themselves to the theme of the saints. It is not particularly surprising therefore that hymnody does not surface in existing academic discussions as an element of saints' cult before the eighth century, with the first proliferation of the so-called 'monastic' hymnody by authors hailing from Palestine. The same tacitly embraced assumption has also invigorated the ever-growing flow of publications on Romanos the Melodist as a tangibly authorial voice of late antique liturgy. Voices, experiences, and ritual contexts that do not involve identifiable (literary) actors, however, have been almost entirely left beyond the scope of discussion.

In the remaining space of this contribution, I will seek to address one stretch of the mostly uncharted territory of late antique devotion to saints in liturgical contexts. I will argue that the cult of saintly martyrs as healing figures — accessible through the fascinating evidence of early miracle

---

[17] Among those hymns that have been deemed genuine, only the Forty Martyrs of Sebaste feature as distinct subject matter (two *kontakia* are devoted to them), with one hymn on 'all martyrs'.

[18] For an informed overview and discussion, see Ágnes T. Mihálykó's two publications: 'Mary, Michael and Twenty-Two Angels: Saints and Angels in Christian Liturgical and Magical Texts', in *Proceedings of the 29th International Congress of Papyrology, Lecce, 28 July – 3 August 2019*, ed. by Mario Capasso, Paola Davoli & Natascia Pellé (Lecce: Centro di Studi Papirologici dell'Università del Salento, 2022), pp. 722–31, and '"Intercede for Our Souls, Holy Martyr": Saints in Late Antique Hymns on Papyri', in *Resonant Faith in Late Antiquity: Literature, Music, and Devotion in Early Christian Hymns*, ed. by Arkadiy Avdokhin (New York: Routledge, forthcoming).

collections in Greek — was solidly rooted in liturgical rituals of hymn-singing and prayer. Practiced at their healing shrines and enacted by thousands of pious travellers on site, these rituals constituted the core of people's experience of the saints — but they remain totally unseen as long as we remain within the frame of analysis based on literary texts and elites' perspectives. In my approach, I broadly follow Harvey's, Booth's, and Parker's earlier interest in the powerful contribution of liturgy to the structuring of late antique devotion, doctrine, and social history, as well as acknowledging Wendy Mayer's recent call for a history of liturgy and ritual as part of the 'Christianity of the many' in late antiquity[19].

Encountering Saints: Pilgrims' Liturgy and the Soundscape of Deliverance

The miracle collections that will form the main focus of this study were composed between the mid-fifth and mid-seventh centuries AD across the Greek-speaking Mediterranean: the *Miracles of Thekla* (*BHG* 1718, c. 467–76, Seleukeia, Asia Minor), the *Miracles of Kosmas and Damian* (two extant versions — *BHG* 372–79 made up of smaller subcollections, sixth-century Constantinople), the *Miracles of Artemios* (*BHG* 173, c. 660, Constantinople), and Sophronios's *Miracles of Cyrus and John* (*BHG* 477–79i, c. 610–14, Alexandria, Egypt)[20]. I leave out of my analysis other Greek collections as

---

[19] Wendy Mayer, 'The Changing Shape of Liturgy: From Earliest Christianity to the End of Late Antiquity', in *Liturgy's Imagined Past/s: Methodologies and Materials in the Writing of Liturgical History Today*, ed. by Teresa Berger & Bryan D. Spinks (Collegeville, MN: Liturgical Press, 2016), pp. 271–98.

[20] For editions, commentary, and translations, alongside *MTh* cited in n. 1 above, see *Kosmas und Damian. Texte und Einleitung*, ed. by Ludwig Deubner (Leipzig: B. G. Teubner, 1907) (Chalcedonian collections) [subsequent reference *MKD* Deubner, with miracle number, page and lines]; *Cosmae et Damiani sanctorum medicorum vitam et miracula e codice londinensi*, ed. Ernestus Rupprecht (Berlin: Junker und Dünnhaupt, 1935) (Miaphysite collection) [subsequent reference *MKD* Rupprecht, with miracle number, page and lines]; *The Miracles of St Artemios: a Collection of Miracle Stories by an Anonymous Author of Seventh-Century Byzantium*, comm. and trans. by Virgil S. Crisafulli, John W. Nesbitt & John F. Haldon (Leiden: Brill, 1997) [subsequent reference *MA*, with miracle number, page and lines] (Greek text is a reprint from the 'Miracula Sancti Artemii', in *Varia Graeca Sacra*, ed. Athanasios Papadopoulos-Kerameus (St Petersburg, 1909), 1–75); *Los Thaumata de Sofronio: contribución al estudio de la incubatio cristiana*, ed., trans and comm. by Natalio Fernández Marcos (Madrid: Instituto Antonio de Nebrija, 1975) [subsequent reference *MCJ*, with miracle number, page, and section], and *Sophrone de Jérusalem: Miracles des saints Cyr et Jean (BHG 477–79)*, comm. and trans. by Jean Gascou (Paris: De Boccard, 2006) (provides important emendations on the text). For an analytical overview, with further bibliography which is ample, see now Stephanos Efthymiadis, 'Collections of Miracles (Fifth–Fifteenth Centuries)', in *The*

they do not present such a rich source of evidence for liturgical rituals (they will, however, enter the discussion a couple of times)[21].

All of the collections listed above comprise accounts of miraculous encounters with saint martyrs at their shrines where incubation for healing purposes was practiced (I use the term in its widest sense of receiving a saint's vision when in her or his shrine, rather than pressing for a historically and theoretically valid category of 'Christian incubation' as a strictly ritualized, self-consciously implemented practice)[22]. These cultic centres — the Hagia Thekla at Meriamlik near ancient Seleukeia (Thekla), the Kosmidion at Blachernae (Kosmas and Damian), and the church of John the Baptist 'the Forerunner' in Constantinople (Artemios) — were major attractions for pilgrims from both near and far who would flock there in search of relief from a variety of (mostly, but not exclusively) medical afflictions[23]. The pilgrimage, of whatever distance, involved a number of rituals practiced across the many

---

Ashgate Research Companion to Byzantine Hagiography, vol. 2, Genres and Contexts, ed. by Stephanos Efthymiadis (Farnham: Ashgate, 2014), pp. 103–42.
[21] Among the most important early collections not included are the *Miracles of Menas*, the *Miracles of Theodore the Recruit* (*BHG* 1765c), the *Miracles of Demetrios*, and the *Miracles of Anastasios the Persian* (*BHG* 89g–90).
[22] For Christian incubation in Late Antiquity, including in early miracle collections, see (all the studies giving extensive further bibliography) Fritz Graf, 'Dangerous Dreaming: the Christian Transformation of Dream Incubation', *Archiv für Religionsgeschichte*, 15 (2014), 117–42; Hedvig von Ehrenheim, 'Pilgrimage for Dreams in Late Antiquity and Early Byzantium: Continuity of the Pagan Ritual or Development within Christian Miracle Tradition?', *Scandinavian Journal of Byzantine and Modern Greek Studies*, 2 (2016), 53–95; Gil H. Renberg, *Where Dreams May Come: Incubation Sanctuaries in the Greco-Roman World* (Leiden: Brill, 2017), Appendix XVI 'Incubation in Late Antique Christianity: A Bibliographical Survey and Analysis of the Sources', pp. 745–807, who problematizes the notion of 'Christian incubation' and makes the useful distinction between 'solicited' and 'unintentional incubation' on p. 783 (the latter instance significantly more typical in miracle collections); Robert Wiśniewski, *Christian Divination in Late Antiquity* (Amsterdam: Amsterdam University Press, 2020), Chapter 7 'Incubation', pp. 201–48, follows Graf's distinction, if not his theory-rich perspective (I am thankful to the author for providing me advance access to the book and pointing out Graf's article).
[23] For Hagia Thekla, see *MTh*, 'Hagia-Thékla', pp. 55–79, and now Troels M. Kristensen, 'Landscape, Space, and Presence in the Cult of Thekla at Meriamlik', *Journal of Early Christian Studies*, 24 (2016), 229–63 (with further bibliography); for the early cult of Kosmas and Damian, see Michel van Esbroeck, 'La diffusion orientale de la légende des saints Cosme et Damien', in *Hagiographie, Cultures et Sociétés: IVᵉ–XIIᵉ siècles*, ed. by Évelyne Patlagean & Pierre Riché (Paris: Institut des Études Augustiniennes, 1981), pp. 61–77; for their incubation site at Blachernae (Kosmidion), see Cyril Mango, 'On the Cult of Saints Cosmas and Damian at Constantinople', in Θυμίαμα στη μνήμη της Λασκαρίνας Μπούρα, ed. by Maria Vassilaki et al. (Athens: Benaki Museum, 1994), pp. 189–92; Dominic Montserrat, 'Pilgrimage to the Shrine of SS Cyrus and John at Menouthis in Late Antiquity', in *Pilgrimage and Holy Space in Late Antique Egypt*, ed. by David Frankfurter (Leiden: Brill, 1998), pp. 257–79; the best discussion of the origins of the cult of Cyrus and John as well as their veneration at

healing shrines[24]. The extant collections offer narratives (compiled at a later date) that were likely based on both local archives of specific shrines (*libelli miraculorum*) and accounts of those successfully healed[25]. The authors of the collections, who often profess their own experiences of healing at the shrines themselves, vary significantly in the framing of their narratives, in what emphases — including apologetic and rationalizing — they introduce into their accounts of saintly apparitions and miracles, and in their idiom, style, and compositional techniques[26].

Miracle collections open up a unique window on the late antique cult of saints and its liturgical enactments exactly because they are a potent, and motley, literary presence[27]. Their stylistic registers range from the archaizing finesse of the *Miracles of Thekla* and the incipiently medieval brand of literary refinement found in Sophronios's *Miracles of Cyrus and John*, to the archive-like curtness of the *Miracles of Kosmas and Damian* in their Egyptian

---

Alexandria is Jean Gascou, 'Les origines du culte des saints Cyr et Jean', *Analecta Bollandiana*, 125 (2007), 241–81.

[24] For incubation shrines as attractions for pilgrims, see the classic Pierre Maraval, *Lieux saints et pèlerinages d'Orient: histoire et géographie des origines à la conquête arabe* (Paris: Cerf, 1985), pp. 224–29; more recent studies include Dominic Montserrat, 'Pilgrimage to the Shrine of SS Cyrus and John', Phil Booth, 'Saints and Soteriology in Sophronius Sophista's Miracles of Cyrus and John', *Studies in Church History*, 45 (2009), pp. 52–63. Maraval, pp. 105–06, and Brouria Bitton-Ashkelony, *Encountering the Sacred: The Debate on Christian Pilgrimage in Late Antiquity* (Berkeley, CA: University of California Press, 2005), Chapter 5 'Local Versus Central Pilgrimage' (but also passim), pp. 184–206, argue that local pilgrimage, most centrally to martyrs' shrines, played a large role in Late Antiquity, which is important for my discussion, as the majority of devotees at the healing shrines came from the nearby cities (Seleukeia, Constantinople, and Alexandria).

[25] For the *libelli*, see Hippolyte Delehaye, 'Les premiers libelli miraculorum', *Analecta Bollandiana* 29 (1910), 427–34.

[26] The author of subcollection (series) 3 of the *MKD* Deubner presents his own healing at the Kosmidion as the impetus that prompted him to recount his experience; Sophronios claims to have been cured of cataract at the shrine of Cyrus and John at Alexandria — an emphasis with antecedents in Aelios Aristides' self-presentation in his *Sacred Tales*. For the rhetoric of apology and doctrinal rationalizing likely offered in response to doubt and criticism of the practices of the veneration of saints at the healing shrines and beyond, see Vincent Déroche, 'Tensions et contradictions dans les recueils de miracles de la première époque byzantine', in *Miracle et Karāma. Hagiographies médiévales comparées*, ed. by Denise Aigle (Turnhout: Brepols, 2000), pp. 145–66, and Matthew Dal Santo, *Debating the Saints' Cults in the Age of Gregory the Great* (Oxford: Oxford University Press, 2012), Chapter 3.

[27] See Phil Booth, 'Between Texts and Shrines in the Greek Cult of Saints (5th–7th centuries)', in *Culte des saints et littérature hagiographique: accords et désaccords*, ed. by Vincent Déroche, Bryan Ward-Perkins & Robert Wiśniewski (Leuven: Peeters, 2020), pp. 39–54, who, independently from my discussion here, offers a pertinent analysis of how various ideological and doctrinal agendas are pursued in the different collections, including the ones that purported to narrate miracles worked by the same saints (I thank the editors for offering me an advance copy of the volume).

(Miaphysite) version, and to the patchwork of authors and styles found in the Chalcedonian collection of narratives (now known as the Deubner collection), with its signature mixture of stark physicality and lofty liturgicality that reaches its peak in the *Miracles of Artemios*[28]. This impressive range of literary takes — stylistically self-conscious, remarkably artless, unremarkably driven by doctrinal and cultic agendas, but in all instances marked with profound devotion to healing martyrs — dances with mesmerizing speed before the eyes of its bewildered readers. Yet, it is precisely this tantalizing literary variation that highlights the constant presence of a non-literary core around which these texts would have circulated orally, then would have been written down, re-written, copied, and refined, and finally sent around and read both at the incubation centres and far beyond[29].

These ritual practices at the various healing shrines formed a core aspect of their authors', listeners', and readers' lived experience that ultimately gave the *raison d'être* to all the collections. Visitors to the healing sites were

---

[28] A general discussion of the literary features and authorial takes in the miracle collections is offered in Ildikó Csepregi, 'The Compositional History of Greek Christian Incubation Miracle Collections: Saint Thecla, Saint Cosmas and Damian, Saint Cyrus and John, Saint Artemios' (unpublished doctoral thesis, Central European University, 2007), with a brief reiteration of its central points in Ildikó Csepregi, 'Who is Behind Incubation Stories? The Hagiographers of Byzantine Dream-Healing Miracles', in *Dreams, Healing, and Medicine in Greece. From Antiquity to the Present*, ed. by Steven M. Oberhelman (Farnham: Ashgate, 2013), pp. 161–87. Key bibliography on individual collections: *Miracles of Thekla* — see *MTh*, 'Lange, style, structure de récit', 152–62; Ángel Narro, 'The Influence of the Greek Novel on the Life and Miracles of Saint Thecla', *Byzantinische Zeitschrift*, 109 (2016), 73–96; for a book-length literary study, see Scott F. Johnson, *The Life and Miracles of Thekla: A Literary Study* (Cambridge, MA: Centre for Hellenic Studies, 2006); *Miracles of Kosmas and Damian* — for the doctrinal underpinnings of the two extant Greek versions, see Phil Booth, 'Orthodox and Heretic in the Early Byzantine Cult(s) of Saints Cosmas and Damian', in *An Age of Saints? Power, Conflict and Dissent in Early Medieval Christianity*, ed. by Peter Sarris, Matthew Dal Santo & Phil Booth (Leiden: Brill, 2011), pp. 114–28; *Miracles of Artemios* — see *MA*, 'Translator's preface', pp. xvi–xvii, and the 'Supplementary essay' on pp. 33–73 for considerations of style; *Miracles of Cyrus and John* — see *MCJ*, pp. 4–6 for Sophronios's rhetorical culture, and 'Introduction' in *Sophrone de Jérusalem: Miracles de saints Cyr et Jean*; see also the more recent Gianfranco Agosti, 'Le brume di Omero. Sofronio di fronte alla paideia classica', in *Il Calamo della memoria. Riuso di testi e mestiere letterario nella tarda antichità* IV, ed. by Lucia Cristante & Tommaso Mazzoli (Trieste: Edizioni Università di Trieste, 2011), pp. 33–50, as well as Alan Cameron's discussion of the author's overall literary competence in his 'The Epigrams of Sophronius', *Classical Quarterly*, n.s. 33 (1983), 284–92.

[29] For miracle collections as read to pilgrims at incubation churches, see e.g. Pierre Maraval, 'Fonction pédagogique de la littérature hagiographique d'un lieu de pèlerinage: l'exemple des Miracles de Cyr et Jean', in *Hagiographie, cultures et societes*, pp. 383–97. *Libelli miraculorum* were likely also read at liturgical assemblies — Delehaye, 'Les premiers libelli'. For the function of miracle stories to prepare pilgrims psychologically for liminal experience, see Victor W. Turner & Edith L. B. Turner, *Image and Pilgrimage in Christian Culture: Anthropological Perspectives* (New York: Columbia University Press, 1978), especially pp. 46–49.

confronted with a broadly shared set of ritualized actions: processions, petitions, prayers, and (para)medical prescriptions — most centrally following a *diaita* (dietary, but also broader, recommendations) and the application of *kērōtē* (a wax-based mixture to be smeared on ailing parts of body), and, ultimately, incubation during which saintly martyrs mostly made their appearances that led to healing[30]. Significantly, pilgrims as well as cult impresarios on site perceived this motley array of practices as a kind of ritual unity. Authors and audiences of miracle collections, while differing slightly over specific appellations, referred to it as 'doing the common thing' (τὰ συνήθη was what Bassiana did)[31] or performing 'the customary things'[32]. As I will argue below, hymnody and prayers galore were also an integral part of the customary rituals of pilgrims' liturgy and of their experience of saints and their shrines.

The martyrial churches where incubation was regularly practiced were quite obviously places where the physical presence of people and substances made itself felt in powerful ways. The rituals performed, and the sheer number of people simultaneously present would be overwhelming: the fragrance of burning incense and lamp oil, alongside the bodily odours of people crammed inside for days at a time, and even starker smells arising from paramedical procedures such as emptying one's stomach or cutting open a wound[33].

The spaces of the healing shrines were also sonorous places. They resonated with shrieks of terror and triumph, of pain and piety[34]. These outcries would have mingled with the chant of all-night vigils, shouted and recited petitions, prayers offered at the top of one's voice, thanksgiving prayers, and

---

[30] For a detailed overview of pilgrims' rituals at a healing shrine based on the *Miracles of Artemios*, see *MA*, 'Introduction', pp. 23–25. For the use of *kērōtē*, see von Ehrenheim, 'Pilgrimage for Dreams', p. 75 n. 94, Maraval, *Lieux saints,* p. 223.

[31] *MTh* 19 (p. 340. 11).

[32] τὰ ἤθη — *MA* 12 (p. 100. 6), τὰ ἐν ἔθει — *MA* 23 (p. 140. 12), 33 (p. 174. 12–13), 36 (p. 190. 10), 37 (p. 194. 11), 38 (p. 198. 15), 41 (p. 210. 18), 44 (p. 220. 6), 45 (p. 222. 26); τὰ πρὸς συνήθειαν — *MA* 32 (p. 166. 25).

[33] For an overview of the material and sensory aspects of the shrines, see Béatrice Caseau, 'Ordinary Objects in Christian Healing Sanctuaries', in *Objects in Context, Objects in Use: Material Spatiality in Late Antiquity*, ed. by Luke Lavan, Ellen Swift & Toon Putzeys (Leiden: Brill, 2007), pp. 625–54.

[34] Examples of powerful human voices of prayer and hymn-singing contributing to the soundscape of the shrines are many and may merit a separate study; see e.g. *MKD* Rupprecht 16 (p. 47. 2–8) — frightening outcries, *MKD* Rupprecht 19 (p. 48) — weeping and wailing; visitors to the shrine of Cyrus and John often cry and pray out loud (μεγαλοφώνως) — e.g. *MCJ* 26 (p. 290. 1) and 31 (p. 304. 7); prayer to saints shouted out — *MKD* Deubner 9 (p. 115. 35).

the singing of hymns. This liturgical and human soundscape was clearly a key feature of pilgrims' experience of seeking healing and of their encounters with saints[35]. Within this ritual soundscape, making your voice heard would have been key to obtaining the much sought-after miraculous healing.

Although there were various rites and rituals shaping the sensory aspect of pilgrims' experience at healing shrines, one particular ritual is of central importance when discussing hymnody and prayer as elements of the pilgrims' liturgy — the all-night vigil (παννυχίς)[36]. As I will discuss, hymn-singing and prayers were central to the enactment of vigils from at least the fourth century on. The large crowds present at such events would eagerly participate in hymnody and ritualized prayers; it is doubtful that the two were terminologically, or ritually, well-distinguished by their pious performers[37].

The centrality of *pannychis* as *the* key element of such rituals may have to do with its broad derivation from earlier liturgical celebrations of martyrs at their tombs, most centrally during their yearly memorial festival of πανήγυρις. *Panēgyris* as a memorial celebration of martyrs was a widely popular event attested at least since the fourth century AD in different regions of the late empire[38]. Attending these services would, in itself, constitute an experience of pilgrimage, as the celebrations attracted great crowds of excited devotees from neighbouring (as well as more distant) cities and villages. Healing could be sought and gained by visitors of martyrs' shrines during their sleep, as e.g.

---

[35] For soundscapes as contributing to the making of liturgical and, more broadly, religious spaces in late antique Christianities, see Chapter 3 in Paul Dilley, *Monasteries and the Care of Souls in Late Antique Christianity: Cognition and Discipline* (Cambridge: Cambridge University Press, 2017), pp. 110–47, and Harvey, 'Patristic Worlds'.

[36] For vigils as part of pilgrimage, including at incubation churches, see Maraval, *Lieux saints*, 216–17. For vigils at the church of the Forerunner, see *MA*, 'Introduction', 23–25.

[37] For hymns, psalms, and prayers used interchangeably in early Christian writings starting from the New Testament, see e.g. Ralph Brucker, '"Songs", "Hymns", and "Encomia" in the New Testament?', in *Literature or Liturgy? Early Christian Hymns and Prayers in their Literary and Liturgical Context in Antiquity*, ed. by Clemens Leonhard & Hermut Löhr (Tübingen: Mohr Siebeck, 2014), pp. 1–14 (with further bibliography). For Egeria's terminological non-distinction of various liturgical compositions as part of vigil (*ymni et psalmi* in her *Itinerary* 24.1), which is particularly important as evidence of pilgrimage experience at a *pannychis*, see the editor's ample commentary, with wider *comparanda*, in *Égérie, Journal de voyage (itinéraire)*, ed., trans. and comm. by Pierre Maraval & Manuel C. Díaz, SC 296 (Paris: Cerf, 1982), p. 235 n. 5. See below pp. 117-18 for instances of interchangeable use of 'hymn' and 'prayer'.

[38] Key discussions of the *panēgyris* in Christian Late Antiquity that I rely on below are Maraval, *Lieux saints*, 216–21; Johan Leemans, 'Celebrating the Martyrs: Early Christian Liturgy and the Martyr Cult in Fourth Century Cappadocia and Pontus', *Questions Liturgiques/Studies in Liturgy* 82 (2001), 247–67; Vasiliki Limberis, *Architects of Piety: The Cappadocian Fathers and the Cult of the Martyrs* (New York: Oxford University Press, 2011), section 'Celebrating the Martyr: The Panegyris', pp. 13–31 (with further literature).

at the shrine of the Forty Martyrs of Sebaste at Ibora, as Gregory of Nyssa relates[39].

Vigils that centred around the liturgical celebration of saintly martyrs were therefore by no means something novel for visitors to the healing shrines. They would have experienced fundamentally similar cultic enactments when attending a local martyr's *panēgyris*, which, given the potent presence of martyrs in the liturgical calendar at least from the fourth century on, would be a typical rather than an exceptional experience.

Pilgrims' pannychis: *Singing Hymns, Encountering Saints*

Firmly embedded into broader ritual enactments on site, and sometimes enshrining the very essence of its miraculous ambience, hymnody was at the heart of the all-night vigils. Ritual sensibilities about hymnody, as expressed in miracle collections, clearly suggest that all-night vigils, their hymns, and their prayers would be perceived, described, and quite likely orchestrated on site, as the liturgical core of pilgrims' ritual actions and experience of encountering the saints.

The *Miracles of Thekla* stand somewhat apart, as it speaks explicitly of the 'night-long waking service' (νυκτεγερσία) only as a service held during the memorial day of the martyr[40]. For the authors and audiences of the *Miracles of Kosmas and Damian*, it would be natural to see the liturgical ambience of all-night vigils as conducive to particularly intense mystical experiences (although this is never spelled out, unlike in the *Miracles of Artemios*). Expectant visitors typically stayed at the shrine at least until the end of the week, as the vigil would be celebrated on Saturday night with the distribution of *kērōtē* and the visitation by the saints forming part of the ritual, as illustrated in the account of a man with an abscess:

> He stayed there for some days. On Saturday when the time of the all-night vigil with *kērōtē* (τῆς παννυχίδος τῷ σαββάτῳ καὶ τῆς κηρωτῆς) came [...] at the ninth hour of the vigil (ἐνάτην τῆς αὐτῆς παννυχίδος), he was overwhelmed and fell asleep, and he beholds (θεωρεῖ) the saints who had carried

---

[39] For the Forty Martyrs, see Gregory of Nyssa, *Encomium in xl martyres ii*, ed. by Gunterus Heil, Johannes P. Cavarnos & Otto Lendle, *Gregorii Nysseni Opera* vol. 10.1, Gregorii Nysseni Sermones pars II (Leiden: Brill, 1990), pp. 159–69, at pp. 166–67 (PG 46, 784. 56–785. 30); Delehaye, *Les légendes*, 145; Limberis, *Architects*, 21; Wiśniewski, *Christian Divination*, 207–08, 220–21. For incubation at martyrs' shrines during the *panēgyris*, see e.g. Delehaye, *Les légendes*, 143; Limberis, *Architects*, 21; Delehaye, *Les origines du culte*, p. 169; Renberg, *Where Dreams May Come True*, 754–56; Wiśniewski, *Christian Divination*, 238–46.
[40] *MTh* 26 (p. 356. 9), 29 (p. 368. 35), 33 (p. 378. 17).

for him a chest full of *kērōtē* (ἁγίους ἐνέγκαντας αὐτῷ ῥάκιον πεπληρωμένον τῆς κηρωτῆς)[41].

All-night vigils and their hymnody are regularly mentioned as the natural context in which religious conversions take place. In Miracle 26, a 'heretical' priest spends the Saturday vigil (παννυχίδα τοῦ σαββάτου) at the shrine with an express wish to obtain healing during what was apparently a designated time for this[42]. In Miracle 10, the ailing pagan who is brought by his desperate friend to the incubation church (perceived, admittedly, as a shrine of Castor and Pollux) has a life-changing experience during the vigil:

> When the all-night vigil was celebrated (γινομένης γὰρ τῆς παννυχίδος), he reached full compunction and saw, as they say, in a vision, very close to the sacred baptistery, three children greedily eating bread soaked in wine (βουκάκρατον)[43].

This vision, with its characteristic mix of Eucharistic symbolism and somewhat gross amusement, prompts the pagan's conversion and baptism, to which the sonorous atmosphere of the vigil evidently contributes.

Lastly, the all-night vigil is self-consciously framed as *the* rite that is recommended to whoever is willing to encounter the saints and obtain healing from them. In his proem to subcollection 3, the compiler addresses his patron Florentios by exhorting him to frequent the Saturday *pannychis* and framing his literary narrative as based directly on first-hand accounts of those successively healed during the service:

> When the crowd goes running together for the regularly held all-night vigil, whenever Saturday comes (κατ' ἔθος γινομένη ἐκεῖσε παννυχίδι σαββάτου ἐπιφωσκοῦντος), those who have been healed by them (the saints) told me in what way that had happened[44].

In the *Miracles of Artemios*, the role of the all-night vigil and, most centrally, hymn-singing as its core ritual element is paramount. Throughout the collection, vigils, their liturgical ambience, and the hymnodic soundscape form a constant background to incubation and visitations by the saint. For petitioners, taking part in the hymnody of the all-night vigil is an integral part of incubation and of the usual rituals observed on site.

Performing the hymnody of the all-night vigil (πληρῶσαι τὴν πάννυχον ὑμνῳδίαν) — apparently participating in a liturgical ritual that involved the

---

[41] *MKD* Deubner 30 (p. 175. 54–59).
[42] *MKD* 26 Deubner (p. 166. 4–5).
[43] *MKD* Deubner 10 (pp. 118–19. 39–41).
[44] *MKD* Deubner Series 3 Proem (p. 154. 24–26).

crowds gathered at the church — is a necessary step in progressing from one customary rite to another, and is to be sung immediately before the incubatory sleep, as part of Artemios's yearly *panēgyris*.

> So he (Peter) took the one who was suffering in his private parts and took him to the church of the Forerunner. It was the memorial day of martyrdom (ἡμέρα τῆς ἀθλήσεως) of the saint wonder-worker Artemios. They follow the usual local observances (τὰ ἐν ἔθει γινόμενα τῷ τόπῳ) [...] Peter was staying up during the night of the vigil (παννύχιον νύκτα ἀγρύπνως διετέλεσεν) while the ailing Andrew fell asleep lying on his bed [...] So Peter [...] after performing the hymnody of the all-night vigil (μετὰ τὸ πληρῶσαι τὴν πάννυχον ὑμνῳδίαν) lay down next to Andrew and went to sleep[45].

However, the all-night vigils and the performance of hymnody during them are more than a concomitant ritual of the incubation. In the *Miracles of Artemios*, hymn-singing, in which the pilgrims take an active part themselves, is indeed the ritual enactment that ensures an encounter with the saint. It is a ritual through which direct contact with the healing saint is made. Liturgical hymnody is not only remarkably routinized and spiritualized in the *Miracles of Artemios*, but the saint's presence at the shrine is intimately linked with the time and place of the performance of the ritualized hymnody:

> The evening of Saturday (τῆς ἑσπέρας τοῦ Σαββάτου) came and Sunday was drawing close (ἐπιφωσκούσης) [...] As he (Polychronios, who suffered from testicle pain) was on his own, thinking over what he had seen in a dream, and as the doxology of the all-night vigil was being performed, he falls asleep (τῆς παννυχίου δοξολογίας ἐκτελουμένης, τρέπεται εἰς ὕπνον) [...] and in his dream he sees the saint, as it were, coming from the choirs of those singing the all-night vigil and going down the little stairs on the sacred coffin (ἐκ τῶν χορῶν τῶν παννυχευόντων ἐρχόμενον καὶ κατιόντα τὰ τῆς ἁγίας σοροῦ γραδίλια)[46].

Similarly to the episodes above, hymn-singing as the central element of closely observed liturgical enactments is invested with the mystical force to bring the petitioner into intimate contact with the saint. Not only is the visitor's encounter with the saint often conditional on her or his participation in the hymnody of the vigil — quite apart from incubation and the application of *kērōtē* — the mystical workings of locating the saint and addressing him are inextricably twined into the spatially embedded enactments of hymn-singing. Artemios is securely located in that part of the sacred topography of the church which is a designated place for the hymnody — the choirs.

---

[45] *MA* 37 (p. 194. 8–28).
[46] *MA* 41 (p. 212. 13–23).

Hymn-singing is therefore a mystical *sine qua non* for establishing contact with the saint and obtaining healing from him. Liturgical hymn-singing here is the sacred apex of pilgrims' experience and the most direct route to the encounter with the saints. The presence of healing saints is emphatically fixed not only spatially — they come from the choirs — but also temporally and performatively. It is during the singing of hymns as part of the all-night vigil that the apparition is effected, and it is from among those singing in the choirs that saints make their healing appearance. Hymn-singing is the ritual to which pious readers are introduced, and towards which they are thereby ushered.

This spatial pinning-down of the saint's presence is tantalizing in the comparative perspective of other sites where miracle collections were composed, primarily that of St Demetrios of Thessalonike. Within the late antique basilica, Demetrios famously has his regular seat in the coffin, where he is to be found on inspection by the doubtful[47]. For the author(s) and audiences of the *Miracles of Artemios* who gathered regularly at the church of the Forerunner in seventh-century Constantinople to celebrate the saint in the hymns of the all-night vigil, the saint is liturgically locatable not only through his relics, but also through the spatial and temporal unity of the performance of the hymnody sung at his shrine. Where and when hymns are sung, there and then is the saint.

This temporal, and not only spatial, emphasis is borne out in the ability of hymn-singing, as the ritual context of the saint's apparition, to become disembedded from the space of its shrine in Constantinople. In Miracle 39, we read about George, who had previously served as reader at the Oxeia church during his childhood years and, after being ordained priest, lived on the island of Plateia. At some point in his adult life, George developed an intestinal condition, but he refused to leave the island and seek healing at the Constantinopolitan shrine. Curiously enough, Artemios, in an unprecedented act of exhibiting utmost care for a former member of his shrine's clergy, makes a visitation to George:

> He (George) only invoked the prospect of God's, and saint martyr Artemios's, help, and had hopes only in them. The One who knows the desires of the heart of hearts sends to him his servant Artemios. The latter came to the island at the hour of the hymnody of the lamp-lighting service vigil, and appeared visibly at the spot where he (George) was lying (τῆς ἐπιλυχνίου ὑμνῳδίας τῇ ὥρᾳ ὤφθη τῷ νοσοῦντι ὀφθαλμοφανῶς)[48].

---

[47] For a detailed description of the ciborium, see *Les plus anciens recueils des miracles de Saint Démétrius et la pénétration des Slaves dans les Balkans*, ed., trans. and comm. by Paul Lemerle, 2 vols (Paris: CNRS, 1979–81), vol. I, pp. 114–15, § 87.

[48] *MA* 39 (p. 202. 17–21).

The liturgical ambience of the saint's apparition is spelled out with revealingly technical precision here. Not only does Artemios make his visitation at the general time of the vigil and the hymns sung during it. He comes specifically during a particular part of the *pannychis* — the lamp-lighting service, a liturgical ritual of ancient origins in which Christian and non-Christian influences are detectable[49].

Artemios's visible, mystical, and healing self-manifestation is effected within the frame of the ritualized hymn-singing of the all-night vigil. It takes on a power of its own, overcoming as it does its embeddedness in the sacred power of the shrine and the physical trappings of the proximity of relics.

A sense of the centrality of liturgical hymn-singing during vigils for coming into an intimate contact with the saint pervades the *Miracles of Artemios*. One of its most spectacular manifestations is the account of a poor widow Sophia, who travels to the church of the Forerunner to petition for her young ailing son after failing to obtain healing from doctors. She is confronted by Artemios, who contrasts his magnanimity with the doctors' avidity, and puts forward a single condition for her son's treatment:

> 'The doctors wanted from you no less than twenty-eight golden coins for treating your child. And what will you be willing to give me if I heal your son?' In the same dream, she answered that she was not well-off: 'I have some wretched little things. I will sell them and I will give you what I can'. But he told her: 'I do not want anything from you; but if your son gets better, make sure to come often to the all-night vigil celebrated in this place (σύχνασον ἐν τῇ ἐνταῦθα ἐκτελουμένῃ παννυχίδι)'. And she dreamed that she gave him an oath not to quit from the hymnody at the (church of) Forerunner (μὴ ἀπαναχωρῆσαι τῆς ὑμνῳδίας τοῦ Προδρόμου) till her death[50].

Hymns therefore are presented to the pious audience of the collection as *the* liturgical ritual for lay devotees to follow throughout their lifetime; their centrality is ultimately endorsed by the saint's direct injunction.

Significantly, other collections reveal comparable emphases on the mystical power of hymn-singing during vigils at incubation shrines, so that these hymns become ritual frames of encounter between expectant visitors and martyr saints. Striking evidence comes from the *Miracles of Kosmas and*

---

[49] A 'lamp-lighting hymn' features already in the *Apostolic Traditions* VIII. 35. 2; the hymn 'Joyous light' (Φῶς ἱλαρόν) may be one ancient liturgical composition used during these services. The bibliography is substantial; see e.g. the standard discussion, with further literature, in Paul Bradshaw, *Daily Prayer in the Early Church: A Study of the Origin and Early Development of the Divine Office* (Eugene: Wipf & Stock, 2008), pp. 75–76. For the centrality of the *lychnikon* in the *Life of Martha*, see Parker, *Symeon Stylites*, pp. 184, 190–92.

[50] *MKD* Deubner 36 (p. 190. 15–22).

Damian (Deubner). In it, a deaf and mute girl comes to the saints' shrine seeking a remedy, and her desire is granted, somewhat unexpectedly, just as one of the most solemn hymns is being performed as part of the wider hymnody of the *lychnikon*:

> And the deaf and mute girl who kept mentally reciting the Trisagion in her mind (ἐν τῇ διανοίᾳ μελετῶσα το τρισάγιον) before the moment of healing, was cured by the grace of Kosmas and Damian exactly through it (the hymn) and by it (δι' αὐτοῦ καὶ ὑπ' αὐτοῦ). When the lights-on service was finished in their church and, as was habitual, the Trisagion was said, the deaf girl suddenly could hear the man singing psalms, and the mute one joined in loudly with those singing psalms (κράξασα μετά τῶν ψαλλόντων ἔψαλλε), and sang together with them the Trisagion. The girl, deeply moved by the two miraculous things which had happened with her at one and the same time, stopped singing psalms (τοῦ ψάλλειν) for a little while and made thanksgiving to God and the saints, crying out and loudly proclaiming to everybody (ἐποιεῖτο εὐχαριστίαν κράζουσα καί βοῶσα καί εἰσαγγελλουσα) the awe-inspiring deeds of God and the grace of his saints, Kosmas and Damian[51].

Aside from the titillating question of why the extant text of the pro-Chalcedonian collection misses the opportunity to furnish the episode with partisan vignettes about the notorious differences between the Miaphysite and Chalcedonian Trisagion[52], the episode powerfully highlights the importance with which hymn-singing during evening services would be invested, and the intensity of the devotional expectations connected with it. The deaf and mute supplicant receives the miraculous treatment emphatically through, and thanks to, the singing of the hymn. Hymnody is therefore presented to the audiences of the text as a quintessential strand of the mystical experience of encountering saints and of successfully seeking their miraculous intervention.

At one juncture at least, however, we do seem to be able to get a glimpse of a different literary and liturgical dynamic at work in late antique veneration of saints through hymns, and of how this dynamic structured the experience of the believer. As I will discuss in the final section of this paper, Sophronios's *Miracles of Cyrus and John* — a collection that bears not just the unmistakable stylistic stamp but also the doctrinal commitments of its erudite author — can tell a story of particular hymns *about* the two healing saints being keenly promoted as a crucial element of their cult at Menouthis.

---

[51] *MKD* Deubner 7 (p. 112. 16–26).

[52] The differences between the Miaphysite and Chalcedonian versions of the hymn famously led to a riot in Constantinople in AD 512 — see now Mischa Meier, 'Σταυροθείς δι'ἡμᾶς — Der Aufstand gegen Anastasius im Jahr 512', *Millennium*, 4 (2007), 157-237 (with earlier literature).

I will also suggest that the hymns may be compositions by Sophronios, and that they were introduced into the liturgical patterns of the shrine, with their literary and ritual agency cloaked in the powerful — if pseudepigraphic — authority of an earlier Christian luminary of particular local significance.

Those Special Hymns: Integrating Literary Texts into the Cult of Saints?

Sophronios of Jerusalem, the author of the *Miracles of Cyrus and John*, shows substantial literary refinement through his keen pursuit of compositional and stylistic games and classicizing allusions[53]. Sophronios's authorial self-consciousness, however, should not make us oblivious of the tremendous doctrinal pressures that he experienced when composing the collection, and which left their mark on it despite the author's best intentions to achieve the contrary. Appointed as Chalcedonian patriarch of the Alexandrian church, Sophronios was faced with the task of promoting the emperor-supported doctrinal variation of Christian faith in a region that was heavily dominated by the Miaphysite commitments of the local populace, the clergy, and the ascetics[54]. Promoting the incubation cult of Cyrus and John at Menouthis near Alexandria as ostensibly Chalcedonian saints was no mean feat for Sophronios, who strove to present the cult as founded by Cyril of Alexandria, a champion of Chalcedonian orthodoxy[55]. Writing the thoroughly erudite collection of accounts of their miracles was one step in this direction. This literary enterprise, as I will argue, tapped into Sophronios's broader efforts to ensure both popularity and the perceived Chalcedonian identity of the saints, while making arrangements for liturgical actions, including hymns to the saints, to be followed on the site of their veneration.

Standing out clearly in Sophronios's collection is his remarkable consistency to round off individual miracle accounts with an emphasis on thanksgiving hymns (as performed by characters in the narrative). This narrative coda almost invariably involves an injunction addressed to the readers — or indeed listeners — to give thanks to the saints by singing a hymn, and only then to proceed to the following episode:

> So Anna the nun in this manner escaped the death prepared for her by demons [...] and encouraged the people who had seen her healing to (use)

---

[53] For the literary quality of the collection, see nn. 20 p. 104 and 28 p. 107 above.
[54] For the doctrinal context of the collection, see Booth, *Crisis of Empire*, Chapter 2 'Sophronius and the Miracles', pp. 44–89 (with further literature).
[55] For the history of the cult, and the poor reliability of Sophronios's account of its Cyrillian foundation, see Gascou, 'Les origines'.

the hymns to the saints (πρὸς ὕμνους τῶν ἁγίων ὀτρύνασα), and having sung praises to them (ἀνυμνήσασα,) together with the others, she left the church. We therefore, who have heard about this just now [...] after having sung praises to the saints as they deserve it (ἀξίως ὑμνήσαντες), let us turn our ears and mouths to <singing> more hymns (πρὸς ἑτέρους ὕμνους) and (hearing) more miracles[56].

She stood up [...] and sang hymns to the saints in a loud voice (τοὺς ἁγίους μεγαλοφώνως ἀνύμνησε) [...] and those watching her sang along (συνυμνοῦντας). So having sung hymns to saints (ἀνυμνήσαντες) to the best of our ability, [...] let us begin the narration about miracles that happened to Egyptians and Libyans[57].

The wonderful Philemon, escaping in this manner from his diseases [...] and praising in a hymn the ones who gave it (healing) to him (τοὺς δεδωκότας ὑμνῶν), went away. So singing hymns to the martyrs twice (διττῶς ὑμνοῦντες τοὺς μάρτυρας) for the double healing, let us move on to the next narrative as the mother of further hymns (ἄλλων ὕμνων μητέρα)[58]. She (Theodora), after voicing thanksgiving for her deliverance (σωτηρίους φωνὰς προσενέγκασα) to the [...] martyrs, left the church. After raising our singing voices in praise of them (βοὰς εὐφήμους αὐτοῖς μελῳδήσαντες) and on her account as well, let us move to a narrative that will bring about more melodies (μελῳδίας)[59].

True, in his emphasis on thanksgiving hymns as the required final step of the ritual enactments at healing shrines, Sophronios follows a pattern well-established in other miracle collections; his narrative rhetoric, however, bespeaks the very special, and personal, role they had for him. Significantly, the phrasing used to speak of thanksgiving hymns and prayers in various collections is remarkably similar and formulaic (typically expressed through participial constructions); the ritual invariably takes place after healing, and its description comes usually at the close of individual accounts. The recently healed and grateful protagonists 'give thanks to the saints' (εὐχαριστῶν(οῦσα)/εὐχαριστήσας(α) τοῖς ἁγίοις, ἀποδοὺς τὴν εὐχαριστίαν)[60], 'confess gratefulness' (χάριν ὁμολογῶν/οῦσα)[61], 'fulfill his/her/their prayers'

---

[56] *MCJ* 44 (p. 349. 8).
[57] *MCJ* 35 (p. 322. 13).
[58] *MCJ* 61 (p. 378. 6).
[59] *MCJ* 26 (p. 291. 3).
[60] *MKD* Deubner 1 (p. 101. 71), 3 (p. 107. 55), 5 (p. 109. 20), 10 (p. 128, 99–100), 12 (p. 132. 113), 14 (p. 137. 60), 16 (p. 141. 94), 20 (p. 153. 74–75), 24 (p. 164. 39–40); *MKD* Rupprecht 7 (p. 24. 2), 16 (p. 40. 19–20), 31 (p. 66. 12–13), 35 (p. 75. 34), 37 (p. 80. 32).
[61] *MKD* Rupprecht 12 (p. 30, 8–10) 'he confessed his gratitude (χάριν ὁμολόγησεν / ὁμολογῶν / ὁμολογοῦσα) to the saints, but rather to Christ who had granted them his grace', 14 (p. 36.

(πληρώσας τὰς εὐχάς)[62] — often with the extension 'of/with thanksgiving' (τῆς εὐχαριστίας/σὺν εὐχαριστίᾳ)[63] — or give thanks to Christ, rather than to the saint, as the ultimate source of healing power (an emphasis that is easy to read as a rationalizing gloss over a practice not entirely unassailable from strict theological perspectives)[64]. Sometimes less formulaic wording can be used[65].

In fewer cases, thanksgiving hymns, rather than prayers, are mentioned[66]. Offered after healing, the hymns take the same place as thanksgiving prayers within the broader script of incubation, and are described similarly. Given their compositionally similar position as well as the generally blurry line between hymns and prayers in late antique sources, it seems safe to suggest that there was a continuous spectrum of practices involved in thanksgiving, and actual practitioners would not particularly distinguish between singing a hymn or performing a prayer as two distinct enactments.[67] The practice of offering a hymn or a prayerful address to saints was therefore one of the standard steps in the often-complex ritual script that a pilgrim was supposed to follow at a healing shrine. Apparently Sophronios makes a general reference to this wide-spread practice, but, as I will argue, for him the hymnic ritual is invested in even greater significance.

Quite apart from the numerically impressive descriptions of thanksgiving hymns and their compositionally persistent description, Sophronios gives them an unequivocally ideological prominence. Outside the miracle collection, although in a text closely connected with it, and quite probably composed so as to circulate alongside the collection — the *Laudatio* of the two

---

24–25), 19 (p. 49. 10), 22 (p. 54. 10–11), 23 (p. 56. 4–6), 25 (p. 59. 4–6), 28 (pp. 62. 7–8), 32 (pp. 68. 17–18), 33 (pp. 72. 10–11), 36 (pp. 77. 18–19).

[62] *MDK* Deubner 23 (p. 162. 54), 24 (p. 164. 39–40), 28 (p. 173. 26), 30 (p. 176. 77–78).

[63] *MKD* Deubner 6 (p. 111. 32–33), 13 (p. 134. 56–57).

[64] *MKD* Deubner 15 (p. 138. 24–26); *MKD* Rupprecht 13 (p. 34. 20–22), 23 (p. 56. 4–6), 25 (pp. 59. 4–6), 31 (p. 66. 12–13), 32 (p. 68. 17–18), 33 (p. 72. 10–11), 35 (p. 75. 34), 36 (p. 77. 18–19), 37 (p. 81. 1–2). For the rhetoric of doctrinal apology in miracle collections, see Dal Santo, *Debating the Saints' Cults*, pp. 149–236.

[65] *MKD* Deubner 26 (p. 167. 37–38) 'he left venerating the servants of Christ' (σέβων τοὺς θεραπευτάς τοῦ Χριστοῦ), 28 (p. 170. 556) 'he left glorifying and singing praise to God [...] through his saint servants' (δοξάζοντα καὶ αἰνοῦντα τὸν θεόν [...] διὰ τῶν ἁγίων αὐτοῦ θεραπόντων), 'he gave praise to God (αἶνον ἔδωκεν θεῷ) who effected such miracles through his saints'; *MKD* Rupprecht 18 (p. 46. 18–19) 'offering many praises (πολλαῖς εὐφημίαις εὐλογῶν) to the saints', 'he praised saints in thousands of encomia' (p. 46. 26–27).

[66] E.g. *MTh* 12 (p. 316. 38) 'singing hymns' (ἀνυμνοῦντες); *MKD* Rupprecht 2 (p. 12. 15–17) 'they sang hymns' (ὕμνουν), 8 (p. 25. 15–16), 'they sent up a hymn' (ὕμνον ἀνέπεμψαν), 26 (p. 60. 5), 'they extolled Christ through hymns' (ὕμνοις Χριστόν ἐγέραιρεν).

[67] See n. 37 p. 109 above for this non-distinction.

saints — he presents an account of the origin of the 'two melodies' sung in honour of Cyrus and John:

> Cyril rushed to (the church of) St Mark and found there the venerable reliquary of Cyrus, and inside the thrice-blessed John as well [...] Afterward, he attuned his spiritual and God-inspired lyre so that it followed the Melodist (Μελῳδὸν) himself, and he praised the martyrs in two melodies (μελῳδίαις δύο τοὺς μάρτυρας ᾔνεσεν) [...] thus becoming an icon and a role model for the pious of how to rejoice in the saints (εἰκὼν καὶ ὑπόδειγμα τῆς ἐπὶ τοῖς ἁγίοις εὐφροσύνης)[68].

The two hymns to be sung — apparently combining a set text and melody — are therefore woven both into Sophronios's narrative, and into the broader, purportedly Chalcedonian, foundation myth of the incubation shrine of the two saints.

As if reinforcing the importance of particular thanksgiving hymns to Cyrus and John with the joint authority of Cyril and David ('the Melodist himself') were not sufficient, in his miracle collection Sophronios introduces a further narrative focus on the centrality of the hymns to the healing martyrs. One of the final episodes portrays an aristocratic female afflicted with a terrible colic, from which she is healed. The enthusiastic traveller who, having been cured, is about to embark upon a further pilgrimage to the Holy Land, receives a singular blessing from the saints alongside a prescription that she is to carry out on her prospective tours:

> And the saints, appearing to her once again, give her a complete healing: they offered her a pastry item to eat (πάστελλον αὐτὴν ἐσθίειν ὀρέξαντες) and gave her a psalm in their honour written (on the pastry item?) as if it were a writing pad (καὶ ψαλμόν τινα δόντες τῶν εἰς αὐτοὺς λεγομένων γεγραμμένον ὡσεὶ εἰς πιττάκιον), and commanded that she say it frequently. And she, after eating the pastry and receiving perfect health now and after singing the hymn, promised to always sing the melodious hymns (μελῳδεῖν) in their honour, and set out on a trip to Palestine and Caesarea[69].

While building on the emphases on the paramount importance of thanksgiving hymns to the saints introduced in earlier episodes (miracle 68 comes nearly at the end of the collection), this episode pushes them further. First, hymnody, according to the script practiced at the Menouthis shrine, receives direct endorsement from the saints who give it their personal recommendation. Second, it is made crystal clear that very specific, textually

---

[68] *Panégyrique des saints Cyr et Jean*, ed. by Pauline Bringel (Turnhout: Brepols, 2008), p. 53.
[69] *MCJ* 68 (pp. 390–91. 6).

stable thanksgiving hymns are offered to pilgrims as they are set in writing for further use.

In his major study of Christian amulets, Theodore De Bruyn has recently discussed this episode as potential evidence of the amuletic use of hymns by adducing comparanda from papyri inscribed with psalms and prayers[70]. While it would be tempting to follow De Bruyn's interpretative path, and to frame (the relatively few) late antique papyri with hymns to saint and martyrs as potential amulets — physical objects falling little short, in their portable physicality, of pilgrim tokens — I will not press this interpretation, as other papyrologists remain more cautious[71]. Yet in the *Miracles of Cyrus and John* we are undoubtedly dealing with a portable object inscribed with hymns used as an aide-memoire for a pious traveller. Whether and by how much actual practices would differ from Sophronios's account is difficult to ascertain. What can be established with clarity, however, is that for Sophronios, an impresario of Cyrus and John as allegedly Chalcedonian healing saints, promoting two specific hymns to the saints was one element of his wider agenda that he pursued when composing his very own collection of their miracles and, apparently, when circulating the book — and the hymns — locally. It seems safe to assume that Sophronios, as far as his ritual authority allowed, would seek to arrange for the hymns to be incorporated into actual liturgies on site. While these ritual arrangements may have been beyond what was practically achievable for the doctrinally marginalized Sophronios immersed in a hostile Miaphysite context, putting together a literary composition that would attribute to the two hymns a truly remarkable significance was something he could hope to rely on.

Lastly, I would like to advance an admittedly conjectural theory concerning the actual origin of the two hymns. Sophronios's ascription of them to Cyril is rendered dubious by at least two considerations. First, Cyril's role in the foundation of the cult of Cyrus and John is highly doubtful, as Jean Gascou has shown, and it is quite likely Sophronios's fabrication or a pre-existing tradition that he channels for his own ends[72]. The unprecedented focus on two specific thanksgiving hymns in the *Miracles of Cyrus and John* almost inevitably leads to speculation about Sophronios's authorship. Given what we know of Sophronios's versatile literary expertise as a rare poet who

---

[70] Theodore De Bruyn, *Making Amulets Christian: Artefacts, Scribes, and Contexts* (Oxford: Oxford University Press, 2017), pp. 203–04.

[71] See Ágnes T. Mihálykó, *The Christian Liturgical Papyri: An Introduction* (Tübingen: Mohr Siebeck, 2019), who briefly mentions the episode on p. 198 yet does not include it in her broader discussion of hymns and prayers on papyri used as amulets on pp. 191–99.

[72] Gascou, 'Les origines'.

was still capable of composing metrically correct anacreontics, and who quite possibly tried his pen at writing liturgical hymnody (attested in later Byzantine manuscript tradition), it seems entirely possible, and maybe indeed probable, that the two hymns were of Sophronios's own composition[73]. If this was the case, Sophronios's personal agency in creating the various aspects of the incubation cult of Cyrus and John would be even greater, as he would be the author of hymnic texts to be used for their liturgical celebration. In the light of what I have discussed earlier, Sophronios, in composing and promoting the hymns, would be tapping into broad patterns whereby hymnody formed a key aspect of pilgrims' experience of the saints. For him, a cult would probably be somewhat bare without a hymnic core that structured pilgrims' experience and scripted their ritual behaviour, and that formed the apex of their liturgical enactments on site while offering an opportunity to further spread the popularity of the cult through established pilgrim routes.

Conclusions: Liturgy and the Cult of Saints 'of the Many'?

For pilgrims to healing shrines who sought deliverance through their encounters with saintly martyrs, liturgical hymn-singing constituted *the* ritual script through which to proceed. In their ritualized experience at incubation churches, singing a hymn to saints was a mystical experience which involved intimate contact between saint and petitioner. Hymnody therefore lay at the very heart of the *cult* of saints as it was practiced and experienced by thousands of pious visitors to shrines across the eastern Mediterranean.

This insight into the inner phenomenology of liturgy-centred devotion is enabled by a turn towards miracle collections as important sources — a choice that de-centres both the individual writing agency and the study of literary texts such as those of Romanos the Melodist that are typically the subject of academic discussion of late antique Christian hymn-writing and singing. Once the experiences of the devoted and venerating 'many', rather than the writing few, come into focus, the formative role of liturgical scripts in shaping the everyday workings of the cult of saints manifests itself. My discussion above has purposefully tended to description rather than conceptual analysis; sources, when approached with attention to voices beyond the usually heeded literary voices of the educated elites as shapers of late antique religion, make themselves heard almost on their own. As I have suggested, the popular appeal of hymn-singing as the liturgical manifestation of devotion to

---

[73] Twelve Nativity hymns are attributed to him in the Byzantine manuscript tradition — see Egon Wellesz, 'The Nativity Drama of the Byzantine Church', *Journal of Roman Studies*, 37 (1947), 145–51.

saints was overwhelming. Individual figures such as Sophronios, if they were serious about making arrangements for the cult of specific saintly figures, would have been wise to fit into this ritual frame.

I have also made a point of abstaining from a question of considerable significance in itself. What exactly were the hymns or thanksgiving prayerful compositions that were sung by pilgrims and that were, quite likely, suggested to them by cult personnel on site? Can we recover them, or at least try to make an educated guess as to what specifically were the texts performed? Beyond a few easy findings, such as Romanos's hymns sung at the vigils of the Forerunner's church in Constantinople,[74] this is a question that, given our current knowledge of late antique sources, is somewhat premature and, in a sense, not central. Whichever particular hymnic texts pilgrims might have used at healing shrines or beyond (as discussed, their liturgical experiences there would not have been unique to these sites), what mattered most to them was *what* hymns allowed them, as ritual actors, to do, and *why*, rather than *how*, in literary and textual terms, that function was achieved. The attention paid to the phenomenology of the veneration of saints, as well as the turn to sources composed beyond the easily accessible yet incurably circumscribed pool of the self-conscious literary hymns, can offer glimpses into a cult of saints in Late Antiquity that is significantly different from the one that we are accustomed to envisage.

---

[74] *MA* 18 (p. 114. 5–6) mentions a member of the church community 'singing the poems' (ψάλλων τὰ στίχη) of Romanos.

Les saints myroblytes en Orient et en Occident jusqu'à l'an mil

Prolégomènes à l'histoire d'un phénomène miraculeux

Xavier Lequeux
(Société des Bollandistes)

Parmi les saints, la qualité de myroblyte est accordée à ceux dont la dépouille ou des éléments de celle-ci ou encore le récipient qui contient ces reliques ont la propriété de distiller (βλύζω) un liquide, souvent odorant et doué de vertus thérapeutiques. Ma première rencontre avec les saints myroblytes remonte au tout début de ce siècle[1]. Depuis lors, j'ai accumulé les références au hasard des lectures, pour constater que ces saints au singulier comportement posthume étaient bien plus nombreux que ne le laissent entendre les listes disponibles[2]. La contribution aborde les problématiques inhérentes à cette facette particulière du culte des saints : la nature du liquide exsudé par la dépouille ou la sépulture de certains saints, le contexte du miracle, l'universalité du phénomène, la variété des sources à prendre en considération, et l'historicité parfois douteuse du prodige. La présente synthèse constitue les premiers jalons d'une histoire d'un aspect du culte des saints, qui reste à écrire[3].

---

[1] Xavier Lequeux, « Saint Nicolas d'Andrinople. À propos d'une inscription de Thrace Orientale », *Analecta Bollandiana*, 119 (2001), 45–47.

[2] Lequeux, « Nicolas d'Andrinople », p. 46, n. 5. Ajouter, pour l'Occident, Sylvia Elizabeth Mullins, *Myroblytes : Miraculous Oil in Medieval Europe* (diss. Washington, D.C.: Georgetown University, 2016).

[3] Je remercie les Professeurs Bryan Ward-Perkins (Oxford University) et Robert Wiśniewski (Uniwersytet Warszawski) de m'avoir donné l'occasion d'exposer les premiers résultats d'une recherche en cours.

Interacting with Saints in the Late Antique and Medieval Worlds, ed. by Robert Wiśniewski, Raymond Van Dam, and Bryan Ward-Perkins, Hagiologia, 20 (Turnhout, 2023), pp. 123–137.
© BREPOLS ❧ PUBLISHERS   DOI 10.1484/M.HAG-EB.5.133624

Myron — manna — liquor

Lorsqu'il publie son *Glossarium ad scriptores mediae et infimae Graecitatis* en 1688, du Cange enrichit considérablement la lexicographie grecque, jusque là cantonnée à la langue classique. À la colonne 979 de l'ouvrage, figure le lemme μυροβλύτης, défini en ces termes : μυροβλύτες *dicti Sancti, quorum reliquiae odoriferum unguentum miraculose exsudant.* L'érudit renvoit ensuite à la rubrique *Manna* dans son *Glossarium ad scriptores mediae et infimae Latinitatis*, paru 10 ans plus tôt. Il précise encore que le martyr myroblyte par excellence est Démétrius de Thessalonique, et il en mentionne trois autres, tirés du Synaxaire byzantin : Myrope (2 déc.), Mirax (11 déc.) et Florus (18 août). La rubrique *Manna* dans le *Glossarium...Latinitatis* est plus étoffée. On y lit la définition suivante : *liquor, vel pulvis odorus qui de sepulchris aut corporibus Sanctorum effunditur et effluit.* Du Cange fournit comme premier exemple la Manne de l'évangéliste Jean, d'après le témoignage de Grégoire de Tours[4] notamment ; il ajoute que la manne est appelée μύρον par les Grecs, avant de fournir 26 attestations du miracle[5]. Le lemme μύρον apparaît également dans le *Glossarium... Graecitatis* ; il y est qualifié de *liquor e Sanctorum cadaveribus promanans, quem alii Μάννα vocant.* La notice énumère ensuite une dizaine d'attestations supplémentaires tirées, pour la plupart, de textes grecs alors inédits.

Du Cange hésitait à propos de la nature de la manne : *liquor vel pulvis*, liquide ou poussière. Cette hésitation provient d'un autre témoignage de Grégoire de Tours, qui relate à deux reprises le miracle qui se produisait régulièrement sur la sépulture d'André (CSLA E00502), à Patras : le jour de sa fête, de la manne sous forme de farine ou d'huile au parfum agréable suinte de la tombe de l'apôtre, et la substance sert à fabriquer des baumes et des potions bénéfiques pour les malades[6]. Pourquoi parler de farine ou d'huile ? La réponse se trouve dans le *Carmen* 21 récité par Paulin en l'honneur de Félix de Nole, le 14 janvier 407. L'année précédente, les vases censés recueillir le parfum dont on arrosait la dépouille du saint se remplirent d'une mixture faite de crasse, de poudre, de micros débris d'os et de tessons, et on constata la présence de terre dans un second temps. Craignant la présence d'un parasite dans la tombe, l'évêque Paul fit ouvrir le tombeau, et constata que le corps

---

[4] *Gregorii ep. Turonensis liber in gloria martyrum*, 29, éd. par Bruno Krusch, MGH SRM 1.2, p. 505. Voir CSLA E00496 (Marta Tycner et David Lambert).

[5] *Glossarium mediae et infimae Latinitatis... auctum a monachis Ordinis S. Benedicti...*, editio nova, 10 vol. (Niort : Favre, 1883–87), t. V, p. 223.

[6] *Gregorii ep. Turon. liber in gloria martyrum*, 30, pp. 505–06 (*mannam in modum farinae vel oleum cum odore nectareo*) et *Eiusdem de miraculis beati Andreae ap.* (*BHL* 430), 37, pp. 845–46 (*De quo sepulchro manna in modum farinae et oleum cum odore suavissimo defluit*). Voir CSLA E00502 (Marta Tycner).

était intact, ce qui rassura les dévots du saint[7]. La substance s'écoulant d'un tombeau pouvait donc avoir une consistance variable...

Plusieurs matières ont été proposées pour la Manne de saint Jean (CSLA S00042) citée en exemple par du Cange[8]. Comme le rapporte Augustin d'Hippone[9], certains pensaient que le *pulvis* récolté sur la sépulture située à Éphèse montait des profondeurs, poussé par la respiration de l'évangéliste qui y dormait enterré ; c'est à cette tradition que se rattachent les *Virtutes Iohannis* composées à la fin du VIe siècle[10] et la double notice du *Synaxaire de Constantinople* en l'honneur de Jean[11]. La substance prélevée par les fidèles est qualifiée de *manna in modum farinae* par Grégoire de Tours, lorsqu'il évoque le même miracle[12]. Toutefois, il existait une autre tradition relative à la mort de Jean. Selon une recension annexe des *Actes grecs de Jean*, l'apôtre avait persuadé ses disciples de le laisser seul dans une fosse pour prier, et lorsqu'ils revinrent un jour plus tard, ceux-ci ne trouvèrent sur place que des sandales et de la terre couverte de végétation (βρύουσαν τὴν γῆν), transformée en fontaine jaillissante (βρύουσαν/βρύοντα τὴν πηγήν) dans plusieurs manuscrits[13]. S'appuyant vraisemblablement sur cette variante, Éphrem d'Antioche prétendit, au VIe siècle, que le corps ne fut pas retrouvé, mais que l'on découvrit une source de myron[14]. Désormais, manne et myron allaient pouvoir se confondre. Il n'est donc pas étonnant que, de nos jours, on utilise encore le terme « manne » pour désigner le liquide qui s'écoule des reliques de Nicolas à Bari, de celles

---

[7] Paulin de Nole, *Carmen* 21. 583–642, éd. par Guilelmus de Hartel, CSEL, 30, pp. 177–79. L'incident est évoqué dans Dennis E. Trout, *Paulinus of Nola. Life, Letters, and Poems* (Berkeley: University of California Press, 1999), pp. 160–61 ; Paola Marone, « Alle origini del culto di S. Felice a Nola », *Studi e Materiali di Storia delle Religioni*, 80 (2014), 282–99 (p. 291).

[8] Dossier des textes avec traduction française : Arietta Papaconstantinou, « La manne de saint Jean, à propos d'un ensemble de cuillers inscrites », *Revue des Études Byzantines*, 59 (2001), 239–46.

[9] *In Ioannis evangelium tractatus* 124. 2, PL 35, col. 1970–71.

[10] *Virtutes Iohannis* 9, 107–20, éd. par Éric Junod et Jean-Daniel Kaestli, *Acta Iohannis*, CCSA 2, pp. 831–32.

[11] 8 mai : *Synaxarium Ecclesiae Constantinopolitanae e codice sirmondiano*, éd. par Hippolyte Delehaye, Propylaeum ad Acta Sanctorum Novembris (Bruxelles : Société des Bollandistes, 1902), col. 663–65, où le terme utilisé est κόνις. S. Willibald fit étape au VIIIe s. à Éphèse : *Vita Willibaldi ep. Eichstetensis* (*BHL* 8931 ; VIIIe s.), 4, éd. par Oswald Holder-Egger, MGH Scr. 15, p. 93 ; la *Vita* III (*BHL* 8933 ; XIe s.), 5 (ibid.) précise que le voyageur fut témoin oculaire du prodige de la manne. Clive Foss, « Pilgrimage in Medieval Asia Minor », *Dumbarton Oaks Papers*, 56 (2002), 129–51 (p. 141) manque de précision.

[12] *In gloria martyrum*, 29, p. 505. Voir CSLA E00496 (Marta Tycner et David Lambert).

[13] *Metastasis* γ, 115, éd. par Junod et Kaestli, *Acta Iohannis*, p. 336, apparat critique.

[14] *Responsio ad Anatolium scholasticum* (voir *CPG* 6908), extrait cité par Photius, *Cod.* 229, éd. par Nunzio Bianchi et Claudio Schiano, *Fozio : Biblioteca* (Pisa : Scuola Normale Superiore, 2016), p. 446.

de Félix à Nole et de celles de Walburge à Eichstätt[15]. Au cours des siècles précédents, le privilège d'émettre une poussière à vertu thérapeutique a été reconnu à d'autres saints : le martyr Hyacinthe d'Amastris (IVᵉ siècle)[16], la thaumaturge Élisabeth (Vᵉ siècle)[17] et Théophane le Confesseur († 818)[18].

Les huiles parfumées constituaient un remède essentiel, utilisé dans la médecine populaire comme dans la médecine savante, depuis la haute Antiquité. Toutefois dans les recueils anciens de miracles, ces huiles traditionnelles sont laissées de côté : pour se démarquer de la médecine profane, on évitait dans les sanctuaires de proposer des remèdes suggérés par la pharmacopée païenne, dont l'huile parfumée fournissait la base commune[19]. On consentit une exception si l'huile parfumée provenait du tombeau ou des reliques d'un saint, et on réserva l'antique terme qui désignait le parfum, — lui-même le plus souvent disponible sous la forme d'huile — au liquide parfumé s'écoulant de certaines tombes.

Le myron ne doit pas être confondu avec l'huile provenant de la lampe suspendue au-dessus de la tombe des saints. Ces huiles sanctifiées par la proximité du saint étaient également utilisées à des fins thérapeutiques : à l'époque de Grégoire de Tours († 594), l'huile de la lampe (*oleum sanctum*) éclairant la tombe de Martin dans la cité épiscopale était réputée lutter efficacement contre les douleurs, les blessures et les états de possession[20]. Cette huile pouvait même être directement ingurgitée par les malades, comme le rapporte Théodore Stoudite († 826) dans son *Éloge de Théophane le Confesseur*[21] ou encore Sabas, dans la *Vie de Pierre d'Atroa* († 837)[22] et, avant eux, le recueil des

---

[15] Nicolas de Myre : prélèvement, le 9 mai (commémoraison de la translation à Bari). Félix de Nole : récolte soit le 15 novembre (fête patronale), soit le 8 décembre. Walburge : production entre le 12 oct. (fête de la translation) et 25 février (anniversaire du décès).

[16] *Synaxarium Ecclesiae Constantinopolitanae*, col. 827–28.

[17] *Synaxarium*, col. 625–27.

[18] *Methodii patr. CP Vita S. Theophanis conf.* (*BHG* 1787z ; prononcé en 822), 54 et 60–62, éd. par Basile Latyšev, *Mémoires de l'Académie des Sciences de Russie*, VIIIᵉ série, vol. XIII, nᵒ 4 (Petrograd, 1918), pp. 35 et 39–40. Il est abusif de parler de myrrhe, comme le fait Stephanos Efthymiadis, « Le miracle et les saints durant et après le second iconoclasme », in *Monastères, images, pouvoirs et société à Byzance*, éd. par Michel Kaplan, Byzantina Sorbonensia, 23 (Paris : Publications de la Sorbonne, 2006), pp. 156–57.

[19] Béatrice Caseau, « Parfum et guérison dans le christianisme ancien et byzantin : des huiles parfumées des médecins au *myron* des saints byzantins », in *Les Pères de l'Église face à la science médicale de leur temps*, éd. par Véronique Boudon-Millot et Bernard Pouderon, Théologie historique, 117 (Paris : Beauchesne, 2005), pp. 151–70.

[20] *Gregorii ep. Turonensis liber de virtutibus S. Martini* (*BHL* 5618), 24, éd. par Bruno Krusch, MGH SRM I/2, pp. 638–39.

[21] Théodore Stoudite, *Éloge de Théophane* (*BHG* 1792b), 17, éd. par Stephanos Efthymiadis, « Le panégyrique de S. Théophane le Confesseur par S. Théodore Stoudite (*BHG* 1792b). Édition critique du texte intégral », *Analecta Bollandiana*, 111 (1993), 282–83.

[22] Relevé des miracles (*BHG* 2365) lors du vivant et après la mort de Pierre d'Atroa, dans Efthymiadis, « Le miracle et les saints », pp. 174–82 : voir en particulier le chap. 102.

miracles des saints anargyres, Cosme et Damien, persécutés sous Dioclétien[23]. Au IXe siècle toujours, dans la *Vie de Nicétas le Patrice* († 836), le biographe anonyme, qui était moine dans le monastère fondé par le saint à Katèsia (sur la côte de la mer Noire, en Bithynie), fait clairement la distinction entre les deux substances miraculeuses. En effet, aux miracles obtenus par l'usage de l'huile bénite (ἅγιον ἔλαιον)[24], l'hagiographe ajoute le miracle qu'il considère comme le plus fameux d'entre tous : l'écoulement occasionnel d'un myron jaillissant de la châsse et servant de remède (φάρμακον) pour ceux qui l'emportent[25].

Les lampes entourant le tombeau d'un saint peuvent également faire l'objet de prodiges. Dans l'*Éloge d'Agathe de Catane* (CSLA S00794), qu'il composa peut-être peu après 843, le patriarche Méthode, qui était natif de Syracuse en Sicile, évoqua un prodige auquel il assista dans l'église dédiée à la martyre à Constantinople : lors de la fête annuelle de cette dernière, l'huile contenue dans certaines lampes se mit à déborder, et c'était la troisième fois de suite que le prodige s'opérait[26]. Dans la *Vie de Théodora de Thessalonique*, le neuvième jour suivant le décès, la lampe qui éclairait la tombe de la sainte se mit à briller avec intensité, et l'huile ne s'épuisa jamais ; deux jours plus tard, cette huile déborda même de la lampe, provoquant l'afflux au monastère d'une foule désirant s'oindre d'huile miraculeuse[27].

L'huile sanctifiée pouvait également provenir d'une libation, une pratique en vogue pour le culte des martyrs durant les premiers siècles[28]. L'huile était

---

[23] Pour les miracles de Cosme et Damien (*BHG* 385–92), voir Luigi Canetti, « *Olea sanctorum* : reliquie e miracoli fra Tardoantico e Alto Medioevo », in *Olio e vino nell'Alto Medioevo*, Spoleto, 20–26 aprile 2006, t. II, Settimane di studio della Fondazione CISAM, 54 (Spoleto : CISAM, 2007), p. 1366, n. 66.

[24] *Vie de Nicétas* (*BHG* 1342b), 28–30, éd. par Denise Papachryssanthou, « Un confesseur du second iconoclasme : la Vie du patrice Nicétas († 836) », *Travaux et Mémoires*, 3 (1968), 346–47.

[25] *Vie de Nicétas* (*BHG* 1342b), 32 (p. 349).

[26] Méthode le Patriarche, *Éloge de S. Agathe* (*BHG* 38), 32, éd. par Carmelo Crimi, « Metodio patriarca di Costantinopoli, *Encomio di S. Agata* (*BHG* 38) », *Rivista di Studi Bizantini e Neoellenici,* n. s. 57 (2020), 83–84 (texte grec) et 125–27 (traduction italienne). Cf. Carmelo Crimi, « L'*Encomio di S. Agata* (*BHG* 38) di Metodio patriarca di Costantinopoli e la *Passio BHG* 37 », in *Ἀνατολὴ καὶ δύσις. Studi in memoria di Filippo Burgarella*, éd. par Giocchino Strano et Cristina Torre, Testi e studi bizantino-neoellenici, 117 (Roma: Nuova Terra, 2020), pp. 136–52. Sur le dossier d'Agathe voir le texte d'Anna Lampadaridi dans ce volume.

[27] Grégoire, *Vie de Théodora de Thessalonique* (*BHG* 1737), 47, éd. par Syméon Paschalidès, *Ὁ Βίος τῆς ὁσιομυροβλύτιδος Θεοδώρας τῆς ἐν Θεσσαλονίκῃ...*, Κέντρον Ἁγιολογικῶν Μελετῶν, 1 (Thessalonique: 1991, Ἱερὰ Μονὴ τῆς Ὁσίας Θεοδώρας), pp. 160–63. Sur cet épisode, voir Michel Kaplan, « L'ensevelissement des saints : rituel de création des reliques et sanctification à Byzance à travers les sources hagiographiques (v[e]–xiie siècles) », in *Mélanges Gilbert Dagron = Travaux et Mémoires*, 14 (Paris, 2002), 319–32 (p. 329).

[28] Sur cette pratique, voir Wilhelm Gessel, « Das Öl der Märtyrer. Zur Funktion und Interpretation der Ölsarkophage von Apamea in Syrien », *Oriens Christianus*, 72 (1988),

introduite dans le sarcophage de pierre au moyen d'un ou de plusieurs petits trous percés dans la plaque supérieure ; elle était ensuite recueillie à la base au moyen d'orifices, après avoir été sanctifiée au contact des reliques. Dans la *Vie d'Euthyme de Palestine* (CSLA E06468), Cyrille de Scythopolis, qui avait séjourné dans le monastère du saint entre 544 et 555, raconte que peu après le décès de ce dernier survenu le 20 janvier 483, on décida de construire une chapelle funéraire dans la grotte où le défunt avait passé ces débuts. On érigea une chapelle voûtée, où on installa le sépulcre du saint. Le 7 mai, l'archevêque de Jérusalem, Anastase, y déposa la dépouille d'Euthyme. On scella le couvercle du tombeau, que l'on perça pour y disposer un entonnoir en argent (χώνη) juste au dessus de la poitrine du défunt. Cet entonnoir, rapporte Cyrille, fit jaillir toutes sortes de bienfaits pour ceux qui l'approchaient avec foi[29]. La sanctification mécanique de l'huile se pratiquait également en Occident : il suffit de rappeler l'incident survenu sur la tombe primitive de Félix de Nole.

Quelques mots sur la nature du myron ou du *liquor* qui s'échappe des saints tombeaux[30]. Pour l'homme médiéval, le myron est au myron ce que l'huile est à l'huile. Les pèlerins et les hagiographes ne se posent pas de question. On a vu précédemment que la consistance du liquide pouvait considérablement varier. Les émanations du tombeau d'Euphémie de Chalcédoine (CSLA S00017), dès le VIe siècle[31], sont assimilées sans équivoque à du sang[32] : cette identification s'appuie vraisemblablement sur la couleur foncée du fluide. Le liquide qui s'échappe des sépultures ne doit pas être confondu

---

183–202 ; pour les siècles suivants, voir Vincenzo Ruggieri, « Ἀπομυρίζω (μυρίζω) τὰ λείψανα, ovvero la genesi d'un rito », *Jahrbuch der Österreichischen Byzantinistik*, 43 (1993), 21–35.

[29] Cyrille de Scythopolis, *Vie d'Euthyme* (BHG 647–648b), 42, éd. par Eduard Schwartz, *Kyrillos von Skythopolis*, Texte und Untersuchungen, 49/2 (Leipzig : Hinrichs, 1939), pp. 61–62 ; description du procédé : Yizhar Hirschfeld, *The Judean Desert Monasteries in the Byzantine Period* (New Haven : Yale University Press, 1992), pp. 130–31 ; contresens dans la traduction d'André-Jean Festugière, *Les moines d'Orient*, III/1 : *Les moines de Palestine* (Paris : Cerf, 1962), p. 116, où le substantif χώνη est traduit « urne ». Voir CSLA E06468 et E06470 (les deux par Efthymios Rizos).

[30] La dépouille d'un saint peut également exhaler un parfum, une bonne odeur, une fragrance : sur ce signe d'élection préfigurant le Paradis, voir Martin Roch, *L'intelligence d'un sens. Odeurs miraculeuses et odorat dans l'Occident du haut Moyen Âge (Ve-VIIIe siècles)* (Turnhout : Brepols, 2009).

[31] Évagre le Scholastique, *Histoire ecclésiastique*, II. 3, éd. par Joseph Bidez et Léon Parmentier, *The Ecclesiastical History of Evagrius with the Scholia* (Londres : Methuen, 1898), p. 41, 7–13 ; Théophylacte Simocatta, *Historiae* 8. 14 (pp. 312, 5 sq.). Voir Albrecht Berger, « Die Reliquien der heiligen Euphemia und ihre erste Translation nach Konstantinopel », *Hellenika*, 39 (1988), 311–32.

[32] Même apparence pour les émanations du tombeau de Marie la Jeune († 902) d'après sa Vie, composée après 1025 : *Vie de Marie la Jeune* (BHG 1164), 12 et 16, éd. par Paul Peeters, *AASS* Nov. t. IV, p. 698A et E.

avec l'huile sacramentelle, appelée Chrême ou myron : ce mélange de quarante huiles essentielles et d'huile d'olives est utilisé pour certains sacrements (baptême, confirmation et onction des malades)[33]. Il ne faut pas non plus confondre μύρον et μύρρα. En effet, ce dernier terme désigne la myrrhe, une gomme résineuse suintant d'un arbre appelé arbre à myrrhe et utilisée comme parfum depuis la plus haute Antiquité. La myrrhe offerte par les Rois mages n'a rien à voir avec le myron qui s'écoule des tombeaux. En 1925, en pleine crise moderniste, les Dominicains de Bari avec l'accord de leurs supérieurs, firent analyser par l'Université de Bari un échantillon du myron prélevé sur les reliques de saint Nicolas, dont l'Ordre dominicain a encore et toujours la garde. Les résultats de l'analyse scientifique furent rapidement rendus publics : *acqua quasi pura*[34].

Quand survient le prodige ?

La plupart du temps, le prodige de la myroblysie survient peu après le décès du saint : l'événement est alors logiquement relaté dans la *Vita* et/ou dans le recueil de miracles qui y est annexé. Quelques exemples :

– D'après Nicéphore le Sceuophylax des Blachernes, des aveugles recouvrèrent la vue en utilisant du myron provenant du cercueil de Théodore de Sykéon († 22 avril 613), peu avant son transfert à Constantinople par l'empereur Héraclius[35].

– Selon la *Vie de Constantin le Juif* (*BHG* 370), composée sous le règne de Léon VI (886–912), le cercueil du saint laisse échapper, à partir du troisième jour de sa mort, un myron intarissable[36].

– Lors du premier anniversaire du décès d'Athanasie d'Égine, survenu avant 916, on constate, après l'ouverture intempestive de son tombeau par trois possédés, que du myron perle sur toutes les faces internes du cercueil[37].

---

[33] Luciano Zappella, « 'Elaion-Myron' : l'olio simbolo dello Spirito Santo nelle catechesi battesimali di Cirillo di Gerusalemme », *Cristianesimo nella Storia*, 11 (1991), 5–27.

[34] Pio Scognamiglio, *La manna di S. Nicola nella storia, nell'arte, nella scienze* (Bari : Società tipografica editrice Barese, 1925).

[35] *Éloge de Théodore de Sykéon* (*BHG* 1749), 43, éd. par Conradus Kirch, « Nicephori sceuophylacis encomium in S. Theodorum Siceotam », *Analecta Bollandiana*, 20 (1901), 267–68.

[36] *Vie de Constantin le Juif* (*BHG* 370), 84, éd. par Hippolyte Delehaye, *AASS* Nov. t. IV, p. 654D.

[37] *Vie et Miracles d'Athanasie d'Égine* (*BHG* 180), 15, éd. par François Halkin, *Six inédits d'hagiologie byzantine*, Subsidia Hagiographica, 74 (Bruxelles : Société des Bollandistes, 1987), p. 191 ; pour la rédaction du texte, le *terminus ante quem* est fourni par la date de copie du seul témoin conservé, le ms. *Vaticanus Gr.* 1660.

- Dans la *Vie de Luc de Steiris* composée peu après 961, le myron provenant de la tombe du saint († 953) opère deux guérisons[38].
- Selon le biographe de Nikon le Métanoeite († fin x[e] / début xie siècle), le corps du défunt déposé dans le cercueil produit aussitôt un myron qui coule sans discontinuer[39].

Le prodige du myron peut faire irruption dans le dossier d'un saint, lorsque son culte prend de l'ampleur. Après l'euphorie du triomphe sur l'iconoclasme, le moine Sabas compose une *Vie de Pierre d'Atroa*, un ascète de Bithynie mort le 1er janvier 837. Le texte rapporte tout naturellement les dernières paroles de Pierre, et précise que la dépouille fut déposée dans une châsse, source de toutes sortes de prodiges[40]. Mais le lieu devient apparemment de plus en plus fréquenté, et Sabas doit revoir sa copie : il retravaille des portions de la Vie, et ajoute des miracles *post mortem*. Dans le texte revu, la fameuse *Vita retractata*, il ne manque pas d'évoquer le transfert de la dépouille, le 19 août 838. À cette date, les moines déposent la dépouille de Pierre, dans la grotte qu'il occupait jadis, et depuis ce moment, le myron, dont Sabas lui-même fera usage, s'écoule par intermittence du cercueil, ce qui permet à l'hagiographe de présenter la tombe miraculeuse comme une nouvelle fontaine de Siloé (Jean 7, 9–11)[41].

À Chypre, au viie siècle, les miracles du myron se multiplient. Béatrice Caseau a pu observer un lien entre attaque arabe et apparition du myron[42]. C'est dans ces circonstances dramatiques, selon le témoignage d'Anastase le Sinaïte, que la châsse d'Épiphane (CSLA S00215), à Constantia, se mit subitement à produire l'équivalent de plus de trente jarres de myron et que, des reliques de Tychon (CSLA S02634), s'échappa un myron qui inonda le sol de l'église où se trouvait la tombe[43] !

---

[38] *Vie et Miracles de Luc le Jeune* (*BHG* 994), 69 et 75, éd. par Carolyn L. Connor et W. Robert Connor, *The Life and Miracles of Saint Luke of Steiris* (Brookline, MA : Hellenic College Press, 1988), pp. 112–17 et 124–25. Dans les paragraphes 71–73, le terme utilisé pour désigner le liquide présent sur la tombe, νοτίς, fait penser à la condensation, d'autant plus qu'il est récolté au moyen d'une éponge (paragraphe 83).

[39] *Vie de Nikon Metanoeite* (*BHG* 1367), 48, éd. par Denis F. Sullivan, *The Life of Saint Nikon* (Brookline, MA : Hellenic College Press, 1987), pp. 164–65.

[40] *Vie de Pierre d'Atroa* (*BHG* 2364), 86, éd. par Vitalien Laurent, *La Vie merveilleuse de saint Pierre d'Atroa († 837)*, Subsidia Hagiographica, 29 (Bruxelles : Société des Bollandistes, 1956), pp. 222–25.

[41] *Vita retractata de Pierre d'Atroa* (*BHG* 2365), 98–99, éd. par Vitalien Laurent, *La Vita retractata et les miracles posthumes de saint Pierre d'Atroa,* Subsidia Hagiographica, 31 (Bruxelles : Société des Bollandistes, 1958), pp. 148–51.

[42] Caseau, « Parfum et guérison », p. 179.

[43] Anastase le Sinaïte, *Récits utiles à l'âme* (*BHG* 1448q), II. 2, éd. par André Binggeli, *Anastase le Sinaïte, Récits sur le Sinaï et Récits utiles à l'âme* (diss. Paris IV-Sorbonne, 2001), t. I, p. 219 (texte), et II, p. 531 (traduction).

Dans plusieurs dossiers hagiographiques de saints reconnus, la mention du myron arrive même très tardivement :

- Le cas de Démétrius de Thessalonique († début du IVe siècle), le saint myroblyte par excellence, est emblématique[44]. Contrairement à ce que l'on pourrait croire, le myron n'a pas toujours fait partie du culte du saint patron de Thessalonique : on n'en trouve aucune mention dans les anciens recueils de miracles compilés durant le VIIe siècle. L'attestation la plus ancienne du prodige remonte au tout début du Xe siècle, si l'on admet l'authenticité du *De expugnatione Thessalonicae* de Jean Kaminiatès, qui relate le siège de Thessalonique par Léon de Tripoli en 904[45] ; une mention du myron de Démétrius dans la *Synopsis des Miracles d'Eugenius de Trébizonde* pointe vers la même époque[46]. Il est même probable que les habitants de Thessalonique usaient déjà du myron de Démétrius dans les années 890 : l'insistance avec laquelle Grégoire, le biographe de Théodora de Thessalonique, vante la qualité du myron qui s'écoulait du sarcophage de la sainte depuis la translation intervenue en 893, laisse entrevoir l'existence d'une rivalité avec le sanctuaire de Démétrius[47].

- La première mention du myron de Nicolas de Myre († 355 ?) figure dans la Vie composée au VIIIe siècle par Michel l'Archimandrite, avant que n'éclate la première crise iconoclaste[48].

- On signalera également la mention du myron thérapeutique surgissant des os du prophète Élie (CSLA S00217) dans le *Traité sur la vénération des images* composé par Théodore Abū Qurrah, entre 815 et 820[49].

---

[44] La bibliographie est gigantesque : voir en dernier lieu, Franz Alto Bauer, *Eine Stadt und ihr Patron, Thessaloniki und der Heilige Demetrios* (Regensburg : Schnell & Steiner, 2013). Voir CSLA S00761.

[45] Iohannes Caminiata, *De expugnatione Thessalonicae*, 2. 4, éd. par Gertrudis Böhlig, *Ioannis Caminiatae de expugnatione Thessalonicae*, Corpus Fontium Historiae Byzantinae, 4 (Berlin : De Gruyter, 1972), p. 5.

[46] Joseph Lazaropoulos, *Synopsis des miracles d'Eugène de Trébizonde* (*BHG* 612), 20, éd. par Jan Olof Rosenqvist, *The Hagiographic Dossier of St Eugenios of Trebizond in Codex Athous Dionysiou 154*, Studia Byzantina Upsaliensia, 5 (Uppsala : Acta Universitatis Upsaliensis, 1996), pp. 302 (texte) et 431 (commentaire).

[47] Stephanos Efthymiadis, « Medieval Thessalonike and the Miracles of its Saints : Big and Small Demands Made on Exclusive Rights (Ninth-Twelfth Centuries) », in Efthymiadis, *Hagiography in Byzantium : Literature, Social History and Cult* (Burlington : Ashgate, 2011), XIII, pp. 11–12.

[48] Michel l'Archimandrite, *Vie de Nicolas* (*BHG* 1348), 41, éd. par Gustav Anrich, *Hagios Nikolaos. Der heilige Nikolaus in der griechischen Kirche*, t. I : *Die Texte* (Leipzig : Teubner, 1913), p. 134.

[49] Théodore Abū Qurra, *Traité sur la vénération des saintes images*, 21, trad. par Sidney H. Griffith, *Theodore Abū Qurrah, A Treatise on the Veneration of the Holy Icons*, Eastern Christian Texts in Translation (Leuven : Peeters, 1997), pp. 88–90. Sur cette œuvre, voir désormais Vasile-Octavian Mihoc, *Christliche Bilderverehrung im Kontext islamischer Bilderlosigkeit*.

- Parfois, le *Synaxaire de Constantinople* constitue la seule source à faire état du prodige du myron, alors que les autres pièces du dossier hagiographique demeurent silencieuses. C'est notamment le cas pour Antipas évêque de Pergame (Ier siècle)[50], Florus et Laurus martyrs dans l'Illyricum (IIe siècle)[51], Hermione fille de l'apôtre Philippe[52], Luc le Sicilien (*Tauromenitanus*)[53], un jeune homme nommé S. Mirax par du Cange[54], et Théodore Trichinas (Ve siècle)[55].

Universalité du prodige

Contrairement à ce qu'on pourrait penser, le prodige du myron n'est pas une spécialité de l'Orient chrétien. Dans le corpus de textes, tel qu'il se présente actuellement, le même phénomène miraculeux semble apparaître en Occident, à une époque moins haute :

- D'après le recueil de miracles posthumes de Gertrude de Nivelles († 659 ; CSLA E07666), composé vers 700, les aveugles recouvraient la vue et les malades leur santé après s'être oints du *liquor* émanant du tombeau en marbre de la sainte[56].
- La Vie anonyme de Sigolène, la fondatrice du monastère féminin du Troclar dans les environs d'Albi (CSLA E06494), mentionne l'existence d'un vase placé à la tête du tombeau pour récolter le *liquor olei* suintant en permanence[57]. Cette *Vita* est un agrégat d'emprunts qui passe pour avoir été confectionné durant la seconde moitié du VIIIe siècle[58].
- La présence d'un vase collecteur pour récolter l'huile provenant du tombeau est aussi mentionnée dans la *Vie de l'abbé Berchaire*, fondateur de Hautvillers et de Montier-en-Der († 685), rédigée au Xe siècle par son lointain successeur, l'hagiographe Adson († 992)[59].

Der Traktat über Bilderverehrung von Theodor Abū Qurrah (c. 755 bis c. 830), Göttinger Orientforschungen, 1. R., Syriaca, 53 (Wiesbaden : Harrassowitz, 2017).

[50] *Synaxarium Ecclesiae Constantinopolitanae*, col. 598.

[51] *Synaxarium*, col. 908.

[52] *Synaxarium*, col. 271–72.

[53] *Synaxarium*, col. 200.

[54] *Synaxarium*, col. 301–02.

[55] *Synaxarium*, col. 616.

[56] *Miracula* (*BHL* 3499), 2, éd. par Bruno Krusch, MGH SRM 2, p. 472.

[57] *Vita* (*BHL* 7570), V. 35, *AASS* Iul. t. V, pp. 636–37.

[58] État de la question : Nelly Pousthomis-Dalle et al., « Sainte Sigolène, sa Vie, ses églises au Troclar (Lagrave, Tarn) », *Archéologie du Midi Médiéval*, 15–16 (1997–98), 1–65 (pp. 8–21).

[59] *Vita Bercharii* (*BHL* 1178), 21, 700–03, éd. par Monique Goullet, *Adsonis Dervensis opera hagiographica*, CCM 198 (Turnhout : Brepols, 2003), pp. 331–32.

LES SAINTS MYROBLYTES

- À Canosa, dans les Pouilles, sous le règne du prince Grimoald IV (806–17), l'évêque Pierre procéda à l'invention des reliques de l'évêque Sabinus (CSLA S01729), un contemporain de Grégoire le Grand. Le jour suivant l'ouverture du tombeau, lorsqu'on voulut déplacer les reliques, on constata que les plaques de marbre étaient couvertes d'un *inenarrabili odore liquor*[60].
- La Passion de l'évêque d'Autun, Révérien/Riran († IIIe siècle) rapporte que sa dépouille distillait un *liquor olei*, qui guérissait infirmes et aveugles[61]. Ce texte rédigé à une époque inconnue fut utilisé par Usuard, au IXe siècle[62].
- Lors de l'ouverture, en 893, de la tombe de Walburge, abbesse d'Heidenheim, décrétée par l'évêque d'Eichstätt, Erkanbald, pour prélever des reliques, les envoyés du prélat s'aperçurent que les os de la sainte exsudaient des *stillae roris*[63].

Il faut évidemment ajouter à ces exemples les reliques de Félix de Nole, qui se mirent entretemps à produire épisodiquement un liquide miraculeux sans intervention humaine cette fois...[64] Le cas d'Éloi, l'évêque de Noyon († 660 ; CSLA S02032) est problématique, car le liquide ne provient pas directement de la dépouille, ni du tombeau lui-même : dans la seconde partie de sa Vie, l'évêque Ouen de Rouen († 686) rapporte l'apparition d'un *ros* sur le tissu de soie doublé de lin recouvrant le tombeau à l'occasion du Carême[65] ; on tordit le tissu au-dessus d'un vase pour recueillir le précieux *liquor*, qui opéra plusieurs guérisons[66].

---

[60] *Historia Vitae, Inventionis, Translationis S. Sabini episcopi* (*BHL* 7443), VI. 22, *AASS* Febr. II, p. 328. Sur l'événement : Ada Campione, « La *Vita di Sabino*, vescovo di Canosa : un *exemplum* di agiografia longobarda », in *Bizantini, Longobardi e Arabi in Puglia nell'Alto Medioevo*. Atti del XX Congresso internazionale di studio sull'alto medioevo, Savelleteri di Fasano (BR), 3–6 nov. 2011, Atti dei congressi, 20 (Spoleto : CISAM, 2012), 365–403.

[61] *Acta S. Reveriani ep.* (*BHL* 7200), 6–7, *AASS* Iun. I, p. 41.

[62] Joseph van der Straeten, « Actes des martyrs d'Aurélien en Gaule », *Analecta Bollandiana*, 80 (1962), 135–39.

[63] Wolfardhus mon. Haserensis, *De Vita S. Walburgis* (*BHL* 8765), 10, *AASS* Febr. t. III, p. 525 ; au XIe siècle, le passage sera repris par *l'Anonymus Haserensis* (*De episcopis Eischtetensibus*, 5 éd. par L. C. Bethmann, MGH Scr. 5, pp. 255. 41–256. 3), qui attribue au liquide prélevé un pouvoir thérapeutique analogue à celui de l'huile provenant de la tombe de S. Nicolas.

[64] La mention de la manne apparaît pour la première fois dans l'ouvrage *De Nola* II. 11 publié par Ambrogio Leone (Venise, 1514). On consigne depuis 1753 l'occurrence du prodige. Dernière attestation : 2011 ; avant-dernière : 1979.

[65] Audoenus ep. Rotomagensis, *Vita Eligii ep. Noviomensis* (*BHL* 2474–76), II. 42, éd. par Bruno Krusch, MGH SRM 4, p. 725. L'authenticité de cette *Vita*, autrefois débattue par Krusch, ne semble plus devoir être mise en doute : François Dolbeau, « Vie et Miracles de sainte Aure, abbesse jadis vénérée à Paris », *Analecta Bollandiana*, 125 (2007), 20–22.

[66] *Vita Eligii*, II. 43, 48, 61, 67 et 80, pp. 725–26, 727–28, 731–32, 734 et 739–40, voir CSLA E06301.

Variété des sources

Le suintement miraculeux constitue pour les hagiographes une preuve de la sainteté du défunt, qu'ils s'empressent de mettre en avant. Toutefois, pour élaborer un répertoire des saints myroblytes, le dépouillement des autres types de littérature qui ne relèvent pas du culte des saints, peut s'avérer utile :

– Dans le premier livre du *De aedificiis*, composé vers 560[67], Procope de Césarée rapporte que, du temps de Justinien (527–65), la vieille église Sainte-Irène dans le quartier de *Sykae* à Constantinople avait été incendiée, et qu'elle fut reconstruite de fond en comble[68]. À l'occasion de ces travaux, on découvrit des reliques, que l'on attribua aux Quarante martyrs de Sébastée (CSLA E04395). Comme l'empereur souffrait alors de la goutte, les reliques, dont la nature n'est pas non plus précisée, furent appliquées sur son genou ; une huile miraculeuse s'écoula de celles-ci, et le mal disparut. La dédicace de la nouvelle église a lieu en septembre 551[69]. En réalité, ces reliques avaient été découvertes une première fois sous l'épiscopat de Proclus (434–37) et la supervision de l'Augusta Pulchérie. Durant la première moitié du Vᵉ siècle, l'historien Sozomène, qui rapportait en détail les circonstances de la trouvaille, précisait — déjà — que les reliques dégageaient les bonnes odeurs des parfums (μύρων εὐωδίας)[70].

– La première attestation du culte rendu à Glycérie, martyre à Héraclée au IIᵉ siècle (CSLA S00018), se lit chez un historien du VIIᵉ, Théophylacte Simocatta, qui rapporte deux anecdotes : l'interruption momentanée du prodige suite à un changement malencontreux du bassin récoltant

---

[67] On hésite sur la date exacte de composition : Denis Roques, « Les *Constructions de Justinien* de Procope de Césarée », in *Le De aedificiis de Procope : le texte et les réalités documentaires* = *Antiquité Tardive*, 8 (2000), p. 43, n. 90.

[68] *De aedificiis*, I. 2, 13 et I. 7, éd. par Jakob Haury, *Procopii Caesariensis opera omnia*, vol. III/2 (Leipzig : Teubner, 1913), pp. 19 et 31–33. Traces épigraphiques de la restauration justinienne : Denis Feissel, « Les édifices de Justinien au témoignage de Procope et de l'épigraphie », dans le même volume, p. 91.

[69] L'usage du myron à des fins thérapeutiques est donc bien antérieur au IXᵉ siècle, contrairement à ce que laisse entendre Stephanos Efthymiadis, « L'incubation à l'époque mésobyzantine : problèmes de survivance historique et de représentation littéraire (VIIIᵉ–XIIIᵉ s.) », in *Le saint, le moine et le paysan. Mélanges d'histoire byzantine offerts à Michel Kaplan*, éd. par Olivier Delouis, Sophie Métivier et Paule Pagès, Byzantina Sorbonensia, 29 (Paris : Publications de la Sorbonne, 2016), 155–69 (p. 169).

[70] Sozomène, *Histoire ecclésiastique*, IX. 2, éd. par Joseph Bidez et Günther Chr. Hansen, *Sozomenus. Kirchengeschichte*, Die griechischen christlichen Schriftsteller, 50 (Berlin : Akademie Verlag, 1960), pp. 392–94, voir CSLA E04058.

le myron[71], et la visite de l'empereur Maurice au sanctuaire, dont il ordonna des travaux de restauration[72]. Le culte rendu à Glycérie constitue l'exemple le mieux documenté de la commémoraison d'un saint myroblyte. La *Vie d'Élisabeth la thaumaturge*, abbesse à Constantinople au Ve siècle, et elle-même originaire d'Héraclée, décrit les festivités qui ont lieu dans cette localité, chaque année durant une semaine en l'honneur de Glycérie : le chef de la sainte était porté en procession dans la ville en liesse[73]. On a également conservé le présentoir médiéval du chef de Glycérie, dont une inscription précise la fonction sans ambiguïté : la stèle est visible au Musée d'Archéologie et d'Ethnographie de Tekirdağ (inv. n° 671)[74].

– Comme il se doit, le *Synaxaire de Constantinople* signale la présence de la tombe de Jean Chrysostome dans l'église des Saints Apôtres à Constantinople[75]. Toutefois, d'après Mésaritès qui avait composé, à la fin du XIIe siècle, une description du même édifice, la tombe, couverte d'une plaque d'argent à l'effigie du saint, laissait s'écouler un myron miraculeux abondant[76].

Historicité parfois problématique du prodige

Alors que dans l'immense majorité des dossiers, la production de myron et sa récolte constituent un événement dont il n'y pas lieu de contester la réalité, il

---

[71] Théophylacte Simocatta, *Histoires*, I. 11, éd. par Carl de Boor, *Theophylacti Simocattae Historiae*, Bibliotheca Teubneriana (Leipzig: Teubner, 1887), p. 60, voir CSLA E00017.

[72] Théophylacte Simocatta, *Histoires*, VI. 1, pp. 220–21. Deux dates possibles : 590 ou 598, d'après Michael Whitby, *The Emperor Maurice and his Historian : Theophylact Simocatta on Persian and Balkan Warfare* (Oxford : Clarendon Press, 1988), p. 156, voir CSLA E00016.

[73] *Vie d'Élisabeth d'Héraclée* (*BHG* 2121), 3, éd. par François Halkin, « Sainte Élisabeth d'Héraclée, abbesse à Constantinople », *Analecta Bollandiana*, 91 (1973), 249–64 (p. 253). La datation du texte est disputée ; une date antérieure à la moitié du Xe s. est possible : voir Valerie Karras, « Life of St. Elisabeth the Wonderworker », in *Holy Women of Byzantium : Ten Saints' Lives in English Translation*, éd. par Alice-Mary Talbot, Byzantine Saints' Lives in Translation, 1 (Washington, DC : Dumbarton Oaks Research Library and Collection, 1996), pp. 117–20.

[74] Description du monument : Holger A. Klein, 'Materiality and the Sacred : Byzantine Reliquaries and the Rhetoric of Enshrinement, Saints and Sacred Matter, in *The Cult of Relics in Byzantium and Beyond*, éd. par Cynthia Hahn et Holger A. Klein, Dumbarton Oaks Byzantine Symposia and Colloquia (Washington DC : Dumbarton Oaks Research Library and Collection, 2015), pp. 241–42.

[75] *Synaxarium Ecclesiae Constantinopolitanae*, col. 425 (Ian. 27. 1).

[76] Glanville Downey, « Nikolaos Mesarites : Description of the Church of the Holy Apostles at Constantinople », *Transactions of the American Philosophical Society*, 47 (1957), 914–15 (§ XXXVIII, 3–4) ; passage traduit par Bernard Flusin, « Le panégyrique de Constantin VII Porphyrogénète pour la translation des reliques de Grégoire le Théologien (*BHG* 728) », *Revue des Études Byzantines*, 57 (1999), 23–24.

peut parfois arriver que l'historicité du prodige puisse être mise en question. Voici un cas qui éveille le doute. Dans la *Vie de Matrone de Pergé*, qui vécut au Ve siècle, l'hagiographe, actif après 543, rapporte que la sainte séjourna dans la ville d'Émèse, et que l'on découvrit alors une urne contenant le chef de Jean Baptiste (CSLA S00020). De la relique suintait une huile parfumée. Sollicitée par un aveugle, Matrone enduisit les yeux de ce dernier, qui recouvra la vue[77]. Pour l'hagiographe, ce miracle vient évidemment confirmer la sainteté de Matrone, même si celle-ci s'était auparavant travestie en homme pour rejoindre la communauté de Bassianos à Constantinople. Or, il se fait que l'on a conservé une autre version de la découverte du chef de Jean Baptiste, à Émèse. Il s'agit du texte grec autrefois traduit en latin par Denys le Petit : le récit de cette découverte, que l'on situe en 452/3, consigné par l'archimandrite Marcel, qui se présente comme le découvreur de la relique dans la grotte qui sert de crypte à son monastère[78]. Malheureusement, le découvreur ne mentionne à aucun moment la présence de Matrone, ni encore moins l'apparition d'huile parfumée sur le vase qui contient la tête du Précurseur. Il est hautement probable que le don de guérison attribué à Matrone soit la pieuse invention d'un hagiographe soucieux de fournir un portrait conventionnel pour une sainte qui ne l'était pas. Par contre, une autre distribution de baume, évoquée par le même hagiographe, tirée cette fois des reliques de Laurent (CSLA S00037) conservées dans la basilique qui porte son nom à Constantinople[79], n'a pas lieu d'être contestée, car elle n'accroît pas la sainteté de Matrone : elle sert tout simplement de contexte à la première rencontre entre la sainte et Athanasia, une femme noble qui la rejoindra dans son monastère[80].

Conclusion

Le dossier des saints myroblytes est complexe. En effet au cours des siècles, en Orient et en Occident, ce label englobe des récits de guérisons, où interviennent des fluides de nature différente et d'origines diverses.

---

[77] *Vie (I) de Matrone de Pergé* (BHG 1221), 12, éd. par Hippolyte Delehaye, *AASS* Nov. t. III, pp. 796–97. Cette Vie aurait été composée entre 529 et 565, d'après Georges Sidéris, « Bassianou et de Matrônès (V[e]-VIe siècles) », in *Le saint, le moine et le paysan*, 631–56 (pp. 633–38).

[78] Marcellus archimandrita Spelaei, *Historia secundae Inventionis* (BHG 840–40bc) ; le texte a reçu le n° 4291–92 dans la *BHL*.

[79] *Vie (I) de Matrone de Pergé* (BHG 1221), 38, p. 807.

[80] Sur ces péripéties, voir dernièrement Sidéris, « Bassianos, les monastères de Bassianou et de Matrônès », pp. 651–54.

Une lecture attentive des sources permet de distinguer deux types de liquide opérant ces guérisons miraculeuses :
- les substantifs *oleum*/ἔλαιον sont d'habitude réservés à l'huile puisée dans les lampes situées à proximité de la sépulture d'un saint ;
- Les substantifs μύρον/*liquor/ros* désignent le fluide s'échappant du tombeau d'un saint ou de ses reliques. C'est aux saints gratifiés de ce prodige *post mortem* qu'ils convient de réserver la qualité de myroblytes.

La confusion actuelle des termes pour désigner le liquide extrait de plusieurs sépultures célèbres — manne de saint Nicolas et de saint Félix, huile ou manne de sainte Walburge — vient inutilement embrouiller les esprits.

De tous temps, le miracle de la myroblysie a suscité la curiosité des foules, et a alimenté la dévotion des fidèles. Il n'est guère étonnant que le prodige soit particulièrement mis en évidence par les hagiographes pour la *gloria posthuma* des saints dont les reliques exsudent effectivement le myron.

II

Local and Cosmopolitan Cults

Reinvented by Julius, Ignored by Damasus

Dynamics of the Cult of Callixtus in Late Antique Rome

András Handl
(KU Leuven)

If one can trust the toxic account of the *Refutatio omnium haeresium* (henceforth *Refutatio*) — and one can trust it, as I have argued extensively elsewhere[1] — bishop Callixtus I of Rome (*c.* 217-*c.* 222) had quite a turbulent life. A fugitive bankrupt slave sentenced to die in the mines of Sardinia but freed by favourable circumstances, then the manager of the first collective cemetery, he eventually became bishop about 1800 years ago[2]. A *passio*, the so-called *Acta Martyrii Sancti Callisti* (*BHL* 1523, henceforth *Acta*) attests to a similarly turbulent end to his life. After failing to starve him to death, his persecutors tied a stone to his neck

---

[1] András Handl, 'Bishop Callistus I. of Rome (217?-222). A Martyr or a Confessor?', *Zeitschrift für Antikes Christentum*, 18 (2014), 390–419. For a critical study of Callixtus's life, ecclesiastical career, and controversies surrounding him, see András Handl, 'From Slave to Bishop. Callixtus' Early Ecclesial Career and Mechanisms of Clerical Promotion', *Zeitschrift für Antikes Christentum*, 25 (2021), 53–73 and András Handl, *Callixtus I, der Bischof von Rom und der Konflikt um seine Person in der Refutatio omnium haeresium*, Supplements to Vigiliae Christianae (Leiden: Brill, forthcoming).

[2] *Refutatio omnium haeresium*, IX. 11–12, ed. by Paul Wendland, GCS 26.3 (1916), pp. 247–48. This edition is still the best available. An English translation and commentary: Hippolytus, *Refutation of All Heresies*, ed. & trans. by M. David Litwa, Writings from the Greco-Roman World, 40 (Atlanta: SBL Press, 2016). For the reliability of the *Refutatio*, see Handl, *Callixtus, der Bischof.*

Interacting with Saints in the Late Antique and Medieval Worlds, ed. by Robert Wiśniewski, Raymond Van Dam, and Bryan Ward-Perkins, Hagiologia, 20 (Turnhout, 2023), pp. 141–160.
© BREPOLS ❧ PUBLISHERS   DOI 10.1484/M.HAG-EB.5.133625

and threw him into a well[3]. It seems the turbulences did not end with his burial. Rather, the emerging cult of the saint marked the start of further turbulences.

The Beginnings

The *Refutatio*, an anonymous heresiological tractate which is traditionally, but highly improbably, attributed to the 'anti-pope' and martyr Hippolytus Romanus (d. 235), constitutes the only extant contemporary account of Callixtus. This account, presumably composed after Callixtus's death[4], not only lists him alongside thirty-one other 'heretics', but also presents the 'Callixtian heresy' as the culmination point of all heresies. The *Refutatio*'s condemnation, however, does not represent the majority opinion; rather, it is the product of a strongly marginalized minority group. Yet, the *Refutatio*'s main argument against the bishop provides an important reference point for the question of whether Callixtus was considered as an authentic martyr and, if so, how he earned this title. The anonymous author undermines very efficiently the apparently widespread view that Callixtus's public confession before the urban prefect Fuscianus and his subsequent condemnation to the mines of Sardinia made him a martyr or, more precisely, a confessor[5]. The author's extensive efforts to prove the opposite, that is, that Callixtus was a con artist rather than a martyr, would have been a completely worthless line of argumentation if the bishop was eventually killed in a persecution, as later sources claim and the scholarly world often repeats[6]. If this conclusion is cor-

---

[3] 'Acta Martyrii Sancti Callisti' (*BHL* 1523) in AASS, Octob. VI, 12–14, Acta Sanctorum, 54, 2nd ed. (Brussels: Culture et civilisation, 1853), pp. 439–441. A useful introduction as well as an English translation is offered by Michael Lapidge, *The Roman Martyrs: Introduction, Translations, and Commentary*, Oxford Early Christian Studies (Oxford: Oxford University Press, 2018), pp. 287–96; for the sources on the cult of Callixtus up to *c.* 700 see <u>CSLA S00145</u>.

[4] Handl, 'Martyr or a Confessor?', p. 401, n. 37.

[5] *Refutatio omnium haeresium*, IX. 11. 4–12. 13, pp. 246–48.

[6] Giovanni Nino Verrando, in 'La Passio Calisti e il santuario della via Aurelia', *Mélanges de l'École Française de Rome. Antiquité*, 96 (1984), 1039–83 has made extensive efforts to underpin the *Acta*'s historical reliability. The results are repeated in Giovanni Nino Verrando, 'Cal(l)isti Coemeterium (via Aurelia)', ed. by Vincenzo Fiocchi Nicolai & Adriano La Regina, *Lexicon topographicum urbis Romae. Suburbium* (Rome: Edizioni Quasar, 2004), pp. 44–50 and accepted by Mara Minasi, *La tomba di Callisto: appunti sugli affreschi altomedievali della cripta del papa martire nella catacomba di Calepodio*, Scavi e restauri, 6 (Città del Vaticano: Pontificia Commissione di Archeologia Sacra, 2009), p. 63. While Lapidge, *The Roman Martyrs*, pp. 287–89 has rightly not given historical credit to the *Acta*'s account, he expressed 'some doubt whether Callistus was genuinely a martyr'. Although it remains somewhat unclear what 'genuinely' means here, it seems that Lapidge has not made a distinction between a martyr and confessor. In Handl, 'Martyr or a Confessor?', I argued extensively against both positions and pointed out that Callixtus did not die as a martyr, but that he was a confessor.

rect and the bishop did indeed die peacefully, the popular thesis concerning the bishop's burial place has to be reconsidered as well.

According to the *Acta*, Callixtus's burial had to be carried out hastily under the cover of night due to the brutality the persecutors unleashed on anybody attempting to bury executed Christians[7]. Previous research accepted this testimony as the most likely explanation for the entombment of Callixtus in a small *hypogeum* on the via Aurelia[8] close to the place of his supposed martyrdom at Trastevere[9]. Yet, the novel-like character of the *Acta*[10] lessens the traditional explanation's persuasive power. Moreover, the fact that the bishop was one of the first occupants in the newly established subterranean complex suggests that his tomb must have been prepared well in advance[11]. What is more, the bishop's decision for the *hypogeum* on the via Aurelia was also a decision against the community κοιμητήριον that he used to manage.

---

[7] *Acta Martyrii Sancti Callisti*, 9, p. 441.

[8] The catacomb was rediscovered and excavated in the 1960s. Cf. Aldo Nestori, 'La catacomba di Calepodio al III miglio dell'Aurelia vetus e i sepolcri dei papi Callisto I e Giulio I', *Rivista di Archeologia Cristiana*, 47 (1971), 169–278 and 48 (1972), 193–233; Aldo Nestori, 'Ultimi lavori a Calepodio', *Rivista di Archeologia Cristiana*, 61 (1985), 237–53; Giovanni Nino Verrando, 'L'attività edilizia di papa Giulio I e la basilica al III miglio della "via Aurelia ad Callistum"', *Mélanges de l'École Française de Rome. Antiquité*, 97 (1985), 1021–61 (p. 1049); Philippe Pergola, *Le catacombe romane: storia e topografia*, ed. by Palmira Maria Barbini, Argomenti, 8 (Rome: Carocci, 1998), pp. 237–39; Danilo Mazzoleni, 'Le iscrizioni della catacomba di Calepodio', *Rivista di Archeologia Cristiana*, 75 (1999), 597–694; Verrando, 'Cal(l)isti Coemeterium (via Aurelia)'; Antongiulio Granelli, 'Osservazioni sulla regione primitiva del cimitero di Calepodio', in *Origine delle catacombe romane*, ed. by Vincenzo Fiocchi Nicolai & Jean Guyon, Sussidi allo studio delle antichità cristiane, 18 (Città del Vaticano: Pontificio Istituto di Archeologia Cristiana, 2006), pp. 237–49; Minasi, *La tomba di Callisto*, pp. 11–22; Barbara Borg, *Crisis and Ambition: Tombs and Burial Customs in Third-Century CE Rome*, Oxford Studies in Ancient Culture and Representation (Oxford: Oxford University Press, 2013), pp. 77–78.

[9] Emanuela Prinzivalli, in 'Callisto I, santo', ed. by Sara Esposito and Giulia Barone, *Enciclopedia dei Papi* (Rome: Istituto della Enciclopedia Italiana, 2000), pp. 237–46 (p. 245), based on Marta Sordi, in *Il Cristianesimo e Roma*, Storia di Roma, 19 (Bologna: L. Cappelli, 1965), pp. 238–39, stated that it was far too risky to carry Callixtus's body across the city to bury him in the community cemetery at the via Appia. An additional but similarly speculative explanation is offered by Peter Lampe, in *Die stadtrömischen Christen in den ersten beiden Jahrhunderten: Untersuchungen zur Sozialgeschichte*, Wissenschaftliche Untersuchungen zum Neuen Testament, 2nd Series, 18, 2nd edn. (Tübingen: Mohr, 1989), p. 23.

[10] Handl, 'Martyr or a Confessor?', pp. 404–17; Cécile Lanéry, 'Hagiographie d'Italie (300–550). I. Les Passions latines composées en Italie', in *Hagiographies: histoire internationale de la littérature hagiographique latine et vernaculaire en Occident des origines à 1550. Vol. 5: Hagiographie d'Italie (300–550)*, Corpus Christianorum Hagiographies, 5 (Turnhout: Brepols, 2010), pp. 15–369 (pp. 156–59). Lapidge, pp. 1–3 claimed in general terms that the *passiones* are works of fiction'.

[11] The tomb is located at the very beginning of the gallery A1, on the right side, *c.* 2 metres from the end of staircase S1, at the oldest access to the subterranean complex. See fig. 1 and cf. Nestori, 'Catacomba di Calepodio', p. 273; Verrando, 'L'attività edilizia', p. 1050; Minasi, p. 87; Borg, *Crisis and Ambition*, p. 77.

In any case, Callixtus was apparently not interested in establishing any kind of burial tradition or in visualizing his succession.

The slander of the *Refutatio* remains the only extant written source about Callixtus for more than a century. Archaeological evidence, however, has shed some light on the beginning of cultic veneration at the via Aurelia *hypogeum*. Although the origins of Callixtus's liturgical veneration must remain in the dark, his tomb became over time the physical focal point of a small-scale collective commemoration. The installation of a *mensa oleorum* in front of the tomb appears to be its first still tangible customization to meet such cultic needs[12]. Whether the furnishing of the floor with a marble pavement was part of the same intervention or whether it belonged to the original ensemble, is hard to decide. Several radical refurbishments over the centuries resulted in an almost complete dis- and reassembling of the subterranean room. While scholars traditionally opt for the first alternative[13], there is no evidence that would rule out the latter option. To be sure, the *mensa* was installed after the pavement was laid, as fragments still *in situ* underneath the *mensa* demonstrate[14]. It is not easy to provide a reliable dating for the *mensa's* installation. Based on similar *mensae* in other early complexes, scholars tend to date it — often confidently — between the mid-third and early fourth century[15]. Unfortunately, the lack of an absolute or at least more reliable dating makes it impossible to refine the cultic activities' early chronology.

Despite this shortcoming, the archaeological evidence demonstrates that the tomb played a crucial role at the early stage of the cult's formation. As a warrant of Callixtus's memory, it served as a place of remembrance. In the beginning, the annual remembrance was probably maintained by the family, because in Roman society funeral-related practices were primarily a family concern. Over time, the tomb became the focal point of a slowly developing and likely rather small scale collective commemoration, probably limited to

---

[12] Nestori, 'Catacomba di Calepodio', pp. 195–96, 274; Verrando, 'L'attività edilizia', pp. 1050–54; Minasi, p. 87.

[13] While Verrando, 'L'attività edilizia', p. 1050 has considered, but eventually rejected the possibility of two separate phases, Minasi, p. 87 has taken it for granted that the pavement and the *mensa* were installed at the same time.

[14] Cf. Minasi, pp. 34, fig. 17.

[15] Whether the *mensa oleorum* (and the marble pavement) was indeed installed at the end of the third or beginning of the fourth century, is rather uncertain. While Minasi, p. 87 based on Verrando, 'L'attività edilizia', p. 1053 and Paul-Albert Février, 'Le culte des morts dans les communautés chrétiennes durant le IIIe siècle', in *Atti IX Congresso Internazionale di Archeologia Cristiana*, Studi di antichità cristiana, 32 (Città del Vaticano: Pontificio Istituto di Archeologia Cristiana, 1978), vol. 1, pp. 211–75 (p. 239), presented the early dating as a fact, Paul-Albert Février is far more cautious in his study: 'La *mensa* est-elle du IIIe siècle? Je n'oserais l'affirmer, bien que rien ne paraisse aller contre.'

144

a few Christian communities located in or close to Trastevere[16]. When this shift from family remembrance to collectively organized commemoration took place — and it is possible that there was continuity between both forms — is difficult to substantiate. It is certain, however, that the *hypogeum* was actively used during the third century by a smaller group or collective. It can neither be confirmed nor excluded that this group shared a common identity or faith and was organized at least to some extent, because the epigraphic evidence is far too scattered to be conclusive. Despite the uninterrupted use, the subterranean cemetery remained modest in size, particularly compared to other complexes frequently used by Christians[17]. At some point the annual commemoration took a more ritualized form, which demanded some customization of the tomb's ensemble in the form of a *mensa oleorum*.

This more ritualized form is reflected in the famous Roman martyrial calendar (*Depositio martyrum*), preserved in the Chronography of 354. A substantial part of this calendar goes back to an earlier compilation, which originates probably in 336[18]. The calendar lists Callixtus alongside a good number of overwhelmingly local martyrs. His record reads as follows: *pri. idus Octob. Callisti in via Aurelia. miliario III*[19]. This entry, like all the others, is as condensed as it can be, containing nothing more than the basic coordinates: name, date, and place of the annual liturgical commemoration. Notable is the entry's topographic reference. Instead of specifying an exact toponym, that is, the cemetery's name, it refers only to the (quite imprecise) distance of the *memoria* from the city walls. The lack of a precise topographic identification in the earliest witness and the partly contradictory testimonies found in later sources has provoked some scholarly discussion in the past[20], which

---

[16] Cf. below, p. 149.

[17] For the inscriptions see Mazzoleni, 'Le iscrizioni della catacomba di Calepodio', p. 597. Granelli, 'Osservazioni sulla regione primitiva', pp. 242 and 244, fig. 4, offers a size comparison to other early Christian cemeteries.

[18] Cf. Michele Renee Salzman, *On Roman Time: The Codex-Calendar of 354 and the Rhythms of Urban Life in Late Antiquity*, The Transformation of the Classical Heritage, 17 (Berkeley: University of California Press, 1990), pp. 43–44, 280; Steffen Diefenbach, *Römische Erinnerungsräume: Heiligenmemoria und kollektive Identitäten im Rom des 3. bis 5. Jahrhunderts n. Chr.*, Millennium-Studien zu Kultur und Geschichte des ersten Jahrtausends n. Chr., 11 (Berlin: De Gruyter, 2007), p. 172, n. 345; Johannes Divjak & Wolfgang Wischmeyer, *Das Kalenderhandbuch von 354, Bd. II: Der Textteil - Listen der Verwaltung* (Vienna: Holzhausen, 2014), p. 499. Instructive for this edition is the review of Richard W. Burgess, 'The New Edition of the Chronograph of 354: A Detailed Critique', *Zeitschrift für Antikes Christentum*, 21 (2017), 383–415.

[19] *Depositio martyrum*, ed. by Theodor Mommsen, MGH AA 9 (1884), pp. 71–72 (p. 72): 'On the 14th of October, Callixtus at the 3rd mile of the Aurelian way'.

[20] Johann Peter Kirsch, in *Le memorie dei martiri sulle vie Aurelia e Cornelia*, Studi e Testi, 38 (Rome: Tipografia del Senato, 1924), p. 84 and Paul Styger, in *Die römischen Katakomben:*

has so far failed to reach satisfactory conclusions[21]. In any case, Callixtus's inclusion in the *Depositio martyrum* marked the first and most crucial step in establishing a permanent cult centre. Because Callixtus was 'officially canonized' as a martyr, his veneration was no longer limited to a small number of communities around Trastevere, but was promoted in the Roman church.

Bishop Julius and the (re)invention of Callixtus

Another prominent Christian text of the Chronography of 354, the *Catalogus Liberianus* (Liberian catalogue), is a succession list of the bishops of Rome from Peter to Liberius (352–66). It was completed roughly a year after the death of Bishop Julius I of Rome (337–52). In contrast to the vast majority of the entries, which merely note basic coordinates[22], the entry for Julius is fairly detailed and also attests to his building activities[23].

> [Iulius] hic multas fabricas fecit: basilicam in via Portese miliario III: basilicam in via Flaminia mil. II quae appellatur Valentini; basilicam

---

archäologische Forschungen über den Ursprung und die Bedeutung der altchristlichen Grabstätten (Berlin: Verlag für Kunstwissenschaft, 1933), p. 292 have accepted that the initial name of the complex was Calepodius. Giulio Belvederi and Enrico Josi, in 'Note di topografia cimiteriale romana. Il sepolcro del papa Giulio I e il cimitero di Callisto sulla via Aurelia', in *Miscellanea Giulio Belvederi*, Amici delle catacombe, 23 (Rome: Pontificio Istituto di Archeologia Cristiana, 1954), pp. 321–33 and Verrando, in 'Cal(l)isti Coemeterium (via Aurelia)' opted for the name Callixtus. Agostino Amore, in *I martiri di Roma*, Spicilegium. Pontificio Ateneo Antonianum, 18 (Rome: Antonianum, 1975), pp. 276–82 argued, in my opinion convincingly, that the cemetery had no name in the beginning. Lapidge, p. 289, followed Amore's verdict.
[21] The lack of a stable toponym until the fifth century and the limited dimensions of the initial burial ground, as well as the cemetery's rather sporadic use during the third century suggest that the complex was initially not intended as a (Christian) community burial ground. See Granelli, 'Osservazioni sulla regione primitiva', p. 242; Borg, *Crisis and Ambition*, pp. 77–78. Borg suggested also that Callixtus's former master, the imperial freedman Carpophorus, could be considered as a potential benefactor of the burial ground. The suggestion is rather unlikely because Carpophorus had hardly any interest in providing further for his former slave. Moreover, her claim that 'he [Carpophorus] is known to have supported the Christian community with various large donations', finds no confirmation in the *Refutatio* (or elsewhere). Borg, p. 78, n. 51 and cf. *Refutatio omnium haeresium*, IX. 12. 1–13, pp. 246–48.
[22] Exceptions are the Apostle Peter, Pontianus († 235), Fabius († 250), Cornelius († 252), Lucius († 254) and Julius († 352). Cf. *Catalogus Liberianus*, ed. by Theodor Mommsen, MGH AA 9 (1884), pp. 73–76.
[23] John R. Curran, in *Pagan City and Christian Capital: Rome in the Fourth Century*, Oxford Classical Monographs (Oxford: Oxford University Press, 2000), pp. 119–27 pointed out that all the building activities took place in untouched parts of the *(sub)urbium*, usually at the periphery of imperial interests. The claim of Verrando, in 'L'attività edilizia', p. 1023, that the entries of the Liberian Catalogue are arranged in chronological order is possible, but difficult to substantiate.

Iuliam, quae est regione VII iuxta forum divi Traiani; basilicam trans Tiberim regione XIIII iuxta Callistum; basilicam in via Aurelia mil. III ad Callistum.

[Julius] constructed many buildings: a basilica on the via Portuensis at the third milestone; a basilica on the via Flaminia at the second milestone which is called 'of Valentinus'; the *basilica Iulia*, which is in the seventh region near to the forum of the deified Trajan; a *basilica* across the Tiber in the fourteenth region in close proximity to Callixtus; a basilica on the via Aurelia at the third milestone at Callixtus[24].

Julius's construction activities are remarkable *sui iuris*, as they took place both within and outside the walls of Rome and, for the first time, without any imperial support[25]. Two basilicas he endowed in the suburbs 'at Callixtus' and 'of Valentinus' are clearly connected to martyrs' tombs in the suburbs, whereas the one located at the via Portuensis is problematic to interpret. While the Liberian catalogue explicitly links Callixtus and Valentinus to concrete places, it does not mention a name in connection to the basilica on the via Portuensis. The lack of archaeological evidence not only complicates any attempts at identification, but also makes it challenging to determine the basilica's function[26]. In contrast, recent excavations and a systematic reassessment of earlier studies confirmed the Liberian catalogue's claim that Julius endowed a basilica at Valentinus's *memoria*[27]. The third basilica, located at

---

[24] *Catalogus Liberianus*, p. 74 and see the commentary at Divjak and Wischmeyer, pp. 567–69. Unless otherwise indicated the translations are by the Author.

[25] Curran, *Pagan City*, pp. 117–27.

[26] The suggestion by Diefenbach, *Römische Erinnerungsräume*, pp. 455–57 that the primary purpose of the basilica was to provide burial places in the suburbs is possible, but in the light of the meagre evidence is challenging to substantiate. His argumentation is, however, convincing that the basilica of Julius was initially not dedicated to the memory of a martyr Felix; this is rather a later development. His further observation that the *memoria* of Felix as we know it from the sources is based on a longer hagiographic evolution appears to be plausible. For the building activities of Julius at the via Portuense, see Giovanni Nino Verrando, 'Il santuario di S. Felice sulla via Portuense', *Mélanges de l'École Française de Rome*, 100 (1988), 331–66. For the evidence on the cult of Felix see 'Felix, martyr of Rome buried on the via Portuensis', CSLA S02672.

[27] For the recent excavations and for the revision of the chronology see Cinzia Palombi, 'Nuovi studi sulla Basilica di San Valentino sulla Via Flaminia', *Rivista di Archeologia Cristiana*, 85 (2009), 469–540; Cinzia Palombi, 'La basilica di S. Valentino sulla via Flaminia. Nuove ricerche sull'assetto della zona presbiteriale', in *Scavi e scoperte recenti nelle chiese di Roma*, ed. by Federico Guidobaldi & Hugo Brandenburg, Sussidi allo studio delle antichità cristiane, 24 (Città del Vaticano: Pontificio Istituto di Archeologia Cristiana, 2012), pp. 153–88. This does not change, however, the fact that very little is known about the martyr Valentinus. On his cult see 'Valentinus, priest and martyr of Rome', CSLA S00433.

the via Aurelia *ad Callistum*, has so far not been archaeologically identified beyond any doubt. Itineraries from the early Middle Ages suggest that it was a *sub divo* rather than a subterranean structure. Moreover, it was presumably a brick-made building similar to the basilicas at the *memoria* of Valentinus, in Trastevere, or at the forum of Trajan[28]. Therefore, the suggestion that the *basilica Iulia* of the Liberian catalogue is identical to the subterranean shrine at Callixtus's tomb called the *basilichetta* is hardly convincing, and it has rightly been rejected by scholars[29]. An entry of the *Depositio episcoporum*, the third Christian text of the Chronograph of 354, points in the same direction. It implies that the basilica must have been erected in close proximity to Callixtus's tomb, because Julius chose it as his final resting place: *prid. idus Apr. Iuli, in via Aurelia miliario III, in Callisti*[30]. Julius apparently opted for placing his sepulchre basilica next to Callixtus's shrine instead of sharing his episcopal predecessors' custom and choosing one of the well-established episcopal burial places in the catacombs[31].

Whatever might have been the purpose of the endowed basilicas in the suburbs, it is obvious that Julius made a distinction between Callixtus's and Valentinus's *memoriae* on the one hand and all the other (ignored) martyrs' tombs on the other. By marking them with fairly modest-sized church buildings[32], he literally made visible the otherwise hidden subterranean *memoriae*, and thus he increased Christianity's presence in the suburbs. Yet the episcopal attention significantly differs between the two promoted martyrs Callixtus and Valentinus. According to the Liberian catalogue, Julius erected not only

---

[28] Likewise, the seventh-century pilgrim itineraries suggest that the basilicas were *sub divo* buildings. Cf. Herman Geertman, 'Forze centrifughe e centripete nella Roma cristiana: il Laterano, la Basilica Iulia e la Basilica Liberiana', *Rendiconti. Pontificia Accademia Romana di Archeologia*, 59 (1986), 63–91 (pp. 68–69). For the identification see also below, n. 32.

[29] Verrando, 'L'attività edilizia', pp. 1045–48; 1054–55; and repeated in Verrando, 'Cal(l)isti Coemeterium (via Aurelia)'.

[30] *Depositio episcoporum*, ed. by Theodor Mommsen, MGH AA 9 (1884), p. 70.

[31] Yet, he was not the first who broke the rule. His immediate predecessor Marcus chose to rest in the Catacombs of Balbina next to his newly founded *basilica*. *Depositio episcoporum*, p. 70; and see Lucrezia Spera, *Il paesaggio suburbano di Roma dall'antichità al medioevo: il comprensorio tra le vie Latina e Ardeatina dalle Mura Aureliane al III miglio*, Bibliotheca archaeologica, 27 (Rome: L'Erma di Bretschneider, 1999), pp. 80–82 for the identification of Marcus's tomb.

[32] Although the basilicas at the via Aurelia and via Portuensis cannot be identified, the 'basilica' at the *memoria* of Valentinus might give an impression of the dimensions of the Julian building activities. The single nave complex with a semicircular apse (phase C) was built between two already existing *mausolea*. The walls of both mausolea have been heavily reused and thus constituted substantial parts of the church's north and south side walls. According to Palombi, 'Nuovi studi', pp. 499–501, the structure had 'dimensioni estremamente modeste', hardly exceeding 4.40 × 13.50 m.

a basilica in the suburbs *ad Callistum*, but also another church within the walls in Trastevere *iuxta Callistum*[33]. This complex *intra muros* was known in 499 as *titulus Iuli*[34], a century later in 595 as *titulus ss. Iulii et Calisti*[35], and today as Santa Maria in Trastevere. Excavations have successfully identified the remains of several earlier church structures, including Julius's basilica[36]. Some evidence, like a small bronze tag for a dog or a slave, confirms that Callixtus's name was associated with the neighbourhood around the basilica Santa Maria in Trastevere already in the mid-fourth century. The entry of the Liberian catalogue merely reflects this firmly established tradition when using *iuxta Callistum* as a matter of course[37]. No evidence suggests, however, that this had already been the case for a longer period prior to the mid-fourth century. Considerable efforts to locate the *domus Callisti*, that is, Callixtus's former house or a *domus ecclesiae*, have failed so far[38].

Julius's (sub)urban building activities are particularly significant for Christianity in Rome, because they mark a ground-breaking development. Julius experimented with and, as Callixtus's case demonstrates, succeeded in forming and instrumentalizing martyrs' cults for collective identity marking and space contestation. The (re)invention and 'official' propagating of (some) martyrs' cults without imperial support must be therefore considered as a genuine innovation by bishop Julius. Subsequently, Damasus I of Rome (366–84) perfected the experimental attempts of his predecessors

---

[33] For the problem of *iuxta* as a topographical reference, see Dale Kinney, 'S. Maria in Trastevere from its founding to 1215' (unpublished PhD Dissertation, New York University, 1975), pp. 18–24; for the church's identification see Kinney, pp. 24–26 and Stefano Coccia, Federico Guidobaldi & Francesco Scoppola, 'Titulus Iulii (Santa Maria in Trastevere): nuove osservazioni sulle fasi più antiche', in *Scavi e scoperte recenti nelle chiese di Roma*, ed. by Federico Guidobaldi & Hugo Brandenburg, Sussidi allo studio delle antichità cristiane, 24 (Città del Vaticano: Pontificio Istituto di Archeologia Cristiana, 2012), pp. 33–62.

[34] *Acta synhodorum habitarum Romae*, ed. by Theodor Mommsen, MGH AA 12 (1894), pp. 393–455 (pp. 411–13), No. 7; 28; 51.

[35] Gregory the Great, *Registrum epistolarum*, ed. by Ludo M. Hartmann, MGH Ep. 1 (1891), I, p. 367: *Petrus presbyter tituli sancti Iulii et Calisti*.

[36] Cf. above n. 33.

[37] CIL XV, 7193: *tene me ne / fugia(m) et revo/ca me ad dom(i)nu(m) m/eu(m) Viventium / in ar<e>a Callisti* (British Museum, 1975, 0902. 6), dated to the mid-fourth century.

[38] Lampe, *Die stadtrömischen Christen*, pp. 13 and 29 argued for a *titulus Callisti*. Kinney, 'S. Maria in Trastevere', pp. 5–18, rejected both the existence of a *domus ecclesiae* founded by the bishop-martyr and a *memoria Callisti*. Prinzivalli, 'Callisto I, santo', p. 244, labelled the *Liber pontificalis* note as an 'obvious anachronism', Manlio Simonetti, 'Giulio I, santo', ed. by Sara Esposito & Giulia Barone, *Enciclopedia dei Papi* (Rome: Istituto della Enciclopedia Italiana, 2000), pp. 334–40 (p. 340) advocated the pre-existence of an 'urban memory of Callixtus', yet he also admitted that nothing certain can be said about it.

Julius, Liberius (352–66), and Felix II (355–65)[39] and turned it into a success story[40].

Julius's efforts to put the tomb and therewith Callixtus's cult as a landmark on the slowly forming Christian map of the suburbs, as well as his promotion of Callixtus's memory *intra muros*, is hard to overlook but rather challenging to explain. The bishop may have had close ties to Trastevere[41] and was possibly in one way or another involved in the organisation of liturgical activities at the shrine on the via Aurelia. That would at least explain his obvious interest in Callixtus and his otherwise rather isolated cult centre.

Remarkably but not surprisingly, Julius's first attempts to promote some martyrs' *memoriae* coincides with the updating of the Roman martyrial calendar. While numerous Roman martyrs were ignored at this update of the *Depositio martyrum* (Damasus will 'rediscover' a good number of them), Julius's patron-martyr Callixtus was included. It cannot be substantiated beyond doubt that Julius's involvement was decisive for Callixtus's inclusion, but the circumstances are suspicious to say the least[42]. The bishop's particular affinity for Callixtus is even more striking when contrasted with the attention devoted to Valentinus. Although Julius promoted the latter's *memoria*

---

[39] According to the *Liber pontificalis* (37. 7 and 38. 2), Liberius decorated Agnes's tomb with marble, and Felix II endowed a basilica with some land on the via Aurelia, two miles from the walls. *Le liber pontificalis. Texte, introduction et commentaire*, ed. by Louis Duchesne, Bibliothèque des Écoles françaises d'Athènes et de Rome, II. 3 (Paris: de Boccard, 1886), vol. 1, pp. 207–11.

[40] Cf. Dennis E. Trout, 'Damasus and the Invention of Early Christian Rome', *Journal of Medieval and Early Modern Studies*, 33 (2003), 517–36; Ursula Reutter, *Damasus, Bischof von Rom (366–84): Leben und Werk*, Studien und Texte zu Antike und Christentum, 55 (Tübingen: Mohr Siebeck, 2009), pp. 111–53; Marianne Sághy, 'Pope Damasus and the Beginnings of Roman Hagiography', in *Promoting the Saints: Cults and Their Contexts from Late Antiquity until the Early Modern Period. Essays in honour of Gábor Klaniczay*, ed. by Ottó Gecser, József Laszlovszky et al., Medievalia, 12 (Budapest: CEU Press, 2011), pp. 1–15; Marianne Sághy, '*Renovatio Memoriae*: Pope Damasus and the Martyrs of Rome', in *Rom in der Spätantike: historische Erinnerung im städtischen Raum*, ed. by Ralf Behrwald & Christian Witschel, Heidelberger althistorische Beiträge und epigraphische Studien, 51 (Stuttgart: Steiner, 2012), pp. 251–66; Markus Löx, *Monumenta sanctorum: Rom und Mailand als Zentren des frühen Christentums: Märtyrerkult und Kirchenbau unter den Bischöfen Damasus und Ambrosius*, Spätantike, frühes Christentum, Byzanz. Reihe B, Studien und Perspektiven, 39 (Wiesbaden: Reichert, 2013), pp. 43–87, 171–80.

[41] The *Liber pontificalis*, 36, vol. 1, p. 205 claims that Julius was born in Rome, which is possible but difficult to verify.

[42] Jörg Rüpke, in 'Geteilte und umstrittene Geschichte: Der Chronograph von 354 und die Katakombe an der Via Latina', in *Antike Mythologie in christlichen Kontexten der Spätantike*, ed. by Hartmut Leppin, Millennium-Studien, 54 (Berlin: De Gruyter, 2015), pp. 221–38 (p. 232) suggests that the Carthaginian martyrs were recorded on the Roman martyrs' calendar because active 'lobbyists' promoted their veneration in Rome. This could also apply to other cults and martyrs.

with a newly endowed basilica, Valentinus's name was nevertheless ignored when the Roman martyrial calendar was updated. Interestingly, Damasus's actions were diagonally opposite to those of Julius. While he honoured Valentinus with a self-composed *carmen* displayed in a large-scale inscription and engraved in beautiful Philocalian calligraphy, he completely ignored Callixtus and his cult centre[43]. But why?

Archaeological evidence provides a possible explanation. It clearly shows that a reconstruction radically changed the subterranean space around Callixtus's tomb at some point during the fourth century. As mentioned before, the tomb is located at the *hypogeum*'s entrance, at the bottom of the staircase (S1), right at the beginning of the main gallery (A1; cf. Figure 1, phase I). Opposite the tomb, two perpendicular galleries used to branch off to the south (α and C1). These two galleries were destroyed to create a voluminous space of *c.* 30 sqm, the so called *basilichetta*. This subterranean room was about three times larger than a typical burial chamber (*cubiculum*) and thus it must have impressed visitors. An additional wall of brick and tufa provided structural support[44]. Remarkably, this wall was erected with particular sensitivity to the already existing but fragile liturgical inventory. The *mensa oleorum* was not only spared, but a small apse above the *mensa* ensured its full functionality[45]. Finally, the walls were covered by a characteristic greyish plaster, painted in red and decorated with lineal patterns in white[46]. Unfortunately, the extant evidence provides no concrete indications to the date of the reconstruction or to the question whether Julius or one of his successors developed the tomb to a subterranean shrine. Yet, some observations support the rather intuitive suggestion of previous scholarship to link the monumentalization to Julius[47]. The bishop's affinity towards Callixtus, which was manifested in his building activities, points clearly in this direction. Moreover, it would make perfect sense if, in addition to the basilica at the surface, he would have monumentalized his patron-martyr's tomb as well. Once the tomb was extended to a subterranean shrine and marked by a basilica on the surface, there was probably no space left and, more importantly, no need (and hardly any benefit) for an additional Damasian 'reinvention' and appropriation. Damasus's ignorance,

---

[43] From the large scale inscription only three fragment-groups were discovered: ICUR X, 27271, 27272, 27273 = *Epigrammata Damasiana* 49. For text and commentary see *Damasus of Rome: The Epigraphic Poetry: Introduction, Texts, Translations, and Commentary*, ed. by Dennis E. Trout, Oxford Early Christian Texts (Oxford: Oxford University Press, 2015), pp. 175–77.

[44] Nestori, 'Catacomba di Calepodio', p. 275.

[45] Nestori, 'Catacomba di Calepodio', pp. 275–76; Verrando, 'Passio Calisti', pp. 1053–54.

[46] Nestori, 'Catacomba di Calepodio', pp. 199–200; Minasi, *La tomba di Callisto*, pp. 87–90.

[47] Nestori, 'Catacomba di Calepodio', p. 276; Minasi, *La tomba di Callisto*, p. 90.

therefore, provides an additional argument for the hypothesis that Julius monumentalized Callixtus's tomb, and in turn, Julius's monumentalization explains Damasus's ignorance about Callixtus.

Whatever role Julius played in these developments, his interventions demonstrate the rising interest in the martyr's cult in Rome and mark the first autonomous attempts of Roman bishops to take control over *memoriae*, promote cultic activities, and instrumentalize them for their own agenda.

The Cult Centre at the Via Aurelia and the Invention of the Acta martyrii sancti Callisti

Extant archaeological evidence at Callixtus's cult centre shows that Julius's efforts to establish and promote the shrine were not in vain. Thanks to donations, the subterranean *basilichetta* was further monumentalized between the end of the fourth and the first half of the fifth centuries. In most cases it is impossible to date the modifications, but the suggested relative chronology appears to be *grosso modo* reliable. The tomb's surrounding was decorated with *opus sectile*, and an otherwise unknown Alfius donated a white marble pergola, which was supported by a pair of marble columns[48]. Remarkably, the monumentalization did not inhibit the shrine's use for funerals: hardly a square inch remained untouched, as fourteen shaft tombs (*forma a tomba*) in the floor impressively demonstrate. Once all available space was exhausted, the excavation of a new gallery level begun. This new section was situated below the first level, and was accessible by a staircase (S3), which directly linked the second level to the martyr's tomb (cf. Fig. 1, phase II). The construction of an additional level corresponds to the increasingly popular fashion of that time, the burial *retro sanctos*[49]. The dating of this development is challenging, but it is reasonable to assume that it took place after the creation of the *basilichetta* at some point during the second half of the fourth century[50].

Apparently, not only the shrine's appearance changed in this period. The *Liber pontificalis*, composed around 530, documents for the first time

---

[48] The inscription is dated between the end of the fourth and mid-fifth century and reads as follows: *SANC(to) CALLISTO ALFIVS VOT(um) SOL(vit)*. Nestori, 'Catacomba di Calepodio', pp. 212–14, 276; Verrando, 'L'attività edilizia', pp. 1055–56; Mazzoleni, 'Le iscrizioni della catacomba di Calepodio', p. 643; Minasi, *La tomba di Callisto*, p. 90.

[49] Aldo Nestori, 'La tomba di S. Callisto sull'Aurelia antica', in *Atti VIII Congresso Internazionale di Archeologia Cristiana* (Città del Vaticano: Pontificio Istituto di Archeologia Cristiana, 1972), vol. 1, pp. 367–72 (p. 371); Verrando, 'L'attività edilizia', pp. 1054–55; Granelli, 'Osservazioni sulla regione primitiva', p. 240.

[50] Nestori, 'Catacomba di Calepodio', p. 276; Verrando, 'L'attività edilizia', pp. 1054–55; Minasi, *La tomba di Callisto*, p. 90.

a new toponym for the burial ground at the via Aurelia. In the concluding part of Callixtus's short biographical note, the complex is called the 'cemetery of Calepodius': *Qui etiam sepultus est in cymiterio Calepodi, uia Aurelia, miliario III, prid. id. Octob*[51]. This name appears also in the entry of Julius, which implies that the toponym must already have been well established in the times when the *Liber pontificalis* was compiled[52]. Scholars have, however, traditionally argued that the *Liber pontificalis* merely reflects a *fait accompli*, because the *Acta*'s author must have invented the name and the story's rising popularity helped to spread the new toponym[53]. According to this hypothesis, the composition of the *Acta* is dated to the end of the fifth century, before the compilation of the *Liber pontificalis*. Yet, the arguments of an early dating of the *Acta* are circumstantial and therefore far from certain[54].

Regardless of whether the *Acta* was composed as late as the seventh or as early as the end of the fifth century, virtually no written record existed about Callixtus. The *Refutatio*'s toxic contemporary account had long been forgotten[55], and there is no evidence that would point to an independent and trustworthy alternative source. One knew for sure that Callixtus was a bishop and suffered martyrdom. But it seems that no one knew why or how. With the increasing popularity of the subterranean shrine among pilgrims, the 'pressure from the street' gradually increased[56]. Visitors from near and far were eager to learn about the life and death of their pious hero. But there was nothing to tell.

---

[51] 'He also was buried in the cemetery of Calepodius on the via Aurelia at the third milestone, 14th of October.' *Liber pontificalis,* 17, vol. 1, p. 141; András Handl, 'Globale Strategie oder Belange lokaler Verwaltung? Anmerkungen zu den bischöflichen Dekreten im vorkonstantinischen Abschnitt des Liber Pontificalis', in *Das Buch der Päpste: Der Liber Pontificalis — Ein Schlüsseldokument europäischer Geschichte,* ed. by Klaus Herbers & Matthias Simperl, Römische Quartalschrift Supplementbände, 67 (Freiburg: Herder, 2020), pp. 78–94 discussed the historical reliability of the pre-Constantininan *vitae.*

[52] *Liber pontificalis*, 36, vol. 1, p. 205: *Qui etiam sepultus est uia Aurelia, in cymiterio Calepodi, miliario III, prid. id. April.* 'He also was buried on the via Aurelia in the cemetery of Calepodius, third milestone, 12th of April.'

[53] Cf. Nestori, 'La tomba di S. Callisto', p. 371; Nestori, 'Catacomba di Calepodio', p. 276; Verrando, 'L'attività edilizia', p. 1056.

[54] See CSLA E02485 (M. Pignot).

[55] The *Acta* does not draw upon any information originating from the *Refutatio*, although the latter provides a good number of important and for a hagiographical text compelling or even 'juicy' material. The *Refutatio*'s marginal late antique (and modern) reception suggests a strongly limited circulation. Handl, 'Martyr or a Confessor?', p. 392, n. 5.

[56] Lapidge, *The Roman Martyrs*, p. 3 observed that 'there is a clear link between the composition of *passiones* and the explosion of pilgrim interest in visiting martyrial sites from the late fourth century onwards.'

An anonymous, probably *ad hoc* hagiographer interpreted the 'signs of the times' correctly when he composed the *Acta*, a typical example of Roman 'epic' *passiones*[57]. Because the hagiographer had almost nothing to go on, he was forced to exploit the little he had, consisting of the shrine, the traditions connected to the toponyms[58], and the meagre record of the Roman martyrial calendar. The result was an entirely fictive but vivid novel-like narration about Callixtus and his quite numerous companions. The hagiographer offered far more than just a story full of bloodlust, violence, and cruelty on the one hand and miracles, swarms of converts, and suffering for faith on the other hand. He diligently filled all the biographical gaps, exhaustively exploited the little tradition at his disposal, and masterfully explained some quite disturbing oddities. The *Acta* tackles a good number of issues, such as the mismatch of the toponym Calepodius and the most famous martyr venerated there (Callixtus), Calepodius's identity, and the missing link between him and the bishop-martyr. The hagiographer invented surprisingly original answers to these issues. He made Calepodius, for instance, Callixtus's presbyter. According to the *Acta*, the old presbyter was devoted to serve his bishop and eager to convert people. One day the persecutors captured and beheaded him, dragged his body through the city, and eventually threw it into the Tiber. Callixtus, who asked fishermen to recover his presbyter's *corpus sanctum*, buried him *in cymiterio suo*, that is, in the catacomb of Calepodius[59].

On the one hand, a person named Calepodius almost certainly existed, as fragments of an inscription confirm. Oddly enough, however, the part of the *basilichetta* where the inscription had been found was in later times almost entirely isolated from the tomb and the shrine[60]. On the other hand, virtually nothing else can be confirmed, not even the fundamental claims about his office or martyrdom. Once the link between Calepodius and the bishop was established and the catacomb's toponym explained, the hagiographer exploited

---

[57] For definition see Hippolyte Delehaye, *Les passions des martyrs et les genres littéraires*, SH 13B (Brussels: Société des Bollandistes, 1921), pp. 171–226. The *Acta* can be considered an epic cycle, as a number of martyrdoms (Calepodius, Asterius, Palmatius, Blanda and Felix, etc.) are grouped around one individual's martyrdom. Remarkably, the hagiographer refrained here from inventing a trial, which marks in other *passiones* the zenith of the storyline.

[58] The hagiographer systematically exploited all the places connected to Callixtus's life with one exception: the catacombs of Callixtus at the via Appia. This ignorance is all the more remarkable as the via Appia complex is the best-known and by far most famous toponym connected to the bishop.

[59] *Acta Martyrii Sancti Callixti*, 6, p. 441.

[60] The fragment records the letters *[‑‑‑]lepodi[‑‑‑]*. Cf. Nestori, 'Catacomba di Calepodio', p. 226–28; Verrando, 'Passio Calisti', pp. 1060–61; Handl, 'Martyr or a Confessor?', p. 408, n. 69. For Calepodius's identity see Handl, 'Martyr or a Confessor?', p. 408 n. 69 and CSLA S01411.

Callixtus's strong local tradition in Trastevere. He located there a certain Pontianus's house, where Callixtus had spent his last days, and also the well into which the bishop had been thrown with a stone tied to his neck[61].

Many elements of the narration (Calepodius's styling as Callixtus's presbyter, their shared destiny, and the geographical proximity between the place of martyrdom in Trastevere and the burial in the via Aurelia cemetery) are concerned with the question of why Callixtus was buried in the catacomb of Calepodius rather than in 'his' cemetery at the via Appia. The answer of the *Acta* was so convincing that modern scholarship adopted it as the most likely explanation[62]. The invention of an almost entirely fictive protagonist gave the hagiographer virtually unlimited freedom to construct a story line that was not limited by any established tradition. This freedom apparently unleashed the hagiographer's creative potential, because the *senex presbyter* dominates large parts of the narration. It is difficult to decide who is the actual epic hero of the story: Callixtus or Calepodius[63]. After Callixtus's martyrdom, the hagiographer introduced a further protagonist, Asterius. He was made, like Calepodius, Callixtus's presbyter. Asterius and his companions have only one task: to take care of Callixtus's mortal remains[64]. Burying the dead, however, turned out to be an offence against the emperor and was immediately 'rewarded' by Asterius's being thrown into the Tiber[65]. On this occasion, Asterius's involvement did not serve as an explanation for oddities or toponyms, but aimed to wrap up the story's loose end. By letting the faithful presbyter's body float to Ostia, the hagiographer left the problem of Asterius's burial to others. Such an ending was not only creative but also demonstrates the hagiographer's familiarity with the hagiographical traditions of Rome and beyond. As it seems, Asterius was indeed an authentic martyr of Ostia[66].

Despite all the obvious hyperbole, the extremely violent imagination of the pre-Constantinian period, and the historical anachronisms, the new story about Callixtus's last days and death struck the right cord. The martyrdom narrative spread slowly but irresistibly across Europe, as the existence

---

[61] *Acta Martyrii Sancti Callixti*, 6, p. 441. For the toponym, see the discussion at Handl, 'Martyr or a Confessor?', p. 405, n. 59.

[62] Cf. above, p. 143.

[63] Handl, 'Martyr or a Confessor?', pp. 408–09.

[64] One of the great concerns of the *passiones* is to provide a detailed description of the recovery of the martyr's body as well as the place, the time, and the manner of burial. Cf. Lapidge, *The Roman Martyrs*, p. 29.

[65] *Acta Martyrii Sancti Callisti*, 9, p. 441.

[66] For the various identities attached to Asterius see Handl, 'Martyr or a Confessor?', p. 406, n. 63; Lapidge, *The Roman Martyrs*, pp. 424–25 and 'Asterius, martyr of Ostia', CSLA S01550.

of almost 140 manuscript copies impressively illustrates[67]. The strategy of inventing and popularising a martyrdom narrative paid off also for the cult centre. By the seventh century at the latest, the shrine was a firmly established attraction on the pilgrims' itinerary to Rome[68]. The increasing number of visitors pushed the accessibility of the shrine to its limits, because the single narrow staircase was not designed to grant access to larger groups. The 'pressure from the street' triggered the shrine's last, but all the more radical refurbishment.

The installation of a second staircase (S4) eliminated the bottleneck at the tomb's entrance and created additional direct access from the surface to the shrine (cf. Figure 1, phases III–IV). One staircase served now as a separate *gradus descensionis*, and the other as a *gradus ascensionis*. This advanced technology for guiding pilgrims largely facilitated visits to the sanctuary and made the narrow space suitable for mass pilgrimage. This innovation, however, came with a high price. The *basilichetta* had to be destroyed, because the new staircase occupied a larger part of the available space, and additional supporting structures were also needed to ensure the staircase's stability[69]. The radical spatial reconstruction destroyed existing decoration as well, but it also created an opportunity for something new. The so far dominant bichrome ornamental patterns were replaced by a pictorial cycle. Although it is challenging to reconstruct the entire circle due to considerable fragmentation and bad preservation, yet it is obvious that it was inspired by *Acta's* narrative. It depicts some emblematic scenes, such as 'Callixtus is thrown into a well with a stone tied to his neck' or 'Callixtus's funeral in the presence of his clergy'[70]. Even though there is some discussion about the precise dating, both

---

[67] Cf. *Bibliotheca Hagiographica Latina Manuscripta* database and Lanéry, 'Hagiographie d'Italie', p. 157, n. 336.

[68] The *Notitia Ecclesiarum Urbis Romae*, also known as the *Itinerarium Salisburgense*, was probably composed between 625 and 645, roughly during the pontificate of Honorius (625–38). Callixtus's basilica is mentioned in the concluding sentence. *Notitia ecclesiarum urbis Romae*, ed. by Roberto Valentini & Giuseppe Zucchetti, in *Codice topografico della città di Roma: scrittori, secoli IV–XII*, Fonti per la storia d'Italia, 88, 4 vols. (Rome: Tipografia del Senato, 1942), vol. 2, pp. 67–99 (p. 94). The *De Locis Sanctis Martyrum Quae Sunt Foris Civitatis Romae* is slightly later and dated usually between 635 and 645. It lists the suburban cemeteries and, from a seventh-century perspective, the most important martyrs venerated there, among them Callixtus and Calepodius. *De locis sanctis martyrum quae sunt foris civitatis Romae et Ecclesiae quae intus Romae habentur*, ed. by Valentini & Zucchetti, in *Codice topografico della città di Roma*, vol. 2, pp. 106–31 (p. 107). Also the *Itinerarium Malmesburiense*, compiled between 648 and 682, mentions the basilica of *sanctus Callixtus et Calepodius* at the fourth mile from the gates. *Itinerarium Malmesburiense*, ed. by Valentini & Zucchetti, in *Codice topografico della città di Roma*, vol. 2, pp. 133–53 (p. 152).

[69] Nestori, 'Catacomba di Calepodio', p. 277; Verrando, 'L'attività edilizia', p. 1057.

[70] Minasi, *La tomba di Callisto*, pp. 63–73.

traditional and more recent attempts situate the refurbishment and redecoration in the first half of the eighth century[71].

The invention of the *Acta* illustrates in an exemplary way the rich and versatile interplay between the shrine, the cult, the existing local traditions, pilgrimage, and literary and artistic production. The few extant records about Callixtus were combined with the contemporary *status quo* at Callixtus's shrine and other local traditions in Trastevere. These elements were masterfully interwoven with fictional, novel-like elements to create an epic narrative of his martyrdom. The narrative's growing popularity as well as the increasing number of visitors shifted the *status quo* at the tomb again. The latter triggered the shrine's radical refurbishment and turned a subterranean sanctuary into a pilgrim-friendly attraction. The narrative largely influenced the shrine's pictorial redecoration, serving as an authentic backdrop for cultic activities and an improved subterranean 'Callixtus experience'.

Conclusions

From a broader perspective, a single constant pattern dominates the development of Callixtus's cult: the interaction between the tomb and its visitors of all sorts. In this setting the tomb serves as a focal point and central hub, because by preserving the martyr's remains, it transcends the strict boundaries between heaven and earth. This particular agency of divine powers attracted the first non-family visitors and facilitated the interaction between involved parties. The interaction is not limited to expressions of popular devotion, even if the vast majority of visitors hardly moved beyond this horizon. Diverse construction works, donations for decorating the shrine and its surroundings, and literary production shed some light on the versatility of piety concentrated around the tomb. Lived religion often, but not always, followed current fashions, reflected the *Zeitgeist*, and shifted when those instances shifted.

In the beginning, Callixtus's tomb on the via Aurelia was not different from any other tomb. It accommodated human remains and served as a place of memorial mainly for family members[72]. Yet, this common function turned out to be crucial, simply because it preserved the confessor-bishop's body in times when Rome's Christian population did not show any interest in the commemoration of their very own 'heroes in faith'. The first traces of community driven cultic activity are tangible at some point in the late third

---

[71] Verrando, 'L'attività edilizia', pp. 1059–60; Minasi, *La tomba di Callisto*, pp. 75–86.
[72] Cf. above, n. 21.

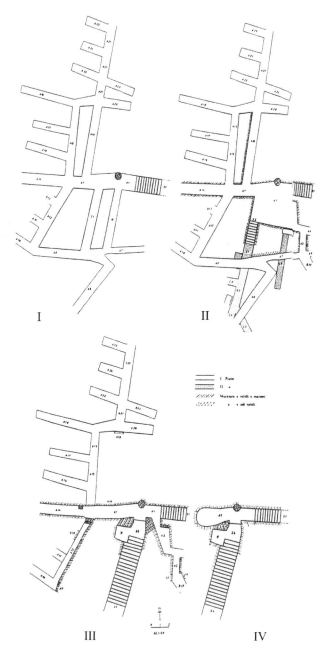

Fig. 1: Phases of the development of Callixtus's shrine in the Calepodio catacomb. Nestori, 'Catacomba di Calepodio', Tavola V. Courtesy of the Pontificio Istituto di Archeologia Cristiana.

or early fourth century. The construction of a *mensa oleorum* reflects actual liturgical needs on the spot. But the veneration was likely restricted to a few Christian communities active in Rome and remained likely in isolation until the mid-fourth century. The *status quo*, that is, the ongoing veneration at the tomb was recognized by the Roman church, when Callixtus was recorded on the Roman martyrs' calendar. He was the first Roman martyr to be included after the Apostles Peter and Paul. Whether bishop Julius was involved in this process remains uncertain but not unlikely. The episcopal activities marked a milestone in the development of the martyrs' cult in Rome in general and that of Callixtus in particular. For the first time without imperial support, he promoted two martyrs' cults by endowing modest-size basilicas at the martyrs' *memoriae* in the suburbs. One of them, Callixtus, received more attention than the other, Valentinus. Julius endowed another basilica to honour 'his' patron-martyr in Trastevere as well. Moreover, it is not unlikely that the bishop initiated the transformation of Callixtus's cult centre, which turned the narrow space of a catacomb corridor around the tomb into a spacious shrine. Finally, Julius let himself be buried in close vicinity to Callixtus's tomb, which stresses the close link between him and his 'patron-martyr'.

In the course of the fourth and fifth centuries, several donations were made for furnishing the shrine with additional decorative elements. Such donations contributed to the further monumentalization of the shrine, attracted and impressed visitors, and offered an opportunity for benefactors to put their wealth and piety on public display. An anonymous hagiographer remedied the lack of an engaging story by composing an 'epic' *passio* at some point between the late fifth and the seventh century. The *Acta*'s fictional but original story was a clever combination of the existing traditions with an exciting and touching storyline, which tried to explain the oddities surrounding Callixtus's tomb. The already rich interaction between the tomb and its visitors, now boosted by a powerful narrative, continued to flourish. The growing number of visitors eventually triggered yet another radical refurbishment of the shrine. A newly installed second staircase facilitated visits to the martyr's tomb, and the *Acta*'s martyrdom story provided the narrative context for its pictorial redecoration in the first half of the eighth century.

Despite political instability and destruction by barbarian invaders, the veneration was never permanently interrupted. Not even an empty tomb could put a definite end to the cultic activities, when translations set the agenda and relics from the eternal city, including those of Callixtus, conquered Western Europe[73]. As late as the twelfth century, the author of the *Mirabilia urbis Romae* still considered the shrine worth mentioning[74].

---

[73] Cf. Sönke Lorenz, 'Papst Calixt I. (217–22). Translationen und Verbreitung seines Reliquienkultes bis ins 12. Jahrhundert', in *Ex ipsis rerum documentis: Festschrift für Harald Zimmermann zum 65. Geburtstag*, ed. by Klaus Herbers (Sigmaringen: Thorbecke, 1991), pp. 213–32; Charles Mériaux, 'La *Translatio Calixti Cisonium* (*BHL* 1525): une commande de Gisèle, fille de Louis le Pieux, au monastère de Saint-Amand?', in *Parva pro magnis munera. Études de littérature tardo-antique et médiévale offertes à François Dolbeau par ses élèves*, ed. by Monique Goullet, Instrumenta patristica et mediaevalia, 51 (Turnhout: Brepols, 2009), pp. 585–611; András Handl, 'A Roman Saint on the Move: Relic Migration and the Dissemination of Bishop Callixtus I's Cult in Rome and in the Carolingian Francia', *Annali di storia dell'esegesi*, 38 (2021), 327–48.

[74] *Mirabilia urbis Romae*, ed. by Gerlinde Huber-Rebenich (Freiburg: Herder, 2014), p. 76.

The Cult of Saints in Constantinople (Sixth-Twelfth Century)

Some Observations

Stephanos Efthymiadis
(Open University of Cyprus)

In the six centuries or so that separate the reign of Justinian from the disastrous conclusion of the Fourth Crusade (1204), Constantinople intersected with the sphere of the holy and more specifically the 'cult of saints' in two ways. On the one hand, as a city the Byzantine capital displayed the largest and most illustrious collection of relics in Eastern Christendom and competed in that respect only with the holy treasures of Rome. Just four years before it saw the crusaders looting its holy treasures, the Russian pilgrim Dobrinia Iadreikovich, the future Anthony archbishop of Novgorod, recorded his visit to some seventy-six churches within the city and to another twenty-one in its suburbs, almost every one of which hosted at least one pious relic[1]. On the other hand, as a location the city became home to the great majority of Byzantine saints. Even when it was not their native city, Constantinople provided the space where Byzantine holy men and women embarked on

---

[1] See ed. Chrisanf M. Loparev, *Kniga palomnik, skazanie mest sviatych vo Caregrade Antonia arhiepiskopa Novgorodskago vo 1200 god*, (St Petersburg: Izdanie Imperatorskago pravoslavnago palestinskago obschchestva, 1899), pp. 1–39; and, more recently, ed. with German trans. by Anna Jouravel, *Die Kniga palomnik des Antonij von Novgorod*, Imagines Medii Aevi 47 (Wiesbaden 2019), pp. 229–347. On the evidence of this text and of other Russian pilgrims' accounts see George Majeska, 'Russian Pilgrims in Constantinople', *Dumbarton Oaks Papers*, 56 (2002), 93–108.

Interacting with Saints in the Late Antique and Medieval Worlds, ed. by Robert Wiśniewski, Raymond Van Dam, and Bryan Ward-Perkins, Hagiologia, 20 (Turnhout, 2023), pp. 161–180.
© BREPOLS ❧ PUBLISHERS   DOI 10.1484/M.HAG-EB.5.133626

pious activities and demonstrated their sacred paradigm. It was where their cults, chiefly centred round the veneration of their relics in particular holy sites, found a posthumous home. Remarkably, this dual primacy can in no way be disputed, even if the Byzantine capital is defined in terms of its narrowest possible geographical extent, delimited by the walls and bereft of its European and Asian hinterland.

As expressions of religious devotion, both the acquisition of relics and the admission of holy men/women into the city are hardly surprising for the period of Late Antiquity and must be seen as part of a continuum that existed in conjunction with the development of Constantinople as a Christian *megalopolis*[2]. From the mid-fourth century onwards, there was a growing inclination to increase the relic collection of the new Roman capital and a notable trend for either hosting holy men coming from the East or venerating the city's prelates and monastic founders as saints[3]. Whether peacefully or not, old and new saints coexisted in the city and its suburbs, occasioning different manifestations of religious belief and practice. In this study I shall briefly discuss some questions arising from the cult of saints in Constantinople, maintaining, as far as possible, the distinction between what was old and established (on the one hand) and the new and promising (on the other). After outlining the place that the veneration of saints held in the religious life of the urban population, it is important to see how their cult was promoted by emperors and other patrons as well as to inquire, with Late Antiquity as a crucial chronological axis, into the effects that this promotion had on such phenomena as building activity[4] and the increase in popularity of particular saints.

---

[2] See Gilbert Dagron, *La naissance d'une capitale. Constantinople et ses institutions de 330 à 451* (Paris: Presses Universitaires de France, 1974), and Cyril Mango, *Le développement urbain de Constantinople (IVᵉ-VIIᵉ siècle)* (Paris: Travaux et Mémoires du Centre de Recherche d'Histoire et Civilisation de Byzance, Collège de France, Monographies: 2004), pp. 23–36.

[3] On the presence of monks in the capital, see the seminal study of Gilbert Dagron, 'Les moines et la ville. Le monachisme à Constantinople jusqu'au concile de Chalcédoine (451)', *Travaux et Mémoires*, 4 (1970), pp. 229–76; and, more recently, Peter Hatlie, *The Monks and Monasteries of Constantinople, c. 350–850* (Cambridge: Cambridge University Press, 2007), pp. 25–171.

[4] On this question, see Ann Marie Yasin, 'Sacred Installations. The Material Conditions of Relic Collections in Late Antique Churches', in *Saints and Sacred Matter. The Cult of Relics in Byzantium and Beyond*, ed. by Cynthia Hahn & Holger Klein (Washington, DC: Dumbarton Oaks Research Library and Collection, 2015), pp. 133–52; also Vasileios Marinis & Robert Ousterhout, '"Grant us to Share a Place and Lot with Them": Relics and the Byzantine Church Building (9ᵗʰ-15ᵗʰ Centuries)', in *Saints and Sacred Matter*, pp. 153–72; and Vasileios Marinis, 'Sacred Dimensions: Church Building and Ecclesiastical Practice', in *The Cambridge Companion to Constantinople*, ed. by Sarah Bassett (Cambridge: Cambridge University Press, 2022), pp. 180–99.

Acquiring Relics and Hosting Cults

To begin with, importing relics to the Byzantine capital was typical of the fourth and fifth centuries, and the lack of mentions of many of them in the extant sources should not be taken as evidence of their absence[5]. Later attestations of functioning shrines make up for this earlier silence and, what is more, reveal the extent of the cultic phenomenon in a new Roman capital initially lacking in specific Christian associations. The poor record of the town of Byzantium in terms of local martyrs is reflected in the existence there of only three martyria, i.e. the churches dedicated to Mokios, Akakios, and Agathonikos, saints who were far from enjoying widespread acclaim in the Christian world. Things took another turn first in 337 with the burial of the first Christian emperor in the mausoleum he had prepared for himself, then in the 350s when a series of relics of such holy figures as St Timothy (St Paul's disciple), St Luke, and St Andrew were imported into the city[6]. All of these were to be deposited at the altar of what was then the most important Christian temple of the city, the church of the Holy Apostles.

---

[5] For recent discussions on the cult of relics and its emergence in the fourth century see Estelle Cronnier, *Les inventions de reliques dans l'Empire romain de l'Orient (IVe-VIe s.)* (Turnhout: Brepols, 2015); and Robert Wiśniewski, *The Beginnings of the Cult of Relics* (Oxford: Oxford University Press, 2019), pp. 48–69 (where their role as defenders of cities is discussed). Also, more diachronically, Holger A. Klein, 'Sacred Relics and Imperial Ceremonies at the Great Palace of Constantinople,' in *Visualisierungen von Herrschaft. Frühmittelalterliche Residenzen - Gestalt und Zeremoniell. Internationales Kolloquium 3./4. Juni 2004 in Istanbul*, ed. by Franz A. Bauer, BYZAS 5 (Istanbul: Ege Yayınları, 2006), pp. 79–99.

[6] See Cyril Mango, 'Constantine's Mausoleum and the Translation of Relics', *Byzantinische Zeitschrift*, 83 (1990), 51–62 and 'Constantine's Mausoleum: Addendum', in the same volume, p. 434 (repr. in Mango, *Studies on Constantinople* (Aldershot: Ashgate, 1993), no. V. Also, Paul Magdalino, 'The Apostolic Tradition in Constantinople', *Scandinavian Journal of Byzantine and Modern Greek Studies*, 2 (2016), 115–24. The date of the translation of the relics of Sts Andrew and Luke to Constantinople is still debated: see Richard W. Burgess, 'The *Passio S. Artemii*, Philostorgius, and the Dates of Invention and Translation of the Relics of Sts Andrew and Luke', *Analecta Bollandiana*, 121 (2003), 5–36. For the later tradition that made Constantine a 'relic-provider' for Constantinople see John Wortley, 'The Legend of Constantine, the Relic-Provider', in *Daimonopylai: Essays in Classics and the Classical Tradition Presented to Edmund G. Berry*, ed. by Rory B. Egan and Mark Joyal (Winnipeg, MB: University of Manitoba Centre for Hellenic Civilization, 2004), pp. 487–96; and John Wortley, 'The Earliest Relic-Importations to Constantinople', *Pecia*, 8–11 (2005), 207–25 (repr. in idem, *Studies on the Cult of Relics in Byzantium up to 1204* (Farnham: Ashgate, 2009), nos III and IV). Recently, the question of early Constantinopolitan cults has been addressed by Alessandro Taddei, *Hagia Sophia before Hagia Sophia. A Study of the Great Church of Constantinople from its Origins to the Nika Revolt of 532* (Rome: Campisano Editore, 2017), pp. 30–50. Especially on St Mokios see Albrecht Berger, 'Mokios und Konstantin der Große: Zu den Anfängen des Märtyrerkults in Konstantinopel,' in *Antecessor Festschrift für Spyros N. Troianos zum 80. Geburtstag*, ed. by Vassiliki A. Leontaritou, Kalliopi A. Bourdara & Eleutheria S. Papagianni (Athens: Ant. N. Sakkoulas, 2013), pp. 165–85.

It was well into the fifth century before the desire to bring out the high status and the outstanding role of the new city in the Christian geography of the empire became fully evident in a well-known passage by the church historian Sozomen: writing in the 440s, he eulogizes Constantinople as a city particularly conducive to the Christian faith[7]. And, after him, the author of the *Vita of St Daniel the Stylite*, a text dating to a few decades later, characterizes New Rome as 'a second Jerusalem replete with martyria and great churches'[8]. Moreover, the two hundred years between 425 and 626 saw intimate and lasting ties developing between the city and the cult of the Virgin Mary. The cult in question was formed and validated through the construction of Marian churches and shrines, attestations of the Mother of God as a wonderworker, her appearances on imperial coins and lead seals[9], and, last but not least, her miraculous intervention in the Avar-Persian siege of Constantinople in 626[10]. After this formative stage, in the period up to the ninth and tenth centuries, several other decisive steps cemented this close relationship and account for Constantinople being designated *Theotokoupolis* (the Virgin's city)[11]. Thus it is no surprise to find 123 establishments dedicated to the Virgin Mary in Raymond Janin's useful catalogue of churches and monasteries of Constantinople[12]. Among them we must include some of the most famous shrines in the city (e.g. the Chalkoprateia, the Blachernai, the Hagia

---

[7] See Sozomen, *Historia ecclesiastica*, II. 3. 7, ed. by Joseph Bidez, repr. SC 306 (1983), p. 240: εἰς τοσοῦτον γὰρ τῆς εἰς Χριστὸν πίστεως ἐπαγωγός ἐστιν, ὡς πολλοὺς μὲν Ἰουδαίους, Ἕλληνας δὲ σχεδὸν ἅπαντας αὐτόθι χριστιανίζειν.

[8] See ch. 10, ed. by Hippolyte Delehaye, *Les saints stylites* (Brussels: Société des Bollandistes, 1923), p. 12. For a discussion of this passage and of the question of 'New Jerusalem' see Petre Guran, 'The Byzantine "New Jerusalem"', in *New Jerusalems: The Translation of Sacred Spaces*, ed. by Alexei Lidov (Moscow: Indrik, 2006), pp. 17–23.

[9] See Vasso Penna, 'The Mother of God on Coins and Lead Seals', in *Mother of God: Representations of the Virgin in Byzantine Art*, ed. by Maria Vassilaki (Athens-Milan: Skira, 2000), pp. 209–17; and John Cotsonis, 'The Virgin and Justinian on Seals of the *Ekklesiekdikoi* of Hagia Sophia', *Dumbarton Oaks Papers*, 56 (2002), 41–55.

[10] For an account of the events see James D. Howard-Johnston, 'The Siege of Constantinople in 626', in *Constantinople and its Hinterland. Papers from the Twenty-seventh Spring Symposium of Byzantine Studies, Oxford, 1993*, ed. by Cyril Mango and Gilbert Dagron (London: Routledge, 1995), pp. 131–42.

[11] See also Cyril Mango, 'Constantinople as Theotokoupolis', in *Mother of God*, pp. 17–25. For the various aspects this devotion was manifested at earlier and later times see studies collected in *Images of the Mother of God. Perceptions of the Theotokos in Byzantium*, ed. by Maria Vassilaki (Abingdon: Routledge, 2016²). Also, Bissera V. Pencheva, 'The Supernatural Protector of Constantinople: the Virgin and her Icons in the tradition of the Avar Siege', *Byzantine and Modern Greek Studies*, 26 (2002), 2–41.

[12] Raymond Janin, *La géographie ecclésiastique de l'empire byzantin*, I: *Le siège de Constantinople et le patriarchat oecuménique*, 3: *Les églises et les monastères* (Paris: Publications de l'Institut français d'études byzantines, 1969), pp. 164–253.

Soros chapel, the Pege, the Hodegetria), which were integrated into the cycle of imperial and ecclesiastical ceremonies while remaining attractions meriting a pilgrim's visit for as long as the empire existed. What is more, the veneration of the Theotokos in some of these shrines came to be associated with precise representations on icons, symbolizing her role as spiritual protector of the reigning city[13].

Since the Theotokos held such a central place in the religious life of Constantinople, we may legitimately wonder how much room was left for the development of the cult of saints in that city. Was there any chance that the cult of a saint could compete with that of the Virgin Mary and contest her exclusive rights? Or, to look at it another way, were these rights really as exclusive as was the case with saints in many other cities and towns of the late antique and medieval empire?

As a matter of fact, most Constantinopolitan cults arrived on the scene in Late Antiquity in a rather obscure fashion. The sources shed little light on their provenance and the circumstances surrounding the translation of their relics, thereby discouraging any serious attempts to reconstruct the history of these cults' reception, integration, and diffusion in the capital. The texts that provide us with a panoramic and by and large comprehensive view of the Byzantine city's sacred topography, namely the *Synaxarion of Constantinople* and the accounts of foreign travellers and pilgrims, are of a much later date, when things were settled and the sacred geography of the city was clearly delineated. As we can legitimately assume, it was by then felt that the age of saints had come full circle[14]. Moreover, as texts, *synaxaria* were also meant to serve as topographical guides, i.e. to record 'what was where', while saying nothing about the history of the holy sites they refer to[15]. As for the *Patria*, the idiosyncratic and simplistic compilation that provides a survey of Constantinopolitan buildings and monuments, both sacred and secular, and which supposedly offers a historical account of their construction, there is no discernible sign of its ever having been seriously intended to elucidate the

---

[13] See Christine Angelidi & Titos Papamastorakis, 'Picturing the Spiritual Protector: from Blachernitissa to Hodegetria', in *Mother of God: Representations of the Virgin in Byzantine Art*, pp. 209–23.

[14] See Claudia Rapp, 'Byzantine Hagiographers as Antiquarians, Seventh to Tenth Centuries', in *Bosphorus. Essays presented in honour of Cyril Mango*, ed. by Stephanos Efthymiadis, Claudia Rapp & Dimitris Tsougarakis, *Byzantinische Forschungen*, 21 (1995), p. 31.

[15] *Synaxarium Ecclesiae Constantinopolitanae, Acta Sanctorum, Propylaeum ad Acta Sanctorum Novembris*, ed. by Hippolyte Delehaye (Brussels: Société des Bollandistes, 1902). See also Andrea Luzzi, 'Synaxaria and the Synaxarion of Constantinople', in *The Ashgate Research Companion to Byzantine Hagiography*, vol. 2: Genres and Contexts, ed. by Stephanos Efthymiadis (Farnham: Ashgate, 2014), pp. 197–208.

history of the establishment of any cults. In this jumbled material the focus is on merely recording the name of the monument, indicating its location, and offering some explanation, whether plausible or not, for that name[16]. All in all, we may conclude that these works represent the medieval mind which, to the disappointment of our modern inquisitive disposition, took things for granted and did not delve into their origins. Nonetheless, these texts allow us to observe, if not the vigour, then at least the survival of particular cult centres over time.

The Piety of Emperors

At any rate, the translation of holy relics to Constantinople and their veneration in particular churches contributed first of all to enhancing and then to maintaining the attraction and importance of the capital. Far from relying solely on the initiatives of Christian emperors and patriarchs, this extensive project owed a great deal to the private sphere. When, by the mid-sixth century, the Queen of the Cities found itself teeming with magnificent churches and shrines housing precious relics from all corners of the empire, this was not simply due to imperial patronage and piety. Splendid edifices that owed their rebuilding and renovation to the artistic patronage of Justinian, such as for instance the churches of Hagia Sophia and the Holy Apostles, were not the only ones dominating the urban landscape. Alongside them other impressive architectural constructions, such as those of St Polyeuktos and Sts Sergios and Bakchos, were also there to captivate the beholder. As was the case with many other patrons of places of worship in the city, Anicia Juliana's choice of the saint to whom she dedicated her church was not an obvious one. On the basis of literary evidence it can be deduced that her new building, which is later known to have housed the skull of Saint Polyeuktos, replaced an older one, a church built on the same site by the Empress Eudocia, known for her devotion to this saint. Anicia had imperial family connections with the famous and learned wife of Theodosius II, a fact that must have determined her choice of this particular saint[17]. As has been shown, on the other hand, the church of Sts Sergios and Bakchos was a martyrium initially built

---

[16] On the version drawn up in the last decade of the tenth century see now Albrecht Berger, *Accounts of Medieval Constantinople. The Patria*, (Washington, DC: Dumbarton Oaks Medieval Library, 2013), pp. 2–227.

[17] See Cyril Mango & Ihor Ševčenko, 'Remains of the Church of St Polyeuktos at Constantinople', *Dumbarton Oaks* Papers, 15 (1961), 243–47. Also R. Martin Harrison, 'The Church of St Polyeuktos in Istanbul and the Temple of Solomon', *Harvard Ukrainian Studies*, 7 (1983) (= *Okeanos: Essays presented to Ihor Ševčenko on his Sixtieth Birthday by his Colleagues and Students*), 276–79; and Harrison, 'Discovery and Background', in L. B. Hill,

for a large Miaphysite monastery and sponsored by a well-known Miaphysite sympathizer, the Empress Theodora[18]. In sum, noble patrons, or upper-class *impresarios*, as Peter Brown likes to call them in a recent reappraisal of his favourite subject[19], often had a particular axe to grind, over and above promoting their patron saint and the potential of his/her cult.

Churches in Byzantium and in Constantinople admitted different identities, depending on their type: public, parish, private, or monastic. The most famous public churches in Constantinople were not only the ones that were impressive by virtue of their size and material treasures, but also those that housed outstanding relics that could be venerated by the faithful, both the people of the city and the pilgrims coming from other parts of the empire or elsewhere. However, with the exception of the Holy Apostles and, to a lesser degree, the basilica of Stoudios dedicated to St John the Baptist, no major Constantinopolitan church, renowned in the *longue durée*, was dedicated to a Christian saint. Or, to put it another way, the most famous churches of the Byzantine capital were not those dedicated to Christian saints. Moreover, we can be pretty sure that, for different reasons, even those highly distinguished churches that I have just mentioned never functioned as shrines, i.e. holy sites intended to attract pilgrims seeking some sort of cure. The fact that no miraculous story pertaining to these illustrious edifices has come down to us endorses the theory that they were not designed to support a saint's cult.

Naturally enough, this observation does not suggest that the cults of traditional saints in Constantinople failed to achieve any prominence in Late Antiquity or later, as they did in many other cities and places in the empire. Rather, it points to the fact that these cults were never institutionalized, that

---

R. Martin Harrison, *Excavations at Sarachane in Istanbul*, vol. 1 (Princeton: Princeton University Press, 2014), pp. 3–10.

[18] Cyril Mango, 'The Church of Saints Sergius and Bacchus at Constantinople and the Alleged Tradition of Octagonal Palatine Churches', *Jahrbuch der Österreichischen Byzantinistik*, 21 (1972), 189–93; and Mango, 'The Church of Saints Sergius and Bacchus Once Again', *Jahrbuch der Österreichischen Byzantinistik*, 23 (1974), 251–54 (repr. in Mango, *Studies on Constantinople* (Aldershot: Ashgate, 1993), nos XIII and XIV). In the light of new evidence the church was studied by Jonathan Bardill, 'The Church of Sts Sergius and Bacchus in Constantinople and the Monophysite Refugees', *Dumbarton Oaks Papers*, 54 (2000), 1–11; and Bardill, 'The Date, Dedication, and Design of Sts Sergius and Bacchus in Constantinople', *Journal of Late Antiquity*, 10 (2017), 62–130. On the same church see Thomas F. Mathews, *The Early Churches of Constantinople: Architecture and Liturgy* (University Park, PA: Penn State University Press, 1971), pp. 42–51; and Irfan Shahīd, 'The Church of Saints Sergios and Bakhos in Constantinople: some new perspectives', in *Byzantium, State and Society. In Memory of Nikos Oikonomides*, ed. by Anna Avramea, Angeliki Laiou & Evangelos Chrysos (Athens: Institute of Byzantine Research, 2003), pp. 467–80.

[19] 'Concluding Remarks', in *Des dieux civiques aux saints patrons (IVᵉ-VIIᵉ siècle)*, ed. by Jean-Pierre Caillet, Sylvain Destephen, Bruno Dumézil & Hervé Inglebert (Paris: Picard, 2015), p. 375.

is 'promoted by the Palace or the Patriarchate'. Again, a cursory glance at Janin's most useful catalogue of churches and monasteries in Constantinople confirms the large number of them that were dedicated to saints as well as their variety and dispersal over space and time. No doubt, those saints who could boast of many establishments were the most popular and prominent in the Christian pantheon, i.e. the apostles and the martyrs. To cite just three examples of prominent saints, Janin has eight entries for St George, ten for St Demetrios and eighteen for St Theodore[20], while there are thirty-five entries for St John the Baptist under the name of Πρόδρομος. Strangely enough, no such plurality was reserved for St Andrew, whose remains lay under the altar of the Holy Apostles. As is well known, at some point that scholars have placed between the sixth and the late eighth century, a tradition had developed which claimed that the first man called to be an apostle had been ordained the first bishop of the city[21]. Yet the apostle who, according to Francis Dvornik, had become the counterpart of St Peter, the first bishop of Rome, saw only a very modest number of religious establishments built in his honour[22]. If anything, this poor record suggests that we should not attach too much significance to the emergence of this legend or at least to its dynamic and potential.

The case of St Demetrios, on the other hand, is interesting in many respects. The Emperors Maurice and Justinian were said to have tried to bring his relics or parts thereof to the imperial city but to no avail[23]. The Thessalonicans must have claimed exclusive rights to their holy martyr and patron,

---

[20] Janin, *La géographie ecclésiastique de l'empire byzantin*, pp. 74–83 (St George), 93–99 (St Demetrios), 155–63 (St Theodore). On these military saints, see Monica White, *Military Saints in Byzantium and Rus, 900–1200* (Cambridge: Cambridge University Press, 2013), pp. 13–31.

[21] See Francis Dvornik, *The Idea of Apostolicity in Byzantium and the Legend of the Apostle Andrew* (Cambridge, MA: Harvard University Press, 1958), pp. 138–80. New reconsiderations of St Andrew's hagiographical dossier place the emergence of St Andrew's 'Byzantine' legend as early as the sixth/seventh century: see Andrey Vinogradov, 'André: du prédicateur encratite à l'apôtre byzantin', *Apocrypha*, 22 (2011), 105–14 (pp. 110–12); or as late as the end of the eighth century: Wolfram Brandes, 'Apostel Andreas vs. Apostel Petrus? Rechtsraum und Apostolizät', *Rechtsgeschichte — Legal History*, 23 (2015), 120–50. See also the remarks of Magdalino, 'The Apostolic Tradition in Constantinople', pp. 128–31.

[22] Janin, *La géographie ecclésiastique*, pp. 31–36.

[23] See *Miraculum* 5 of the collection of the Miracles of St Demetrios by Archbishop John, ed. by Paul Lemerle, *Les plus anciens recueils des Miracles de Saint Démétrius et la pénétration des Slaves dans les Balkans*, vol. 1 (Paris: Éditions du CNRS, 1979), pp. 88–90. Note that in 519 and 594 respectively, the same emperors, Justinian (before he ascended the throne) and Maurice (via his wife Konstantina), are recorded to have made similar unsuccessful requests for the partial translation of relics from Rome; see CSLA E000615, E00616, E00617 (David Lambert) and CSLA E06351 (Frances Trzeciak).

and the same thing must have happened, under very different circumstances, in the reign of Leo VI the Wise (886–912). Three of his forty-two surviving Homilies (nos 17–19, *BHG* 536–38) were dedicated to St Demetrios[24]. Notably, the third of these homilies was pronounced on the occasion of the inauguration of the church of St Demetrios built in the Great Palace. Its title reads: 'Homily of Leo Emperor in Christ the eternal king <pronounced> when the church in the Palace was dedicated to the celebrated fighter of the right faith and the one who patrols in the heavens'[25]. No doubt the learned emperor took a personal interest in this martyr's cult, and the way he worked out the story of this military saint is perhaps revealing of his inner intentions. Strangely enough, neither in the first and longest of these homilies, where he rehearses Demetrios's virtues as a child and man before treating the story of his martyrdom in great detail, nor in the other two short sermons, does he give any hint about the city where the saint was believed to have suffered martyrdom and that, more specifically, monopolized his cult, i.e. Thessalonica[26]. This reticence no doubt betrays Leo's hidden agenda on behalf of the partial transfer of the cult of this saint, to whom he showed a personal devotion and whom, as a result, he wanted to portray not as a local but as a universal martyr to Constantinople. Apparently, the devotion he showed to the patron saint of Thessalonica was not sufficient to justify any relocation of the saint's remains, which were kept intact to be venerated in Thessalonica[27]. Local patriotism must have been aroused, and as a result no serious attempt to establish a parallel cult centre elsewhere would have been successful. In fact, Leo's devotion was of a personal and private nature and had little to do with his public identity.

As a further proof of his efforts to establish the official veneration of significant prelates, the same Leo issued his Novel 88, in which he specifically decreed that, in addition to the holy days when the Almighty and the

---

[24] *Leonis VI Sapientis Imperatoris Byzantini Homiliae*, ed. by Theodora Antonopoulou, CCSG 63, pp. 243–65. On these Homilies see Antonopoulou, *The Homilies of the Emperor Leo VI* (Leiden: Brill, 1997), pp. 132–36.

[25] *Leonis VI Homiliae*, 263: Λέοντος ἐν Χριστῷ βασιλεῖ αἰωνίῳ βασιλέως ὁμιλία, ὅτε τῷ ἀοιδίμῳ τῆς εὐσεβείας ἀγωνιστῇ καὶ τὰ οὐράνια περιπολοῦντι ἀνάκτορα Δημητρίῳ ὁ οἶκος ἐν βασιλείοις ἀνιερώθη.

[26] Notably, Symeon Metaphrastes, who, in composing his *Passio of St Demetrios* (*BHG* 498), drew on Leo VI's Homilies (cf. Antonopoulou, *The Homilies of the Emperor Leo VI*, pp. 135–36), did not omit to mention in his preamble that the holy martyr came from 'great Thessalonica'; see PG 116, col. 1185: '...ὃν μὲν ἤνεγκε ἡ μεγάλη Θεσσαλονίκη ...'.

[27] On developments in the cult of St Demetrios and the motives that may have led Leo VI to show such an interest in the matter see Ruth J. Macrides, 'Subversion and Loyalty in the Cult of St Demetrius', *Byzantinoslavica*, 51 (1990), 189–97 (pp. 191–92); and Paul Magdalino, 'Saint Demetrios and Leo VI', *Byzantinoslavica*, 51 (1990), 198–201.

martyrs were celebrated, such saints as Athanasios, Basil, Gregory the Theologian, Gregory of Nyssa, John Chrysostom, Cyril, and Epiphanios (of Salamis) should be duly commemorated in feasts celebrated on the holy day of their demise. To the feasts sanctioned for the Holy Apostles the Emperor Leo added another seven, arguably in order to enlarge the official *sanctorale* of the Byzantine capital[28]. Notably, this Novel fails to include any of the sanctified patriarchs or bishops of later times, i.e. after the 'Golden Age' of the Greek Church Fathers (fourth-fifth centuries)[29].

Some years later, on the nineteenth of January 946, under very different circumstances, Leo's son, Constantine VII Porphyrogennitos, delivered a long panegyric (*BHG* 728) on the return of the relics of Gregory of Nazianzos from Cappadocia to Constantinople. This fine piece of eloquence has been preserved anonymously, yet it can safely be ascribed to the emperor-patron of letters or someone from his literary circle[30]. Prior to this, St Gregory's relics had been deposited in the Church of the Holy Apostles, to which the same author devoted a eulogy in the form of a rhetorical description (chs. 6–8). Another source, the *Chronicle* of Symeon Magistros, places this translation in the late part of Constantine's reign, after the death of Patriarch Theophylaktos (933–56) and the enthronement of Patriarch Polyeuktos (956–70). More precisely, this source states that St Gregory's relics were split up, one part being housed in the church of the Holy Apostles, the other being transferred to Saint Anastasia, the church closely associated with St Gregory's short tenure as bishop of Constantinople (379–81)[31].

Nearly all emperors who reigned after the end of iconoclasm strove to associate their name with inventions of relics and/or their translation to the capital, which, of course, they celebrated in triumphal fashion. The sequence begins with Michael III and the translation of St John the Baptist's head, continues with Leo VI and the translation of St Lazaros's and St Mary

---

[28] Sp. N. Troianos, *Οι Νεαρές Λέοντος Στ΄ του Σοφού* (Athens: Herodotos, 2007), pp. 252–54 (edition based on the earlier one by Pierre Noailles and Alphonse Dain). For an analysis of this Novel, see pp. 461–62. On the question of the celebration of saints by Byzantine emperors and members of the imperial family see Symeon A. Paschalides, 'Οἱ ἑορτὲς τῶν ἁγίων', in Paschalides, *Ἐν Ἁγίοις. Εἰδικὰ θέματα βυζαντινῆς καὶ μεταβυζαντινῆς ἁγιολογίας*, vol. 1 (Thessaloniki: P. Pournara, 2011), pp. 285–310, esp. pp. 297–98 (on Leo's initiatives).

[29] On the same question, see below pp. 178-79.

[30] See Bernard Flusin, 'L'empereur et le Théologien: à propos du retour des reliques de Grégoire de Nazianze (*BHG* 728)', in *Aetos: Studies in Honour of Cyril Mango*, ed. by Ihor Ševčenko & Irmgard Hutter (Stuttgart: Teubner, 1998), pp. 137–53; and Flusin, 'Le *Panégyrique* de Constantin VII Porphyrogénète pour la translation des reliques de Grégoire le Théologien (*BHG* 728)', *Revue des Études Byzantines*, 57 (1999), 5–97 (edition of the text on pp. 41–80).

[31] Ed. Immanuel Bekker, *Symeonis Magistri et Logothetae Annales* (Bonn, 1838), pp. 755$^{8-10}$. See Flusin, 'L'empereur et le Théologien', p. 138.

Magdalen's relics, followed by Romanos I Lakapenos's transfer of the Holy Shroud (*Mandylion*) of Edessa[32], and ends with Porphyrogennitos himself who, apart from St Gregory's remains, had also deposited in the church of the Holy Apostles a hand of St John the Baptist and the once lost but later recovered garments of the apostles. Predictably, in sponsoring all these pious transfers, each emperor had an axe to grind and Porphyrogennitos was no exception.

We know that after his forced resignation from the patriarchal throne of Constantinople, Gregory withdrew to his domains in Cappadocia where he met his death and where his body was buried. Recurring references in the text and indeed the title of the work alone serve to emphasize that this transfer of relics represented their natural return to the city that St Gregory had served as a prelate but from which he had been unceremoniously expelled. In several instances the author draws parallels between the present (σήμερον) and the past (χθές), thereby highlighting a comfortable current situation that had been preceded by a dreadful anomaly[33]. In fact, by that time, now that the Lakapenos family had ceased to usurp imperial power, Constantine was reigning as sole ruler and could wipe away the distress of earlier years[34]. The transfer of St Gregory's relics represented a personal vindication.

The practice of bringing relics into Constantinople did not die out on the demise of this learned emperor. The reigns of such military emperors as Nikephoros Phokas (963–69) and his murderer and successor Ioannes Tzimiskes (969–76) were also marked by the celebration of translations of holy objects from places in the East. These included the piece of the holy cross from Tarsos; the icon of Christ brought from Hierapolis (Manbij), from which blood and water gushed; the κεραμίδιον, the Holy Tile, again from Hierapolis[35]; the icon of Christ in Beirut; and the sandals of Christ. All these precious relics were sacred booty resulting from some victorious military campaigns undertaken on the Eastern front and triumphantly celebrated with litanies

---

[32] On the circumstances of the Mandylion's deposition see Sysse G. Engberg, 'Romanos Lekapenos and the Mandilion of Edessa', in *Byzance et les reliques du Christ*, ed. by Jannic Durand & Bernard Flusin (Paris: Centre de Recherche d'Histoire et Civilisation de Byzance, 2004), pp. 123–42.

[33] See ch. 13, ed. by Flusin, 'Le *Panégyrique* de Constantin VII', p. 49.

[34] On the whole question of Constantine VII's seizure of imperial power see now Jean-Claude Cheynet, 'Une querelle de famille: la prise du pouvoir par Constantin VII', in *Mélanges Bernard Flusin* (Paris: ACHCByz, 2019) (= *Travaux et Mémoires*, 23/1), pp. 121–39.

[35] On this event see François Halkin, 'Translation par Nicéphore Phocas de la brique miraculeuse d'Hiérapolis (*BHG*³ 801n)', in Halkin, *Inédits byzantins d'Ochrida, Candie et Moscou* (Brussels: Société des Bollandistes, 1963), 253–60. See Anthony Kaldellis, *Streams of Gold. Rivers of Blood. The Rise and Fall of Byzantium. 955 A.D. to the First Crusade* (Oxford: Oxford University Press, 2017), p. 49.

and parades in Constantinople. As a tool of domestic propaganda, they sustained the game of imperial legitimization which had been an issue for some time, since both Nikephoros and Ioannes were usurpers who had seized the throne of the Macedonian dynasty. A few decades later, in 1032, after conquering Edessa in Mesopotamia, another ambitious and successful military man, Georgios Maniakes, would triumphantly carry back to the capital the very letter that Christ had sent to King Abgar[36]. In a sense, medieval Byzantium continued to gain in piety by being supplied with holy objects preserved in regions that had historic connotations for Christianity, though they were located outside its orbit or in the fragile borderland.

The continuity of this tradition was interrupted in the eleventh and twelfth centuries, when the only mention of it concerns Manuel I Komnenos, who in 1169 is reported to have imported the so-called stone of unction, the slab on which Christ's body was anointed prior to the laying in the tomb (ἁγία λίθος), from Ephesos to Constantinople[37]. The emperor took the relic on his shoulders and carried it from the harbour of Boukoleon to the Pharos church at the Great Palace. The event was recorded by the historian Niketas Choniates in the concluding paragraph of his final book on the reign of this emperor, perhaps reflecting some intention to counterbalance his portrayal of Manuel elsewhere as a loose character with an act of piety[38]. On the occasion of the same transfer, Georgios Skylitzes, a Byzantine administrator and scholar, composed an office whose title states that this happened in the twenty-seventh year of Manuel's reign, i.e. 1169[39]. Naturally, no such acts of piety were expected in an age when what we might call secularization was gaining currency in Byzantium and when imperial initiatives in the religious sphere were manifested in other ways. In this period the personal piety of members of the imperial family introduced the practice of sponsoring the construction or the restoration of imposing monastic foundations, some of

---

[36] On all these translations of relics see Bernard Flusin, 'Construire une nouvelle Jérusalem: Constantinople et les reliques', in *L'Orient dans l'histoire religieuse de l'Europe: l'invention des origines*, ed. by Mohammad A. Amir-Moezzi & John Scheid (Turnhout: Brepols, 2000), pp. 54–57.

[37] See Paul Magdalino, *The Empire of Manuel I Komnenos, 1143–1180* (Cambridge: Cambridge University Press, 1993), pp. 291 and 455.

[38] Ed. Joannes L. van Dieten, *Nicetae Choniatae Historia*, vol. I, CFHB II. I, Series Berolinensis, p. 222. 71–86. For Niketas's criticism of Manuel I, see Magdalino, in the same volume, pp. 4–14. For the episode of this relic transfer see Robert Ousterhout, 'Sacred Geography and Holy Cities: Constantinople as Jerusalem', in *Hierotopy: The Creation of Sacred Space in Byzantium and Medieval Russia*, ed. by Alexei Lidov (Moscow: Progress-Tradition, 2006), p. 108.

[39] Ed. Theodora Antonopoulou, 'George Skylitzes' Office on the Translation of the Holy Stone: A Study and Critical Edition', in *The Pantokrator Monastery in Constantinople*, ed. by Sofia Kotzabassi (Berlin: De Guyter, 2013), pp. 109–41.

which were soon to win general acclaim and continued to function until the fall of the empire. These foundations include St Mary Peribleptos (Sulu Manastır)[40], the Pantepoptes Monastery (Eski Imaret Camii?)[41], St Mary Pammakaristos (Fethiye Camii)[42], and the Pantokrator Monastery (Zeyrek Camii)[43]. Significantly, none of these establishments, which were, after all, works of personal piety, is dedicated to a saint. For such dedications we must turn our attention to the private sphere, made up of other groupings of people and supported by particular social milieus.

The Piety of Benefactors

Indeed, it is this private element, represented by influential individuals or groups of people assembled under a common identity, that fostered the cult of saints in the imperial capital. This trend or tradition, which harks back to the early days of Constantinople[44], predated and determined the imperial sponsorship that, as mentioned above, would emerge after the end of iconoclasm in 843 and would more or less come full circle with Constantine VII Porphyrogennitos and his successors. Wherever they were located and whenever they were built, religious foundations dedicated to saints owed their existence to private benefactors, supporting or supported by certain groups of people, i.e. religious communities settled in specific districts of the capital. It is again from Janin's lengthy list of Constantinopolitan religious foundations that we can single out churches dedicated to minor, i.e. not widely known

---

[40] On this monastery, restored by Romanos III Argyros (1028–1034), see Cyril Mango, 'The Monastery of St Mary Peribleptos (Sulu Manastr) at Constantinople Revisited', *Revue des Études Arméniennes*, 23 (1992), pp. 473–93; and Ken Dark, 'The Byzantine Church and Monastery of St Mary Peribleptos in Istanbul', *The Burlington Magazine*, 141, no. 1160 (1999), 656–64.

[41] On this monastery, founded by Anna Dalassene in 1087, see Cyril Mango, 'Where at Constantinople was the Monastery of Christos Pantepoptes?', *Deltion tes Christianikes Archeologikes Etaireias*, 20 (1998), 87–88; and Nesilhan Asutay & Arne Effenberger, 'Eski Imaret Camii, Bonoszisterne und Konstantinsmauer', *Jahrbuch der Österreichischen Byzantinistik*, 58 (2008), 13–44.

[42] On this monastic church see Hans Belting, Cyril Mango & Doula Mouriki, *The Mosaics and Frescoes of St Mary Pammakaristos (Fethiye Camii at Istanbul)* (Washington, DC: Dumbarton Oaks Studies, 1978), and Arne Effenberger, 'Zu den Gräbern in der Pammakaristoskirche', *Byzantion*, 77 (2007), 170–96.

[43] On this imperial monastery see now *The Pantokrator Monastery in Constantinople*, ed. by Sofia Kotzabassi (Berlin: De Gruyter, 2013) and *Piroska and the Pantokrator, Dynastic Memory, Healing and Salvation in Comnenian Constantinople*, ed. by Marianne Sághy & Robert G. Ousterhout (Budapest: CEU Press, 2019).

[44] See Kim Bowes, *Private Worship, Public Values, and Religious Change in Late Antiquity* (Cambridge: Cambridge University Press, 2008), pp. 106–24.

saints, such as the ones dedicated to St Bari(y)psabbas[45], founded some time before the twelfth century, or to St Pancharios[46] and St Procla, the legendary wife of Pontius Pilate[47]. Churches or chapels of this sort shed light on another dimension of the cult of saints. The fame of a saint sometimes counted for less than the personal devotion shown to him/her by an individual or group. How should we interpret the founding of all these small sanctuaries? Janin has an answer for the first example: St Baripsabbas was a Syrian and must have been venerated by his fellow countrymen, refugees, or émigrés, who at some point in Late Antiquity settled in Constantinople. As has been shown in a recent study, this phenomenon of ethnic communities being attached to a shrine was not typical of the Byzantine capital but can be paralleled in Old Rome[48].

We hear more explicitly about such a community of provincials established in Constantinople and the ties that it developed with a particular saint thanks to a miracle collection written in the late seventh or early eighth century, after the end of Antiquity. This is the *Miracles of Therapon*, a saintly bishop of Cyprus, about whom we know next to nothing and whose relics were translated from Cyprus to the capital to be laid in the church of the Theotokos of Elaia, in all likelihood located on the hill of Galata[49]. The particular bonds that Cypriot Christianity developed with bishop-saints in Late Antiquity was a remarkable phenomenon, and the case of St Therapon's cult that was transferred to the capital is further proof of this attachment[50]. The translation of this enigmatic saint's relics must have occurred in the aftermath of the two Arab attempts to conquer the island in the mid-seventh century and must have been connected with the migration of Cypriot refugees

---

[45] See Janin, *La géographie ecclésiastique*, p. 63. For this saint, who purportedly lived in the apostolic age, only a short *vita* (*BHG* 238) has been preserved in Greek: see *AASS Sep.* III, pp. 498–500.

[46] See Janin, *La géographie ecclésiastique*, p. 399.

[47] See *La géographie ecclésiastique*, p. 457.

[48] See Maya Maskarinec, *City of Saints. Rebuilding Rome in the Early Middle Ages* (Philadelphia: University of Pennsylvania Press, 2018), pp. 117–37.

[49] See ch. 6. 1–5 and 10–12, ed. by Ludovicus Deubner, *De incubatione capita quattuor* (Leipzig: Teubner, 1904), p. 123. On the shrine of Elaia and its possible location on the hill of Galata see Janin, *La géographie ecclésiastique*, p. 183. See also Cyril Mango, 'Constantinople's Mount of Olives and Pseudo-Dorotheus of Tyre', *Nea Rhome*, 6 (2009), 157–70.

[50] See John Haldon, '"Tortured by my Conscience". The *Laudatio Therapontis*: A Neglected Source of the Later Seventh or Early Eighth Centuries', in *From Rome to Constantinople. Studies in Honour of Averil Cameron*, ed. by Hagith Amirav & Bas ter Haar Romeny (Leuven: Peeters, 2007), pp. 262–78. For the identity of the late antique saints of Cyprus, see now Stephanos Efthymiadis, 'The Cult of Saints in Late Antique Cyprus and the Apostolicity of its Churches', in *From Roman to Early Christian Cyprus*, ed. by AnneMarie Luijendijk, Laura Nasrallah & Charalambos Bakirtzis (Tübingen: Mohr Siebeck, 2020), pp. 211–23.

to Bithynia and the hinterland of Constantinople. The text, which has been attributed to Andrew of Crete[51], chronicles this translation and gives a rather dry account of incubatory cures; nonetheless, it documents the driving force that prompted the establishment of particular cults and gives useful insights into the 'microcosms' that sustained them in the melting pot that was Constantinople. New or previously unknown saints like St Therapon could be transplanted into its rich soil and enjoy a cult for brief periods or longer.

The significance of an earlier collection, the *Miracula* of St Artemios, dated between 658 and 668, lies in the vivid picture that it paints of the devotion to a shrine shown by rather low-to-middle-class people living in a Constantinopolitan district. How St Artemios, the *dux* of Egypt, allegedly martyred in Antioch under the pagan Julian, was transformed into a healer of hernias in male genitalia, an interesting development in itself, is hard to trace; it is equally unknown whether this healing identity was likewise a feature of the cult of St Artemios in other places outside the Byzantine capital.

The collection that promotes this saint's cult in Constantinople brings together forty-five stories of miraculous cures, in a location set apart from the city-centre traffic and bustle, the district of Oxeia on the southern bank of the Golden Horn. This saint was neither the primary nor even the second individual tenant of the shrine where these miraculous cures were performed. It was dedicated to St John the Baptist, and apart from the relics of St Artemios, it housed those of a female saint, Febronia[52]. As said, the collection is unique in reconstructing the conditions in which a shrine of this kind operated and its appeal within and beyond the confines of the parish and the neighbourhood in which it was located. Through longer and shorter accounts marked by notable diversity, the author does not hide his intention to bolster, on the one hand, the 'monopoly' of the shrine in curing a precise disease and, on the other hand, the kind of loyalty that the community attached to it should demonstrate. Some miracles, placed toward the beginning of the collection, promote the ecumenical potential of the shrine; in these stories people coming from afar are advised or are self-motivated to practice incubation

---

[51] See Marie-France Auzépy, 'La carrière d'André de Crète', *Byzantinische Zeitschrift*, 88 (1995), 9–11.

[52] On the cult of St Febronia at this particular shrine see Michel Kaplan, 'Une hôtesse importante de l'église Saint-Jean-Baptiste de l'Oxeia à Constantinople: Fébronie', in *Byzantine Religious Culture. Studies in Honor of Alice-Mary Talbot*, ed. by Denis Sullivan, Elizabeth Fisher & Stratis Papaioannou (Leiden: Brill, 2012), pp. 32–52; and Aude Busine, 'The Dux and the Nun: Hagiography and the Cult of Artemios and Febronia in Constantinople,' *Dumbarton Oaks Papers*, 72 (2018), 93–111. On St Febronia more generally see Jeanne-Nicole Saint-Laurent, 'Images de femmes dans l'hagiographie syriaque', in *L'hagiographie syriaque*, ed. by André Bìnggeli (Paris: Geuthner, 2012), pp. 214–20.

in the church at Oxeia. And the same holds for people of the capital who sought refuge in other churches. The woman carrying her son suffering from testicular hernia to the well-known church of the Theotokos in the quarter *ta Kyrou* is directed by the Virgin Mary in a dream to St John's church, where lay the relics of St Artemios[53].

In another instance, the same collection allows us to similarly glimpse a spirit of opposition, if not competition. A victim of burglary from this neighbourhood, seeking his stolen clothes, was advised to visit the church of St Pantaleon in the *ta Rouphinou* district, where exorcisms were performed and information could be elicited about the burglar. Upon entering the church and hearing the shouts of a possessed man, the hero of the story became aware that he was being disloyal to his local saint and said to himself: 'Now I am forsaking God and approaching demons; now I have been robbed of and sold my soul'[54]. Apart from bearing witness to the practice of consulting demoniacs[55], the passage leaves hints at a critical point. Attachment to St Artemios was supposed to be unswerving; no betrayals or recourse to other shrines were permitted.

St Artemios's relics, as deposited in St John the Baptist's church at Oxeia, are documented to have still attracted pilgrims as late as the end of the eleventh century[56]. Yet the city enjoyed a more durable and conspicuous relationship with much more acclaimed medical specialist-saints, whose establishments may be called institutional as they were firmly connected to public welfare and philanthropic activity. Suffice it to mention St Sampson and his

---

[53] *Miraculum* 12, ed. by Athanasios Papadopoulos-Kerameus, *Varia Graeca Sacra* (St Petersburg: Tipografia V. Th. Kiršbauma, 1909), p. 1213; reprinted with English translation by Virgil S. Crisafulli and John W. Nesbitt, *The Miracles of St Artemios: a Collection of Miracles* (Leiden: Brill, 1997), pp. 98–101.

[54] *Miraculum* 18, see Papadopoulos-Kerameus, p. 20; English trans. pp. 114–15. On the text in general and this episode in particular, see Vincent Déroche, 'Pourquoi écrivait-on des recueils de miracles? L'exemple des miracles de saint Artémios,' in *Les saints et leurs sanctuaires: textes, images et monuments à Byzance*, ed. by Catherine Jolivet-Lévy, Michel Kaplan & Jean-Pierre Sodini (Paris: Publications de la Sorbonne, 1993), pp. 95–116; and Stephanos Efthymiadis, 'A Day and Ten Months in the Life of a Lonely Bachelor: The *Other Byzantium* in *Miracula S. Artemii* 18 and 22', *Dumbarton Oaks Papers*, 58 (2004), 1–26 (pp. 5–9), repr. in Efthymiadis, *Hagiography in Byzantium: Literature, Social History and Cult* (Farnham: Ashgate, 2011), no. III. On the popularity of St Panteleemon as a healer and the centre of his cult in Nikomedia, see Sharon E. J. Gerstel, '"Tiles of Nicomedia" and the Cult of Saint Panteleimon', in *Byzantine Religious Culture*, pp. 173–86.

[55] On this matter see Robert Wiśniewski, 'La consultation des possédés dans l'Antiquité tardive: pythones, engastrimythoi, arrepticii', *Revue d'Études Augustiniennes et Patristiques*, 51 (2005), pp. 127–52.

[56] See Krijnie N. Ciggaar, 'Une description de Constantinople traduite par un pèlerin anglais', *Revue des Études Byzantines*, 34 (1976), 211–68 (p. 259, ch. 36).

Xenon (hospital) in the northern vicinity of Hagia Sophia[57], and St Zotikos and his leprosarium somewhere in the region of Pera, on the opposite side of the Golden Horn[58]. Legends developed around the last two saints, Sampson and Zotikos, that they were local, i.e. Constantinopolitan, benefactors and that they had launched their charitable projects during the reigns of such prominent emperors as Justinian and Constantine respectively. These legends point to a particular endeavour to enhance the leading role of the Byzantine *metropolis* in the sphere of philanthropy. Besides these two saints, a word must be said about the most reputable pair of medical saints, Cosmas and Damian, whose Constantinopolitan shrine at Kosmidion, at the end of the Golden Horn, was a prominent holy site that knew periods of flourishing and decline[59]. From the late fifth century down to the Paleologan era, the shrine witnessed several destructions and restorations, the latter proving that it never lost its significance and was firmly integrated into the religious history of the reigning city. In a recent discussion, it has been shown that the late antique miracle collections dedicated to the so-called *Anargyroi* intersected with imperial policy regarding doctrinal polemic and opposition. The shrine at Kosmidion may have admitted a varied clientèle of both 'orthodox' and 'heretics'[60]. Its venerated saints, however, never became emblematic of the imperial capital nor were they invested with a role larger than that defined by their healing identity.

Apart from the old and long-established saints whose relics, according to the accounts of Russian pilgrims dating to the late Byzantine period, were

---

[57] On St Sampson's *xenon*, see Timothy S. Miller, 'The Sampson Hospital of Constantinople', *Byzantinische Forschungen*, 15 (1990), 105–13; and Miller, *The Birth of the Hospital in the Byzantine Empire* (Baltimore: Johns Hopkins University Press, 1997²), pp. 80–85. On the most important piece of hagiography dedicated to this saint, see Vincent Déroche, 'Des miracles pour la bonne société: La *Vie de Sampson* par Syméon Métaphraste', in *Οὗ δῶρόν εἰμι τὰς γραφὰς βλέπων νόει, Mélanges Jean-Claude Cheynet*, ed. by Béatrice Caseau, Vivien Prigent & Alessio Sopracasa (Paris: ACHCByz, 2017) (= *Travaux et Mémoires*, 21/1), pp. 109–22.
[58] Cf. Timothy S. Miller & John W. Nesbitt, *Walking Corpses: Leprosy in Byzantium and the Medieval West* (Ithaca, NY: Cornell University Press, 2014), pp. 72–95. The most important text regarding this saint is by the famous late Byzantine hagiographer Constantine Akropolites, ed. by Timothy S. Miller, 'The Legend of Saint Zotikos according to Constantine Akropolites', *Analecta Bollandiana*, 112 (1994), 339–76.
[59] On the location of Kosmidion and its function, see Grigori Simeonov, 'Die Anlegestellen beim Kosmidion', in *Die byzantinischen Häfen Konstantinopels*, ed. by Falko Daim (Mainz: Verlag des Römisch-Germanischen Zentralmuseums, 2016), pp. 147–200.
[60] See Phil Booth, 'Orthodox and Heretic in the Early Byzantine Cult(s) of Cosmas and Damian', in *An Age of Saints? Power, Conflict and Dissent in Early Medieval Christianity*, ed. by Peter Sarris, Matthew Dal Santo & Phil Booth (Leiden: Brill, 2011), pp. 114–28.

to be revered in nearly a hundred religious shrines[61], Constantinople could also boast of the new saints, patriarchs, and monks, whose holiness found acclaim in the social conditions of the Byzantine metropolis rather than in the isolation of the periphery. No doubt, the process of becoming a saint in the capital was far from being consistent and did not always follow the same, homogeneous pattern in terms of the reception and promotion of the cult. The chapter on the history of sainthood in Byzantium in the period from the age of Justinian to the Comnenian era is yet to be written, but the entanglement of sainthood with the main axes of power, imperial, patriarchal or other, is as self-evident as it was fluid.

It is in an entry taken from the extremely valuable Database on the Cult of Saints in Late Antiquity (CSLA) that we read about the ascetic Patriarch of Constantinople John the Faster (Ioannes Nēsteutēs) (see CSLA E00021 — Efthymios Rizos), whose death in 595 is recounted by the seventh-century historian Theophylact Simocatta. The pious emperor Maurice, who was highly engaged with the veneration of saints, collected the patriarch's humble personal belongings, which he revered as relics for the promotion of his cult[62]. In later centuries emperors demonstrating a similar zeal to that of Maurice become thin on the ground. In fact, most of the saintly patriarchs of the eighth to the tenth century were distinguished for opposing themselves to emperors who interfered with religious and canonical issues. The list starts with Tarasios (784–806), who restored the doctrine of icon worship in Nicaea II, includes such influential figures as Nikephoros (806–15), Ignatios (847–56, 867–77), and Photios (856–67, 877–86), and extends to the early tenth century with Euthymios (907–12) and Nikolaos Mystikos (901–07, 912–25), both involved from opposite standpoints in the conflict over the fourth, sinful marriage of Leo VI[63]. Not unlike that of patriarchs, the cult of bishop-saints during the middle Byzantine period was at odds with the prevailing tendency to highlight the monastic saintly paradigm, especially of founders of influential monasteries to which the Constantinopolitan and provincial aristocracy provided financial and social support. The few bishop-saints that fall into this period were either defenders of icon-worship during

---

[61] See the count and analysis of Paul Magdalino, 'Medieval Constantinople', in *Studies on the History and Topography of Byzantine Constantinople* (Aldershot: Ashgate, 2007), no. I, pp. 67–75.

[62] See book VII. 6. 1–5, ed. Carolus de Boor, *Theophylacti Simocattae Historiae* (Leipzig: Teubner, 1985²), pp. 254–65.

[63] On the ninth- and tenth-c. patriarchs who came to be venerated as saints see Stephanos Efthymiadis, *The Life of the Patriarch Tarasios (BHG 1698)* (Aldershot: Ashgate, 1998), pp. 3–6.

the Second Iconoclasm (815–43) or occupied sees of provincial towns[64]. The original version of the *Synodikon of Orthodoxy*, the liturgical document produced by the partisans of icon-worship after 843, celebrates the memory of a large cohort of confessors of the right faith, of whom some were distinguished bishops, yet most were holy monks[65].

Monastic sanctity, as manifested in the capital, took various paths and explored different historical circumstances in order to emerge and find approval in Constantinopolitan society. Holy monks were the obvious victims of iconoclasm, but they enjoyed widespread recognition when this crisis was resolved. Nonetheless, one must be sceptical as to the impact and persistence of their cults over time. Compared to bishop-saints, the founders of monasteries were no doubt on safer ground in this respect if their cult rested, on the one hand, on the strength of their name and historical presence and, on the other, on the survival and prestige of their monastic establishments. Among the very few saintly names postdating Late Antiquity that I would single out from the rich account of holy treasures given by Anthony of Novgorod, the Russian pilgrim who visited Constantinople in the year 1200, are Theodore and Joseph the Stoudites, whose relics lay in their eponymous monastery, and St Stephen the Younger, the martyr par excellence of the First Iconoclasm[66].

The modest place that the cults of near contemporary saints could occupy in the urban environment of the capital after the end of Late Antiquity did not always discourage the emergence of new saints. The hagiography of the tenth and eleventh centuries includes a group of *Lives* that blur the borders between historical reality and fiction, extolling the exploits of saints who probably never existed. Andrew the Fool, Basil the Younger, Irene of Chrysobalanton, and, to a lesser extent, Niphon are the names of saints well-known to Byzantinists. Each text has its own *causa scribendi*, yet it is noteworthy that for three of them the action in their *Lives* is entirely set in Constantinople, while the protagonist of the fourth is a native of the city[67]. Should we infer that all these saints emerged because of a need for new cults

---

[64] On the whole question see Stephanos Efthymiadis, 'The Place of Holy and Unholy Bishops in Byzantine Hagiographical Narrative (Eighth–Twelfth Centuries). In *Saintly Bishops and Bishops' Saints*, ed. John S. Ott & Trpimir Vedriš (Zagreb: Hagiotheca, 2012), pp. 169–82.

[65] See Jean Gouillard, 'Le Synodicon de l'Orthodoxie. Édition et commentaire', *Travaux et Mémoires*, 2 (1967), pp. 138–92 and for the edition p. 297.

[66] See Loparev, *Kniga palomnik*, pp. 22 and 25–26. Also, ed. with German trans. by Anna Jouravel, *Die Kniga palomnik des Antonij von Novgorod*, 292–93, 304–05, and 316–17.

[67] On all these *Lives* see Stephanos Efthymiadis, 'Hagiography from the "Dark Age" to the Age of Symeon Metaphrastes (Eighth–Tenth Centuries)', in *The Ashgate Research Companion to Byzantine Hagiography*, vol. 1: Periods and Places, ed. Efthymiadis (Farnham: Ashgate, 2011), pp. 125–28.

and for new holy men and women integrated into an otherwise secular city? Regardless of the answer to this question, the fact is that at least Andrew the Fool and Irene of Chrysobalanton constitute rare examples where hagiography alone decisively contributed to promoting cults that, sooner or later, enjoyed remarkable popularity in the Orthodox world.

Conclusion

There are several puzzles to solve when dealing with the histories of cults in Constantinople. The evidence discussed here suggests the following observations. The cult of saints in the Byzantine capital was a manifestation of a highly localized, popular religiosity rather than a phenomenon consistent with a centralized policy continuously promoted by the imperial and ecclesiastical authorities. It can be described as a conglomeration of microcosms, venerating particular saintly figures who bore the marks of ethnic or local identities. On the one hand, cults were established and developed along with the coming and settling of immigrants in precise districts. On the other hand, a network of parish churches and monastic foundations, each of which shared a small part in the wide distribution of relics in the imperial city, existed in the shadow of prominent official shrines and establishments. In the few instances where emperors manifested an interest in certain cults, this can be interpreted in terms of personal piety and private interest. Naturally enough, this is the domestic picture of the phenomenon, seen through the prism of the lived experience of the city's inhabitants, not the outward, rich, and pluralistic one that the visitors to Constantinople, whether welcome or unwelcome, record in their accounts. As a matter of fact, in the light of this plurality, which was the result of many cultic microcosms being put together in a large space, no saint could impose his/her monopoly on the Christian *megalopolis*. Unlike other cities and places in the empire, Constantinople could take pride in her democracy in terms of saints and their cults.

The Origins and Later Development of the First Italo-Greek Hagiographies

The *Dossiers* of the Sicilian Martyrs Agatha, Lucia, and Euplus

Anna Lampadaridi
(CNRS HiSoMA UMR 5189)

This chapter will focus on the first period of Sicilian hagiographical production, as Lancia di Brolo defined it at the end of the nineteenth century in his *Storia della Chiesa in Sicilia*[1]. This categorisation was adopted and further elaborated a century later by Guy Philippart, who dealt with Sicilian hagiography in the context of the hagiography of the West and identified an 'archaic' period, prior to the edict of Milan (313), followed by a period of 'transition' (300–600)[2]. Stephanos Efthymiadis, in his recent study on Greek hagiography of Italy, also followed the broad lines of this scheme and referred to an early Sicilian hagiographical production dealing with local martyrs[3].

---

[1] Domenico Gaspare Lancia di Brolo, *Storia della Chiesa in Sicilia nei primi dieci secoli del cristianesimo*, 2 vols (Palermo: Stabilimento poligrafico Lao, 1880), I, pp. 37–41.

[2] Guy Philippart, 'L'hagiographie sicilienne dans le cadre de l'hagiographie de l'Occident', in *La Sicilia nella tarda antichità e nell'alto medioevo. Religione e società. Atti del Convegno di Studi (Catania-Paternò 24–27 settembre 1997)*, ed. by Rossana Barcellona & Salvatore Pricoco (Soveria Manelli: Rubbettino, 1999), pp. 167–204 (p. 178).

[3] Stéphanos Efthymiadis, 'L'hagiographie grecque d'Italie (VIIe-XIVe siècle)' in *Hagiographies. Histoire internationale de la littérature hagiographique latine et vernaculaire en Occident des origines à 1550*, ed. by Guy Philippart and others, VII, ed. by Monique Goullet (Turnhout: Brepols, 2017), pp. 345–421 (pp. 367–68). See also Mario Re, 'Telling the Sanctity in Byzantine Italy' in *A Companion to Byzantine Italy*, ed. by Salvatore Cosentino (Leiden: Brill, 2021), pp. 609-40 (pp. 609-10).

Interacting with Saints in the Late Antique and Medieval Worlds, ed. by Robert Wiśniewski, Raymond Van Dam, and Bryan Ward-Perkins, Hagiologia, 20 (Turnhout, 2023), pp. 181–210.
© BREPOLS ❧ PUBLISHERS　　　　　　　　　　　DOI 10.1484/M.HAG-EB.5.133627

This phase includes the hagiographical *dossiers* of the Sicilian martyrs Agatha, Lucia, and Euplus. These Sicilian *Passiones* can be dated roughly between 300 and 550, prior to the Byzantine conquest of the island by Justinian (535). Taking into consideration both Greek and Latin versions of these martyrdoms, we will be discussing the cult of these three Sicilian martyrs in Byzantium, as described in their liturgy and literary reception by later writers. In other words, we will be looking into the transformations and re-semantisations of these martyrs and their legends in the Byzantine world, trying to figure out the pattern of their religious and cultural transfer[4].

Agatha

Agatha, a beautiful consecrated virgin, scion of a prominent family, was martyred in Catania under Decius, reportedly on 5 February 251[5]. Quintinianus, the governor of Sicily, who fell in love with her beauty as well as with her fortune, ordered her to be entrusted to the *matrona* Aphrodisia. He hoped that Aphrodisia and her young daughters would manage to pervert Agatha and persuade her to venerate idols. Despite their machinations, Agatha's faith rested on a rock. She was summoned to court and interrogated by Quintinianus. As she kept despising the pagan gods, the governor ordered his men to beat her and then to put her in jail. The next day the virgin was ordered to appear at the tribunal, where she refused once more to change her mind. The governor ordered his men to cut off her breast and sent her again to prison. At about midnight, an old man visited her and brought many medicines. She did not let him take care of her, but the old man revealed to her that he was the apostle Peter. Her breast recovered. Four days later, she appeared once again before the governor, who ordered Agatha to be thrown on broken pottery and coals heated in fire. The city of Catania was severely shaken by an earthquake, and some ruins fell on the governor's assistant, Silvanus, and on his friend, Falconius. Profoundly confused, Quintinianus ordered his men to lead Agatha back to prison, where she gave up the ghost. The crowd hastened to safeguard Agatha's body, and a young man, completely unknown to the people of Catania and suspected to be an angel, left a tablet with an inscription praising Agatha's holiness next to her head and then went away, never to be seen again. The crowd started venerating the tomb. Quintinianus,

---

[4] On the notion of cultural transfer and the dynamic of re-semantization of a cultural object passing from one context into another, see Michel Espagne, 'La notion de transfert culturel', *Revue Sciences/Lettres*, 1 (2013) <http://journals.openedition.org/rsl/219> [accessed 3 September 2019].

[5] On the Latin martyrdom of Agatha, see CSLA E01916 (Matthieu Pignot).

wanting to get hold of Agatha's wealth, drowned in a river. One year after Agatha's death, Mt. Etna erupted. The pagans removed the covering from the martyr's tomb and placed it in front of the fire, which ceased right away.

Possibly the earliest evidence for the cult of Agatha is a now lost Greek funerary inscription found on the island of Ustica, near Palermo, in the beginning of the nineteenth century[6]. The dating of this inscription that commemorated Lucifera is highly uncertain and cannot provide a secure *terminus ante quem* for the development of Agatha's cult. A Latin inscription, probably from the early fourth century, commemorating the last hours of an eighteen-month old infant, Julia Florentina, who was buried close to a local martyrs' shrine, has been evoked as further proof for the veneration of unnamed martyrs in Catania[7]. However, this inscription, whose dating remains uncertain, cannot provide secure evidence for Agatha's cult.

Her cult was attested in Rome[8] by the end of the fifth century in a letter attributed to Pope Gelasius I (492–96), which mentioned a church dedicated to Agatha in *Caclanus fundus*, located probably near Rome[9]. The *Liber Pontificalis* mentioned another basilica consecrated by Pope Symmachus (498–514) on the via Aurelia[10], which had been destroyed already by the time of

---

[6] The funerary inscription was first edited by Salvatore Morso, *Giornale di Scienze per la Sicilia* (Palermo, 1823), IV, p. 168; the text reprinted in *IG* 14. 592 is barely legible. We follow the text found in Packard Humanities Institute, Greek Inscriptions: Λουκιφέρ[α] / ἀ<πέ>θανεν [τῇ] {sc. ἑορτῇ} / κυρίας Ἀ / γάθης ('Lucifera died on the festival of mistress Agatha'). On this inscription, see also: Carla Morini, *La Passione di S. Agata' di Ælfric di Eynsham, Bibliotheca Germanica*, Studi e testi, 4 (Alessandria: Edizioni dell'Orso, 1993), pp. 31–36; Daniela Motta, *Percorsi dell'agiografia. Società e cultura nella Sicilia tardoantica e bizantina* (Catania: Edizioni del Prisma, 2004²), p. 30, n. 24.

[7] *CIL* 10. 7112. She was born when Zoilus was the *corrector* of the province of Sicily; by *c.* 330 the governor had the title of *consularis* [*PLRE* 1:994, 'Zoilus']. For a revised text, see Giacomo Manganaro, 'Iscrizioni latine e greche di Catania tardo-imperiale', *Archivio Storico per la Sicilia Orientale*, 11–12 (1958–59), 5–30 (p. 23).

[8] See also Lellia Cracco Ruggini, 'Il primo cristianesimo in Sicilia (III–VIII secolo)', in *Il cristianesimo in Sicilia dalle origini a Gregorio Magno. Atti del Convegno di Studi organizzato dall'Istituto teologico pastorale 'Mons. G. Guttadauro', Caltanissetta (28–29 ottobre 1985)*, ed. by Vincenzo Messana & Salvatore Pricoco (Caltanissetta: Edizioni del seminario, 1987), pp. 85–125 (pp. 91–95); Cesare Pasini, 'Chiesa di Milano e Sicilia: punti di contatto dal IV all'VIII secolo', in *Sicilia e Italia suburbicaria tra IV e VIII secolo. Atti del Convegno di Studi (Catania, 24–27 ottobre 1989)*, ed. by Salvatore Pricoco (Soveria Mannelli: Rubbettino, 1991), pp. 367–98; Cécile Lanéry, *Hagiographies d'Italie (300–550)*, vol. 1: *Les Passions latines composées en Italie*, CCHAG, 5 (2010), pp. 278 and 284, n. 608.

[9] Pope Gelasius I, *Letters, Fragment* 12, ed. by Victor W. von Glanvell, *Die Kanonessammlung des Kardinals Deusdedit* (Paderborn: Ferdinand Schöningh, 1905; repr. Aalen: Scientia Verlag, 1967), I. Die Kanonessammlung Selbst, p. 318; Motta, p. 30, n. 24; CSLA E02007 (Matthieu Pignot).

[10] *Liber Pontificalis* 53, ed. by Louis Duchesne, *Le Liber Pontificalis* (Paris: R. Thorin, 1886), I, pp. 262 and 267; Vincenza Milazzo & Francesca Rizzo-Nervo, 'Lucia tra Sicilia, Roma

Hadrian IV. In his *Dialogues*, written in Rome around 593, Gregory the Great described the re-consecration of an Arian church in Rome (*Subura*), presumably the present-day church of Saint Agatha of the Goths, and its dedication to the martyrs Sebastian and Agatha along with the transfer of their relics[11]. According to Aldhelm, Gregory the Great introduced the names of Agatha and Lucia in the daily canon of the service[12]. Gregory the Great also provided secure evidence for the establishment of Agatha's cult in Palermo by the end of the sixth century. In two of his letters (598/99) he referred to a monastery dedicated to Maximus and Agatha, called *Lucuscanum*, in Palermo[13].

Agatha's cult seems to have spread to Milan, according to liturgical evidence[14]. Rossi Taibbi mentions a church dedicated to Agatha and Lucia that was built by Bishop Ursus in Ravenna in 384. However, evidence concerning this church is highly dubious[15]. Moreover, the two virgins were portrayed next to Roman virgins in the mosaics of the basilica of Sant'Apollinare Nuovo in the first quarter of the sixth century.

The *Passio* of Agatha survives in Greek (*BHG* 36–37) and Latin versions (*BHL* 133–36)[16]. The Latin *Passio* was one of the most popular pieces of Latin hagiography[17], surviving in 171 manuscripts[18], the oldest ones dating back to the eighth/ninth century, whereas the Greek versions have survived in approximately 28 manuscripts[19]. The dating of the Latin *Passio* is debatable;

---

e Bisanzio: itinerario di un culto', in *Storia della Sicilia e tradizione agiografica nella tarda antichità. Atti del Convegno di Studi (Catania, 20–22 maggio 1986)*, ed. by Salvatore Pricoco (Soveria Manelli: Rubbettino, 1988), pp. 95-135 (p. 100, n. 22); CSLA E01350 (Robert Wiśniewski).

[11] Gregory the Great, *Dialogues* III. 30, ed. by Adalbert de Vogüé, *Grégoire le Grand, Dialogues*, SC 260 (1979), pp. 279–81; Milazzo & Rizzo-Nervo, p. 119, n. 107; CSLA E04501 (Frances Trzeciak); CSLA E01419 (Robert Wiśniewski).

[12] Aldhelm, *De virginitate* 42, ed. by Rudolf Ehwald, MGH AA 15. 1, p. 293; Milazzo & Rizzo-Nervo, pp. 116-17, 124.

[13] Gregory the Great, *Register of Letters* IX. 67 and IX. 83, ed. by Dag Norberg, CCSL 140A (1982), pp. 622-23, 637; Motta, pp. 77-78; CSLA E06391 (Frances Trzeciak).

[14] Lanéry, p. 184.

[15] Giuseppe Rossi Taibbi, *Martirio di santa Lucia. Vita di santa Marina. Testi greci e traduzioni*, Vite dei santi siciliani 2, (Palermo: Istituto siciliano di studi bizantini e neogreci, 1959), p. 14; Milazzo & Rizzo-Nervo, pp. 112-44.

[16] Valentina Zanghi & Sandra Isetta, 'Passio Agathae *BHL* 133', in *Le légendier de Turin. Ms. D.V.3 de la Bibliothèque Nationale Universitaire*, ed. by Monique Goullet (Florence: SISMEL-Edizioni del Galluzzo, 2014), pp. 357-71.

[17] Philippart, p. 183.

[18] Zanghi & Isetta, p. 359, n. 15.

[19] According to the database *Pinakes*: https://pinakes.irht.cnrs.fr/notices/oeuvre/14395/ and https://pinakes.irht.cnrs.fr/notices/oeuvre/14396/. See also Maria Stelladoro, 'Ricerche sulla tradizione manoscritta degli Atti greci del martirio di S. Agata', *Bollettino della Badia Greca di Grottaferrata*, 49-50 (1995-96), 63-89.

according to Cécile Lanéry, on the basis of liturgical evidence it should be dated before the mid-fifth century[20]. Even if the precise date of its composition is difficult to ascertain, it must have been written by the late seventh century, since one of its versions (*BHL* 134) — not necessarily the version that we have now — was used by Aldhelm (639–709) writing in Anglo-Saxon Britain[21].

Nowadays the Latin *Passio BHL* 133 is widely recognised by scholars as the original version[22]. The Latin text is more precise than the Greek concerning several points, such as the date of the martyrdom (at the time of the third consulship of Decius) and the title of Quintinianus (*consularis* instead of ἡγεμών, as mentioned in *BHG* 36)[23]. Some other narrative details indicate that the Greek versions resulted from a rewriting of the Latin text[24]. For example, in the episode of the apparition of the apostle Peter, the hagiographer of the Greek text revealed right away the identity of the visitor ('the apostle Peter appeared in front of her in the form of a priest')[25], but repeated the information at the end of the scene, creating a narrative incoherence ('I am an apostle of Christ')[26].

In fact, Agatha was known to the Greek-speaking world as early as the end of the third century, since Methodius of Olympus dedicated to Agatha the sixth discourse of his *Symposium*[27], written around 290. This dialogue conducted by women on the subject of chastity, the most famous among Methodius's works,

---

[20] Lanéry, p. 284.

[21] Lanéry, p. 282; CSLA E06576 (Benjamin Savill).

[22] Lanéry, pp. 280–82; Zanghi & Isetta, p. 359, n. 9 with bibliography.

[23] Motta, p. 25.

[24] According to *Pinakes* (https://pinakes.irht.cnrs.fr/notices/oeuvre/14395/), the two manuscripts transmitting *BHG* 36 are the ms. Biblioteca Centrale della Regione Siciliana «Alberto Bombace», II. E. 08, fols 197–200v (16th-17th century) [siglum P] and the ms. Bibliothèque des Bollandistes, 193 [285], fols 126–30 (17th-18th century) [siglum B]. The Palermitan manuscript, copied by Ottavio Gaetani, has been examined *in situ*. I thank Xavier Lequeux for making available to me the reproduction of the folios of the manuscript kept in the Library of the Bollandists in Brussels. For a recent critical edition of *BHG* 36, see Mario Re, 'La Passio di S. Agata *BHG* e Nov. Auct. *BHG* 36. Introduzione, edizione del testo, traduzione', *Rivista di Studi Bizantini e Neoellenici*, 56 (2019), 249–89. For a Latin translation, see *AASS* Febr. I, 1658, 618–20.

[25] *BHG* 36: ἐφάνη αὐτῇ ἐν ὁμοιώματι πρεσβυτέρου ὁ ἀπόστολος Πέτρος (B, fol. 127; P, fol. 199).

[26] *BHG* 36: ἐγὼ ἐκείνου Ἀπόστολος τυγχάνω (B, fol. 128; P, fol. 199v). For a comparative study of this episode in *Passio BHG* 37 and the Methodius's *Oratio* (*BHG* 38) see Carmelo Crimi, 'Pietro o l'angelo. A proposito della *Passio Agathae* (*BHG* 37) e di Metodio patriarca di Constantinopoli, *Encomio di sant'Agata* (*BHG* 38)', in *Ripensare la santità in Sicilia*, ed. by Vincenzo Lombino & Mario Re, Ho theológos. Collana della Facoltà Teologica di Sicilia 15 (Rome: Città Nuova Editrice, 2022), pp. 115-39.

[27] Methodius of Olympus, *Banquet*, 6, ed. by Herbert Musurillo & Victor-Henry Debidour, SC 95 (1963), pp. 165–77.

was modelled on Plato's *Symposium*. It depicted a festive meal of ten virgins, during which each of the participants praised Christian virginity.

However, Methodius's praise of virginity inspired by Agatha is not related to any of the Greek versions of her *Passio*. Both basic Greek versions, *BHG* 36 and 37[28], seem to be derived from the Latin *BHL* 133. The *Passio BHG* 36 survived in only two manuscripts[29], whereas the *Passio BHG* 37 can be read in more than twenty codices[30].

Rather than being translations of the Latin model, these two Greek *Passiones* of Agatha represented rewritings of the legend with variations that are worth noting. One basic difference concerns the mention of the city of Palermo, which was totally absent from the Latin versions. In the Greek *Passio BHG* 36, Agatha was depicted as a native of Catania ('Catania was her hometown') who happened to live in Palermo ('who was living in Palermo, outside the city of Catania'), when Quintinianus summoned her[31]. A whole passage was devoted to the description of her journey from Palermo to Catania, with an episode concerning the disappointing attitude of the citizens of Palermo:

> While recounting such things, she kept moving forward in tears; on her way, she set her foot on a stone and retied one of her shoelaces that was loose. As she turned backwards, she saw that none of the citizens, who were previously escorting her, were following her anymore. Saint Agatha, deeply upset, prayed and said: My Lord, the King of the universe, perform a miracle for those who refused to believe in your servant, who intends to compete [as a martyr] on behalf of Your name. And an olive tree that cannot bear fruit appeared right away, censuring the attitudes of these unfaithful people who were moving away from their city[32].

---

[28] This Greek version was published by Migne among the writings of Symeon Metaphrastes: PG 114, coll. 1331–46. On the discussion concerning the imputed authorship of the Greek *Passio BHG* 37 to Metaphrastes, see Christine Angelidi, 'Translationes Agathae. Note sur le culte d'une sainte entre Byzance et la Sicile Normande', in *Χρόνος συνήγορος*. Mélanges André Guillou, ed. by Lisa Benou & Cristina Rognoni (Rome: Università degli Studi di Roma « Tor Vergata », 2013) (= *Νέα Ῥώμη*, 9 [2012]), II, pp. 123–32 (pp. 126–27) and Carmelo Crimi, 'L'Encomio di S. Agata (*BHG* 38) di Metodio Patriarca di Constantinopoli e la *Passio BHG* 37', in *Ἀνατολὴ καὶ δύσις*. Studi in memoria di Filippo Burgarella, ed. by Gioacchino Strano & Cristina Torre, Testi e Studi Bizantino-Neoellenici 21 (Rome: Edizioni Nuova Cultura, 2020), pp. 135-52 (p. 136, n. 6).

[29] See *supra*, note 24.

[30] According to *Pinakes*, see https://pinakes.irht.cnrs.fr/notices/oeuvre/14396/.

[31] πατρίδος μὲν Κατάνης (B, fol. 125; P, fol. 197) ἔξω Κατάνης ἐν Πανόρμῳ διατρίβουσαν (B, fol. 125; P, fol. 125 s.l.: τὴν διατριβὴν ποιοῦσαν). For this confusing indication, see *infra* p. 191.

[32] Ταῦτα δὲ καὶ τὰ τοιαῦτα μετὰ δακρύων λέγουσα ἐπορεύετο καὶ καθ'ὁδὸν στήσασα τὸν πόδα αὐτῆς ἐπί τινος λίθου, ἔδησε τὸν σπάρτον (μετὰ τὸν cdd.) τοῦ ὑποδήματος λυθέντα· καὶ στραφεῖσα οὐδένα οἶδεν συνακολουθοῦντα (-ντι P) αὐτῇ προπεμπόντων (προκραπόντων P)

Concerning the episode of the death of Quintinianus, the Greek *Passio BHG* 36 specified that he was attacked by his own horses and drowned in a river named 'Psimethos', which is presumably the present-day Simeto river[33]. This geographical indication was absent from the Latin *Passio BHL* 133, whose text is mutilated at this point[34].

The *Passio BHG* 36 had some similarities with the patriarch Methodius's *Oratio* dedicated to saint Agatha (*BHG* 38)[35], pronounced after 843 in Constantinople according to its editor, Elpidio Mioni[36]. Methodius, a native of Syracuse, also included the episodes related to Palermo, especially the olive tree miracle and the unfriendly attitude of the people of Palermo: 'And straightaway an olive tree, one of the most perfect trees, grew without any grace, as it was condemned never to bear fruit'[37].

Methodius's sermon offered important evidence for Agatha's cult in nineth-century Constantinople (if we accept Mioni's assessment that the discourse was pronounced in the capital). It was the only source to mention a miracle consisting of the bubbling of the oil of the martyr's lamp. This miracle referred to the present time of the narration and happened every year; Methodius himself claimed to have attended this scene already twice during the last two years. He did not give the name of the martyrium where this miracle took place, but he implied that there was more than one place in which Agatha was venerated in Constantinople:

> This speech, my fathers, dedicated to the martyr, the athlete of the race, was delivered in front of you on the occasion of the annual miracle. As during the last two years, I was honoured to see it for a third time, even if I am not rightfully worthy of it, as my sins are an impediment. But thanks to you,

---

αὐτὴν πολιτῶν. Ἡ δὲ ἁγία Ἀγάθη (Ἀγάθα P) σφόδρα λυπηθεῖσα (μειθοῦσα P) ηὔξατο λέγουσα· Κύριε παντοκράτορ, διὰ τοὺς ἀπιστήσαντας τῇ σῇ δούλῃ μελλούσῃ (μελ- B) ἀθλῆσαι ὑπὲρ τοῦ ὀνόματός σου, δεῖξον θαῦμα. Καὶ παραχρῆμα ἀνῆλθεν ἐλαία ἄκαρπος ἐξελέγχουσα τὰς γνώμας τῶν ἀπίστων ἐκείνων ἀποδήμων (-μῶν B; ὑποδῶν P).

[33] B, fol. 129; P, fol. 200.

[34] Zanghi & Isetta, p. 370.

[35] Elpidio Mioni, 'L'encomio di S. Agata di Metodio patriarca di Constantinopoli', *Analecta Bollandiana*, 68 (1950), 76–93. See also Dirk Krausmüller, 'Being, Seeming and Becoming: Patriarch Methodius on Divine Impersonation of Angels and Souls and the Origenist Alternative', *Byzantion*, 79 (2009), 168–207; Efthymiadis, p. 352.

[36] Mioni, pp. 74–75. The composition of the sermon in Rome, where Methodius lived between 815 and 821, cannot be excluded, see Angelidi, pp. 125–26. See also Carmelo Crimi, 'Agata e Bisanzio nel IX secolo. Rileggendo Metodio patriarca di Constantinopoli', in *Euplo e Lucia 304–2004. Agiografia e tradizioni cultuali in Sicilia*, ed. by Teresa Sardella & Gaetano Zito, Quaderni di Synaxis 18 (Catania: Studio Teologico S. Paolo, 2005), pp. 143–63 (pp. 155–61).

[37] καὶ παρευθὺ ἐλαία φυτὸν τελειότατον ἐν ἀχαρεῖ αὐξήματι ἀναβέβηκεν, ὅτι μὴ φέρειν καρπὸν κατακέκριται (Mioni, p. 81 [Chapter 10]).

God, I was able to see it through my prayers. I do not know for how many years this will be granted to me. But I am asking all of you who have gathered today in this church or another shrine of the martyr and have been judged worthy of the oil of the martyr's happiness[38], either through your faith or through the bubbling, to remember me and keep me in your mind every time you pray, to remember me who once was judged worthy to experience this miracle through the most divine grace. In fact, it is possible for you to evaluate this miracle, as you have heard of it and have recently experienced its performance, as you have learned it and have seen it. You can appreciate how the presence of the martyr provokes the bubbling of the oil in some lamps[39].

The allusion to Palermo was further developed in the *Passio BHG* 37, where the city actually became Agatha's homeland ('the saint and magnanimous Agatha was a native of the city of Palermo')[40]. The author of this Greek version also described her journey by adding some geographical precisions that made the story clearer. The soldiers who arrested Agatha moved from Catania to Palermo, Agatha departed from Palermo, and she arrived at Catania, where her martyrdom would take place[41]. These indications allowed the audience to visualise the unfolding narrative[42].

The episode concerning the disappointing attitude of the Palermitan citizens who abandoned Agatha was rewritten with some stylistic changes, including the use of more high-style vocabulary; for instance, the verb ἐξελέγχω was replaced by στηλιτεύω:

As she was on her way, her shoelace came loose. She set her foot on a stone and retied it. As she turned back, she saw that none of the citizens, the men and women who were previously escorting her, were following her

---

[38] See Psalm 45. 7 (= LXX 44. 8).

[39] Οὗτος ὁ λόγος — ὦ πατέρες — τῆς μάρτυρος τοῦ ἀθλητικοῦ διανύσματος, ὃν μεθ᾽ ὑμῶν ὁμιλῆσαι τῇ ἐναγωγῇ τοῦ ἐτησίου θαύματος, καὶ τῷ νῦν τρίτῳ ἐν τοῖς πρόσθεν δυοῖν χρόνοιν εὐδοκηθεὶς ὅμοια, ἴσως παραποδισμοῖς ἁμαρτίας οὐκ ἐπαξίως ἔχων ὁρᾶν, δι᾽ ὑμᾶς παρακληθέντι Θεῷ ἰδεῖν συγκεχώρημαι. Οὐκ οἶδα δ᾽ εἰς ὅσα καὶ ἔτη συγχωρηθήσομαι, ἀλλ᾽ αἰτῶ ὑμᾶς πάντας, τούς τε κατ᾽ αὐτὴν ἡμέραν, εἴτε ἐν τούτῳ τῷ ναῷ, εἴτε ἐν ἄλλῳ τῆς μάρτυρος ἀθροιζομένους, ἀξιωθέντας τοῦ ἐλαίου τῆς μαρτυρικῆς ἀγαλλιάσεως, ἢ πίστει ἢ καὶ τῷ ἐκβλύσματι, μνημονεῦσαι καὶ ἐμοῦ προσευκτικῶς ἐν τῇ διανοίᾳ, τοῦ πότε καὶ τὴν ὄψιν τοῦ θαύματος ἰδεῖν ἀξιωθέντος θεοχαρέστατα. Ἔστι γὰρ τοῦτο ἔστιν ὑμῖν τε τοῖς ἀκούσασι, καὶ πείρᾳ ἐσχάτῃ παραλαβοῦσι τὸ θαῦμα τῆς ὄψεως, τοῖς τε προμαθοῦσι καὶ προσιδοῦσι κρινόμενον, ὡς ἡ παρουσία τῆς μάρτυρος τὸν ἐκβλυσμὸν τοῦ τινων κανδήλων ἐλαίου ἐργάζεται. (Mioni, pp. 91–92 [Chapter 32]). Mioni's edition is problematic in places and needs revision.

[40] ἡ ὁσία καὶ μεγαλόφρων Ἀγάθη, ὁρμωμένη μὲν ἐκ τῆς Πανορμητῶν πόλεως (PG 114, 1332A).

[41] PG 114, coll. 1332C–33BD.

[42] On this point, see Anne Alwis, 'The Hagiographer's Craft: Narrators and Focalisation in Byzantine Hagiography', in *The Hagiographical Experiment. Developing Discourses of Sainthood*, ed. by Christa Gray & James Corke-Webster, Vigiliae Christianae, Supplements 158 (Leiden: Brill, 2020), pp. 300–32 (p. 306).

anymore. On the contrary, they forsook her and went away. Saint Agatha, deeply upset, prayed and said: My Lord, the almighty King, perform a great miracle for those who refused to believe in your servant, who intends to compete [as a martyr] on behalf of Your name. And an olive tree that cannot bear fruit appeared right away, reprimanding the people of Palermo for their attitude[43].

The author of the *Passio BHG* 37 further elaborated the episode of Quintianus's death. He stated that the governor, having been informed of Agatha's death, was heading towards Palermo in order to collect her fortune, and he specified that the river Psimethos where he drowned was situated near Catania. The fact that Agatha came from Palermo, as we can read at the beginning of the *Passio BHG* 37, explained the governor's journey to this city. The author therefore constructed a coherent narrative and explained the reason why Quintinianus left the city of Catania and how he met his death:

> When Quintinianus learned that Agatha had taken leave of this world, he moved forward in order to take hold of her possessions. Accompanied by all the members of his military parade, he hurried straight off to Palermo. While he was on his way, through the right judgement of God he was killed in a river called Psimethos, situated close to the city of Catania. As he wanted to cross this river, he entered on a ford along with his two horses. Both horses attacked him. The first one tackled his face and wiped him out, while the second one kicked him ruthlessly and finally plunged him into the river Psimethos. Although many people have searched for his body, nobody has found it up until now[44].

This information confirms the assumption that this is the Simeto river, which constituted the boundary between the province of Catania and that of Enna.

---

[43] Πορευομένης αὐτῆς, ἐλύθη τὸ περικείμενον σπαρτίον τοῦ ὑποδήματος αὐτῆς, καὶ στήσασα τὸν πόδα ἐπὶ λίθου, ἔδησεν· καὶ στραφεῖσα εἰς τὰ ὀπίσω, οὐδένα ἴδεν (*sic*) συνακολουθοῦντα αὐτῇ τῶν προπεμπόντων αὐτῇ πολιτῶν καὶ πολιτίδων, ἀλλ'ἐάσαντες αὐτὴν ἀνεχώρησαν. Ἡ δὲ ἁγία Ἀγάθη σφόδρα λυπηθεῖσα ηὔξατο λέγουσα· Δέσποτα Κύριε παντοκράτορ, διὰ τοὺς ἀπιστήσαντας τῇ σῇ δούλῃ τῇ μελλούσῃ ἀθλεῖν (ἐλθεῖν ed.) ὑπὲρ τοῦ ὀνόματός σου, δεῖξον μέγα θαῦμα. Καὶ παραχρῆμα ἀνῆλθεν ἐλαία ἄκαρπος, στηλιτεύουσα τὰς γνώμας τῶν Πανορμητῶν (PG 114, 1333C).

[44] Ἀκούσας δὲ ὁ Κυντιανός, ὅτι ἀπέστη τῶν ἐνθάδε ἡ ὁσία μάρτυς, κατὰ τῶν αὐτῆς πραγμάτων ἐχώρει καὶ λαβὼν πᾶσαν τὴν τάξιν αὐτοῦ ἐπείγετο παραγενέσθαι ἐν Πανόρμῳ· καὶ δὴ αὐτοῦ ἀπερχομένου κατὰ τὴν ὁδόν, κρίσει Θεοῦ δικαίᾳ ἀπολέσθαι αὐτὸν συνέβη ἔν τινι παρακειμένῳ ποταμῷ τῇ πόλει Κατάνῃ, ὀνόματι Ψημίθῳ. Βουλομένου γὰρ αὐτοῦ τοῦτον διαπεράσαι, εἰσῆλθεν ἐν πορθμείῳ μετὰ τῶν ἵππων αὐτοῦ, καὶ δὴ δύο ἵπποι ὥρμησαν κατ'αὐτοῦ· καὶ ὁ μὲν εἰς εἰσδραμὼν κατὰ πρόσωπον αὐτὸν ἠφάνισεν· ὁ δὲ ἕτερος λακτίσμασιν πλήσσων οὐ διέλιπεν, μέχρις ἂν αὐτὸν ἐνέβαλεν ἐν τῷ ποταμῷ Ψημίθῳ, καὶ πολλῶν ζητησάντων τὸ σῶμα αὐτοῦ, οὐχ εὑρέθη μέχρι τῆς σήμερον (PG 114, 1344C).

The symbolic punishment of the citizens of her hometown Palermo through the miracle of a tree without fruit gradually became an important element of Agatha's legend. This scene was also found in a liturgical hymn dedicated to Agatha[45] that is difficult to date with certainty but must have been inspired by the *Passio BHG* 37, as the use of similar vocabulary indicates[46]. This hymn also referred to a 'feast celebrating the martyr's memory', presumably held in Constantinople[47].

The martyrdom of saint Agatha was narrated in various strata of the Synaxarion of Constantinople[48]. Her entry was preserved even in the most ancient family of this major liturgical book, recension H according to H. Delehaye's edition[49], dating back to the time of Constantine Porphyrogenitus (mid-tenth century)[50]. The entry in this family was basically the same as the entry in recension S, edited by Delehaye in his full-page edition. The existence of the legend of saint Agatha in the most ancient strata of the Synaxarion, as well as in the *Typikon* transmitted by the Patmos manuscript[51], offered important evidence of her cult in Constantinople, attested at least by the tenth and presumably by the ninth century.

The text of the Synaxarion bears no resemblance to the *Passio BHG* 37. However, the rewriting of the legend is interesting. Not only was Palermo defined as Agatha's hometown ('She was a native of the city of Palermo, which is located in Sicily'[52]) but Catania also totally disappeared from the narrative. In other words, readers had the impression that the action took place entirely in Palermo, and Agatha thus became a Palermitan martyr. Agatha was also commemorated in the *Menologion* of Basil II[53]; the entry had some similarities with the text of recension S of the Synaxarion[54] and also made the martyr a native of Palermo[55].

---

[45] Giuseppe Schirò & Elpidios Tomadakis, *Analecta hymnica graeca e codicibus eruta Italiae inferioris* (Rome: Istituto di Studi Bizantini e Neoellenici. Università di Roma 'La Sapienza', 1974), VI, Febr. 5, ode 3.

[46] ἀκαρπίας φυτῷ στηλιτεύεις (ode 3)/ ἐλαία ἄκαρπος στηλιτεύουσα (PG 114, col. 1333C); λακτίσμασι (ode 9)/ (PG 114, col. 1344C).

[47] τὴν πανέορτον μνήμην (*Analecta hymnica graeca*, VI, Febr. 5, ode 1).

[48] *SECP*, col. 445 (Febr. 5).

[49] Library of the Patriarchate, Holy Cross 40, fols 99v–100. The text remains unpublished.

[50] See Andrea Luzzi, *Studi sul Sinassario di Constantinopoli,* Testi e Studi Bizantino-neollenici 8 (Rome: Dipartimento di filologia greca e latina. Sezione Bizantino-Neoellenica. Università di Roma 'La Sapienza', 1995), pp. 5–90.

[51] See Andrea Luzzi, 'Il Patmiacus 266: un testimone dell'utilizzo liturgico delle epitomi premetafrastiche', *Rivista di Studi Bizantini e Neoellenici*, 49 (2012), 239–61.

[52] Αὕτη ἦν ἐκ πόλεως Πανόρμου, τῆς κατὰ Σικελίαν (*SECP*, col. 445).

[53] PG 117, col. 296C-D.

[54] See the following phrases: ἐκκόπτεται, ἐπ'ὀστράκου κεκομμένου σύρεται/ ἐπάνω κεκομμένου ὀστράκου σύρεται (*SECP* 445 and PG 117, col. 296D).

[55] PG 117, col. 296C.

It is worth pointing out that the episode of the eruption of Mt. Etna and the miraculous *post mortem* intervention of the martyr was absent from the narratives of the Synaxarion. This was actually one of the basic features of Agatha's cult in Catania[56] that one can read in the *Passiones BHG* 36 and 37, as well as in Methodius's sermon. This incident was also found in a tenth-century *Oratio* in memory of Athanasius, a native of Catania who emigrated to Patras and became bishop of Methone in the Peloponnese, composed by Peter, the bishop of Argos[57]. The removal of this scene supports the conclusion that Agatha's cult in Catania was of no interest to the authors of the entries of the Synaxarion.

The Greek *dossier* of Agatha clearly reflected a tension between Catania and Palermo, because each city claimed to be the homeland and the place of martyrdom of the saint. This 'dual affiliation' of Agatha has drawn the attention of historians since the time of the historian Jean Levesque de Burigny (1692–1785)[58]. The reference to Palermo first appeared in the *Passio BHG* 36, an understudied text due to the lack of a critical edition until recently. In this text Agatha was a native of Catania who lived in Palermo when the governor summoned her. The *Life of Leo of Catania* (*BHG* 981b), a text that widely echoed the *Passio*, provided additional evidence. In this *Life* of an eighth-century bishop of the city of Catania, composed in Constantinople during the first half of the ninth century according to Alexakis[59], we read that Catania was situated 'on the borders of Panormon'[60]. Alexakis pointed out that this confusion betrayed a misreading of the expression ἔξω Κατάνης ἐν Πανόρμῳ ('in Palermo, outside Catania') found in the *Passio BHG* 36[61]. However, there was no doubt concerning the city of Agatha's martyrdom: 'a remarkable city named Catania, in which the aptly-named virgin martyr Agatha competed in the contest for immortality'[62]. The same clarity was present in Methodius's sermon (*BHG* 38), in which Agatha was also presented as a native of Catania living in Palermo, whereas in the *Passio BHG* 37, Palermo was Agatha's

---

[56] Enrico Morini, 'Sicilia, Roma e Italia suburbicaria nelle tradizioni del sinassario costantinopolitano', in *Sicilia e Italia suburbicaria*, pp. 129–84 (p. 133).

[57] Konstantinos Kyriakopoulos, Ἁγίου Πέτρου ἐπισκόπου Ἄργους Βίος καὶ Λόγοι. Εἰσαγωγή, κείμενον, μετάφρασις, σχόλια (Athens: Metropolis of Argos, 1976), p. 46 (Chapter 3).

[58] Jean Levesque de Burigny, *Histoire générale de Sicile, dans laquelle on verra toutes les différentes révolutions de cette isle depuis le temps où elle a commencé à être habitée, jusqu'à la dernière paix entre la maison de France & la maison d'Autriche* (The Hague: Isaac de Beauregard, 1745), pp. 339–42.

[59] Alexander Alexakis, *The Greek Life of St Leo bishop of Catania*, Subsidia Hagiographica 91 (Brussels: Société des Bollandistes, 2011), p. 73.

[60] ἐν ὁρίοις τῆς Πανόρμου (Alexakis, pp. 140–41).

[61] On this point, see *supra* p. 186.

[62] Alexakis, pp. 140–41.

homeland but her martyrdom still took place in Catania. In the various strata of the Synaxarion, Catania totally disappeared from the narrative and the action took place entirely in Palermo.

Scholars have interpreted the shift of Agatha's cult from Catania towards Palermo in various ways[63] and even associated this phenomenon with the existence of the monastery dedicated to Agatha by the end of the sixth century in Palermo[64]. The growing importance of the role of the city in Agatha's legend could thus be interpreted as an attempt of Palermo to claim the origins of the martyr[65]. However, the image of Palermo depicted in the *BHG* 36, 37 and 38 was rather negative, as its citizens abandoned Agatha and were blamed for their ungratefulness. This negative representation was absent only from the narratives of the Synaxarion, where Agatha was turned into a Palermitan martyr. Moreover, the confusing geographical indications regarding the two cities found in the *Passio BHG* 36 indicated poor knowledge of the local context and did not conform with a Sicilian origin for the narrative. We could thus argue that the association of the martyr with the city of Palermo seems to be of Constantinopolitan origin. It is worth noting that Agatha was the only saint of Palermo mentioned in the Synaxarion of Constantinople, whereas Catania was associated with at least three saints[66].

The entries of the *Typikon* (P) of the Great Church, as well as of recensions H and S of the Synaxarion, ended with an explicit allusion to Agatha's martyrium in Constantinople, situated 'in the Triconch'[67]. According to Janin, this Triconch was located in the Capitolium. Methodius's sermon was presumably pronounced in this martyrium[68]. Recension S$_a$ of the Synaxarion, dating from the twelfth century, implied that there was a second shrine of

---

[63] Alexakis argues that these 'confusing indications in some early Greek texts may have been one of the contributing factors that resulted in the establishment of the cult of Saint Agatha in both Catania and Palermo' (ibid. p. 198). However, Agatha's cult must have been already established in both cities before the composition of these texts. On this discussion, see also *AASS*, Febr. I, pp. 605A–605C.

[64] See *supra*, p. 184.

[65] Motta, pp. 76–80, suggests that the Greek legend of Agatha was composed in Palermo. See also Vivien Prigent, 'Palermo in the Eastern Roman Empire', in *A Companion to Medieval Palermo. The History of a Mediterranean City from 600 to 1500*, ed. by Anneliese Nef, Brill's Companions to European History 5 (Leiden: Brill, 2013), pp. 9–38 (p. 19).

[66] See the entries dedicated to the martyr Euplus (*SECP*, coll. 881–84) and to the bishops of Catania Leo and Beryllus (coll. 479–81, 551–52).

[67] ἐν τῷ μαρτυρείῳ αὐτῆς τῷ ὄντι ἐν τῷ Τρικόγχῳ (*SECP*, col. 445 - Feb. 5).

[68] Milazzo & Rizzo-Nervo, p. 132; Raymond Janin, *La géographie ecclésiastique de l'empire byzantin*, I: *Le siège de Constantinople et le patriarcat œcuménique*, III: *Les églises et les monastères* (Paris: Institut français d'études byzantines, 1969²), pp. 6–7.

the cult of Agatha in the capital, presumably remote[69]. Indeed, the prologue of recension S_a stressed the importance of the μνήμη, with the sense of commemoration, of the saints[70].

The martyrdom of Agatha also inspired the eleventh-century Byzantine writer Michael Psellos. His *Commentarius de mulierum festo* was a result of creative rewriting that indicated no direct dependence on the *Passio BHG* 37 or the entry of the Synaxarion[71]. Although Psellos made no explicit allusion to the martyrium of Agatha in Constantinople, the composition of his *Commentarius* implies that the cult of Agatha was still popular in the eleventh-century city.

The development of Agatha's cult in Constantinople could indicate the presence of her relics in the city[72]. The only source that mentioned their transfer to the capital was an account of Mauritius, the bishop of Catania (1124–1144)[73], who played a key role in the revival of the cult of Agatha during the twelfth century[74]. He composed his narrative in 1126, shortly after the transfer of Agatha's relics from Constantinople back to Catania. According to his account, the relics of the martyr were dispatched to Constantinople by the general Georgios Maniakes in 1043, during the ephemeral Byzantine conquest of the island, along with the relics of other local martyrs. The relics therefore must have been kept in the martyrium mentioned in the Synaxarion of Constantinople, until their removal and their adventurous return to

---

[69] Τελεῖται δὲ ἡ αὐτῆς σύναξις ἐν τῷ μαρτυρείῳ αὐτῆς τῷ ὄντι ἐν τῷ Τρικόγχῳ καὶ πέραν ἐν τῷ κάστρῳ τῶν Ῥῶς (*SECP*, col. 445, Synaxaria Selecta: Sa). Morini, 'Sicilia, Roma e Italia suburbicaria', p. 135, claims that the martyrium of Agatha is situated 'beyond the fortress of Ros' but the construction of the phrase in Greek clearly suggests a second place of worship.
[70] *SECP*, pp. viii–x. On this point see Sophie Métivier, 'Le Synaxaire de Constantinople, une autre manière de raconter et faire l'histoire', in *L'histoire comme elle se présentait dans l'hagiographie byzantine et médiévale*, ed. by Anna Lampadaridi and others, Acta Universitatis Upsaliensis, Studia Byzantina Upsaliensia 21 (Uppsala: Uppsala Universitet, 2022), pp. 199–217 (pp. 200–02).
[71] Konstantinos Sathas, *Μεσαιωνικὴ Βιβλιοθήκη* (Venice & Paris, 1876), V, pp. 527–31. Regarding the Byzantine reception of Agatha's legend, see also a brief homily (or part of a homily) recently edited: Mario Re, 'Agata, la colomba. Un testo inedito in onore della martire siciliana', *Rivista di Studi Bizantini e Neoellenici*, 58 (2021), 57-72.
[72] Janin claims that her relics were transferred to Constantinople at the end of the tenth or the beginning of the eleventh century, without mentioning the source of this information. See Janin, I, III, p. 7.
[73] Mauritius Episcopus Catanensis, *Historia translationis corporis S. Agathae V. M. Constantinopoli Catanam, AASS*, Febr. I, pp. 637–43. See also Angelidi, pp. 128–32 and Edina Bozoky, 'Translations de reliques prestigieuses d'Orient en Italie, fin du XIᵉ-début du XIIIᵉ siècle', *Cahiers d'Études Italiennes*, 25 (2017) https://journals.openedition.org/cei/3534?lang=en [accessed 11 January 2023].
[74] See Paul Oldfield, 'The Medieval Cult of St Agatha of Catania and the Consolidation of Christian Sicily', *Journal of Ecclesiastical History*, 62 (2011), 439–56 (p. 447).

Catania in 1126. In 1204, Enrico Dandolo gave the relics remaining in Constantinople to Sicilians, who brought them back to Catania[75].

Lucia

Lucia of Syracuse[76], often considered as the counterpart of Agatha ('il piu celebre binomio della storia religiosa di Sicilia'[77]), reportedly suffered martyrdom under Diocletian, probably in 304. Accompanied by her mother and suffering from a loss of blood, this noble virgin from Syracuse went to the martyrium of Agatha in Catania, as the martyr had become popular for her healing powers. In a dream Agatha predicted that Lucia would save Syracuse, as she herself had saved Catania. Lucia and her mother returned to Syracuse and Lucia distributed all her money to the poor, after having sold all her belongings. Worried, her betrothed asked her mother why Lucia was selling everything, and she pretended that Lucia meant to buy a property. He informed the governor Paschasios of Lucia's devotion to Christ, and the virgin appeared before him. Paschasios questioned her, threatened to take her to a brothel, ordered that human urine be poured over her, and commanded that she be dragged to the brothel by oxen; but Lucia stood firm. She declared that she would also remain untouched by the flames of the fire that the governor's servants prepared. Paschasios's friend suggested killing her with a sword. Lucia predicted the peace of the church, the fall of Diocletian, and the death of Maximian. She foretold that Syracuse would venerate her, as Catania honoured Agatha. She was beheaded on 13 December; a martyrium was built on the site of her martyrdom, and her corpse performed healing miracles.

An inscription discovered in 1894 in the Catacomb of S. Giovanni in Syracuse celebrated the memory of a 25-year-old woman named Euskia who died on the day of the feast of Lucia (τῇ ἑορτῇ τῆς κυρίας μου Λουκίας)[78]. Paolo Orsi, who discovered the inscription, assumed that it dated to the end of the fourth or the beginning of the fifth century and considered it to be the most ancient evidence for Lucia as a patron saint of the blind, as the name Euskia had been associated with the word σκιά, 'shade'. However, this theory is highly hypothetical, and there is no secure evidence for dating the inscription

---

[75] Andreae Danduli ducis Venetiarum *Chronica per extensum descripta (aa. 46–1280 d.C.)*, ed. by Ester Pastorello, Rerum Italicarum scriptores 12. 1 (Bologna: N. Zachinelli, 1937), p. 280.

[76] See CSLA E02092 (Matthieu Pignot) and CSLA E07563 (Nikolaos Kälviäinen).

[77] Rossi Taibbi, p. 13.

[78] Paolo Orsi, 'Insigne epigrafe del cimitero di S. Giovanni in Siracusa', *Roemische Quartalschrift*, 9 (1895), 299–308; Milazzo & Rizzo-Nervo, pp. 99, 109.

that early. In addition, the representation of Lucia as the protector of sight was attested in iconography no earlier than the fourteenth century[79].

The cult of Lucia in Syracuse was established by the end of the sixth century. At the time of Gregory the Great, a monastery dedicated to Lucia was attested in Syracuse. In his letter to Iohannes, bishop of Syracuse, written in 597, Gregory referred to a dispute between a monastery dedicated to the Apostle Peter and the monastery of Lucia in Syracuse[80]. In another letter to Iohannes, bishop of Syracuse, written in 603, Gregory referred to a former monk of this monastery named Cosmas[81]. In Rome, Lucia's cult was also present by the end of the sixth century. In his *Dialogues* (*c.* 593) Gregory the Great mentioned the monastery of *Renatus* and its abbot Probus[82]. This was actually a monastery dedicated to Andrew and Lucia; in a letter written in 600, Gregory referred to the same person, the abbot Probus, calling him *abbas monasterii sanctorum Andreae et Luciae*[83]. Both names of the monastery were mentioned in the *Liber Pontificalis*[84]. The monastery was also mentioned in the Acts of the Lateran Council of 649, according to which it was occupied by Greek-speaking Armenian monks[85]. Lucia's cult was thus associated with the Greek-speaking diaspora of oriental monks. Traces of her cult could also be found in Catania. In the *Life of Leo of Catania* (*BHG* 981b), we read that Leo was buried in the church of St Lucia, which he himself had built.

> A most beautiful and admired church was built for the great virgin-martyr of Christ, Lucia, brilliantly adorned by his craftsmanship and diligence with the beauty and magnificence of every kind of ornament. Here the immaculate body of Leo's godlike and blessed soul was honoured and laid to rest reverently and gloriously'[86].

---

[79] Milazzo & Rizzo-Nervo, p. 110.

[80] Gregory the Great, *Register of Letters* VII. 36, CCSL 140 (1982), p. 499, CSLA E06376 (Frances Trzeciak).

[81] Gregory the Great, *Register of Letters* XIII. 30, CCSL 140A (1982), p. 1031, CSLA E06434 (Frances Trzeciak).

[82] Gregory the Great, *Dialogues* IV. 13, ed. by Adalbert de Vogüé, *Grégoire le Grand, Dialogues*, SC 265 (1980), III, pp. 52–55.

[83] Gregory the Great, *Register of Letters* XI. 15, ed. by Norberg, CCSL 140A (1982), pp. 881–84.

[84] *Liber Pontificalis* 98, ed. by Duchesne, p. 24.

[85] Rudolf Riedinger, *Concilium Lateranense a. 649 celebratum*, Acta Conciliorum Oecumenicorum II. 1 (Berlin: De Gruyter, 1984), p. 50; Jean-Marie Sansterre, *Les moines grecs et orientaux à Rome aux époques byzantine et carolingienne (milieu du VIᵉ s.–fin du IXᵉ s.)*, 2 vols, Académie Royale de Belgique. Mémoires de la Classe des Lettres II. 64 (Brussels: Palais des Académies, 1982), I, pp. 12–13; Milazzo & Rizzo-Nervo, pp. 119, 133–34.

[86] For the text and the translation, see Alexakis, pp. 148–51 (Chapter 7) and p. 214.

This *Life* remains the only source to mention such a martyrium.

The *Passio* of Lucia has survived in both Greek (*BHG* 995–96) and Latin (*BHL* 4992) versions, considered to represent two different branches of the text's tradition[87]. The Latin legend was widely spread (approximately 200 manuscripts) and used by later writers[88]. Like the *Passio* of Agatha, it was one of the most popular Latin hagiographical texts[89]. Along with Agatha, Aldhelm, in his prose treatise entitled *On Virginity* (c. 675/86), named Lucia as an exemplary virgin; this reference offered a secure *terminus ante quem* for the composition of the Latin martyrdom[90]. As an argument for an early dating of the text, Cécile Lanéry[91] points out that borrowings from the Latin *Martyrdom of Lucia* can be found in the *Passio* of the Roman martyrs Lucia and Geminianus, dated to the second half of the seventh or the beginning of the eighth century[92]. The legend of the Sicilian martyr inspired the *Passio* of the Roman Lucia.

The publication of a Latin translation of the Greek *Passio* by the Jesuit Ottavio Gaetani in the middle of the seventeenth century[93], followed by the edition of the Greek text one century later[94], stirred up debate concerning the relationship between the Greek and Latin versions of Lucia's *Passio*. Scholars have commonly recognized the primacy of the Greek version, generally dated to the fifth century and surviving in fewer manuscripts[95], and considered it to be closer to the earliest version of the story[96]. The Greek text is certainly devoid of some distracting passages. In the Latin version, when a report arrived from Sicily recording that the governor, Paschasios, had plundered the whole province, Lucia's persecutor was enchained and sent to Rome; after a hearing in the Senate, he was sentenced to death[97]. Lucia received communion

---

[87] Ferruccio Bertini & Sandra Isetta, 'Passio Luciae *BHL* 4992', in *Le légendier de Turin*, pp. 373–83 (p. 373).

[88] Bertini & Isetta, pp. 373–74.

[89] Philippart, p. 183.

[90] Aldhelm, *De virginitate* 42, ed. by Ehwald, p. 293; Milazzo & Rizzo-Nervo, p. 102, CSLA E06578 (Benjamin Savill). Also see *supra*, note 12.

[91] Lanéry, pp. 285–86.

[92] Mario Re, 'La Passio dei SS. Lucia e Geminiano (*BHG* 2241). Introduzione, edizione del testo, traduzione e note', *Νέα Ῥώμη*, 5 (2008), 75–146 (pp. 98–99).

[93] Ottavio Gaetani, *Vitae sanctorum siculorum ex antiquis graecis latinisque monumentis...*, I (Palermo, 1657), pp. 114–15.

[94] Giovanni Di Giovanni, *Acta sincera Sanctae Luciae Virginis et martyris siracusanae ex optimo codice graeco nunc primum edita et illustrata*, I (Palermo: 1758).

[95] *BHG* 995 survives in 15 manuscripts, see Taibbi, pp. 34–37. See also the list available on *Pinakes* https://pinakes.irht.cnrs.fr/notices/oeuvre/16724/ (also including other recensions of the *Passio*).

[96] Milazzo & Rizzo-Nervo, pp. 97–98.

[97] Bertini & Isetta, p. 383.

before dying[98]. On the other hand, the Greek *Passio* was the only account to mention the miracles *post mortem*, consisting of the healings accomplished by the martyr's relic.

> A shrine was constructed in her honour in the place where she drew her dying breath. There, through her intercession, those who advance towards her relic with faith receive blessing and are cured from their diseases, while glorifying our Lord Jesus Christ, to whom be glory for ever and ever[99].

The Greek *Martyrdom* of Lucia inspired many Byzantine rewritings in Sicily and beyond. The *Passio BHG* 995d[100] was the work of a native of Syracuse who wrote to honour his fellow citizen, as well as his hometown[101]. For him, Lucia was a 'scion of our own homeland'[102]. This rewriting of the ancient *Passio* was typical of high-style hagiography generally dated to the ninth and tenth centuries[103] and must have been completed before the Arab conquest of Syracuse in 878, as there was no allusion to the conquerors. The text was composed on the occasion of the saint's festival ('she [Lucia] has invited us to a splendid feast today')[104] and thus offers important evidence on the cult of Lucia in Syracuse shortly before the Arab invasion. This *Passio* is written in an elaborated style, including citations from Sophocles, Plutarch, and the Bible, and a more dramatized tone with many dialogues. The first episodes were more developed, stressing the bond between Lucia and her mother and describing the martyr's vision[105]. The hagiographer further described the women's mourning after arrival at Agatha's shrine[106]. Lucia even addressed a long prayer to Agatha, in which she emphasized her affection towards her mother: 'you know how strong is the affection that an only daughter displays for her mother'[107]. She fell asleep and had a vision[108]. The author of *BHG* 995d went as far as to revisit some of the characters. For instance, contrary to the

---

[98] Ibid.

[99] Ἐν αὐτῷ δὲ τῷ τόπῳ ἐν ᾧ τὸ πνεῦμα ἀπέδοτο, ᾠκοδομήθη αὐτῇ ναός· ἐν ᾧ, αὐτῆς πρεσβευούσης εὐεργεσίας καὶ παθῶν ἴασιν λαμβάνουσιν οἱ πίστει προσερχόμενοι τῷ λειψάνῳ αὐτῆς, δοξάζοντες τὸν κύριον ἡμῶν Ἰησοῦν Χριστόν, ᾧ ἡ δόξα καὶ τὸ κράτος εἰς τοὺς αἰῶνας τῶν αἰώνων (Rossi Taibbi, p. 70).

[100] Salvatore Costanza, 'Un «martyrion» inedito di S. Lucia di Syracusa', *Archivio Storico Syracusano*, 3 (1957), 5–53.

[101] Costanza, pp. 11–13; Motta, pp. 61–64.

[102] ἐξ αὐτῆς ἡμῖν τῆς πατρίδος καθάπερ τις ἰθυγενὴς ὄρπηξ ἀναδοθεῖσα (Costanza, p. 11).

[103] Efthymiadis, p. 374.

[104] λαμπρὰν ἡμῖν τὴν πανήγυριν σήμερον συγκεκρότηκεν (Costanza, p. 11).

[105] On the importance of this element for the narrative, see Teresa Sardella, 'Visioni oniriche e immagini di santità nel martirio di S. Lucia', in *Storia della Sicilia*, pp. 137–54.

[106] Costanza, p. 17.

[107] καὶ οἶδας ὅσον ἐστὶ τὸ φίλτρον πρὸς μητέρα μονογενοῦς θυγατρός (Costanza, p. 19).

[108] Costanza, p. 19.

earlier *Passio*, the mother suggested to her daughter to keep her possessions, get married, and not rush to embrace Christianity, but Lucia insisted that she could not care for an earthly bridegroom. On the other hand, the hagiographer cut out information that was not of any interest to him, such as the prophecy of Lucia before her martyrdom.

Lucia's legend also reached Constantinople. The epitome *BHG* 995e, published by François Halkin, was preserved in a premetaphrastic *menologion* of December kept in Istanbul (Library of the Patriarchate, Hagias Trias 88) and copied at the Stoudios monastery at the end of the ninth or the beginning of the tenth century[109]. It seems to be the oldest Constantinopolitan piece of Lucia's *dossier* that we have. A significant number of linguistic similarities between this abridged version of Lucia's martyrdom and the entries concerning the same martyr in families H[110] and S of the Synaxarion of Constantinople (not found in the Greek text *BHG* 995)[111] indicate that this epitome must have been the source for the compilers of the liturgical book[112]. We know that the authors of the Synaxarion tended to draw on shortened versions of *Lives* of saints and *Passiones*, rather than on the original *Lives*, in order to compose their entries[113]. In contrast to the entry on Agatha, Lucia's origins

---

[109] François Halkin, 'Une passion grecque abrégée de sainte Lucie', *Classica et Mediaevalia. Mélanges Carsten Høeg*, 17 (1956), 71–74; Milazzo & Rizzo-Nervo, pp. 130–31. On this manuscript, see *Catalogue des manuscrits conservés dans la Bibliothèque du Patriarcat œcuménique: Les manuscrits du monastère de la Sainte-Trinité de l'île de Chalkè*, 2 vols, ed. by André Binggeli and others (Turnhout: Brepols, 2019), I, fols 237–41.

[110] Library of the Patriarchate, Holy Cross, 40, fols 62–62v. The text remains unpublished.

[111] Morini, 'Sicilia, Roma e Italia suburbicaria', p. 134, suggests that the entry of the Synaxarion is not far from the *Passiones BHG* 995 and 995d.

[112]

BHG 995e (Halkin, 'Une passion', pp. 73–74)	*SECP*, col. 306 (Dec. 13)
Ἡ ἁγία καὶ ἔνδοξος παρθενομάρτυς Λουκία ἦν ἐκ Συρακούσης τῆς Σικελῶν νήσου, **μεμνηστευμένη ἀνδρί·** ἥτις πόθῳ τῆς ἁγίας μάρτυρος Ἀγάθης φερομένη, μετὰ τῆς ἰδίας μητρὸς **αἱμορροίας** πάθος ἐχούσης... **διεβλήθη ὑπὸ τοῦ ὁρμασαμένου αὐτήν·** καὶ κατασχεθεῖσα προσήχθη τῷ ἄρχοντι... ἀρξαμένων οὖν πλήθος στρατιωτῶν ἕλκειν, **μετακινῆσαι αὐτὴν ἐκ τοῦ τόπου** οὐκ **ἠδυνήθησαν...** Διαπορηθεὶς δὲ ὁ ἄρχων **ἀνάπτει πυρὰν** ἐν τῷ τόπῳ ὥστε **καταφλέξαι αὐτήν...**Ἡ δὲ ἀβλαβὴς διὰ τῆς πυρᾶς διαμείνασα **ξίφει τὴν κεφαλὴν ἀποτέμνεται.**	Αὕτη ἦν ἐκ Συρακούσης τῆς πόλεως, τῆς κατὰ Σικελίαν, **μεμνηστευμένη ἀνδρί...** δεηθησομένη τῆς κυρίας μάρτυρος Ἀγάθης ἀπαλλάξαι τῆς **αἱμορροίας** τὴν ταύτης μητέραν...Παρὰ δὲ τοῦ μνηστῆρος **διαβληθεῖσα** παρέστη τῷ ἄρχοντι...**μὴ δυνηθέντων**, καίπερ πολλῶν συνελθόντων, **μετακινῆσαι αὐτὴν ἐκ τοῦ τόπου**, ἔνθα ἐστήρικτο. Ἀπαγορεύσαντες δὲ τὴν αὐτῆς μετάβασιν καὶ μηδὲ **διὰ τῆς πυρᾶς, ἣν ἀνήψαν**, ἔνθα ἡ ἁγία ἵστατο, **αὐτὴν καταφλέξαντες**, διὰ τὸ ὑπὸ Θεοῦ ταύτην φυλάττεσθαι, **ξίφει τὴν αὐτῆς ἀπέτεμον κεφαλήν.**

[113] See e.g. Anna Lampadaridi, 'L'histoire de saint Porphyre de Gaza de la *Vita* aux notices du *Synax. CP*', *Analecta Bollandiana*, 129 (2011), 241–46 (p. 241 with bibliography).

were maintained in the Synaxarion and her adherence to the city of Syracuse was clearly stated. 'She was a native of the city of Syracuse, which is located in Sicily'[114]. The text on Lucia found in the *Menologion* of Basil II was slightly different from that of the Synaxarion, without any clear dependence on the Epitome[115].

In his canon dedicated to the martyr Lucia, the patriarch Methodius referred to the feast celebrated in her memory, drawing on the *Passio BHG* 995[116]. Another canon in honour of Lucia was composed by Ioannes the Monk[117].

In the context of the Norman Conquest of Sicily, the Constantinopolitan scholar Ioannes Tzetzes dedicated an *encomium* to the martyr in the twelfth century (*BHG* 996)[118]. The text was composed in the same high style as the *Passio BHG* 995d, but there were no linguistic borrowings. Tzetzes stressed the Syracusian origins of the martyr ('I am Syracusian by birth')[119] and dedicated a long section to the Greek heritage of the island. The scholar emphasized Lucia's wish for freedom, something that one can read as an implicit allusion to the Norman Conquest[120]. His narrative was indicative of a local patriotism and underlined the importance of Lucia as patron saint of Syracuse; this localism was actually the main feature of her cult, according to the pieces of her Greek *dossier*. Tzetzes also slightly rewrote the legend. For instance, it took longer for Lucia to persuade her mother to go to Catania, and the two women wept over Agatha's shrine in a more dramatized tone, just as in the *Passio BHG* 995d[121].

As already stated, according to the account of Mauritius, the twelfth-century bishop of Catania, Georgios Maniakes transferred the relics of Agatha to Constantinople in 1043 along with the relics of other local martyrs[122]. Two southern Italian sources, the account of the expedition by Amatus de

---

[114] Αὕτη ἦν ἐκ Συρακούσης τῆς πόλεως, τῆς κατὰ Σικελίαν (*SECP*, col. 306).

[115] PG 117, coll. 204D–205A.

[116] Athanasios Kominis & Giuseppe Schirò, *Analecta hymnica graeca e codicibus eruta Italiae inferioris*, IV (Rome: Istituto di Studi Bizantini e Neoellenici. Università di Roma, 1976), Dec. 13, canon 21.

[117] Kominis and Schirò, *Analecta hymnica graeca*, IV, Dec. 13, canon 20.

[118] Athanasios Papadopoulos-Kerameus, *Varia Graeca Sacra* (Saint Petersburg: Kirsbaum, 1910), pp. 80–97. The edition of the text presents various problems. This encomium was interpreted as an attempt to gain the goodwill of William II but this statement remains highly hypothetical. See Milazzo & Rizzo-Nervo, p. 135; Efthymiadis, p. 352.

[119] Συρακουσία τὸ γένος καθέστηκα (Papadopoulos-Kerameus, p. 93).

[120] Papadopoulos-Kerameus, p. 88.

[121] Papadopoulos-Kerameus, p. 86.

[122] See *supra*, p. 193.

Montecassino[123], written around 1080, and the *Chronicle of Montecassino*[124], composed between 1087 and 1105, mentioned the relics of Lucia among the relics 'of other local martyrs' dispatched to Constantinople by Maniakes[125]. In 1204 these relics were transferred from Constantinople to Venice[126].

Euplus

Euplus was reportedly martyred in Catania on 12 August 304, fifty-three years after the martyrdom of Agatha in the same city[127]. The first part of his trial supposedly took place in Catania on 29 April, in the year of Diocletian's ninth consulship. Euplus showed up at the government house, the *secretarium*, and shouted that he was a Christian and wanted to die. He appeared before the *corrector* Kalvisianos, carrying the holy Gospels and stating that he had no home. At the request of the governor, Euplus read from the Gospels and declared that he had received them from Jesus Christ. Kalvisianos ordered him to be brought to a public trial. Euplus stood in public before the tribunal while Kalvisianos told him that his confession had been taken down in the record. He ordered Euplus to hand over the books and to be beaten until he promised to sacrifice to the gods. Euplus endured the contest of martyrdom, and Kalvisianos ordered him to be executed by the sword.

As mentioned above, the Latin inscription, probably from the early fourth century, commemorating the last hours of Julia Florentina does not offer secure evidence for the establishment of the cult of Agatha or Euplus in Catania[128]. At the end of the sixth century a basilica was dedicated to the martyrs Stephen, Pancras of Taormina, and Euplus in Messina by its bishop Felix, according to a letter of Gregory the Great[129]. During the first centuries the cult of Euplus did not seem to spread beyond Sicily. His veneration in Rome was attested for the first time in the seventh century and was associated with the popes of oriental origins. Theodore I (642–49), a native of Jerusalem, built, dedicated, and decorated an oratory in his honour outside

---

[123] Amatus of Montecassino, *The History of the Normans*, 2. 9, trans. by Prescott N. Dunbar & Graham A. Loud (Woodbridge: The Boydell Press, 2004), p. 75.

[124] *Chronica Monasterii Casinensis* II. 66, ed. Hartmut Hoffmann, *Die Chronik von Montecassino*, MGH Scr. 34, p. 298.

[125] Oldfield, p. 441.

[126] Giovanni Musolino, *Santa Lucia a Venezia. Storia, culto, arte* (Venice: Stamperia di Venezia, 1987), p. 67.

[127] See CSLA E00394 and CSLA E00395 (both by Efthymios Rizos).

[128] *CIL* X, 7112; Motta, p. 44, n. 75.

[129] Gregory the Great, *Register of Letters* II. 6, CCSL 140 (1982), p. 94; Maria Stelladoro, *Euplo/Euplio martire. Dalla tradizione greca manoscritta* (Cinisello Balsamo: San Paolo, 2006), p. 78; CSLA E06330 (Frances Trzeciak).

St Paul's Gate, according to the *Liber Pontificalis*[130]; the edifice was later restored by Hadrian I (772–95)[131]. The cult of Euplus arrived in Naples only in the second half of the tenth century and reached Greece by the eleventh century, when he was represented in the mosaics of Daphni[132].

The *Passion* of Euplus was apparently compiled in Catania during the fourth century[133]. It has survived in both Greek and Latin versions; even if their relationship cannot be precisely determined (because many pieces of the Latin *dossier* remain unpublished[134]), the Greek *Passio BHG* 629[135], which survives in a single eleventh-century manuscript (National Library of France, Parisinus gr. 1173), seems to preserve an earlier form of the text than the *Passio BHL* 2728[136], considered to be the earliest Latin version of the martyrdom. The narrative basically consisted of dialogue scenes and described what may have been a genuine account of the trial. The Greek text is thought to have provided more accurate information concerning the two phases of the trial (the Latin only mentions 12 August 304, whereas the Greek also refers to the date of the first phase), and it mentioned the titles of the characters. In the Greek text, Kalvisianos was defined as a *corrector provinciae*, attested in Sicily under the Tetrarchs, whereas the Latin called him *consularis* and *praefectus*; he is not known from any other source.[137]

The legend of Euplus gave rise to many rewritings in the Byzantine world. The metaphrastic *Passio BHG* 630[138], transmitted in ten manuscripts[139], profoundly reshuffled *BHG* 629. To begin with, it introduced Pentagouros, an enigmatic figure supposedly sent by the emperors to Sicily in order to promote paganism and torture Christians[140]. The narrative of the Metaphrastes revealed a good knowledge of the geography of the city; Kalvisianos

---

[130] *Liber Pontificalis* 75, ed. by Duchesne, pp. 333–34, n. 12; CSLA E01629 (Robert Wiśniewski).

[131] *Liber Pontificalis* 97, ed. by Duchesne, pp. 508, 520 n. 94); Stelladoro, *Euplo/Euplio*, pp. 77–79.

[132] Stelladoro, *Euplo/Euplio*, pp. 80–81.

[133] Motta, pp. 65–66.

[134] Philippart, pp. 179–82.

[135] Pio Petro Franchi de' Cavalieri, 'Note agiografiche', Studi e Testi 49 (Rome: Tipografia poliglotta vaticana, 1928), pp. 47–48; Herbert Musurillo, *The Acts of the Christian Martyrs* (Oxford: Clarendon Press, 1972), pp. 310–13.

[136] Musurillo, pp. 314–19.

[137] See *PLRE* 1: 177. The historicity of this governor is rejected.

[138] PG 115, coll. 524B–29C.

[139] According to the list available on *Pinakes*: https://pinakes.irht.cnrs.fr/notices/oeuvre/15509/.

[140] PG 115, col. 524B.

welcomed Euplus and installed his tribunal in a place named Ἀχίλλιον[141]. This was the place of execution where the magician Heliodorus was burned to ashes ('an execution site for the condemned') in the *Life of Leo of Catania* (*BHG* 981b)[142], mentioned above in relation to the *Passiones* of Agatha and Lucia[143]. The people of Catania appeared before him, and Pentagouros and Kalvisianos affirmed that they all worshiped pagan gods. Pentagouros gave to Kalvisianos the edict of the emperors and appointed him prefect of the city. Pentagouros set out to visit the other cities of Sicily, particularly Agrigento. Kalvisianos was informed of the presence of a foreigner named Euplus:

> Some people in the audience told him: 'Our Lord, there is a foreigner here named Euplus, who has a small book with him; with this book he deceives the crowd by saying that the God of the Christians is great'. Having heard that, Kalvisianos was shocked and said: 'Chain and bring me this man quickly'. His servants left and ran through the streets of the city until they finally found him; he was living in a cell and was teaching the Gospel of God to the crowd. They entered, rushed forward, bound him with chains, and brought him before the tribunal of the prefect Kalvisianos[144].

Euplus was no longer a 'voluntary' martyr, but a sort of 'itinerant preacher'[145]. He was asked to worship the gods Zeus, Asklepios, Artemis, and 'Galenos'[146]. His tortures were extensively described: 'he was hanged on a stake and his skin was thoroughly scraped using iron instruments'[147]. As Euplus persevered in his faith, Kalvisianos ordered his lower legs to be beaten with hammers[148]. He was sent to prison with the book of the Gospels tied around his neck to make him look ridiculous[149]. At this point he was refreshed by a

---

[141] Ibid. Gaetani, I, pp. 110–13; Motta, pp. 53–55; Stelladoro, *Euplo/Euplio*, pp. 54–55.

[142] Alexakis, pp. 182–83 (Chapter 34). As we know from other sources, it used to be a bath, which is compatible with the information given in the *Passion* of Euplus (ibid., pp. 240, 259).

[143] See *supra*, pp. 191, 195-96.

[144] Τινὲς οὖν τῶν παρεστώτων εἶπον αὐτῷ· Δέσποτα, ἔστιν ἐνθάδε τις ξένος ὀνόματι Εὔπλος ἔχων βιβλιαρίδιον μεθ᾽ἑαυτοῦ καὶ ἐν τούτῳ ἀπατᾷ τὸ πλῆθος τοῦ λαοῦ. Τότε ἀκούσας ὁ Καλβισιανὸς καὶ ταραχθεὶς εἶπεν· Σπουδαίως δέσμιον προσαγάγετέ μοι αὐτόν. Ἀπελθόντες δὲ οἱ ὑπηρέται, καὶ διαδραμόντες τὰς πλατείας τῆς πόλεως, εὗρον αὐτὸν ἐν κελλίῳ διάγοντα καὶ διδάσκοντα τοὺς λαοὺς τὸ εὐαγγέλιον τοῦ Θεοῦ. Καὶ εἰσελθόντες, ἐπέδραμον πρὸς αὐτόν· καὶ δήσαντες αὐτόν, ἤνεγκαν ἔμπροσθεν τοῦ βήματος Καλβισιανοῦ τοῦ ἐπάρχου (PG 115, 525B).

[145] Morini, 'Sicilia, Roma e Italia suburbicaria', p. 134.

[146] Διῒ καὶ Ἀσκληπιῷ καὶ Ἀρτέμιδι καὶ Γαληνῷ (PG 115, 525C). Galenos may refer to the Roman god Mars, who is mentioned in the Latin *Passio BHL* 2728, but this assessment is highly dubious. See Motta, p. 57.

[147] καὶ κρεμασθῆναι ἐπὶ τοῦ ξύλου καὶ χεῖρας σιδηρᾶς γενέσθαι καὶ καταξέεσθαι τὰς σάρκας αὐτοῦ ἐπιμελῶς (PG 115, 525D).

[148] PG 115, coll. 527A-B.

[149] PG 115, coll. 528B.

miracle. After seven days in prison, when Euplus was thirsty and prayed to God, his cell was filled with water: 'suddenly plenty of water was spraying up inside the prison'[150]. He miraculously made the water disappear and appeared before Kalvisianos, who ordered claws made of iron to be put on his ears. Kalvisianos's throne was placed next to the prison in front of the bathhouse. Before his martyrdom, Euplus once again read the Gospels and enlightened the crowd[151]. His corpse was put in a noteworthy place by some monks and accomplished miraculous healings[152].

Euplus found his place in the Synaxarion of Constantinople and was also commemorated in the Typikon of the Great Church[153]. However, the Synaxarion clearly mentioned Catania as his home city and entirely transformed his identity, defining him as a 'deacon' of the local church[154]. The text related to Euplus found in the *Menologion* of Basil II depended on recension S[155].

The *Epitome BHG* 630d[156] was edited on the basis of the ms. Vindobonensis hist. gr. 45, a premetaphrastic menologium of August compiled in Constantinople in the eleventh century[157]. On the basis of a significant number of linguistic borrowings, we can assume that this abridged version of the *Passio* was the source of the entry of the Synaxarion[158]. Contrary to the other narratives, this *Epitome* was the only Greek version to present Euplus explicitly as a deacon of the church of Catania, an element also found in the entries of the Synaxarion. In terms of the narrative, *BHG* 630d had many

---

[150] ἄφνω ἀνῆλθεν πλησμονὴ ὕδατος ἐνδόθεν τῆς φυλακῆς (PG 115, 528C-D).
[151] PG 115, coll. 529A-B.
[152] PG 115, coll. 529B-C.
[153] *SECP*, coll. 881–84, see also the apparatus. Recension H also contained an entry about Euplus but not on 11 August. His legend should be found on 29 April but the ms. Library of the Patriarchate, Holy Cross 40 that we have examined is mutilated at this point.
[154] *SECP*, col. 881.
[155] PG 117, col. 581A-B.
[156] Franchi de' Cavalieri, pp. 209–10.
[157] Albert Ehrhard, *Überlieferung und Bestand der hagiographischen und homiletischen Literatur der griechischen Kirche von den Anfängen bis zum Ende des 16ten Jahrhunderts*, I Texte und Untersuchungen, 50 (Leipzig: J. N. Hinrichs Verlag, 1937), pp. 682–88. According to *Pinakes*, the *Epitome BHG* 630d can also be read in the eleventh century ms. Benaki Museum, T.A. 141.
[158]

BHG 630d (Franchi de' Cavalieri, pp. 209–10)	*SECP*, col. 881–84 (Aug. 11)
Ὁ ἅγιος μάρτυς **Εὔπλος** ἦν ἐπὶ **Διοκλητιανοῦ** τοῦ βασιλέως ἐκ τῆς πόλεως **Κατάνης** τῆς Σικελῶν ἐπαρχίας, διάκονος τῆς ἐκκλησίας τῆς αὐτῆς πόλεως·	Ἄθλησις τοῦ ἁγίου μάρτυρος Εὔπλου· ὃς ἦν ἐπὶ Διοκλητιανοῦ βασιλέως, ἐκ πόλεως Κατάνης τῆς Σικελῶν ἐπαρχίας, διάκονος τῆς ἐκεῖσε ἐκκλησίας.

similarities with the Metaphrastes' rewriting of the legend. Euplus was no longer a voluntary martyr but was denounced to the governor Kalvisianos, he suffered the same tortures, and he accomplished the same miracle with the source of water as in the metaphrastic *Passio*. But as already stated, the Metaphrastes undertook a radical elaboration of the legend of *Passio BHG* 629. We can even doubt that the latter was the direct model that he used. It is clear that the metaphrastic *Passio* was more closely linked to the *Epitome BHG* 630d. The Metaphrastes may have drawn directly on the abridged *Passio BHG* 630d or on a longer version of this *Epitome* now lost. The *Epitome BHG* 630d thus played an important role in the development of the Greek legend of Saint Euplus.

Euplus also inspired later Byzantine poets, such as Christophoros Mytilenaios (eleventh century)[159] and Theodoros Prodromos (twelfth century), who briefly referred to him. The latter seems to have read the metaphrastic *Passio BHG* 630, on the basis of a linguistic borrowing regarding Euplus's martyrdom[160]. A *Laudatio* dedicated to the martyr has been attributed to the Byzantine scholar of the Palaiologan era Constantinos Akropolites (thirteenth-fourteenth century), who also drew on the metaphrastic *Passion BHG* 630[161]. The novel-like rewriting of the Metaphrastes was more popular than the oldest *Passion BHG* 629 among Byzantine scholars.

...προσέταξεν ὁ ἄρχων τὰς δύο χεῖρας αὐτοῦ δεθῆναι καὶ τὸν ἕνα πόδα τοῖς δυσὶ γόνασιν....ἐκέλευσε παγῆναι ξύλον καὶ ἐν αὐτῷ τὸν μάρτυρα **κρεμασθέντα χερσὶ σιδηραῖς ἀφειδῶς ξέεσθαι**... ...**σφύραις σιδηραῖς τὰς σιαγόνας καὶ τὰς κνήμας αὐτοῦ θλάττεσθαι** προσέταξεν... ποιήσας τε ἐν τῇ εἰρκτῇ ἡμέρας ζ΄ μὴ γευσάμενός τινος, ἐδίψησε, καὶ προσευξαμένου αὐτοῦ **ἀνεδόθη πηγὴ ὕδατος ἐν τῇ φυλακῇ**... ...**τὸν μάρτυρα τῆς φυλακῆς ἐκβαλεῖν**... ...πρῶτον μὲν **σιδήροις ὀξέσι πεπυρακτωμένοις τὰς ἀκοὰς αὐτοῦ κατετρήθη** [...] ἔπειτα δεξάμενος τὴν διὰ τοῦ **ξίφους** ἀπόφασιν τὴν κεφαλὴν ἀποτέμνεται...	...πρῶτον μὲν δεσμεῖται **χεῖρας καὶ πόδας πρὸς τοῖς γόνασιν**. Ἔπειτα κρεμᾶται ἐπὶ ξύλου ὀρθοῦ καὶ **χερσὶ σιδηραῖς ξέεται**... Μετὰ δὲ ταῦτα **σφύραις σιδηραῖς τὰς κνήμας αὐτοῦ θλάττεται** καὶ ἐν τῇ εἱρκτῇ ἀπορριφθεὶς εὐχῇ μόνῃ **πηγὴν ὕδατος** πεποίηκεν **ἀναδοθῆναι ἐν τῇ φυλακῇ**· εἶτα πάλιν ἐκβληθεὶς **σιδήροις ὀξέσι πεπυρακτωμένοις τὰς ἀκοὰς αὐτοῦ κατετρήθη**, καὶ αὖθις τῇ τοῦ **ξίφους** τιμωρίᾳ κατεδικάσθη.

[159] Enrica Follieri, *I calendari in metro innografico di Cristoforo Mitileneo*, Subsidia Hagiographica 63 (Brussels: Société des Bollandistes, 1980), I, Aug. Stichera — canon, l. 17, 54.

[160] ἐτελειώθη διὰ τοῦ ξίφους (PG 115, col. 529C) / Ὁ ἅγιος Εὔπλος ξίφει τελειοῦται. Σῶν, μάρτυς Εὔπλε, τίς λάθοιτο θαυμάτων; (Augusta Acconcia Longo, *Il calendario giambico in monostici di Teodoro Prodromo*, Testi e studi Bizantino-Neoellenici 5 (Rome: Istituto di Studi Bizantini e Neoellenici. Università di Roma, 1983), Aug. 11, l. 1.

[161] Elissavet Chartavella, *Βυζαντινά Εγκώμια για τον Άγιο Εύπλο* (unpublished DPhil Dissertation, University of Thessaloniki, 2014), pp. 35–48 (edition) and 20–23 (relationship with the work of the Metaphrastes).

A thorough reading of the above pieces of the Greek *dossier* of the *Passio* of Euplus demonstrates that the Latin version actually mingled elements found in different Greek recensions and thus bears the marks of a later rewriting. For instance, Euplus was defined as a deacon (*diaconus*), a description found in the *Epitome BHG* 630d and the entries of the Synaxarion; the pagan gods that he was forced to worship were explicitly mentioned (Mars, Apollo, Aesculapius); and his book was fastened to his neck before his execution[162], two details found in the metaphrastic *Passio BHG* 630.

Many mysteries still remain concerning the story of his relics[163]. During the Arab invasion, around 974–75, his relics disappeared from Catania. We do not know if they were transferred to Constantinople along with those of saint Agatha and saint Lucia by Georgios Maniakes. Later they were claimed by Trevico in Campania, where they supposedly rested in the Cathedral of Santa Maria Assunta. In 1284 Euplus became the patron of Trevico.

Overview

Bilingualism clearly distinguished this first phase of Sicilian hagiographical production from the next period of local hagiographical narratives, when Greek texts prevailed over the Latin ones[164]. The study of the three *dossiers* about Agatha, Lucia, and Euplus shows how these different linguistic traditions not only existed side-by-side, but also interacted constantly. Most of the material that we dealt with comes from the eastern part of the island (except the reference to Palermo in the story of Agatha). This emphasis is compatible with what we know about the Christianisation of Sicily, because Syracuse is considered to be the earliest cradle of Sicilian Christianity[165], and epigraphic evidence from the eastern part of the island demonstrates an extensive use of Greek[166]. As our analysis has shown, we cannot actually talk about *Passiones* being translated from Latin into Greek and vice-versa; instead, the different

---

[162] Musurillo, pp. 316, 318.

[163] Stelladoro, *Euplo/Euplio*, pp. 87–90.

[164] Philippart, pp. 177–83; Motta, p. 27; Efthymiadis, pp. 373–82; Re, 'Telling the Sanctity', pp. 614-21; Vincenza Milazzo, 'Bilinguismo e agiografia siciliana. Alcune osservazioni sulle «Passiones» di Agata e Lucia', in *Bilinguismo e scritture agiografiche. Raccolta di studi*, ed. by Vincenza Milazzo & Francesco Scorza Barcellona, Sanctorum. Scritture, pratiche, immagini 4 (Rome: Viella, 2018), pp. 77–110.

[165] Roger J. A. Wilson, *Sicily under the Roman Empire: The Archaeology of a Roman Province, 36 BC AD 535* (Warminster: Aris and Phillips, 1990), pp. 310–12; Motta, p. 43, n. 73.

[166] See, for example: Jonathan R. W. Prag, 'Sicilian Identity in the Hellenistic and Roman Periods: Epigraphic Considerations', in *Epigraphical Approaches to The Post-Classical Polis. Fourth Century BC to Second Century AD*, ed. by Paraskevi Martzavou & Nikolaos Papazarkadas (Oxford: Oxford University Press, 2013), pp. 37–53; Motta, p. 28, n. 21 with bibliography.

versions represented rewritings of the legend that could present major differences in the narrative.

These early rewritings must have been completed in Sicily, where two linguistic audiences existed and the cults of the three martyrs were established very early. The need to make accessible to both Greek-speaking and Latin-speaking audiences the legends of local martyrs was there, as were the writers with the necessary skills in both Greek and Latin. The *Life of Pancras of Taormina* (*BHG* 1410) stated that both languages were spoken in Taormina and referred to an interpreter who had mastered them both[167]. This *Life* presumably dated from the beginning of the eighth or the beginning of the ninth century, although it described the deeds of the first bishop of the city supposedly in apostolic times[168].

These three martyrs were an important part of Sicilian Christian memory; this 'local flavour' was particularly obvious in the case of Lucia, who was presented as the patron saint of Syracuse even in later hagiographies of the ninth and twelfth centuries[169]. The legends of these Sicilians martyrs constituted in a sense the basis of Sicilian hagiography by becoming a common literary heritage providing material that influenced and inspired later Sicilian hagiographical production. Considering the impact of this early hagiography on later Sicilian literary production, including novel-like hagiographies characterized by a strong component of the marvellous, such as the *Life of Pancras of Taormina* and the *Life of Leo of Catania* mentioned above, we can argue that these texts did not go unheeded, as they provided literary motifs for later hagiographers.

As has been stated, the *Life of Leo of Catania* had common elements with the *Passiones* of Agatha, Lucia, and Euplus. We find the confusion between Catania and Palermo[170], an episode about a woman suffering from an excessive flow of blood who traveled from Syracuse to Catania in order to be healed[171], the construction of a martyrium of Lucia[172], and the bathhouse

---

[167] *The Life of Saint Pankratios of Taormina. Greek Text, English Translation and Commentary* by Cynthia Stallman-Pacitti, Byzantina Australiensia 22 (Leiden: Brill, 2018), pp. 316–19 (Chapter 195), 336–37 (Chapter 212).

[168] Stallman-Pacciti, pp. 14–15. See also Anna Lampadaridi, 'La *Vie de Pancrace de Taormine* (*BHG* 1410) et l'histoire des images à Byzance', in *L'histoire comme elle se présentait dans l'hagiographie byzantine et médiévale*, ed. by Anna Lampadaridi and others, Acta Universitatis Upsaliensis, Studia Byzantina Upsaliensia 21 (Uppsala: Uppsala Universitet, 2022), pp. 75–102 (pp. 96–98).

[169] See *supra*, p. 197-99.

[170] See supra, p. 191.

[171] Alexakis, pp. 186–87 (Chapter 37).

[172] See *supra*, p. 195-96.

called Ἀχίλλιον[173]. The theme of the virgin in the brothel[174], found in the *Martyrdoms of Agatha* and *Lucia*, was attested in the *Life of St Pancras*[175]. The *Martyrdom of the Three Brothers of Lentini* (*BHG* 62a) had some similarities with the *Passion* of Agatha. A martyr named Epiphane underwent the cutting off of her breast[176], the martyrs were healed thanks to a miraculous visit of the apostle Andrew[177], and some soldiers drowned in a river called Psimethos[178], attested only in the Greek versions of the *Passion* of Agatha (*BHG* 36 and 37). The legends of Sicilian martyrs also mentioned names that could be found in later local hagiographical production (*Falconius* of the *Passion* of Agatha reminds us of the God *Falcon* destroyed by Pancras[179]). These accounts of martyrdom also included claims to apostolic visitations (such as the visit of the apostle Peter with Agatha in prison) that foreshadowed in some way the development of later legends of apostolicity for the churches of Sicily, such as the *Life of Pancras*. In this narrative the apostle Peter played a central role in the establishment of the bishopric of Taormina, as he is the one who sent Pancras to Sicily. The *Life* thus offered a classic case study of the legendary motif of the apostolic origins of the Sicilian dioceses, here specifically Taormina, as Evelyne Patlagean has pointed out[180].

The cult of Sicilian martyrs extended beyond Sicily and spread to Constantinople; this evolution gave rise to a rich array of different rewritings in Greek. However, the most significant evidence for the importance of their cult in Constantinople is the fact that they were included in major hagiographical collections commissioned by emperors, such as the Synaxarion of Constantinople and, shortly thereafter, the metaphrastic *menologion* and the *Menologion* of Basil II. As no specific procedures for the canonization of saints ever developed in Byzantium, *de facto* recognition resulted from

---

[173] See *supra*, p. 202.

[174] Francesca Rizzo-Nervo, 'La vergine e il lupanare. Storiografia, romanzo, agiografia', in *La narrativa cristiana antica. Codici narrativi, strutture formali, schemi retorici, XXIII Incontro di studiosi dell'antichità cristiana, Roma 5–7 maggio 1994*, Studia Ephemeridis Augustinianum 50 (Rome: Institutum patristicum Augustinianum, 1995), pp. 91–99; Motta, p. 50, note 90.

[175] Stallman-Pacciti, pp. 276–301(Chapters 158–82).

[176] François Halkin, *Six inédits d'hagiologie byzantine*, Subsidia Hagiographica 74 (Brussels: Société des Bollandistes, 1987), pp. 69–70 (Chapter 5).

[177] Halkin, *Six inédits*, p. 67 (Chapter 3).

[178] Halkin, *Six inédits*, p. 66 (Chapter 2).

[179] Stallman-Pacciti, pp. 84–93 (Chapters 26–32); Motta, p. 68.

[180] Évelyne Patlagean, 'Les moines grecs d'Italie et l'apologie des thèses pontificales (VIIIᵉ-IXᵉ siècles)', *Studi medievali*, 3.5 (1964), 579–602.

being included in collections and calendars[181]. Lucia's legend did not come to the attention of the Metaphrastes, probably because of its particular local impact. But her martyrdom did inspire a twelfth-century Constantinopolitan scholar, who also laid emphasis on her close association with the city of Syracuse.

Of course, Sicilian martyrs were not the only Western martyrs who were introduced in Byzantium. Accounts of martyrdoms were an important part of the Latin hagiographical literature translated into Greek, resulting in various rewritings. This activity resulted from a need to re-establish the cults of important figures of both eastern and western martyrs, to renew contact with a mutual Christian heritage, and to return to the roots in a sense[182]. For instance, the exploits of many martyrs associated with Rome and its periphery were translated into Greek[183]. Let us take the example of Agnes, a Roman martyr as popular as Agatha of Sicily. Her Latin *Passio* gave rise to two Greek versions, *BHG* 45 and 46. However, these Greek translations or adaptations of the Latin legend have survived in very few manuscripts; each of the two Greek versions (*BHG* 45 and 46) can be read in only two codices[184]. Moreover, the legend of Agnes of Rome did not inspire other Byzantine rewritings. The Synaxarion of Constantinople included just a short mention (not a complete entry) on Agnes of Rome on 21 January[185], while her *Passio* did not retain the attention of Symeon Metaphrastes. In addition, there is no secure evidence for the existence of a shrine of Agnes in Constantinople[186].

This overview of the Greek *dossier* of Agnes demonstrates that even if her legend had reached Constantinople, her cult was not as popular as those of Sicilian martyrs. The imported Sicilian stories occupied an important place among legends of western saints bequeathed to the East. There was a conscious effort to import and integrate this 'patrimonio martirologico siciliano' into the Byzantine church[187]. In the eighth century, the Church of Sicily

---

[181] On this subject, see Christian Høgel, *Symeon Metaphrastes: Rewriting and Canonization* (Copenhagen: Museum Tusculanum Press, 2002).

[182] On this point, see Anna Lampadaridi, 'Du latin au grec: le voyage linguistique et culturel des vies monastiques dans le monde byzantin', in *Les mobilités monastiques de l'Antiquité tardive au Moyen Âge (IVᵉ-XVᵉ siècle)*, ed. by Olivier Delouis and others, Collection de l'École Française de Rome 558 (Rome: École Française de Rome, 2019), pp. 373–89.

[183] For an illustrative list, see Xavier Lequeux, 'Latin Hagiographical Literature translated into Greek', in *The Ashgate Research Companion to Byzantine Hagiography*, ed. by Stephanos Efthymiadis (Farnham: Ashgate, 2011), I: Periods and Places, pp. 385–99 (pp. 386–87).

[184] According to *Pinakes*: https://pinakes.irht.cnrs.fr/notices/saint/36/.

[185] *SECP*, col. 412. The short mention is also present in recension H of the Synaxarion.

[186] Her cult was probably associated with Saint Lawrence, see Janin, I, III, p. 9.

[187] Morini, 'Sicilia, Roma e Italia suburbicaria', p. 132.

passed to the control of Constantinople[188]. This was an event of major religious and cultural importance that strengthened the existing links between Sicily and Constantinople.

The importation of the cult of Sicilian martyrs in Constantinople was not devoid of political interest. Their existence in the form of a complete entry and not a short note in recension H, the most ancient stratum of the Synaxarion, which was commissioned at the request of Constantine Porphyrogenitus in the mid-tenth century, was therefore no coincidence, because while Romanos Lekapenos was emperor and Constantine VII co-emperor (913–59), the Byzantines made important attempts to regain Sicily[189]. The Synaxarion also provided important information concerning the martyrs' shrines. We know that at least one shrine of Agatha existed in Constantinople by the tenth century (but probably earlier), and another one was mentioned in a later recension of the Synaxarion. The case of these three Sicilian martyrs shows that there was a constant effort to introduce material from the periphery into this universal, 'ecumenical' enterprise; the Synaxarion can also be read as a 'decentralized history' of Byzantium[190]. The need to include as many cities as possible of the important island of Sicily may have been the reason why Agatha became a Palermitan martyr for the Synaxarion; in contrast to Catania, no other saint of Palermo was mentioned in the Synaxarion[191]. The geographical precision adopted in entries of the Synaxarion and the effort to include the names of the locations[192] has made the Synaxarion an importance source for social history in Byzantium[193]. The relics of Agatha, Lucia, and presumably other Sicilian martyrs reached Constantinople at the very beginning of the eleventh century; this circulation confirmed the interest in their cults.

---

[188] On this subject, see Vivien Prigent, 'L'évolution du réseau épiscopal sicilien (VIIIᵉ-Xᵉ s.)', in *Les dynamiques de l'islamisation en Méditerranée centrale et en Sicile: nouvelles propositions et découvertes récentes*, ed. by Annliese Nef & Fabiola Ardizzone (Bari: Edipuglia, 2014), pp. 89–103.

[189] See Vivien Prigent, 'La politique sicilienne de Romain Iᵉʳ Lécapène', in *Guerre et société au Moyen Âge. Byzance — Occident (VIIIᵉ–XIIIᵉ s.)*, ed. by Dominique Barthélemy & Jean-Claude Cheynet, Monographies 31 (Paris: ACHCByz, 2010), pp. 63–84.

[190] See Sophie Métivier, *Aristocratie et sainteté à Byzance (VIIIᵉ-XIᵉ siècle)*, Subsidia Hagiographica 97 (Brussels: Société des Bollandistes, 2019), pp. 219–58.

[191] See *supra*, p. 192.

[192] Motta, pp. 52, 61.

[193] Alexander Kazhdan, 'Constantinopolitan Synaxarium as a Source for Social History of Byzantium', in *The Christian East: Its Institutions and its Thought. A Critical Reflexion. Papers of the International Scholarly Congress for the 75ᵗʰ Anniversary of the Pontifical Institute. Rome 30 May–5 June 1993*, ed. by Robert F. Taft, OCA 251 (Rome: Pontificio Istituto Orientale, 1996), pp. 485–515.

Political, religious, cultural, and linguistic links between Sicily and Constantinople could explain the important penetration of Sicilian martyrs in Byzantium. The role of individuals who functioned as vectors of cultural and religious transfers should not be underestimated[194]. Networks of people who moved from one place to another played a major role in linguistic and cultural exchanges. For instance, the patriarch Methodius proclaimed his Sicilian origins and composed an *Oratio* dedicated to Agatha that was presumably pronounced after 843 in Constantinople on the occasion of the saint's feast. He was also the author of a liturgical hymn on Agatha's counterpart, Lucia, the patron saint of his hometown, Syracuse. His activity promoted the cults of these two Sicilian saints and particularly strengthened the cult of Agatha, whose presence in Constantinople was stronger and attested presumably as early as the ninth century. The case of Theodore Krithinos, another Sicilian who became *oikonomos* of St Sophia in Constantinople, also indicated the impact of individual action within a cultural transfer. He ordered the translation into Greek of the Latin *Passio* of the Roman martyr Anastasia in Rome in 824, so that the text could serve as an argument for iconoclast ideology[195]. He thus played a major role in the transfer of Anastasia's legend from Rome to Byzantium.

There was perhaps a certain exoticism in these Sicilian figures that captured the imagination of the compilers of the Synaxarion, Symeon Metaphrastes, and later Byzantine writers such as Psellos, Tzetzes, and Constantinos Akropolites. Their religious and cultural transfer implies a re-consideration, a re-semantization of their identity in a different historical and cultural setting that leads to the construction of a different narrative[196]. Sicilian martyrs were sometimes subject to radical transformations, as Agatha became a Palermitan martyr in the Synaxarion, whereas Lucia and Euplus maintained their local identity. Euplus was no longer a strange 'voluntary' martyr but a deacon of the church of Catania, perhaps as an attempt to update this character to 'today's taste'. It did not matter that they were no longer totally the same figures; their profound and early penetration into Byzantine sanctity demonstrated an attempt to reconnect with a cultural and religious heritage that was still claiming its rightful place in Byzantine identity.

---

[194] See Espagne, <http://journals.openedition.org/rsl/219>.
[195] Hermann Usener, 'Beiträge zur Geschichte der Legendenliteratur', *Jahrbücher für Protestantische Theologie*, 13 (1887), 219–59; François Halkin, *Légendes grecques de 'martyres romaines'*, Subsidia Hagiographica 55 (Brussels: Société des Bollandistes, 1973), pp. 86–87.
[196] Crimi, 'Agata e Bizanzio', pp. 146, 161.

III

Constructing Paradigms

The Lives of Episcopal Saints in Gaul

Models for a Time of Crisis, *c.* 470–550

Ian Wood

Introduction

The hagiography of Late Roman Gaul/Merovingian Francia has long attracted attention, in part because of the sheer quantity of the material, but largely because of the creation of a corpus published by Bruno Krusch and Wilhelm Levison in volumes 3–7 of the Monumenta Germaniae Historica, Scriptores Rerum Merovingicarum. One should note, however, that the corpus is not complete. It is particularly unfortunate, but understandable, that Krusch left aside almost all the Merovingian *passiones* of Roman-period martyrs, although there are a considerable number of them, and indeed they constitute a significant subset of the hagiography of the time[1].

The corpus itself has not gone unquestioned — Krusch's chronological pronouncements, and his classification of work as forged or authentic, have been much debated[2]. Of the texts relating to saints of the fifth to eighth centuries, some works that he ignored or dismissed have been defended as genuine. In addition, and perhaps more important, scholars have recently concentrated

---

[1] Brigitte Beaujard, *Le culte des saints en Gaule* (Paris: Cerf, 2000), pp. 117–41; Ian Wood, 'The Cult of Saints in the South-East of Gaul in the Fifth and Sixth Centuries', in *L'empreinte chrétienne en Gaule du IVe au IXe siècle*, ed. by Michèle Gaillard (Turnhout: Brepols, 2014), pp. 257–69 (pp. 258–61).
[2] Monique Goullet, 'Introduction', in *L'hagiographie mérovingienne à travers ses réécritures*, ed. by Monique Goullet, Martin Heinzelmann & Christiane Veyrard-Cosme (Ostfildern: Thorbecke, 2010), pp. 11–25.

Interacting with Saints in the Late Antique and Medieval Worlds, ed. by Robert Wiśniewski, Raymond Van Dam, and Bryan Ward-Perkins, Hagiologia, 20 (Turnhout, 2023), pp. 213–228.
© BREPOLS ❧ PUBLISHERS   DOI 10.1484/M.HAG-EB.5.133628

on the possibility of *réécriture* — hagiographical texts were frequently rewritten, sometimes simply to improve the Latin for stylistic reasons[3]. The result is that there are several texts that we can point to as being fifth- or sixth-century in origin, even if they have only survived in later recensions.

Many of the texts in the corpus fall into groups, above all those relating to Columbanus and his followers[4], and to the bishops, especially the martyr bishops, of the seventh and early eighth centuries[5]. Consideration of these groups makes it clear that at certain moments hagiography concerned with a particular model of holiness became a central mode of discourse[6]. From the early fifth century, and thus earlier than the MGH corpus, there is a cluster of works associated with Lérins which are partly concerned to set out the ideals of the island monastery and those trained there[7], just as the monastic hagiography of the seventh century can be seen as constituting a debate about Columbanus and the monastic tradition that he inspired. So too, the martyr acts of the seventh and eighth centuries deal with the role of bishops in the political world[8]. A similar cluster of episcopal and related lives from the fifth to sixth centuries has received less attention because the majority of the texts included were either dismissed by Krusch as forgeries or because he did not include them in the Merovingian corpus at all. Christian Stadermann has looked at most of the individual *vitae* in this cluster, in the context of a study of the representation of the Goths in Merovingian narrative sources[9]. Yet these texts are also worth considering as a group because they allow us to

---

[3] *L'hagiographie mérovingienne à travers ses réécritures.*

[4] Alexander O'Hara & Ian Wood, *Jonas of Bobbio, Life of Columbanus, Life of John of Réomé, and Life of Vedast* (Liverpool: Liverpool University Press, 2017), pp. 79–81.

[5] Paul Fouracre, 'Merovingian History and Merovingian Hagiography', *Past and Present*, 127 (1990), 3–38; Paul Fouracre & Richard Gerberding, *Late Merovingian France, History and Hagiography, 640–720* (Manchester: Manchester University Press, 1996), pp. 3–38.

[6] Ian Wood, *The Missionary Life: Saints and the Evangelisation of Europe, 400–1050* (London: Longman, 2001).

[7] Alongside the *Lives* of Honoratus (ed. by Marie-Denise Valentin, *Hilaire d'Arles, Vie de saint Honorat*, SC 235 (1977)), and Hilary (ed. by Samuel Cavallin & Paul André-Jacob, *Honorat de Marseille, Vie d'Hilaire d'Arles*, SC 404 (1995)), and Faustus's sermon on Maximus of Riez (ed. by Salvatore Gennaro, *Dinamii Vita sancti Maximi episcopi Reiensis: Fausti Sermo de Maximo episcopo et abbate* (Catania: Università di Catania, 1966)), there is the rather neglected *Vita Iusti Lugdunensis* (AASS, September I, September 2nd, pp. 373–75): see the full text (from *Acta Sanctorum*) and a translation (by Philip Beagon) in CSLA E06326. See below n. 52 for recent discussion of the text.

[8] Fouracre, 'Merovingian History and Merovingian Hagiography'.

[9] Christian Stadermann, *Gothus: Konstruktion und Rezeption von Gotenbildern in narrativen Schriften des merowingischen Gallien* (Stuttgart: Franz Steiner Verlag, 2017), pp. 133–34, 495–536. See also Martin Heinzelmann, 'L'hagiographie mérovingienne: Panorama des documents potentiels', in *L'hagiographie mérovingienne à travers ses réécritures*, p. 61.

note a particular set of concerns relating to the role of a bishop, and especially a non-monastic bishop, during the period of the establishment of the Successor States. It is necessary, therefore, to begin by describing the dossier of texts.

The Lives

1. Constantius, the *Life of Germanus of Auxerre*, written for Bishop Patiens of Lyon (449/50–475/80)[10].
2. Verus of Orange, the *Life of Eutropius of Orange*, written for Bishop Stephanus of Lyon (475/80–501/15)[11].
3. Ennodius, the *Life of Epiphanius of Pavia*: written 501–02[12]. It may seem inappropriate to consider this within the late-Gallo-Roman corpus, because it was composed in northern Italy. But although the transmission of Ennodius's works is notoriously un-evidenced before the late eighth century, when Paul the Deacon played a major role in gathering them together[13], Pierre Courcelle argued that two Gallic lives, the *Vita Bibiani* and the *Vita Orientii*, which arguably date to the early sixth century, borrow from the *Vita Epifani*, which suggests that it circulated in Gaul[14]. This argument has been challenged by Andrew Gillett, who has insisted that the *Vita Bibiani* is more likely to have drawn on Sulpicius Severus's *Vita Martini* and the *Life of Germanus of Auxerre* by Constantius[15]. That these other texts did influence the authors of the *Lives* of Bibian and Orientius is highly likely, but the centre of Courcelle's case was the importance of banquets held by Visigothic kings in each of the three works

---

[10] Constantius, *Vita Germani*, ed. by René Borius, *Constance de Lyon, Vie de saint Germain d'Auxerre*, SC 112 (1965). See Andrew Gillett, *Envoys and Political Communication in the Late Antique West, 411–533* (Cambridge: Cambridge University Press, 2003), pp. 115–37. For a new reading of the *Vita Germani*, see Ian Wood, 'La *Vita Germani*: Constance de Lyon et son public' (forthcoming).

[11] Verus, *Vita Eutropii*, ed. by P. Varin, *Bulletin du Comité Historique des monuments écrits de l'histoire de France, Histoire-Sciences-lettres*, vol. 1 (Paris, 1849), pp. 53–64. A new edition has been prepared by Graham Barrett, to whom I am indebted for allowing me to consult his work prior to publication.

[12] Ennodius, *Vita Epifani*, ed. by F. Vogel, MGH AA 7 (1885), pp. 84–109: also G. M. Cook, *The Life of Epiphanius by Ennodius* (Washington: Catholic University of America Press, 1942), and Maria Cesa, *Vita del beatissimo Epifanio vescovo della chiesa pavese* (Como: New Press, 1988).

[13] Stéphane Gioanni, *Ennode de Pavie, Lettres, Livres I et II* (Paris: Belles Lettres, 2006), pp. cxxxvii–cxliv. S. A. H. Kennell, *Magnus Felix Ennodius: A Gentleman of the Church* (Ann Arbor: University of Michigan Press, 2000), pp. 221–22.

[14] Pierre Courcelle, 'Trois dîners chez le roi wisigoth d'Aquitaine', *Revue des études anciennes*, 49 (1947), 169–77 (p. 170) notes parallels with the *Vita Bibiani* and *Vita Orientii*.

[15] Gillett, *Envoys and Political Communication*, p. 138, 144, n. 124: followed by Stadermann, *Gothus*, pp. 508–10.

he was considering, something which does have a parallel in Martin's presence at a feast hosted by the emperor Magnus Maximus[16], but not in the *Vita Germani*. That such literary influence could take place within a generation of the original composition is perhaps less surprising than appeared to Gillett. Ennodius himself came from Provence, and he retained strong family links with the region[17]. His contact with Provence can also be seen in the fact that at some point between 506 and 521 he wrote a *Life of Anthony of Lérins*[18]. In addition, the political context facilitated connections between Italy and southern Gaul: following the death of Alaric II at Vouillé in 507, Theodoric the Ostrogoth took charge of as much Visigothic territory as he could save from the Franks. Moreover, the narrative of the *Vita Epifani* has much to say about southern Gaul. We can, therefore, legitimately consider Ennodius's text in the cluster of episcopal hagiographies with which I am concerned[19].

4. Of the two texts that seem to show dependence on the *Vita Epifani* the *Life of Bibian* or Vivian of Saintes (d. *c.* 478?) is regarded as having been written *c.* 520–30[20].

5. The surviving *Life of Orientius of Auch* (d. *c.* 440) is one of those texts that is now thought to survive only as a *réécriture*. According to Bruno Dumézil, however, it is still possible to see that the original version was composed before the defeat of the Visigoths at Vouillé. If this is correct, it might suggest a very quick dissemination of the *Vita Epifani*, with no more than six years separating the two works[21].

---

[16] Sulpicius Severus, *Vita Martini*, 20. 6, ed. by Jacques Fontaine, *Sulpice Sevère, Vie de saint Martin*, SC 130 (1967), pp. 296–98.

[17] Karl Friedrich Stroheker, *Der senatorische Adel im spätantiken Gallien* (Tübingen: Alma Mater Verlag, 1948), pp. 166–67 and 238, Stammbaum II.

[18] Ennodius, *Vita Antoni*, ed. by Vogel, pp. 185–90. Stéphane Gioanni, 'Une figure suspecte de la sainteté lérinienne: saint Antoine. D'après la *Vita Antoni* d'Ennode de Pavie', *Recherches Augustiniennes et Patristiques*, 35 (2007), 133–87.

[19] On the *Vita Epifani* see also Gillett, *Envoys and Political Communication*, pp. 148–71.

[20] *Vita Bibiani*, ed. by Bruno Krusch, MGH SRM 3 (1896), pp. 94–100: dated to 520/30 by François Dolbeau, 'La vie en prose de Marcel évêque de Die: histoire du texte et édition critique', *Francia*, 11 (1983), pp. 97–130 (p. 108, nn. 63–64); Ferdinand Lot, 'La *Vita Viviani* et la domination visigothique en Aquitaine', *Mélanges Paul Fournier* (Paris: Sirey, 1929), pp. 467–77, reprinted in *Recueil des travaux historiques de Ferdinand Lot*, vol. 2 (Geneva: Droz, 1970), pp. 101–11: Courcelle, 'Trois dîners chez le roi wisigoth'; Heinzelmann, 'L'hagiographie mérovingienne', p. 61; Robert Godding, *Prêtres en Gaule mérovingienne* (Brussels: Société des Bollandistes, 2001), pp. xxxix, noting that it was known to Gregory of Tours. Also Gillett, *Envoys and Political Communication*, pp. 143–48; Stadermann, *Gothus*, pp. 110, 508–10.

[21] *Vita Orientii*, AASS May I, May 1st, pp. 61–62; E. Griffe, *La Gaule chrétienne à l'époque romaine*, vol. 2. *L'église des Gaules au Vᵉ siècle* (Paris: Letouzey et Ané, 1966), pp. 31–33, with comment on the date at p. 32, n. 3; Heinzelmann, 'L'hagiographie mérovingienne', p. 61;

6. Along with this group we can place the *Life of Marcellus of Die*. Our surviving text is unquestionably a *réécriture* of the Carolingian period. Apparent citations of the *Vita Bibiani* that have been noted by François Dolbeau may, however, have been present in the original text[22]. The Ur-text could, therefore, belong to the cluster that includes the *Lives* of Bibian and Orientius.

7. Another Aquitanian *vita* from this period is that of Anianus of Orléans (d. 453): this would seem to have been composed either late in the fifth century or very early in the sixth. It has been identified as influencing the author of the *Life of Genovefa of Paris*, which was written *c.* 520, and it was certainly known to Gregory of Tours[23].

8. The *Vita Genovefae* itself, although not an episcopal text, deserves to be included in this corpus — it has much in common with the other *Lives*, and it has been argued that Genovefa is effectively presented as a bishop — probably because there was no other hagiographical model to describe a holy woman who was politically active in the late fifth century[24]. Although regarded by Krusch as a Carolingian composition, the A recension is now accepted as a work of the third decade of the sixth century[25].

9. Like the *Lives* of Anianus and Genovefa the *Life of Lupus of Troyes* is concerned with the invasion of Attila and the responses to it[26]. Like the *Vita Genovefae*, it was thought by Krusch to be a forgery, but its authenticity was strongly defended by Eugen Ewig, who placed it in the first half of the sixth century[27]. Among Krusch's arguments was a claim the *Vita Lupi*

Bruno Dumézil, *Les racines chrétiennes de l'Europe: conversion et liberté dans les royaumes barbares, Vᵉ-VIIIᵉ siècles* (Paris: Fayard, 2005), p. 728; Stadermann, *Gothus*, pp. 109, 131–32, 524–25. See also, Gillett, *Envoys and Political Communication*, pp. 138–43.

[22] *Vita Marcelli*, ed. by Dolbeau, 'La vie en prose de Marcel évêque de Die', pp. 107–09, on parallels with the *Vita Bibiani*. See also Stadermann, *Gothus*, pp. 521–22.

[23] *Vita Aniani*, ed. by Bruno Krusch, MGH SRM 3, pp. 108–17: Griffe, *La Gaule chrétienne*, vol. 2, pp. 54–55; Heinzelmann, 'L'hagiographie mérovingienne', p. 61; Godding, *Prêtres en Gaule mérovingienne*, pp. xxiii–xxiv; Stadermann, *Gothus*, pp. 109, 370–74, 496–98.

[24] *Vita Genovefae*, ed. by Bruno Krusch, MGH SRM 3, pp. 204–38; Ian Wood, 'Forgery in Merovingian Hagiography', in Monumenta Germaniae Historica: Schriften 33, *Fälschungen im Mittelalter* V (Munich, 1988), pp. 369–84, at pp. 376–79.

[25] For the date, Martin Heinzelmann, '*Vitae sanctae Genovefae*. Recherches sur les critères de datation d'un texte hagiographique', in Martin Heinzelmann & Jean-Claude Poulin, *Les vies anciennes de sainte Geneviève de Paris, Études critiques* (Paris: H. Champion, 1986), pp. 1–111 (pp. 107–11): Stadermann, *Gothus*, pp. 110, 518–20.

[26] *Vita Lupi*, ed. by Bruno Krusch, MGH SRM 7, pp. 284–302.

[27] Krusch, MGH SRM 7, pp. 295–302: Godding, *Prêtres en Gaule mérovingienne*, p. xxxiii: Eugen Ewig, 'Bemerkungen zur *Vita* des Bischofs Lupus von Troyes', in *Geschichtsschreibung und Geistiges Leben im Mittelalter: Festschrift für Heinz Löwe zur 65. Geburtstag*, ed. by Karl Hauck & Hubert Mordek (Cologne: Böhlau, 1978), pp. 14–26: reprinted in Eugen Ewig,

was dependent on the *Vita Severini*, written by Eugippius in 511 — a point dismissed by Ewig, but accepted by Isabelle Crété-Protin, who, however, sees this as providing no more than a terminus *post quem*. According to Crété-Protin the *Vita Lupi* should be accepted as a sixth-century text[28].

10. One Gallic work that we can date with considerable precision is the *Life of Caesarius of Arles*, Book I of which was written shortly after the saint's death in 542 and certainly before 549, by his episcopal disciples Cyprian of Toulon, Firminus of Uzès and Viventius, while Book II was composed shortly after by the priest Messianus and the deacon Stephanus[29].

11. There are five other *vitae* which merit a mention alongside these clustered texts. The first is the *Life of Apollinaris of Valence*, condemned by Krusch, but defended by Angela Kinney, who noted possible verbal links with the *Vita Germani*[30]. Certainly it seems to have points in common with our other *vitae*, and it also seems to reflect the world of the late- and post-Roman Gallic aristocracy that one can see in the *Life of Epiphanius* (and indeed of Marcellus).

12. A further episcopal *Life* is the puzzling *Vita Remedii*, which is seen as an eighth-century text by Marie-Céline Isaïa[31], but has been accepted as the *Life of Remigius of Rheims* known to Gregory of Tours by Stadermann[32]. Curiously it makes nothing of the bishop's connections with Clovis, while, on the other hand, a prominent miracle involves the daughter of a noble from Toulouse, cured by the saint at the request of the girl's parents and of the Visigothic King Alaric[33]. The absence of any reference to the baptism of Clovis, as well as the favourable presentation of Alaric,

---

Spätantikes und fränkisches Gallien, Gesammelte Schriften (1974–2007), vol. 3 (Ostfildern: Thorbecke, 2009), pp. 505–17.

[28] Isabelle Crété-Protin, *Église et vie chrétienne dans le diocèse de Troyes du IVᵉ au IXᵉ siècle* (Villeneuve d'Ascq: Presses universitaires du Septentrion, 2002), pp. 135–50 (on the date of the text) and 151–76 (on the *vita* as a literary, spiritual and historical text).

[29] *Vita Caesarii*, ed. by Bruno Krusch, MGH SRM 3, pp. 457–501; and ed. by Germain Morin, Marie-José Delage & Marc Heijmans, *Vie de Césaire d'Arles*, SC 536 (2010). See Stadermann, *Gothus*, pp. 111, 510–13. Also, Christine Delaplace, 'Pour une relecture de la *Vita Caesarii*: le rôle politique de l'évêque d'Arles face aux représentants des royaumes burgonde, wisigothique et ostrogothique', *Annales du Midi*, 124 (2012), 309–24.

[30] *Vita Apollinaris*. ed. by Krusch, MGH SRM 3, pp. 197–203; Angela Kinney, 'An Appeal Against Editorial Condemnation: A Reevaluation of the *Vita Apollinaris Valentinensis*', *Festschrift für Kurt Smolak zum 70. Geburtstag* (Berlin: De Gruyter, 2014), pp. 157–77.

[31] *Vita Remedii episcopi Remensis male attributa Venantio Fortunato*, ed. by Bruno Krusch, MGH AA 4. 2 (1885), pp. 64–67: Marie-Céline Isaïa, *Remi de Reims: Mémoire d'un saint, histoire d'une Église* (Paris: Cerf, 2010), pp. 376–80.

[32] Gregory of Tours, *Decem Libri Historiarum*, II. 31, ed. by Bruno Krusch & Wilhelm Levison, MGH SRM 1. 1 (1951): Stadermann, *Gothus*, pp. 110–11, 263, 525–28.

[33] *Vita Remedii*, IV–VIII (16–24).

certainly strengthen the case for the text originating in the sixth century. Despite the episode involving the Goths, unlike most of the texts in this dossier, the wider political world does not feature in the *Life*.

13. In addition to these episcopal *vitae* there is that of Eptadius of Cervon[34]. This is another *vita* that was condemned by Krusch as a forgery. Justin Favrod has argued strongly in favour of the text belonging to the sixth century, and Stadermann has added to, but modified his argument[35], yet it remains problematic as a historical source because much of the information it contains is factually suspect. However, other *vitae* whose authenticity is unquestionable include material that is highly unreliable: there is no automatic correlation between authenticity and accuracy[36]. Leaving aside the problems of the narrative contained in the *Vita Eptadii*, we can acknowledge that some of the issues raised by the *vita* are comparable with concerns to be found in works of episcopal hagiography dating from the fifth and sixth centuries, despite the fact that Eptadius does not seem to have ever taken up the post of bishop. Although he is described as *episcopus* in the *Life*, according to an early chapter he refused election to the see of Auxerre[37]. The *vita* may be a late sixth- or early seventh-century outlier of the other works discussed here.

14. There are two *Lives* concerned with martyrs of the period that deserve attention: first, there is that of Memorius (Mesmin) priest of Troyes, which provides an account of the invasion of Attila that has been compared to those in the *Vita Aniani* and the *Vita Lupi*[38].

15. Finally, there is the *Vita Vasii* or *Basii*, which is essentially an account of a property dispute in which a land-grabbing Roman, Proculus, kills the ascetic Vasius, who was supported by the Visigothic King Alaric II[39]. The positive presentation of an Arian ruler is, once again, striking. According to Martin Heinzelmann this is a *réécriture* of the seventh or eighth century[40].

---

[34] *Vita Eptadii*, ed. by Krusch, MGH SRM 3, pp. 184–94.

[35] Justin Favrod, *Histoire politique du royaume burgonde (443–534)* (Lausanne: Bibliothèque historique vaudoise, 1997), pp. 17–18: Stadermann, *Gothus*, pp. 112, 516–18: Martin Heinzelmann, 'Clovis dans le discours hagiographique du VIᵉ au IXᵉ siècle', *Bibliothèque de l'École des Chartes*, 154 (1996), 87–112 (pp. 94–95). See Ian Wood, 'Arians, Catholics, and Vouillé', in *The Battle of Vouillé, 507 CE. Where France Began*, ed. by Ralph Mathisen & Danuta Shanzer, (Berlin: de Gruyter, 2012), pp. 139–49 (p. 142).

[36] Wood, 'Forgery in Merovingian Hagiography', pp. 373–76.

[37] *Vita Eptadii*, 8, 12: Stadermann, *Gothus*, pp. 516–18.

[38] *Vita Memorii*, ed. by Krusch, MGH SRM 3, pp. 102–04: Crété-Protin, *Église et vie chrétienne dans le diocèse de Troyes*, pp. 136–38.

[39] *Vita Vasii*, AASS, April 16th, vol. II, pp. 420–21.

[40] Heinzelmann, 'L'hagiographie mérovingienne', p. 43, who sees the text as a réécriture of the seventh or eighth century: Stadermann, *Gothus*, pp. 109, 507–08.

Discussion

Of course these are not the only hagiographical texts written in this period[41]. Brigitte Beaujard saw this as an age of the composition of the acts of martyrs who suffered during the Roman persecutions[42]. And there are some important works of monastic hagiography from the sixth century, including the *Vita Patrum Iurensium*[43] and the *Vita Abbatum Acaunensium*[44], and, for Aquitaine, possibly the *Vita Maxentii*[45]. But what are we to make of this largely episcopal dossier? There is the obvious point that most of the subjects are bishops, and, with the exception of Caesarius, they are presented as non-monastic bishops, although Lupus, who was married to the sister of Hilary of Arles, did spend time at Lérins[46]. The *Vita Lupi* is, however, not a Lérinian Life — it does not obviously link with the *Lives* of Honoratus or Hilary, or even with the late sixth-century *Life of Maximus of Riez*, which was written by Dynamius of Provence.

More important, it is worth stressing that the dossier is made up of a remarkably coherent group of texts. The hagiographers of the *vitae* in question were quite clearly reading earlier works of the same genre, even works that had been composed no more than a decade or so earlier — we have noted the possible use made of Ennodius's *Vita Epifani* by the hagiographers of Bibian and Orientius, of the *Vita Bibiani* by the hagiographer of Marcellus of Die, as well as the *Vita Aniani* by the author of the *Life of Genovefa*[47], of Eugippius's *Vita Severini* in the *Life of Lupus of Troyes*, and Constantius of Lyon's *Vita Germani*, especially in the *Life of Apollinaris of Valence*.

---

[41] Among the other texts discussed by Stadermann one might note especially the *Passio Vincentii Aginnensis*, ed. by Baudoin de Gaiffier,' La Passion de S. Vincent d'Agen', *Analecta Bollandiana*, 70 (1952), 160–81, dated by Stadermann, *Gothus*, pp. 111–12, 533–36, to *c.* 541/*c.* 549–73.

[42] Beaujard, *Le culte des saints en Gaule*, pp. 117–41.

[43] *Vita Patrum Iurensium*, ed. by François Martine, *Vie des Pères du Jura*, SC 142 (1968).

[44] *Vita Abbatum Acaunensium absque epitaphiis*, ed. by Bruno Krusch, MGH SRM 7 (1920), pp. 322–36.

[45] *Vita Maxentii abbatis Pictavensis*, ed. by Jean Mabillon, Acta Sanctorum Ordinis sancti Benedicti I (Venice, 1733), pp. 578–80; Stadermann, *Gothus*, pp. 112, 522–23. See also Ralph Mathisen, 'Vouillé, Voulon, and the Location of the *Campus Vogladensis*', in *The Battle of Vouillé, 507 CE. Where France Began*, pp. 43–62 (pp. 57–58).

[46] *Vita Lupi*, 3: Crété-Protin, *Église et vie chrétienne dans le diocèse de Troyes*, pp. 153–55; Marc Heijmans & Luce Pietri, 'Le "Lobby" lérinien: le rayonnement du monastère insulaire du Vᵉ siècle au début du VIIᵉ siècle', in *Lérins, une île sainte de l'Antiquité au Moyen Âge*, ed. by Yann Codou & Michel Lauwers (Turnhout: Brepols, 2009), pp. 35–61, at pp. 37, 39–40.

[47] For the use of the *Vita Martini*, and parallels with the *Vita Aniani* and other fifth- and sixth-century texts, see Joseph-Claude Poulin, 'Les cinq premières *Vitae* de sainte Geneviève', in Heinzelmann & Poulin, *Les vies anciennes de sainte Geneviève de Paris*, pp. 115–89 (pp. 127–32, 134–37, 142–43).

The *Vita Germani* is the best known of the texts in the dossier, and in the present context it is particularly interesting, not only because of its narrative, of a bishop dealing with a series of crises relating to theological disagreement (a Pelagian crisis in Britain) and to the threat of barbarians, but also because we know something of its commission. It was written at the request of Bishop Patiens of Lyon by Constantius[48]. It is unclear whether the author was a priest of Lyon, but he was certainly not a priest of Auxerre. The text that he produced was not one that the bishops of Germanus's cathedral city found satisfactory: it was rewritten probably as early as *c.* 600[49]. Patiens does not seem to have intended to promote a cult of Germanus, which is scarcely surprising, since the saint had been bishop not of Lyon but of Auxerre. So we must assume that he wanted to have an account of the saint for other reasons.

Constantius was surely concerned in part to represent a theological position, since he spent a great deal of time dealing with Germanus's conflicts with British Pelagians. His anti-Pelagian stance may indicate reservations about the monastic traditions associated with Cassian, Faustus of Riez, and Eucherius of Lyon, which are sometimes portrayed as semi-Pelagian[50]. Unlike his predecessor, Eucherius, Patiens was not a monastic bishop[51]. Even less was he an ascetic saint like Justus, his fourth-century predecessor, who retired to become a monk in Egypt following a political showdown in which he thought he was the loser, and for whom we have an early fifth-century *vita*[52]. As we know from Sidonius, Patiens was in close contact with the Burgundian *magister militum per Gallias*, Chilperic, who enjoyed the bishop's feasts[53]. This is not to say that Patiens was anti-monastic. Nor indeed was Germanus, who is said to have founded a monastery[54], and there are plenty of similarities between Sulpicius Severus's *Life of Martin* and the *Vita Germani*[55]. Moreover Constantius would seem to have drawn on the *Lives* of

---

[48] Constantius, *Vita Germani*, letter to Patiens.

[49] Wolfert Van Egmond, *Conversing with the Saints: Communication in pre-Carolingian Hagiography from Auxerre* (Turnhout: Brepols, 2006), pp. 107–27.

[50] Wood, 'La *Vita Germani*: Constance de Lyon et son public'. For Eucherius's works, see especially the *De Laude eremi*, ed. by Salvatore Pricoco, *Eucherii De Laude eremi* (Catania: Università di Catania, 1965), and the *Passio Acaunensium Martyrum*, ed. by Bruno Krusch, MGH SRM 3, pp. 20–41.

[51] See Ian Wood, 'Les évêques qui ne s'intéressaient pas dans le monachisme' (forthcoming).

[52] Marie-Céline Isaïa, 'Histoire et hagiographie de saint Just, évêque de Lyon', *Hagiographica*, 19 (2012), 1–30: ead., 'Le saint évêque dans l'hagiographie lyonnaise (IVᵉ-VIIᵉ s.)', in *L'empreinte chrétienne en Gaule*, pp. 111–29 (pp. 115–16).

[53] Sidonius Apollinaris, *ep.* VI. 12. 3, ed. by André Loyen, *Sidoine Apollinaire*, 3 vols (Paris: Belles Lettres, 1960–70).

[54] Constantius, *Vita Germani*, I. 1. 6.

[55] Borius, ed., *Constance, Vie de saint Germain d'Auxerre*, pp. 31–38.

Honoratus and Hilary[56]. But he does not present Germanus as a monastic figure. He is, rather, a politically and theologically active saint, dealing with secular rulers and barbarian leaders, as well as Pelagian dissidents. It would seem that the *Vita Germani* was commissioned at least in part to provide a model of non-monastic episcopal sanctity, where a bishop's role in the political world was fully acknowledged.

The mysterious *Life of Eutropius* provides a further example of a non-monastic bishop, and Heinzelmann has drawn attention to the lack of any monastic reference in the saint's epitaph[57]. Even so, he was unquestionably ascetic: his chastity is highlighted by a remarkable vision in which he dreamt that a column of crows that rose from his genitals was consumed by fire[58]. But Eutropius, as presented by his hagiographer Verus, is scarcely a political figure. In trying to contextualise the *vita*, we may note that it is addressed to a bishop of Lyon, Stephanus. Moreover, the saint is said to have announced his coming death to a Bishop Patiens[59], presumably the bishop of Lyon[60]. The text certainly takes a firm theological position: it is worth noting the use of Augustine made by Verus[61]. This is surely significant, given the debates over what has been called semi-Pelagianism. As we have already noted, the *Vita Germani*, which was commissioned by Patiens, is explicitly anti-Pelagian.

From these texts I turn briefly to the *Life of Epiphanius* by Ennodius: again this is very definitely a non-monastic Life, where the bishop's role in politics, and perhaps above all as a diplomat, using his skills to protect Italians, is central[62]. Diplomacy is also at the heart of the two *Lives* that Courcelle saw as influenced by the *Vita Epifani*: the *Life of Bibian of Saintes* and that of Orientius of Auch[63]. In both cases, as in the *Life of Epiphanius*, we find interesting references to the behaviour of bishops in the face of Arian monarchs, and especially to their differing response to eating with them[64]. In

---

[56] Borius, ed., *Constance, Vie de saint Germain d'Auxerre*, p. 38.

[57] Martin Heinzelmann, *Bischofsherrschaft in Gallien: zur Kontinuität römischer Führungss-chichten von 4. bis 7. Jahrhundert. Soziale, prosopographische und bildungsgeschichtliche Aspekte* (Munich: Artemis, 1976), and esp. pp. 94–98 on Eutropius' epitaph.

[58] Verus, *Vita Eutropii*, 4; Kevin Uhalde, 'Juridical Administration in the Church and Pastoral Care in Late Antiquity', in *A New History of Penance*, ed. by Abigail Firey (Leiden: Brill, 2008), pp. 97–120 (p. 110).

[59] Verus, *Vita Eutropii*, 28.

[60] Heinzelmann, *Bischofsherrschaft in Gallien*, p. 128, n. 199, seems hesitant.

[61] Verus, *Vita Eutropii*, 8.

[62] Ennodius, *Vita Epifani*, 79–94, 136–77.

[63] See Audrey Becker, 'Les évêques et la diplomatie romano-barbare en Gaule au Ve siècle', in *L'empreinte chrétienne en Gaule*, pp. 45–59.

[64] Courcelle, 'Trois dîners chez le roi wisigoth'; See also Ian Wood, 'The Development of the Visigothic Court in the Hagiography of the Fifth and Sixth centuries' (forthcoming).

the *Life of Orientius* we hear how the Arian King of the Goths, Theodoric I, asked the saint to intervene to prevent an attack on Toulouse by Aetius and Litorius. The former received the bishop well, but the latter refused to see him, and was subsequently killed in the siege of the city[65]. We also hear how the saint went to intercede for a Spaniard at the Gothic court, and at dinner with the king was able to secure the man's life[66]. Perhaps a generation later Bibian appealed against Gothic demands for tribute, which had led to confiscation of property and the imprisonment of those unable or unwilling to pay[67]. Having travelled to the royal court at Toulouse, unlike other bishops he refused to accept the drink offered by Theodoric (I or II?), because of the eucharistic echoes of the ritual. In so doing he caused instant offence, but his vigils at the shrine of Symphorian that night led an apparition to calm the irate king, and secured the liberation of the imprisoned[68]. Subsequently the bishop's prayers drove back a Saxon raid on the Gironde[69].

There are clearly a number of recurrent issues here. Saintly bishops deal with barbarian kings, who may well behave better than Roman officials[70]. More specifically there seems to be something of a debate about how Catholic clergy should dine with Arian monarchs. As we have noted, eating with a barbarian ruler is also mentioned in Sidonius's presentation of Patiens[71], but there I would argue that the bishop of Lyon was not faced with an Arian Burgundian, but rather with a Catholic barbarian *magister militum*.

Turning to the *Vita Marcelli*, in which François Dolbeau noted several borrowings from the *Vita Bibiani*, we find Marcellus being driven into exile on the orders of Euric[72]. This is an episode which is difficult to place historically, since the Visigothic king is not known to have ever controlled the city of Die. It may, therefore, be a topos. More interesting is the account of Marcellus's relations with Caretena, the Catholic wife of the Arian Gundobad[73]. Having been invited to the dedication of the church of St Michael in Lyon, the saint asked the queen for help in securing some concession for his city of

---

[65] *Vita Orientii*, 3.

[66] *Vita Orientii*, 4.

[67] *Vita Bibiani*, 4.

[68] *Vita Bibiani*, 6.

[69] *Vita Bibiani*, 7.

[70] For the subject of saints and barbarians see *Les saints face aux barbares au haut Moyen Âge. Réalités et légendes*, ed. by Edina Bozoky (Rennes: Presses univesitaires de Rennes, 2017), which, however, does not deal with the saints discussed here.

[71] Sidonius Apollinaris, *ep.* VI. 12. 3.

[72] *Vita Marcelli Diensis episcopi et confessoris*, 4–5, ed. Dolbeau, 'La vie en prose de saint Marcel de Die', at pp. 117–21.

[73] *Vita Marcelli Diensis episcopi et confessoris*, 9, ed. Dolbeau, 'La vie en prose de saint Marcel de Die', at pp. 124–26.

Die. The queen approached Gundobad on the bishop's behalf, but the king refused. Marcellus left Lyon, but that night a servant of the queen fell ill. Caretena then had a vision of the saint. She hurried to the house where he had been staying in Lyon and collected the dried saliva of the saint — not the saliva of a drunkard, but that of an ascetic (*sputum quod in pariete iecerat, non crapulae squalore confectum sed ieiunii maceratione mundissimum*) — and took it back to the girl, forcing her to drink an infusion. Naturally, the invalid recovered, and the saint secured the concession for his city. We cannot construct an accurate narrative of Marcellus's episcopate from his *vita*, but we can see that the hagiographer was keen to show the saint dealing with good and bad barbarian rulers.

The *Lives* of Anianus, Lupus, Memorius, and Genovefa all treat the same issue of the need for leading ecclesiastics, and holy men and women, to use their influence to protect their cities against hostile barbarian powers — and all of them illustrate the matter in the context of Attila's invasion of Gaul in 451[74]. Anianus saved his city by prayer: indeed the title given to his *vita* is *Virtus sancti Aniani episcopi, quemadmodum civitatem Aurelianus suis orationibus a Chunus liberavit*[75]. But he also interceded with the *magister militum* Agripinus for those in prison[76], and he made sure that Aetius provided relief for Orléans[77]. Lupus is said to have negotiated with Attila over the fate of the city of Troyes, and accompanied the Hunnic king on his retreat to the Rhine (presumably following the Battle of the Catalaunian Plains, though this is nowhere mentioned)[78]. Subsequently, for fear of unnamed threats, he moved his congregation to the defended retreat of Mont Lassois, in the diocese of Langres, forty miles away[79]. Also concerned with the fate of the city of Troyes is the *Vita Memorii*, which Crété-Protin has linked to the *Lives* of Anianus and Lupus[80]. Here Lupus is instructed in a vision to send twelve newly baptized children, the priest Memorius, the deacons Filix and Sinsatus, and the subdeacon Maximian, to intercede with Attila[81]. The king's prefect regarded them as magicians and wanted to have them killed, but Attila himself merely ordered the burning of their crucifixes. One of the servants of the king was struck in the eye, and was cured by Memorius. The prefect, nevertheless,

---

[74] See Crété-Protin, *Église et vie chrétienne dans le diocèse de Troyes*, pp. 136–39, 164–70.
[75] Edited by Bruno Krusch, MGH SRM 3, p. 108. See also *Vita Aniani*, 4, 7–10.
[76] *Vita Aniani*, 3.
[77] *Vita Aniani*, 7, 10.
[78] *Vita Lupi*, 5.
[79] *Vita Lupi*, 6.
[80] Crété-Protin, *Église et vie chrétienne dans le diocèse de Troyes*, pp. 136–37.
[81] *Vita Memorii*, 2–6.

demanded the decapitation of the priest. The martyrdom was followed by a storm that so terrified the Huns that they fled, leaving Troyes unharmed.

Like Memorius, but even more like Anianus and Lupus, Genovefa protected the inhabitants of her city from Attila, through prayer and fasting[82], but she also had dealings with the pagan Childeric[83], while Clovis and Chlothild subsequently promoted her cult[84]. It is worth noting that Genovefa was directly linked by her hagiographer to Germanus of Auxerre and Lupus of Troyes, who consecrated her[85], as well as to Anianus[86]. Perhaps even more striking, Sidonius regarded Anianus, Germanus, and Lupus as equal in merit[87]. Already in the fifth century these figures were regarded as a cluster.

Another saint who is said to have dealt with Clovis is the priest (or bishop) Eptadius. According to the saint's *vita* the Frankish king attempted to persuade Gundobad to elevate him to the see of Auxerre, which the Burgundian ruler refused to do[88]. Yet even when elected bishop, Eptadius simply retired to the Morvand, leaving it unclear as to whether he was ever consecrated. Subsequently he is said to have promised Clovis that he would act on behalf of captives, whether Roman or Burgundian or of any *gens*. According to the hagiographer he did indeed redeem those taken from Italy by the Burgundians, an episode that seems to echo the actions of Epiphanius in ransoming Ligurians seized by Gundobad's army recorded by Ennodius[89]. There is a reference to the redemption of prisoners taken from Dun, in the Limousin, by the Roman troops of Sigismund, and redeemed by the saint[90]. The hagiographer also claims that Eptadius ransomed Gothic captives taken by Clovis after the Battle of Vouillé[91]. These anecdotes are perhaps a blueprint for saintly behaviour in time of war rather than records of actual events[92].

More complicated is the *Life of Apollinaris of Valence*, recently defended by Kinney. Her defence of the authenticity of the text is convincing, but it

---

[82] *Vita Genovefae*, 12.

[83] *Vita Genovefae*, 26.

[84] *Vita Genovefae*, 56.

[85] *Vita Genovefae*, 2–5, 13.

[86] *Vita Genovefae*, 14.

[87] Sidonius, *ep.* VIII. 15. 1: Crété-Protin, *Église et vie chrétienne dans le diocèse de Troyes*, pp. 132–23.

[88] *Vita Eptadii*, 8. Heinzelmann, 'Clovis dans le discours hagiographique', pp. 94–95.

[89] Ennodius, *Vita Epifani*, 136–77.

[90] *Vita Eptadii*, 9, 12.

[91] *Vita Eptadii*, 13.

[92] On the ransoming of captives, especially in the *Vita Caesarii*, see William Klingshirn, 'Charity and Power: Caesarius of Arles and the Ransoming of Captives in Sub-Roman Gaul', *The Journal of Roman Studies*, 75 (1985), 183–203.

does not address the work's oddity: that it is effectively built round two unrelated episodes. It is tempting to draw a parallel with Élie Griffe's description of the *Vita Aniani*, which he stated was not a *vita*, but (in accordance with the work's title, *Virtus sancti Aniani episcopi, quemadmodum civitatem Aurelianus suis orationibus a Chunis liberavit*) an account of the deliverance of Orléans from the Huns[93]. In fact a number of these texts revolve around one or two major incidents, making only the slightest attempt to write an account of the saint's whole career: this is also true of the Lyon *Vita Iusti*, from the early fifth century. In the case of the *Vita Apollinaris* the first incident concerns the saint's prominence in the episcopal opposition to the Burgundian Catholic king Sigismund's condoning of the marriage of his treasurer Stephen to his dead wife's sister[94]. The second part of the text relates to the period after the collapse of the Burgundian state — although the author makes no comment on the different political circumstances. At the end of his life Apollinaris visited Provence, and among those he saw were relatives, who before the collapse of Gibichung Burgundy would have been living in a separate kingdom, as well as Caesarius of Arles and the Ostrogothic regent Liberius[95]. The first half of the text thus deals with a bishop facing up to a king, and doing so over a very specific matter of canon law[96], while the second half deals with his reestablishment of a family nexus, and relates rather to the history of the senatorial aristocracy of sub-Roman Gaul. The text effectively reads as the combination of two short and very distinct pieces, both of which happen to relate to the same man.

All these texts, with the exception of the *Vita Eutropii*, deal with the political situation of the period, and of how a bishop should respond. Interestingly the barbarians are not necessarily 'the bad guys'. Romans are as likely to cause problems for the clerics, as for example Litorius in the *Vita Orientii*. This issue is not confined to episcopal *vitae*: it is equally apparent in the *Vita Patrum Jurensium*, where the Burgundian Chilperic is praiseworthy, but a Roman at court is most certainly not[97]. It is also central to the *Vita Vasii*, another one-episode *Life*, where Alaric II supports the saint over a land dispute with Proculus, who subsequently kills the holy man[98]. Interestingly in this work and in the episcopal hagiographies the Arianism of individual

---

[93] Griffe, *La Gaule chrétienne à l'époque romaine*, vol. 2, p. 54.

[94] *Vita Apollinaris*, 2–6.

[95] *Vita Apollinaris*, 10.

[96] On the issue of canon law, Ian Wood, 'Incest, Law and the Bible in Sixth-Century Gaul', *Early Medieval Europe*, 7 (1998), 291–303.

[97] *Vita Patrum Iurensium*, II. 10, 93.

[98] *Vita Vasii*, 1–6.

barbarian rulers is not usually a problem, except in the case of Euric. Thus, Theodoric I and II and even Alaric II come off remarkably well in the hagiographical narratives. Nor are Catholic barbarians immune from criticism: Attila and Euric apart, the barbarian ruler who causes the most significant problem is the highly orthodox Burgundian ruler Sigismund.

Few of these *vitae* seem to be concerned to establish a saint's cult. There is a marked absence of interest in any tomb or any posthumous miracles. Although most of the *Lives* contain a general statement that miracles were performed at the saint's shrine, only in the case of the *Vita Genovefae*[99] and the *Vita Marcelli*[100] is any detail given. Nor (with the exception of the *Vita Eutropii*) are they greatly concerned with the role of the bishop in his diocese — they do not, therefore, contribute to the establishment of a notion of *Bischofsherrschaft*[101], although the *Vita Remedii* lays stress on the saint's *patronicia*[102]. Rather, as is stated explicitly in the *Vita Apollinaris*, the saint provides *exempla*[103].

It would appear rather that in the eighty years between 470 and 550 bishops and hagiographers were thinking hard about the ideal behaviour of the senior clergy in the new political circumstances following the collapse of the Western Empire — which involved not just kings, but other secular officials, Romans and barbarian. Of course dealing with rulers was not a new concern. It is present in the *Lives* of Ambrose and Augustine. Nor is it an exclusively episcopal concern. In the *Vita Eptadii*, which may have a sixth-century core, we can see some of these issues being considered in the life of an ordinary priest, albeit one who seems to have rejected episcopal office. And, as we have already noted, relations with the new political powers are also an issue in the *Vita Patrum Jurensium*[104]. The same is true of the contemporary *Vita Severini*

---

[99] *Vita Genovefae*, 54–56.

[100] *Vita Marcelli*, 12.

[101] The standard discussion of *Bischofsherrschaft* in the immediately post-Roman period is that of Heinzelmann, *Bischofsherrschaft in Gallien*. The development of episcopal power is summarised by Claudia Rapp, *Holy Bishops in Late Antiquity: The Nature of Christian Leadership in an Age of Transition* (Berkeley, 2005), esp. pp. 290–302. The historiography relating to developments from the sixth century onwards is dealt with by Steffen Patzold, *Episcopus: Wissen über Bischöfe im Frankenreich des späten 8. bis frühen 10. Jahrhundert* (Ostfildern: Thorbecke, 2008), pp. 24–26. That episcopal power developed at different rates in different cities is clear from individual studies: e.g. Jean Durliat, 'Les attributions civiles des évêques mérovingiens: l'exemple de Didier, évêque de Cahors (630–55)', *Annales du Midi*, 91 (1979), 237–54; Ian Wood, 'The Ecclesiastical Politics of Merovingian Clermont', in *Ideal and Reality in Frankish and Anglo-Saxon Society*, ed. by Patrick Wormald (Oxford: Blackwell, 1983), pp. 34–57.

[102] *Vita Remedii*, 26–27.

[103] *Vita Apollinaris*, 14.

[104] *Vita Patrum Iurensium*, II. 10, 93.

of Eugippius[105], which, as we have seen, was apparently read by the author of the *Vita Lupi*. Political reality was, therefore, not irrelevant to monastic writers. And one can see the *Vita Caesarii* as both an episcopal and a monastic text. Here politics are as important as they are in any of the other *vitae* I have mentioned, but at the same time Caesarius's monastic history and his promotion of monasticism are fully considered.

During a period when we know that bishops were heavily involved in crisis management in their dioceses[106], it is notable that hagiographers set down models for the behaviour of church leaders, and that they did this at the same moment that other hagiographers were promoting the cult of martyrs, who were presented as defenders of their cities[107]. The two groups of saints even overlap: Germanus visited the shrine of Alban, and commissioned a *vita* of the martyr[108]: Bibian prayed at that of Saturninus at Toulouse[109]: Genovefa promoted the cult of Denis[110]. Eptadius travelled to the feast of Symphorian at Autun[111]. The protection offered by the martyrs clearly went hand in hand with the more worldly and practical view that the ideal saint in the late fifth and early sixth century was likely to be a politically active bishop. And the model of such a bishop is a recurrent feature of the episcopal *Lives* that were written in Gaul in the closing decades of the fifth century and the first half of the sixth. In so far as there is a dominant discourse in these *Lives*, it would seem to be the role of the bishop in the wider political world.

---

[105] Eugippius, *Vita Severini*, 7, 8, 17, 19, 22, 31, 32, 40, 42, 44, ed. by Philippe Régerat, *Eugippe, Vie de saint Séverin*, SC 374 (1991).

[106] Klingshirn, 'Charity and Power: Caesarius of Arles and the Ransoming of Captives in Sub-Roman Gaul', *The Journal of Roman Studies*, 75 (1985), 183–203; Pauline Allen & Bronwen Neil, *Crisis Management in Late Antiquity (410–590 CE): A Survey of the Evidence from Episcopal Letters*, Vigiliae Christianae Supplement 121 (Leiden: Brill, 2013).

[107] Beaujard, *Le culte des saints en Gaule*, pp. 117–41.

[108] Constantius of Lyon, *Vita Germani*, III. 16: *Passio Albani*, T Text, 21, ed. by Wilhelm Meyer, 'Die Legende des h. Albanus, des Protomartyr Angliae in Texten vor Beda', *Abhandlungen der königlichen Gesellschaft zu Göttingen*, Philologisch-historische Klasse, neue Folge 8 (1904), p. 36; Richard Sharpe, 'The Late Antique Passion of St Alban', in *Alban and St Albans*, ed. by Martin Henig & Phillip Lindley, BAA Conference Transactions 24 (Leeds: Maney, 2001), pp. 30–37 (p. 36). For diplomatic transcripts of two of the manuscripts of what may have been the text commissioned by Germanus, Ian Wood, 'Levison and St Alban', *Wilhelm Levison (1876–1947). Ein jüdisches Forscherleben zwischen wissenschaftlicher Anerkennung und politischem Exil*, ed. by M. Becher and Y. Hen (Bonn: Bonner historische Forschungen, 2010), pp. 171–85; see also Ian Wood, 'Germanus, Alban and Auxerre', *Bulletin 13 du Centre d'études médiévales Auxerre* (2009), 123–29.

[109] *Vita Bibiani*, 5.

[110] *Vita Genovefae*, 17–22.

[111] *Vita Eptadii*, 21.

Saints and Sacred Objects in Eastern Roman Imperial Warfare

The Case of Maurice (582–602)

Michał Pietranik

(University of Warsaw)

It is commonly acknowledged that elements of Christian piety and worship extensively pervaded east Roman warfare in the late sixth century[1]. Evidence from Corippus and the *Strategikon*, a military treatise traditionally attributed to the emperor Maurice (582–602), clearly demonstrates a well-developed set of religious rituals that were intended to ensure God's favour, which at the time was considered the most important factor in victory[2]. Therefore,

---

[1] In general, for the relationship between military service and Christian worship in east Roman warfare, see Jean-René Vieillefond, 'Les pratiques religieuses dans l'armée byzantine d'après les traités militaires', *Revue des Études Anciennes*, 37 (1935), 322–30; Paul Goubert, 'Religion et superstition dans l'armée byzantine à la fin du VIᵉ siècle', *Orientalia Christiana Periodica*, 13 (1947), 495–500; Michael Whitby, '*Deus Nobiscum*: Christianity, Warfare and Morale in Late Antiquity', in *Modus operandi: Essays in Honour of Geoffrey Rickman*, ed. by Michel M. Austin, Jill D. Harries & Christopher J. Smith (London: Institute of Classical Studies, University of London, 1998), pp. 191–208; Michael Whitby, 'War', in *The Cambridge History of Greek and Roman Warfare*, ed. by Philip Sabin, Hans van Wees & Michael Whitby, 2 vols (Cambridge: Cambridge University Press, 2008), II, pp. 336–41; Michael McCormick, *Eternal Victory. Triumphal Rulership in Late Antiquity, Byzantium and the Early Medieval West* (Cambridge: Cambridge University Press, 1990), pp. 237–47.
[2] Pseudo-Maurice, *Das Strategikon des Maurikios*, Praefatio, ed. by George T. Dennis, Corpus Fontium Historiae Byzantinae, 17 (Vienna: Verlag der Österreichischen Akademie der Wissenschaften, 1981), pp. 70–73.

Interacting with Saints in the Late Antique and Medieval Worlds, ed. by Robert Wiśniewski, Raymond Van Dam, and Bryan Ward-Perkins, Hagiologia, 20 (Turnhout, 2023), pp. 229–247.
© BREPOLS ⚜ PUBLISHERS   DOI 10.1484/M.HAG-EB.5.133629

on the eve of battle, troops were supposed to perform special supplicatory prayers to ensure a blessing for the army. A field chapel was usually set up in the middle of the camp where soldiers and officers gathered and carried their war banners[3]. *Kyrie eleison* was recited repeatedly and religious hymns were sung[4]. The presence of priests in a military camp should also be noted, since they were tasked with giving communion to soldiers and blessing banners[5]. Additionally, according to the *Strategikon*, each combat unit was obliged to shout *Nobiscum Deus* three times as it marched out of the camp, but noticeably this did not occur during the charge on the enemy, as it was believed it would make the cowardly more prone to giving in to their fear, or the brave would break ranks by recklessly rushing forward into battle[6].

All these practices demonstrate the special contribution of Christian worship to east Roman warfare in the sixth century. In general, the process of increasingly involving God in war was a continuous and gradual development between the fourth and seventh centuries, but in the last decades of the sixth century this process was distinctly accelerated. This phenomenon cannot be explained without taking into account the process of the so-called 'liturgification' of eastern Roman society which occurred at that time. In brief, the existential challenges which affected the eastern Empire and its population created a specific and complex social process that led to the increasing infiltration of all areas of life with Christian religious content. The increased presence of cults of saints and sacred objects as a significant feature of eastern Roman religiosity could hence be observed at that time[7].

This process did not omit the imaginative and symbolic sphere of war, as was evidenced by Corippus and the *Strategikon*, but in both of these sources there is a lack of elements from which to draw a more comprehensive image of eastern Roman pious warfare. Most of all, in the evidence from Corippus and the *Strategikon* there is no mention of cults of saints, relics, and

---

[3] Corippus, *Iohannidos libri viii*, VIII. 321–23, ed. by James Diggle & Francis R. D. Goodyear (Cambridge: Cambridge University Press, 1970), p. 177.

[4] *Strategikon*, II.1, pp. 138–41.

[5] *Strategikon*, VIIA.1, pp. 232–33.

[6] *Strategikon*, II.18, pp. 138–49.

[7] Averil Cameron, 'The Theotokos in Sixth-Century Constantinople: A City Finds its Symbol', *The Journal of Theological Studies*, 29 (1978), 79–108 (pp. 80–82); Derek Krueger, 'Christian Piety and Practice in the Sixth Century', in *The Cambridge Companion to the Age of Justinian*, ed. by Michael Maas (Cambridge: Cambridge University Press, 2005), pp. 291–315; Mischa Meier, 'Religion, Warfare and Demography', in *A Companion to Religion in Late Antiquity*, ed. by Josef Lössl & Nicholas J. Baker-Brian (Malden: Wiley Blackwell, 2018), pp. 544–48.

sacred images. It must be mentioned that if we were to base our notion of the presence of saints in the military context only on the above two sources, we would have to admit that saints were totally absent from the religious life of the east Roman army. However, this would be very misleading. First, it is very hard to believe that the army was completely separated from the impact of the religious trends which penetrated almost all of east Roman society at this time; and second, we can find many examples which could serve to prove that throughout the second half of the sixth century the use of holy objects was a feature of east Roman warfare.

Significantly, most instances of the use of sacred objects in war coincided with the reign of the emperor Maurice, which is remarkable for several reasons. Maurice had to face several substantial problems inherited from his predecessors, including a lack of stability on the entire Roman border on account of Persian, Avar, Slav, and Lombard incursions; disturbances that arose from disputes between Chalcedonian and non-Chalcedonian doctrines; and the depletion of economic resources by invasions, natural disasters, the resulting depopulation, and large expenditures on the costs of both warfare and peace tributes to the Persians and Balkan tribes[8]. It is often remarked that in the face of these troubles Maurice and his entourage sought to bolster the authority of the imperial office and accent the sacredness of the emperor's power by including an increasing number of objects of Christian piety in the imperial ceremonial and political agendas[9]. More importantly, under Maurice this phenomenon is also noticeable in matters of military significance, and his reign was characterized by many examples of the penetration of particular elements of the Christian cult (saints, relics, images) into the imaginative and symbolic sphere of war. This chapter aims to examine the evidence concerning the presence of sacred Christian objects in east Roman warfare under Maurice in order to show how his policy towards saints and relics differed from that of his predecessors, and to ask whether his pattern of the use of sacred objects can be described in terms of change or continuity.

---

[8] Michael Whitby, *The Emperor Maurice and his Historian: Theophylact Simocatta on Persian and Balkan Warfare* (Oxford: Clarendon Press, 1988), pp. 11–12.
[9] Michael Whitby, 'The Successors of Justinian', in *The Cambridge Ancient History Volume XIV: Late Antiquity: Empire and Successors, A.D. 425–600*, ed. by Averil Cameron, Bryan Ward-Perkins & Michael Whitby (Cambridge: Cambridge University Press, 2000), p. 101; Matthew dal Santo, 'The God-Protected Empire? Scepticism towards the Cult of Saints in Early Byzantium', in *An Age of Saints? Power Conflict and Dissent in Early Medieval Christianity*, ed. by Peter Sarris, Matthew dal Santo & Phil Booth (Leiden: Brill 2011), pp. 131–32.

MICHAŁ PIETRANIK

Before the Campaign

Contemporary Greek sources recognized Maurice as a pious military commander even before he ascended the imperial throne[10]. After he became an emperor, Maurice also was taking care of the proper religious background for his military campaigns. When describing Maurice's preparations for the campaign of 591 against the Avars and the Slavs in the Balkans, Theophylact Simocatta in his *History* noted that because the emperor

> [...] was also eager to obtain some divine guardianship to accompany him on campaign, he spent the night at the great shrine of our religion, the one built by the emperor Justinian: that sanctuary is dedicated to the name of the Wisdom of God. Accordingly, since no dream vision appeared to him, he spent the day at the house of the Mother of God outside the city, joined in prayer by the people and attending the mysteries, and he partook of the banquet of the Incarnate God. The church is known as the one at the Spring[11].

Maurice slept at Hagia Sophia in the hope of receiving a dream vision, but it did not come. Theophylact Simocatta's account of Maurice's vigil refers to 'some divine protection' (θείας τινὸς ἐποπτίας), which is a very unclear term, but the use of an indefinite pronominal adjective may clearly suggest that the emperor's efforts failed. According to Simocatta, the emperor's intention was clear: the word συστρατευσομένη clearly suggested that the emperor wanted the divine powers to fight with him in the approaching war. The way in which Maurice sought to obtain divine assistance in the upcoming campaign is also noteworthy, because it was one of the relatively rare cases when an east

---

[10] According to Evagrius, Maurice obtained a great victory over the Persian forces under Adarmahan and Tamkhosrow near Constantina in 582 solely through his piety and trust in God: Evagrius, *Historia ecclesiastica*, V. 20, ed. Joseph Bidez & Léon Parmentier (Amsterdam: A. M. Hakkert, 1964), p. 216. Menander Protector notes that when the Roman forces were besieging Chlomaron, the Persian commander of the city, Binganes, offered to Maurice sprinklers, chalices, and other precious liturgical vessels as a ransom to raise a siege, but Maurice refused to take them and said that 'he had not come to plunder the holy objects or to wage war on Christ, but with Christ's help to fight and to free those of his own faith from the Persians with their erroneous beliefs': Menander Protector, *The History of Menander of Guardsmen*, fr. 23. 7, ed. Roger C. Blockley, Arca Classical and Medieval Texts, Papers and Monographs 17 (Liverpool: Francis Cairns, 1985), pp. 202–05.

[11] Theophylact Simocatta, *Historiae*, V. 16. 7–8, ed. by Carl de Boor (Leipzig: Teubner, 1887, repr. Stuttgart 1972): τυχεῖν δὲ γλιχόμενος καὶ θείας τινὸς ἐποπτίας συστρατευσομένης αὐτῷ ἐπὶ τὸ μέγα τῆς θρησκείας κατεπαννυχίζετο τέμενος τὸ ὑπὸ Ἰουστινιανοῦ ᾠκοδομημένον τοῦ αὐτοκράτορος· ἐς προσηγορίαν δὲ τῆς τοῦ θεοῦ σοφίας τὸ ἱερὸν ἀνατέθειται. μηδεμιᾶς τοιγαροῦν ὄψεως ἐνυπνίων ἐπιφανείσης αὐτῷ, λιταζόμενος ἅμα τῷ λαῷ εἰς τὴν πρὸ τοῦ ἄστεος τῆς θεομήτορος οἰκίαν διημέρευε μυσταγωγούμενος, καὶ τῆς θεανδρικῆς μετελάγχανε πανδαισίας· ὁ δὲ νεὼς πρὸς τῆς Πηγῇ καταλέγεται, trans. Efthymios Rizos, CSLA E00047.

Roman emperor performed the practice of Christian incubation[12]. Simocatta also described another of the emperor's sacred rituals, which he seems to have performed in order to obtain the support of supernatural powers. This intention may explain Maurice's visit to the church of the Mother of God 'at the Spring', where he partook in collective prayers and liturgy. It is not entirely clear whether Maurice carried out these rites together with the army or with his civilian subjects, because in his narrative about the imperial visit at Pege, Simocatta used the word τό λαός, which might mean both soldiers and people[13]. Obviously the presence of people in collective prayers does not exclude that this act was aimed at gaining divine protection during a military campaign, but the issue would be more evident if soldiers had been present there. In addition, Simocatta's account raises the question of whether the choice of the church of the Mother of God as a place for the emperor's prayers before a campaign was an attempt to engage her as a patroness of the imperial campaign, which may testify to the increased significance of the imperial cult of the Mother of God as the patron and guarantor of imperial military victories. It is also worth mentioning that during this campaign Maurice visited the shrine of the martyr Glykeria, which was partially burned by the Avars, and he granted funds for the restoration of damage[14]. It is possible to consider that imperial generosity towards the sanctuary of Glykeria aimed to persuade the saint to support the emperor against the Avars, who had after all devastated her shrine[15].

---

[12] Procopius of Caesarea reports that when Justinian was seriously ill, he received a vision and was miraculously healed by Kosmas and Damian: Procopius of Caesarea, *De aedificiis*, I. 6. 5–8, ed. by Jacob Haury (Leipzig: Teubner, 1913), CSLA E04389 (Julia Doroszewska). However, it is hard to say whether Justinian practiced incubation here; Procopius does not state whether the emperor fell asleep intentionally in the sanctuary or whether the vision was granted to him regardless of any cult practice, both of which are plausible. Eustratius reports that Justinian appointed Eutychius to the patriarchal throne of Constantinople after a dream vision which he received in the sanctuary of the apostle Peter in Athyra: Eustratius, *Vita Eutychii Patriarchae Constantinopolitani*, ed. by Carl Laga, CCSG 25 (1992), p. 24. These two cases, unlike that of Maurice, fall in the traditionally conceived functions of incubation as a source of healing and a means of seeking the answer to problematic questions. About Christian incubation see: Robert Wiśniewski, *The Beginning of the Cult of Relics* (Oxford: Oxford University Press, 2019), pp. 76–82; Stephanos Efthymiadis 'Collections of Miracles (Fifth–Fifteenth Centuries)', in *The Ashgate Research Companion to Byzantine Hagiography*. 2 vols, *II: Genres and Contexts*, ed. by Stephanos Efthymiadis (Farnham: Ashgate, 2014), pp. 108–13.
[13] In his lexicon, Lampe gives the meaning of τό λαός as 'people', especially in the context of a church community. Geoffrey William Hugo Lampe, τό λαός, in *A Patristic Greek Lexicon*, (Oxford: Clarendon Press, 1961), pp. 792–93; however, the highly classicizing style of the prose of Simocatta makes it possible to use this word in the more ancient sense, which may mean 'soldiers'.
[14] Theoph. Sim. VI. 1. 3, CSLA E00016 (Efhymios Rizos).
[15] Perhaps Glykeria was expected to punish the destructive barbarians, just as saint Alexander of Dryzipera had punished the Avars who burned his church, opened his tomb, plundered

The Wood of the True Cross

The above examples clearly exhibit Maurice's efforts to gain God's favour before the military expedition against the Avars and the Slavs. In general, this campaign was remarkable for an extraordinary religious environment. Since the time of Theodosius, no east Roman emperor had ever gone to war in person. But Maurice was the commander-in-chief of this campaign, and his presence created an aura of uniqueness which was accompanied by a religious setting[16]. The religious resources accompanying this campaign were undoubtedly extremely impressive, and they were not limited to the aforementioned practices. Theophylact Simocatta reported that during the expedition to Thrace in 591, Maurice and his army were preceded by a piece of the True Cross raised on a golden spear.

> [...] The emperor was delighted by the formation of his escorting unit; the soldiery walked behind, while the wood of Christ's cross was raised up high on a golden spear and preceded the Emperor and the imperial guard[17].

This was the first piece of narrative evidence that described the emperor setting out on a war campaign with a relic of the True Cross. This might be somewhat puzzling when the importance of the Cross in the imaginative and symbolic landscape of east Roman warfare is considered. Christian authors had long spoken of the cross as the *tropaion* which symbolized Christ's victory over death, the devil, and the enemies of faith[18]. The cross in the hands of the orthodox emperor was regarded as a guarantee of a victory sent by God himself, while victory achieved through the Cross confirmed the legitimacy of the victorious emperor's power[19].

---

it, and insulted his body. As a result, the invaders were miraculously punished with plague: Theoph. Sim. VI. 5. 2; VII. 14. 11–15. 3, CSLA E00085 (Efthymios Rizos).

[16] Theoph. Sim. VI. 1–3. Joaquín Serrano del Pozo, 'The Cross-standard of Emperor Maurice (582-602 AD)', *Diogenes*, 11 (2021), 1–17 (p. 9).

[17] Theoph. Sim. V. 16. 11: ὁ δὲ αὐτοκράτωρ περιεγάνυτο τῷ σχήματι τῆς ἐκταξέως τῆς προπομπούσης δυνάμεως. τὸ δὲ μάχιμον κατόπιν ἐβάδιζεν, τό τε ξύλον τοῦ σταυροῦ τοῦ Χριστοῦ ἐς ὕψος ἐπὶ δόρατος χρυσοῦ ἀπηώρητο καὶ προηγεῖτο τοῦ τε βασιλέως καὶ τῆς περιπόλου δυνάμεως.

[18] Eusebius of Caesarea, *Vita Constantini*, I. 32. 2, ed. by Friedhelm Winkelmann, GCS 9 (1975). In his homily on the cult of the Holy Cross, John Chrysostom describes the lament of Satan, the infernal serpent, who complains that a nail was stuck in his heart (which was clearly a reference to the Holy Nails), and that he was pierced with a wooden spear, the Cross: John Chrysostom, *In adorationem venerandae crucis*, PG 62, col. 748. The motif of the cross as the wooden spear which pierced Hades also appears in hymnography: Romanus the Melodist, *On the Victory of the Cross*, in *Sancti Romani Melodi Cantica. Cantica Genuina*, ed. by Paul Mass & Constantine A. Trypanis (Oxford: Clarendon Press, 1963), p. 165.

[19] Eusebius of Caesarea, *Oratio de laudibus Constantini* 9, ed. I. A. Heikel, GCS 9 (1902), p. 219.

However, for a long time the cross did not appear in the military sphere in the form of material relic, but rather as a visual sign[20]. The first appearance of a relic of the True Cross as a miraculous apotropaion that rescued the city from the enemy is associated with the siege of Apamea by Persian troops in 544, as reported by Procopius of Caesarea[21]. The inhabitants of Apamea, terrified by the invasion of the Persian forces, asked Thomas, the local bishop, to show them a portion of the wood of the Cross, which was kept in a wooden box covered with gold and precious stones and exposed to the public only once a year. When Thomas complied with the request and walked around the temple in procession with the relic, a miraculous flame followed him. The people of Apamea, witnessing the miracle and trusting in the protection of the Cross, went out on the walls to oppose the 'army of the Medes'. Admittedly, before any regular siege action took place, the residents allowed Khosrow and a group of trusted people to enter the city, and they paid him a substantial ransom to withdraw from the siege. But the city survived, and one could get the general impression that this happened largely due to the relics of the True Cross. Even though in the case described by Procopius there was no military confrontation, nevertheless it is worth looking at closely because the wood of the True Cross had proven itself to be an apotropaic talisman that spreads its protective power over the local community[22].

Although Procopius's evidence testifies to the increased reliance of inhabitants of the eastern parts of the empire on material guarantees of protection against the enemy, this example does not relate to the use of the relics of the True Cross in explicitly military purposes, as occurred in the case of the campaign of 591. The material aspect of the holy object used during this campaign is a crucial issue. In the case of Maurice and his golden spear, the material aspect

---

[20] Quodvultdeus, the bishop of Carthage, claimed that the emperor Arcadius secured his victory in the war with Persia because his soldiers had bronze crosses on their coats when they went into battle. Then, after the successful war, the victorious emperor ordered that the sign of the cross be included on gold coins: Quodvultdeus, *Liber promissionum et praedictorum Dei*, III. 24. 35, ed. René Braun, SC 101–02 (1964), II, pp. 558–61. Quodvultdeus incorrectly associated the persecutions of Christians in Persia and the resulting war with the reign of Arcadius, while most likely his description referred to the time of Theodosius II: Kenneth G. Holum, 'Pulcheria's Crusade A.D. 421–22 and the Ideology of Imperial Victory', *Greek, Roman and Byzantine Studies*, 18 (1977), 153-172 (pp. 155-57). Theodosius II ordered the minting of imperial solidi with the new iconographic type of a figure of the winged victory holding a cross in her right hand: Holum, pp. 153–54, 172.

[21] Procopius, *De bello persico*, II. 11, pp. 354–55, ed. by Henry B. Dewing, (Cambridge MA: Loeb Classical Library, 1914), The miraculous display of the Cross is also reported by Evagrius, IV. 26, p. 173.

[22] Procopius, *The Persian War*, II. 11, pp. 354–55, even states that the men of olden times believed that the Cross would be the protective *phylakterion*.

of the relic is clearly emphasized by referring to the relic as the 'wood' (τό ξύλον). The potential connections between Maurice's banner and the labarum are debatable and very difficult to resolve, because it would be very tempting to see in the banner from the campaign of 591 a further development in the evolution of eastern Roman war insignia, as a traditional labarum modified under the influence of religious trends based on the worship of sacred material objects[23]. In this new labarum, the Christogram would be replaced by the more expressive symbol of a relic of the wood of the Cross. A similar banner was attributed to Heraclius, but information about it is derived from a highly allusive poem by George of Pisidia[24]. It is significant that George of Pisidia likewise emphasized the material aspect of the Cross, which he also described as τό ξύλον. This description may confirm some changes in the understanding of the role of the Cross as an attribute of victory, because at this point not only cross-shaped insignia but also the material relic of the True Cross had become powerful instruments that ensured divine support for the emperor in wars against the empire's enemies.

Armed to the teeth? Relics of Saint Symeon Stylites the Elder

The fact that Maurice took a relic of the True Cross with him on the campaign in Thrace is not the only evidence of the increasing significance of sacred objects in the context of war in the last decades of the sixth century. We have the evidence of Evagrius Scholasticus, who recounted Philippikos's request for relics of Saint Symeon Stylites the Elder in order to secure his units in the East[25]. Philippikos, brother-in-law of the emperor Maurice and a very high-ranking personality at the imperial court[26], was appointed *magister militum per Orientem* to replace the ineffective former commander John Mystakon, and his task was to continue the war with the Persians. It is hard to date this request because Evagrius inserted it as a chronological interpolation in his narrative about the relics, miracles, and shrine of Symeon Stylites the Elder, but it can be possibly dated to the period before 589, when Philippikos was finally replaced

---

[23] Serrano del Pozo, 'The Cross-standard', pp. 9–10.

[24] George of Pisidia, *De expeditione persica*, II. 252–55, ed. by Agostino Pertusi, *Giorgio di Pisidia: Poemi. I. Panegirici epici, edizione critica, traduzione e commento* (Ettal: Buch-Kunstverlag Ettal, 1960), p. 109. Anatole Frolow, *La relique de la Vraie Croix* (Paris: Institut Français d'Études Byzantines, 1961), no. 53, p. 189; *idem*, 'La vraie Croix et les expéditions d'Héraclius en Perse', *Revue des Études Byzantines*, 11 (1953), 88–105 (p. 92); Sophia Mergali-Sahas, 'Byzantine Emperors and Holy Relics. Use, and Misuse, of Sanctity and Authority', *Jahrbuch der Österreichischen Byzantinistik*, 51 (2001), 41–60 (p. 50); Mischa Meier, p. 546.

[25] Evagrius, I. 13, p. 23: Φιλιπικοῦ δεηϑέντος παραφυλακῆς ἕνεκα τῶν ἑῴων ἐκστρατευμάτων τίμια λείψανά οἱ ἐκπεμφϑῆναι, CSLA E04490 (Efthymios Rizos).

[26] See Philippicus 3 in *PLRE* 3: 1022–26; Walter E. Kaegi, in *Oxford Dictionary of Byzantium*, 3 vols, (Oxford: Oxford University Press, 1991) Philippikos, p. 1654.

by another general, Komentiolos. Evagrius reports on the state of the preservation of the saint's head that he saw with his own eyes, which may suggest that Gregory, the patriarch of Antioch, complied with Philippikos's request and sent him a part of the saint's head (most probably a tooth or a hair)[27].

A little earlier Evagrius had inserted into his account a letter sent by the inhabitants of Antioch to Leo I, in which they asked the emperor to leave the relics of the saint with them when Leo I tried to transfer the entire body of the saint to Constantinople. Their concern was defense. 'Because our city does not have a wall, since it collapsed in an earthquake, we have brought the all-holy body to be a wall and protection for us'[28]. Although there is obviously a difference between Leo's attempt to bring the entire body of Symeon to Constantinople and Philippikos' desire to acquire a tiny part of it (perhaps Philippikos' request for only a little piece was some kind of compromise), both cases illustrate the common belief in the protective power of relics. In one case the body of the saint is a source of protection for the city, whereas in the other it is protection for the field army. Local context should be also taken into account here as Philippikos might have believed that a relic of a local saint would be more helpful than any other because the local saint would offer more support with which to defend his cult centre, which for Symeon Stylites was Antioch. It is not without reason that Evagrius's account emphasized that the relics were intended for the eastern armies. This is a very clear indication that they were to be put on the frontlines of the Persian-Roman war. If the troops failed, the capital of Syria would undoubtedly be threatened again by a Persian invasion. This implied threat was motivation for the saint to support Philippikos. On the other hand, it is probable that Evagrius wanted to emphasize the prestige enjoyed by the remains of this local saint by showing that the imperial commander was interested in the relic. Moreover, slightly further on in his work, Evagrius emphasizes that the head of the saint had been deprived of most of its teeth by devout people. In this way, Evagrius tries to show that the saint enjoyed great popularity which even reached the imperial court, as demonstrated by two attempts to obtain the relics: once in the distant past by Leo I, the second time in the author's presence.

The Emperor and the Civic Patron: the case of Demetrios

Another example of an attempt to obtain the relic of a saint for military purposes comes from Book 1 of the *Miracles of Saint Demetrios*, which was

---

[27] I am very grateful to Bryan Ward-Perkins for this suggestion.
[28] Evagrius, I. 13, 23. For more on the role of saints as defenders and protectors of the cities, see Wiśniewski, pp. 48–69.

compiled between 610 and 620 by John, the archbishop of Thessalonica (*BHG* 499–516). In his work John claims that Maurice wanted to obtain relics of Saint Demetrios, because he saw them as a significant way of receiving this saint's help in war:

> [...] the pious emperor, through divine letters sent to the present shepherd of the Christian people of Thessalonica, requested some relic of the Christ-bearing martyr Demetrios, which he wanted to use as an ally in battle[29].

Archbishop John clearly suggests that Maurice sought in the relics of Demetrios aid from the alliance with the saint (τὴν ἐξ αὐτοῦ τῆς συμμαχίας βοήθειαν)[30]. Although Maurice wrote a letter with his request to Archbishop Eusebius, John's predecessor, he was turned down when Eusebius claimed that the saint's burial place was unknown. Eusebius also explained that when Justinian earlier had tried to obtain the relics of Demetrios, the emperor even ordered excavations underneath the basilica, but due to a supernatural intervention — miraculously sent flames had blocked the progress of the works — the emperor had to give up, and he had to be content with some sweet-smelling soil from under the altar[31]. Ultimately, Eusebius sent some of this fragrant earth to Maurice.

It must be emphasized that Maurice's desire to possess the relics of St Demetrios is not as important from the point of view of the account of the Miracles as the saint's strong refusal to dispense his physical remains[32]. In this passage John indirectly expressed the common belief of the inhabitants of Thessalonica that the saint would never abandon their city in times of trouble[33]. The recognition of the saint's military power by the imperial authority was supposed to confirm the saint's ability to resist the invasion of the

---

[29] John of Thessalonica, *Miracula S. Demetrii*, I. 5, ed. Paul Lemerle, *Les plus anciens recueils des miracles de Saint Démétrius et la pénétration des Slaves dans les Balkans*, 2 vols. (Paris: Editions CNRS, 1979), p. 89: ὡς φιλευσεβὴς βασιλεὺς ᾐτήσατο, θείαις χρησάμενος κεραίαις πρὸς τὸν τηνικαῦτα τὸν τῶν Χριστιανῶν λαὸν τῶν Θεσσαλονικέων ποιμαίνοντα πόλεως, ὥστε πεμφθῆναι αὐτῷ λείψανόν τι τοῦ Χριστοφόρου μάρτυρος Δημητρίου, πίστει τὴν ἐξ αὐτοῦ τῆς συμμαχίας βοήθειαν βουλομένῳ καρπώσασθαι.

[30] Interestingly, in his enkomion of Saint Demetrios, John praised the invisible alliance in wars that the people of Thessalonica had with the saint: Anna Philippidis-Braat, 'L'enkômion de Saint Démétrius par Jean de Thessalonique', *Travaux et Mémoires*, 8 (1981), 397–414 (p. 306).

[31] *Miracula S. Demetrii*, I. 5, p. 89.

[32] James Constantin Skedros, *Saint Demetrios of Thessaloniki: Civic Patron and Divine Protector, 4th-7th Centuries CE* (Harrisburg, PA: Trinity Press International, 1999), p. 87.

[33] This belief is the most visible in Miracle 15 which describes a vision of a man from Thessalonica: two angels appeared to call Demetrios back to heaven, since the city would soon be destroyed. Demetrios refused to abandon his people and finally the city survived: *Miracula S. Demetrii*, I. 15, pp. 161–65.

Avars and the Slavs, as Demetrios had been able to do before[34]. However, the *Miracles* is a hagiographical work that uses a set of narrative motifs characteristic of this genre. The inhabitants of Thessalonica, who in the face of various threats (sieges, famine, epidemics) were left alone and unable to count on the help of the imperial army and administration, were dependent only on their holy patron, who did not disappoint them and in some way replaced the ineffective state authority[35]. Moreover, the emperor sought help from Demetrios with his own problems, expecting that his relics would effectively help in the war.

In the aforementioned cases, the beliefs about the relics of two saints, Simeon Stylites the Elder and Demetrios, although they come from different parts of the Empire, were quite similar: first, that the relics of a saint are a source of protective power for the city in which they are located, and second, that this power might as well be used by the emperor or his commander on the battlefield. Another example of the new approach to incorporating the relics of saints into the sphere of war derives unexpectedly from an author in distant Gaul, Gregory of Tours, who describes a rumour heard by the usurper Gundovald in 584 about an eastern king who was rushing into battle with the thumb of Saint Sergios attached to his own right arm[36]. It is unknown whether this eastern king was Maurice, but this case perfectly demonstrates confidence that the power of the martyr's relic has a direct impact on the battlefield.

This confidence is nothing new in terms of the perception of the protective function of saints in war, because the phenomenon had been attested much earlier, but the method of acquisition of this supernatural protection had clearly changed. Previously emperors or their commanders visited the sanctuary and prayed at the grave of a saint instead of taking or trying to take relics on campaigns or to the battlefield[37].

---

[34] In Miracle 13, Demetrios appeared on the walls in military dress and struck the first attacker to mount the ladder with a spear: *Miracula S. Demetrii*, I. 13, p. 135; In Miracle 14, riding a white horse and wearing a white mantle, Demetrios repelled the marauders: *Miracula S. Demetrii*, I. 14, p. 157.

[35] Ruth J. Macrides, 'Subversion and Loyalty in the Cult of St Demetrios', *Byzantinoslavica*, 51 (1990), 189–97 (p. 191); Franz A. Bauer, *Eine Stadt und ihr Patron. Thessaloniki und der Heilige Demetrios* (Regensburg: Schnell und Steiner, 2013), pp. 239–40.

[36] Gregory of Tours, *Decem Libri historiarum*, VII. 31, ed. by Bruno Krusch & Wilhelm Levinson, MGH SRM I. 1 (1951), pp. 350–51, CSLA E02263 (Katarzyna Wojtalik).

[37] Ammianus Marcellinus ironically states that Sabinianus, the commander of the Roman army in the East, visited martyrs' tombs in Edessa in order to ensure protection for the campaign against the Persian king Shapur in 359: Ammianus Marcellinus, *Res gestae*, XVIII. 7. 7, ed. by Wolfgang Seyfarth (Leipzig: Teubner, 1978). This episode is discussed in more detail by John Weisweiler, *Christianity in War: Ammianus on Power and Religion in Constantius'*

Acheiropoietos *of Christ*

The presence of sacred objects in east Roman warfare was not only manifested in the relics of saints; an even more visible change is the appearance of images, because the cult of icons began to embrace a more significant role than it had ever held in previous centuries[38]. Simocatta reported on the presence of an acheiropoetic image of Christ that was presented to soldiers before the battle of Solachon in 586:

> [...] When the enemy came into view and the dust was thick, Philippikos displayed the image of God Incarnate, which tradition from ancient times even to the present day proclaims was formed by divine wisdom, not shaped by a weaver's hands nor adorned by a painter's pigment. For this reason it is celebrated among the Romans as not made by human hand and is thought worthy of divine privileges: for the Romans worship its archetype to an ineffable degree. The general stripped this of its sacred coverings and paraded through the ranks, thereby inspiring the army with a greater and irresistible courage[39].

In his account Simocatta described a dramatic scene, in which before the soldiers rushed into battle, Philippikos paraded through the ranks with the image of Christ stripped of its sacred coverings to inspire the army to be more courageous. Afterwards he began a tearful supplication before the soldiers, which finally filled them with extraordinary bravery that allowed them to strike the enemy and achieve an impressive victory.

Persian War, in *The Power of Religion in Late Antiquity*, ed. by Andrew Cain & Noel Lenski (Burligton: Ashgate, 2009), pp. 384–88. Rufinus of Aquileia records that Theodosius I, before the war against the usurper Eugenius, celebrated a supplicatory prayer at the tombs of the martyrs and apostles, seeking support from the saints in the war: Rufinus of Aquileia, *History of the Church*, XI. 33 trans. by Philip R. Amidon, The Fathers of the Church. A New Translation 133 (Washington D.C.: The Catholic University of America Press, 2017), p. 479.
[38] Ernst Kitzinger, 'The Cult of Images in the Age before Iconoclasm', *Dumbarton Oaks Papers*, 8 (1954), 83–150 (p. 87); Derek Krueger, pp. 310–11. But see also Robin Jensen's article in this volume, who argues that the beginnings of devotional (although not necessarily powerful) images can be traced back to the fourth century.
[39] Theoph. Sim. II. 3: ἐπεὶ δὲ τὸ πολέμιον παρεφαίνετο, καὶ ἦν κόνις πολλή, Φιλιππικὸς τὸ θεανδρικὸν ἐπεφέρετο εἴκασμα, ὃ λόγος ἔκαθεν καὶ εἰς τὰ νῦν διηχεῖθε θείαν ἐπιστήμην μορφῶσαι, οὐχ ὑφάντου χεῖρας τεκτήνασθαι ἢ ζωγράφου μηλιάδα ποικίλαι. διά τοι τοῦτο καὶ ἀχειροποίητος παρὰ Ῥωμαίοις καθυμνεῖται καὶ τῶν ἰσοθέων πρεσβειῶν ἠξίωται· ἀρχέτυπον γὰρ ἐκείνου θρησκεύουσι Ῥωμαῖοι τι ἀάρρητον. Ταύτην ὁ στρατηγὸς τῶν σεβασμίων περιπέπλων γυμνώσας τὰς τάξεις ὑπέτρεχεν, κρείττονος καὶ ἀνανταγωνίστου θράσους ἐντεῦθεν μεταδιδοὺς τῷ στρατεύματι. On the battle of Solachon see: Anna Kotłowska & Łukasz Różycki, 'The Battle of Solachon of 586 in Light of the Works of Theophylact Simocatta and Theophanes Confessor (Homologetes)', *Travaux et Mémoires*, 19 (2015), pp. 315–27.

SAINTS AND SACRED OBJECTS

It should definitely be noted that this was the first reference to the direct participation of an acheiropoetic image in a battle. Their earlier appearances in relation to wartime events were closely related to the defence of the cities in which they were located. The first reference to an *acheiropoietos* was made by Evagrius, and it is remarkable that Evagrius's account concerned the image's miraculous intervention during the siege of Edessa by the Persians in 544[40]. This would mean that the acheiropoietic portrayals were introduced relatively quickly into the arsenal of sacred objects used for the purposes of war. In general, sacred images were treated as a tool of communication with the army, and Simocatta recorded another episode that sheds some light on the role of the sacred objects. He reports that Priskos, another of Maurice's generals in the East, sought to calm some soldiers who were furious because of reductions in their military pay by revealing to them the acheiropoietic image of Christ, which he ordered to be carried before the troops. The soldiers, however, were not convinced that they should submit to the relic, which they instead pelted with stones[41]. The attempt to calm down the rebel soldiers could be regarded as an obvious example of the manipulation of sacred objects by a military commander. Almost all of the sources accused Priskos of stirring up the soldiers with his awkward and arrogant behaviour. In his work Simocatta presents Priskos in a rather unfavourable light. By using a holy image in his narrative, he wants to show that while one commander, Philippikos, was able to achieve an impressive victory with the image of Christ, another one, Priskos, was unable to control a raging mob in spite of his attempts to use the holy icon. Regardless, these two examples were harbingers of the further development of the military function of holy images, which appeared to be fully formed during the wars of Heraclius[42].

---

[40] Evagrius, IV. 27, p. 175.

[41] Theoph. Sim. III. 1. 11–12.

[42] The *coup d'état* of Heraclius in 610 was carried out under the banner of the acheiropoetic image of the Mother of God, which was attached to the mast of his flagship: George of Pisidia, *Heraclias*, II. 15, p. 252. Theophanes alludes to reliquaries and icons of the Mother of God on the masts of the ships of Heraclius, asserting that this information came from George of Pisidia: Theophanes, *Chronographia*, ed. Carl de Boor, Corpus Scriptorum Historiae Byzantinae (Leipzig: Teubner, 1883), AM 6102 [AD 609/10], p. 298. Both George of Pisidia and Theophanes claimed that Heraclius took an acheiropoetic image of Christ on a campaign against the Persians: George of Pisidia, *De expeditione persica*, I. 139–51, p. 91 and II. 86–87, p. 101; Theophanes, *Chronographia*, AM 6113 [AD 620/1], p. 303.

Names of the Saints

It must also be emphasized that in the military context of Maurice's rule sanctity manifested itself not only through relics, sacred objects, and images, but also by invoking the names of saints on the battlefield. An excellent example illustrating this phenomenon is described by Simocatta in his account of the joint campaign of Khosrow II, his troops, and an army provided by Maurice in order to help the former regain his throne from the usurper Bahram. Simocatta reports that the Romans taught the Persian troops of Khosrow the name of Mary as a password in order to distinguish them from the Persian troops of Bahram during the battle:

> [...] The Romans provided a password for their barbarian allies as well, teaching them the name of the Mother of God and Virgin, lest they might kill their allies as enemies because of the difference in race, since in the confusion of the battle those on their own side would present an indistinguishable aspect. And the situation was somewhat strange, as the name of Mary became a means of salvation even for the Chaldaeans[43].

This is quite an interesting example, though it is not the first use of a saint's name in the context of war. Theodoret of Cyrus mentions that during the Persian siege of Theodosiopolis, Bishop Eunomius, who led the defence of the city, used a catapult named after Thomas the Apostle to crush the skull of a Persian magnate who had cursed the city[44]. Furthermore, some evidence confirms the use of the names of saints in this manner in later times. In Book 2 of the Miracles of Saint Demetrios, compiled in the 680s, a catapult stone inscribed with Demetrios' name collides with an enemy projectile in mid-air, causing it to rebound into an Avar siege engine[45].

Although all of these practices relate to the use of saints' names as a strategy that was available to Christian soldiers to fight the enemy or protect their own ranks, there are some differences. The use of the Virgin Mary's name in Simocatta's account of the campaign of Khosrow II applies to a pitched battle in an open field, while in the other two examples the sacred names were intended to invoke aid for the besieged cities. Simocatta's evidence could

---

[43] Theoph. Sim. V. 10. 4–5: Σύμβολον δὲ οἱ Ῥωμαῖοι καὶ τοῖς συμμαχοῦσι βαρβάροις παρείχοντο τὴν τῆς θεομήτορος καὶ παρθένου προσηγορίαν διδάξαντες ἵνα μὴ τῷ διακεκριμένῳ τοῦ γένους ὡς ἀντίπαλον τὸ συμμαχικὸν διαφθαρῶσιν, τῷ συγκεχυμένῳ τῆς συμπλοκῆς ἀδιάρθωτον αὐτοῖς τῶν οἰκειοτάτων παρεχομένων τὴν δήλωσιν. καὶ παράδοξόν τι χρῆμα συνέβαινεν· ἐγίνετο γὰρ καὶ Χαλδαίοις τὸ τῆς Μαρίας σωτήριον ὄνομα (trans. Efthymios Rizos, CSLA E00046).

[44] Theodoret of Cyrrhus, *Historia ecclesiastica* V. 39. 12–14, ed. Léon Parmentier & Günther Ch. Hansen: *Histoire Ecclésiastique. Livres III–V*, SC 501 (2009), pp. 486–87.

[45] *Miracula S. Demetrii*, II, 2, p. 187.

SAINTS AND SACRED OBJECTS

acknowledge the presence of the cult of the Mother of God in the imperial army, despite the fact that using the name of Mary as a battle cry or a military password was far from religious worship and should be considered in the broader context of his account of Khosrow II's restoration to the Persian throne.

Simocatta's narrative about Khosrow's campaign against Bahram is remarkable on account of the prominence of the Christian religious components. Their role in the narrative was to justify Maurice's controversial decision to help Khrosrow II and show that their alliance was approved by God. Consequently, Simocatta's reference to the invocation of the name of the Mother of God in the battle could be regarded as part of an elaborately constructed account of a piously motivated and conducted war. This would be partially true, but another more important factor that should not be forgotten is the presence of the cult of the Mother of God in the imperial army[46]. It is significant that Maurice's piety was also marked by his special attitude to the Mother of God, and that Maurice is known as an enthusiastic promoter of the Theotokos's cult[47]. In the description presented by Simocatta it is not obvious whether the choice of the Virgin's name as a battle password was inspired by the emperor and his entourage, or whether it was a practice of soldiers that had nothing to do with imperial orders.

What has changed?

These examples demonstrate that east Roman warfare under Maurice was marked by a special accumulation and use of the sacred objects. This development would be in line with the overall trend towards the use of relics and holy

---

[46] An interesting example of incorporating some elements of Marian piety into the sphere of war is provided by Evagrius, who claimed that Narses, commander-in-chief of Justinian in Italy, was not to begin any military action before he received a sign from Mother of God: Evagrius, IV. 24, p. 171.

[47] Maurice presumably instituted or reorganized the weekly feast for the Virgin that was celebrated on Fridays at Blachernae with a special procession to the church of the Virgin in the Chalkoprateia; he also inaugurated the feast on 15 August celebrating the Dormition of the Theotokos and attended the liturgy for the feast of Christ's Presentation at the Temple (Candlemas) at the church at Blachernae, where relics of the garment of Mary were kept: CSLA E00040 (Efhymios Rizos). Also, Maurice introduced the Mother Mary holding the Child in front of her chest as a new iconographic image on his imperial seals. This image replaced the winged victory with the Cross, which in turn may indicate that the Theotokos gradually acquired the role of the guarantor of imperial victory: *Catalogue of Byzantine Seals at Dumbarton Oaks and in the Fogg Museum of Art*, VI: Emperors, Patriarchs of Constantinople, Addenda, (Washington D.C.: Dumbarton Oaks, 2009), no. 9. 1–9. On the role of the Marian cult in Maurice's religiosity, see: Whitby, *Emperor Maurice*, pp. 22–23.

images in different areas of life during the reign of this emperor, who was generally regarded as a great enthusiast of the cult of saints. The emperor's piety, which we can observe throughout the sources, was especially focused on his personal contact with objects through which he could obtain divine grace. For instance, during Lent in 596, Maurice slept on a wooden pallet belonging to the patriarch of Constantinople, John the Faster[48]. This need for contact with the holy was also manifested through the feverish collecting of relics. Maurice unsuccessfully attempted to acquire the relics of the prophet Daniel from the Persian king Khosrow II and bring them to Constantinople[49], while his wife sought to acquire St Paul's head from Rome[50]. The Syrian Chronicle of Seert attributes the acquisition of the cap of Sabrisho, the leader of the Nestorian community, to the emperor[51]. In addition, Maurice was eager to contact saintly people during their lifetimes. He invited Saint Theodore of Sykeon[52] and Saint Golinduch of Persia[53] to Constantinople to honour them and gain their blessing.

Admittedly, all this does not distinguish dramatically Maurice from his predecessors, among whom one can find worshippers of relics who very willingly brought to Constantinople the sacred objects which they wanted to keep as close as possible[54]. Justinian's example thoroughly demonstrates this attitude, because the emperor was above all praised for his impressive building programme and the piety he manifested in the worship of saints

---

[48] Theoph. Sim. VII. 6. 5, CSLA E00021 (Efthymios Rizos).

[49] Sebeos, *Armenian History attributed to Sebeos*, 14, trans. by Robert W. Thomson (Liverpool: Liverpool University Press, 1999), p. 30. Sebeos claimed that the imperial attempt to bring Daniel's relics ended in failure due to a miraculous intervention. Having learned about Maurice's intentions, Queen Shirin, the wife of Khosrow II, arranged collective prayers and fasting for the Christians of Persia, thanks to which they obtained the grace necessary to retain the body of the saint: Sebeos, p. 31, CSLA E00129 (Nikoloz Aleksidze).

[50] Gregory the Great, *Registrum epistularum*, IV. 30. 1–7, 32–36, ed. by Dag Norberg, CCSL 140 (1982), CSLA E06351 (Frances Trzeciak,).

[51] Chronique de Seert, *Histoire nestorienne, pt. II*, trans. by Addai Scher, *Patrologia Orientalis*, 13 (1919), pp. 492–93.

[52] *Life of Theodore of Sykeon* 82, trans. by Elizabeth Dawes & Norman H. Baynes, *Three Byzantine Saints* (Oxford: Blackwell, 1948), p. 145.

[53] Eustratius, *Life of Golinduch*, IV. 23, ed. by Athanasios Papadopoulos-Kerameus, Ἀνάλεκτα Ἱεροσολυμιτικῆς Σταχυολογίας, 5 vols (St Petersburg: Kirsbaum, 1897), p. 171. On this episode see: Matthew dal Santo, 'Imperial Power and its Subversion in Eustratius of Constantinople's *Life and Martyrdom of Golinduch (c. 602)*', *Byzantion*, 81 (2011), 138–76 (p. 164).

[54] For example, Theodosius II dressed in the cloak of the late bishop of Hebron, who died in Constantinople, thinking that in this way a portion of the deceased's sainthood would flow into him: Socrates, *Historia ecclesiastica*, VII. 22. 14, ed. by G. C. Hansen, *Histoire Ecclésiastique. Livre VII*, SC 506 (2007), pp. 86–87.

SAINTS AND SACRED OBJECTS

and relics[55]. The same can be said about Justin II[56]. During his reign relics and images were increasingly included in court ceremonies, and the new patterns for adoring the relics of the True Cross clearly imitated the adoration of the emperor[57]. Justin also brought two important sacred objects to Constantinople: a relic of the True Cross from Apamea, and a famous *acheiropoietos* of Christ, the so-called image of Kamouliana[58].

The involvement of saints in war was likewise not a new phenomenon in itself. But now the methods of attracting their attention had changed. Initially, the emperor or a commander prayed at the grave of a martyr or in his sanctuary and then went to war. During the reign of Maurice, relics started to accompany him to the very battlefield. The selection of the saints who would appear on the battlefield was also different. Previously these had been either the Apostles or particular saints. Although these companions did not disappear altogether, it is clear that for Maurice the presence of Christ (in the form of relics of the Cross, acheiropoietic images, or any other form) and the Mother of God became essential. In addition, when analysing the above examples, it should be noted that there was a strong connection between imperial authority and the relics taken to the war. The main possessors and owners of relics were the emperor and his trusted commanders, such as

---

[55] Procopius provides an excellent example of how the cult of saints and relics was involved in the image of the pious emperor. When for a long time the emperor suffered pain caused by excessively rigorous ascetic practices, priests laid the reliquary with the relics of the Forty Martyrs of Sebaste on his knee. After the emperor was cured, further oil suddenly flowed out from the relics and spilled on Justinian's feet and purple tunic. This garment became a relic itself and was kept in the palace as a testimony and source of healing power: Procopius of Caesarea, *De aedificiis*, I. 7. 12–16, CSLA E04395 (Julia Doroszewska & Efthymios Rizos). Interestingly, the Forty Martyrs of Sebaste are also invoked as heavenly protectors of the Empire and the emperor's allies at war in Kontakion 58 of Romanus the Melodist: *On the Forty Martyrs of Sebasteia* II, pp. 495–505, CSLA E05878 (Efthymios Rizos). On his kontakia from a perspective of political ideology and court propaganda, see: Johannes Koder, 'Imperial Propaganda in the Kontakia of Romanos the Melode', *Dumbarton Oaks Papers*, 62 (2008), 275–91.

[56] Averil Cameron, 'The Early Religious Policies of Justin II', in *The Orthodox Churches and the West*, ed. by Derek Baker, Studies in Church History 13 (Oxford: Blackwell, 1976), pp. 51–67 (pp. 65-67).

[57] John of Ephesus, *The Third Part of the Ecclesiastical History of John Bishop of Ephesus*, trans. by Robert Payne Smith (Oxford: Oxford University Press, 1860), II. 29, pp. 140–41.

[58] On the translation of part of the True Cross from Apamea and Kamouliana to Constantinople, see: Georgios Kedrenos, *Historiarum compendium*, Corpus Scriptorum Historiae Byzantinae, ed. by Barthold G. Niebuhr, 2 vols. (Bonn: Weber, 1838), I, p. 685. Among the contemporary authors only Menander Protector refers to the translation of the relic of the True Cross from Apamea and reports that the removal of the holy relic from this city led the inhabitants of Apamea to launch an armed uprising against imperial authority: Menander Protector, fr. 17, pp. 154–57.

245

Philippikos or Priskos, while there is no mention of the possession of relics by simple soldiers. This is especially visible in the narrative of Theophylact Simocatta, who liked to embellish his account with tales of the adventures of ordinary soldiers[59]. But in all of his stories about relics and images, the emperor or any of his commanders are the main protagonists while the soldiers are absent.

The question of Maurice's personal contribution to the development of particular forms of piety related to the cult of saints is extremely difficult to solve, mainly due to the specificity of the sources from which the information about him is derived. The vast majority of the evidence comes from the *History* of Theophylact Simocatta, while other authors who wrote about Maurice's rule are often silent about the acts of the emperor's military piety. But we have to remember that most of the authors were distant from the imperial court, and they were either not particularly interested in reporting all the events and occurrences in the immediate vicinity of the emperor, or they were rather prejudiced against Maurice. Thus, the silence of John of Ephesus, John of Nikiu, John of Epiphaneia, and Menander Protector, while significant, is not really shocking.

As for Simocatta, while he admittedly wrote in the period of Heraclius and may have tried to adapt his narrative to the political circumstances of his time, there is no reason to believe that he manipulated memories about Maurice's attitude towards saints, relics, and sacred objects. First, we have other sources independent of Simocatta that confirm Maurice's special attachment to the cult of relics, sacred objects, and saints. Especially valuable in this regard are the accounts of Evagrius and John, the archbishop of Thessalonica, because they both represent local historiographic or hagiographic traditions uninfluenced by the imperial court. Second, the practices described by Simocatta correspond with changes in eastern Roman religiosity at that time. In practices related to cults of relics and icons in the army, the next step of evolution, which occurred gradually from the second half of the sixth century, can definitely be found in terms of the relations between authority and saints or sacred objects.

In a broader sense, this process should be associated with the liturgification of east Roman society, which from the perspective of imperial power was characterized by an increasing convergence of religion with ceremonial and imperial ideology, with the result that relics and sacred images permeated official ceremonies and court rituals. The emperors were eager to acquire sacred objects and associate themselves with popular cults to strengthen their

---

[59] For instance: Theoph. Sim. II. 6. 6 and II. 18. 14–24.

fading power in the face of various crises by exhibiting the sacerdotal nature of their power, which they held as rulers of an empire endowed by heaven. The novelty in Maurice's attitude towards relics and holy images lies in the fact that these objects, which were preserved in strictly defined, non-military frames, began slowly to enter matters of war. Therefore it can be said, albeit quite paradoxically, that Maurice's policy can be described in terms of both change and continuity.

Martyrs, Hunters and Kings

The 'Political Theology' of Saints' Relics in Late Antique Caucasia

Nikoloz Aleksidze
(Free University of Tbilisi)

Introduction

Medieval Caucasia is the most fertile ground for the study of the historical interplay of religious and cultural practices. Located at a virtual crossroad of civilizations, the late antique Caucasian nations, Albania, Armenia, and Iberia, were exposed to and have internalized major religious beliefs from across Eurasia. From Christianity to Islam and Judaism, and from local mountainous religious practices to Zoroastrianism and Mithraism, all of these traditions, whether in their symbolic form, rhetoric, or political manifestation, contributed to the creation of the extraordinary cultural landscape of Caucasia[1].

Armenia and Iberia/Kartli (eastern Georgia) were Christianized in the first few decades of the fourth century. This dramatic event was followed by the gradual formation of Christian writing, institutions, and local theological traditions. Two centuries later, Armenian writing produced a sizeable

---

[1] For an overview of the interaction of religious traditions in late antique Caucasia, see Nikoloz Aleksidze, 'Caucasia: Armenia, Albania, Georgia', in *A Companion to Religion in Late Antiquity*, ed. Josef Lössl & Nicholas J. Backer-Brian (Chichester: Wiley-Blackwell, 2018), pp. 135–56.

Interacting with Saints in the Late Antique and Medieval Worlds, ed. by Robert Wiśniewski, Raymond Van Dam, and Bryan Ward-Perkins, Hagiologia, 20 (Turnhout, 2023), pp. 249–268.
© BREPOLS ❧ PUBLISHERS   DOI 10.1484/M.HAG-EB.5.133630

corpus of historical, theological, and exegetical literature. The Georgian tradition was equally heavily invested in Christian apologetics and in producing accounts of martyrdoms and saintly lives for the purpose of strengthening Christianity in this religiously volatile region. Nevertheless, throughout Late Antiquity and the early medieval period, Caucasia was a ground of cohabitation, conflict, and syncretism between Christian and Zoroastrian worldviews. Despite the thoroughly Christian nature of early medieval Caucasian literary production, and despite attempts to Hellenize and Byzantinize their identities, the Caucasian cultures remained integral parts of the Iranian Oecumene, with Iranian and Zoroastrian imagery persisting in the language, symbolism, and political imagery of the Caucasian people[2].

The appropriation of Iranian and Zoroastrian imagery by Christian rhetoric emerging in Armenian and Georgian writing throughout Late Antiquity and the early Middle Ages has been demonstrated on multiple occasions[3]. The subject of the present essay is one such conceptual crossroad of Zoroastrianism, Christianity, and traditional Caucasian religious practices that resulted in a unique kind of religious and political representation in late antique Caucasian writing. It provides further evidence for such syncretism of Christian and Iranian representations by illustrating the appropriation and transformation of Sasanian symbolism of royal investiture by Christian rhetoric, through replacing Iranian symbols of the divine *farrah* (glory, splendour, good fortune) with Christian symbolic language[4]. The essay also discusses some related aspects of the 'political theology' of the cult of the relics of the saints in late antique and early medieval Caucasian religious and political rhetoric.

The central theme of the present essay is the discovery of a treasure by a charismatic hunter as a manifestation of his royal investiture. The motif of hunters as liminal figures is certainly universal, and it is attested in all cultures from Polynesia to Iran and the Americas[5]. Equally well studied is the representation of the Zoroastrian concept of royal investiture in Iranian art and religious writing. The novelty that the Caucasian sources provide rests in a unique kind of symbolic appropriation within early Christian writing.

---

[2] For an overview, see Tim Greenwood, 'Sasanian Reflections in Armenian Sources', *E-Sasanika* 3 (2008) (https://cpb-us-e2.wpmucdn.com/sites.uci.edu/dist/c/347/files/2020/01/e-sasanika3-Greenwood.pdf).
[3] See numerous works by James Russell and Nina Garsoïan.
[4] For the definition of *farrah* as used in the present paper, see Gherardo Gnoli, '*farrah*', in *Encyclopædia Iranica*, online edition, 2012 (accessed on 11 February 2018).
[5] Thomas T. Allsen, *The Royal Hunt in Eurasian History* (Philadelphia: University of Pennsylvania Press, 2006), pp. 160–86.

After Christianization, the Zoroastrian symbolism of the royal *farrah* persisted and was internalized by early Christian narratives, in which material royal treasures transubstantiated into equally material relics of the saints that authenticated the king's divine mandate to rule. These relics, however, which possessed the power to bestow royal charisma, were not merely mechanical substitutes for the (divine) treasure, but rather encapsulated crucial political and theological symbolism.

Three Foundation Narratives

For the purpose of our enquiry, two early medieval quasi-historical accounts can be analyzed, with a brief albeit crucial reference to a third. The first is the early medieval Georgian epic chronicle entitled *Life of the Georgian Kings*[6]. The *Life* is a universal history which opens with the story of Noah's grandsons and the eponymous founders of the Caucasian nations, and carries on with describing the foundation of the Georgian kingdom and the lives and deeds of its kings, culminating in its Christianization. The *Life of the Georgian Kings* was incorporated into the large medieval compendium the *Georgian Chronicles* in a way that the reader is led towards the Christianization of the kingdom, even though this was most likely not the intention of the original composition, and the markedly Christian elements were a later development. As has been argued on several occasions, the early medieval Georgian historical corpus has not survived in its original form, and what we possess nowadays is a result of extensive reworking, both textual and ideological, with attempts to override the Sasanian and other Iranian components within the narratives in order to adapt early Sasanian accounts to the ideological demands of the age. Among other influences, the *Life of the Georgian Kings* is also modelled according to Iranian quasi-historical epic narratives. Although the *Life*'s present form is tentatively dated to the eighth century, its individual parts were probably formulated earlier in an oral form[7]. Within this corpus, our interest lies in what can be conventionally called the *Life of P'arnavaz*, a subsection of the *Life of the Georgian Kings*, the story of the ascension to the Iberian throne of its legendary first king in the third century BC. and the creation of the Iberian body politic as known to the authors of

---

[6] *K'art'lis c'xovreba* [The Life of Georgia] 1, ed. by Simon Qaukhchishvili (Tbilisi: Sabchota Sakartvelo, 1955), pp. 1–71; For an English translation, see Robert W. Thomson, *Rewriting Caucasian History: The Medieval Armenian Adaptation of the Georgian Chronicles. The Original Georgian Texts and the Armenian Adaptation* (Oxford: Clarendon Press, 1996).

[7] For discussion of the Sasanian component of the *Life of the Georgian Kings*, see Stephen Rapp Jr., *The Sasanian World through Georgian Eyes: Caucasia and the Iranian Commonwealth in Late Antique Georgian Literature* (Farnham: Ashgate, 2014).

the *Life*. This episode holds a central place among other Georgian historical narratives, as it is specifically dedicated to the fundamentally transformative event in the history of Kartli (also known as Iberia in eastern Georgia)– the foundation and establishment of kingship and the political system.

The second corpus has a comparable textual history and complexity. The historical collection known as the *History of the Albanians* is attributed to a certain Movsēs Kałankatwac'i or Movsēs Dasxuranc'i in the tenth century. Although the chronicle recounts the history of Caucasian Albania, it has survived in Armenian, or, more likely, was originally written in Armenian. Far from being a single or even coherent narrative, the *History of the Albanians* is rather a collection and edition of disjointed historical and quasi-historical accounts related to Caucasian Albania, often revealing awkward attempts to sustain continuity. The earliest strata of Book One of the *History* are conventionally dated to as early as the second half of the sixth century, while the rest is markedly late, with the final parts dating to the eleventh century. Among other events, its opening chapter focuses on the reign of Vač'agan I the Pious, the late fifth-century king who restored Christianity in Albania and thereby founded a new political order. There is a general, albeit a cautious consensus, that the part that can be called the *Life of Vač'agan* must have been created as an independent text and may be dated to the aftermath of the king's death[8].

Both the *Life of P'arnavaz* and the *Life of Vač'agan* chronicle the foundation of the Iberian and Albanian polities and narrate the initiation to kingship of their legendary founders. They recount the rites of passage of the two charismatic figures to legitimate kingship and provide definitions of Iberia's and Albania's *raison d'être*. The major difference, however, is obvious. The former is a story of a pre-Christian king and thus reveals strong Iranian imagery. By contrast, the latter is an account of the deeds of a pious Christian monarch and the final establishment of Christianity in fifth-century Albania. Despite this seemingly crucial difference, I argue that the two narratives are essentially structured identically, and that the strategies of legitimation of their kings' rule follow a single pattern, with P'arnavaz and Vač'agan passing through identical liminal stages on their path to legitimate kingship. Although thoroughly Christian in its rhetoric, the *Life of Vač'agan* achieves this by manifestly Christianizing Iranian symbolism.

---

[8] For these arguments, see Jean-Pierre Mahé, 'Vac'agan III le Pieux et le culte des reliques', *Révue des Études Arméniennes*, 35 (2013), 113–29; Constantin Zuckerman, 'The Khazars and Byzantium. The First Encounter', in *The World of the Khazars: New Perspectives. Selected Papers from the Jerusalem 1999 International Khazar Colloquium*, ed. by Peter B. Golden, Haggai Ben Shamai & András Róna-Tas (Leiden: Brill, 2007), pp. 399–432.

The third narrative antedates the former two and was written down sometime in the middle of the fifth century. Agathangelos's *History of Armenia*, alternatively known as the *Life of Gregory the Illuminator*, recounts in detail the Christianization of Arsacid Armenia in the early fourth century and the establishment of the national Church, patriarchal succession, and other Christian institutions. Agathangelos's account exercised a fundamental impact on subsequent Armenian writing and provided models for the conceptualization of the metaphysical image of the Armenian nation. Crucially, it also set the tone for the perception of the role of the relics of the saints in Armenian and other Caucasian religious and political rhetoric. It will be demonstrated that, while the *Life of Vač'agan* was formally structured according to Iranian models and revealed affinities with the Georgian royal epic, simultaneously it adopted Christian political and theological imagery formulated by Agathangelos, especially with regard to the role of the relics of the saints in the perception of the metaphysical image of the nation.

The Road to Legitimacy

The *Life of P'arnavaz* is a foundation narrative that recounts the beginnings of the political community in Iberia and of those institutions that its authors believed to be fundamental to their ethno-religious and political identity. According to his *Life*, P'arnavaz was a descendant of the original rulers of Kartli, the *mamasaxlisis*. He overthrew the reign of Azon, a foreigner who was enthroned in Kartli by Alexander the Great, and reclaimed what he considered his rightful inheritance. Because he conceptualized the traditional Georgian administrative units, established the royal and centralized cult, created Georgian writing, and prescribed Georgian as the only official language of the kingdom, P'arnavaz is credited with the creation of all the markers of an independent polity. This, however, was the culmination of P'arnavaz's career, preceded by a path towards legitimate kingship. On this path, P'arnavaz, an outstanding hunter (a quality essential for an Iranian king), through a rite of passage, transubstantiated into a political entity[9]. The authors present

---

[9] In Iranian epic tradition, a literary device also adopted and internalized by medieval Georgian heroic epic, e.g. the *Amirandarejaniani* and *The Knight in the Panther's Skin* (eleventh-thirteenth centuries), the hunt is widely used as a literary device to initiate a transitional event in the king's life and career, which is followed by a life-changing discovery — a person, treasure or magic. William Hanaway, 'The Concept of the Hunt in Persian Literature', *Boston Museum Bulletin* 69 (1971), 21–69 (pp. 27–28): 'In addition to being a vehicle through which the poet can idealize the traditional male attributes and project them upon mortal kings, the concept of the hunt appears as a formal literary device. Hunting, as has been shown, was a conventional activity for a king, and therefore the hunt can be convincingly

the formation of the kingdom of Kartli as an essential transformation from wilderness to polity, from barbarian lawlessness to a state, a story that is in itself encapsulated in P'arnavaz's rite of passage[10]. P'arnavaz's political and metaphysical journey to kingship, from being merely a hunter to becoming a divinely sanctioned king, can be broken down into the following stages of investiture.

Legitimacy by heredity: Before the outset of P'arnavaz's adventure, he is revealed to be a native of Kartli and a descendant of Mc'xet'os, the eponymous founder of the city of Mcxeta, Iberia's capital. His direct ancestors were the pre-Alexandrian rulers of Mcxeta, the *mamasaxlisis*, whose rule was abolished following Alexander's invasion. Therefore, from the beginning of the narrative we are told that from the point of view of heredity, P'arnavaz is the rightful pretender to the Iberian throne, unlike Azon, his main rival, who was brought and installed from Greece.

Charismatic Election: The central event in the narrative, and indeed the primary topic of our essay, which is described in detail in P'arnavaz's *Life*, is the king's charismatic election. P'arnavaz's initiation and the descent of *farrah*, the royal splendour or the *tychē basileōs* over him, is manifested through the dream that he saw while hunting in the forests of Tbilisi. The king's vision was immediately followed by the discovery of a wondrous treasure[11]. Through this divine revelation and the virtual descent upon him of the divine light, P'arnavaz assumed the second, political identity, and only after this was he made worthy to uncover and put to use the treasure. Crucially, the treasure was immediately used as an instrument for the cohesion of his realm and for the creation of the Iberian body politic.

Popular acclaim: The legitimacy of P'arnavaz's rule was immediately acknowledged by K'uji, the ruler of Egrisi (western Georgia), who accepted P'arnavaz's gifts and his mandate over both realms, the west and the east[12].

---

used as the setting for an incident. Such an incident can provide a change of direction in the plot by leading the hunter across a threshold to a new world, where he may have extraordinary adventures and from where he returns with special knowledge.'

[10] The association of *farrah* with the royal hunt in Iranian tradition has been pointed out on numerous occasions. See Allsen, *The Royal Hunt*, p. 162. In Iranian imagery 'by virtue of a successful hunt, the king acquires a radiant nimbus as a sign of his acquired Farr (right)'. Abolala Soudavar, 'Farr(ah) ii: Iconography of Farr(ah) /Xvarenah', in *Encyclopædia Iranica*, online edition, 2012, available at https://www.iranicaonline.org/articles/farr-ii-iconography (accessed on 11 February 2018).

[11] This topic is explored in detail in Zurab Kiknadze, *k'art'uli mit'ologia 2: p'arnavazis sizmari* [Georgian mythology 2: The dream of P'arnavaz] (Tbilisi: Ilia State University Press, 2016). Kiknadze provides additional parallels between P'arnavaz's dream and Georgian and Caucasian folk traditions.

[12] *K'art'lis cxovreba*, p. 22; Thomson, *Rewriting*, p. 31.

Immediately after the discovery of the treasure, P'arnavaz dispatched a messenger to K'uji and offered him the opportunity to join his unifying project. A similar deal is struck with the Ossettes and the Leks (Lesgians), again through the aid of the treasure. Eventually P'arnavaz united the Georgian realms and overthrew Azon. Having united the realm and now endowed with divine grace, P'arnavaz promulgated laws and created political institutions. He set off to organize the kingdom administratively and established seven principalities. Further, he established a 'national' cult of Armazi, a local variation of Ahura Mazda, and erected its monument at the entrance of Mcxeta: 'This P'arnavaz was the first king in Kartli from among the descendants of K'artlos. He extended the Georgian language, and no more was a different language spoken in Kartli except Georgian. And he created the Georgian script'[13].

Imperial legitimacy: P'arnavaz's legitimacy was finally sanctioned by the universal emperor, who, according to the authors of the *Life*, was Antiochos I Soter, the king of the Seleucid Empire: 'P'arnavaz sent envoys to King Antiochos of Asurastan, and offered valuable gifts. He promised to serve him, and requested from him help against the Greeks. Antiochos accepted his gifts, called him his son, and presented him with a crown'[14]. P'arnavaz's mandate to rule in Kartli thus received multiple validations and confirmations.

The King's Treasure

The central event in P'arnavaz's rite of passage is his endowment with *farrah* and the subsequent miraculous discovery of the treasure. The dream that P'arnavaz saw is a typical manifestation of the divine grace of Iranian royal investiture narratives and an essential component of the legitimation of kings. Correspondingly, the discovery of treasure serves as a material confirmation of the king's metaphysical investiture. The episode is recounted in particularly solemn terms:

> Then P'arnavaz saw a dream: he was in an uninhabited house and was wishing to depart, yet could not leave. Then a ray of sunlight entered the window and seized him around the waist; it drew him up and brought him out the window. When he had come out into the countryside, he saw the sun bending down. He stretched out his hand, wiped the dew on the sun's face, and anointed his own face. P'arnavaz awoke, was astonished, and said: 'The dream means that I should go to Ispahan, and there I shall find good (fortune).' On that day P'arnavaz went out and hunted alone; he chased a deer in the plain of Digom. The deer fled into the rough ground of Tbilisi. P'arnavaz

---

[13] *K'art'lis c'xovreba*, p. 26; Thomson, *Rewriting*, p. 38.
[14] *K'art'lis c'xovreba*, p. 23; Thomson, *Rewriting*, p. 32.

followed; he shot an arrow and hit the deer. The deer went on a little and fell at the foot of a cliff. P'arnavaz went up to the deer. Now the day, (already) evening, was declining. So he sat down by the deer in order to spend the night; in the morning he would go off. Now at the foot of the cliff was a cave, the entrance of which had been blocked up long since by stones; the ravages of time had caused dilapidation in the edifice. Then a heavy rain began to fall. So P'arnavaz took up an axe and broke away the entrance to the cave in order to keep himself dry from the rain inside. He entered the cave and saw there unparalleled treasures, gold and silver and incomparable dishes of gold and silver. Then P'arnavaz was astonished and filled with joy. He remembered the dream, and closed up the entrance to the cave in the same fashion. He hastened off and informed his mother and two sisters. That same night the three of them returned with donkeys and carts, and began to collect the treasure and to bury it in an appropriate (place). When day dawned, they again closed up the entrance to the cave in the same way. In this fashion they collected the treasure for five nights and planned their opportunity[15].

The discovery of treasure as a manifestation of divine grace and royal investiture is attested in a wide range of cultures from Antiquity to recent ethnographic records[16]. A crucial aspect of the encounter of the future king with the treasure is that eventually it is up to the treasure to find its owner, or to make itself manifest to him or her, and not the other way around. Louis Gernet calls these golden or valuable objects *agalmata*, specifically with reference to treasure that possesses both manifest and hidden powers. Crucially, *agalmata* possess a certain dangerous ambiguity that eventually defines the fate of the owner of the treasure: 'The qualities of power and danger are attached to something that is valuable and a precious possession. To know whether or not it will be wasted — or more precisely trampled on — is crucial'[17]. The

---

[15] *K'art'lis c'xovreba*, pp. 21–22; Thomson, *Rewriting*, pp. 29–30.

[16] Perhaps the most widely known and quoted example is Herodotus's account of Scythian ethnogenesis, according to which Targitaos's children received the divine treasure: 'In the time of their reign, golden products fell from the sky: a plow and also a yoke, a battle ax, and a *phialē* fell to Scythia. Seeing these first, the oldest went close, planning to take them, but as he approached, the gold burst into flame. When he had departed, the second son approached the gold, and it flared up again. And when the flaming gold had repelled them, the fire was extinguished at the approach of the third and youngest son, and he carried it off as his own. The older brothers then accepted that the whole kingship be handed over to the youngest.'

[17] See Louis Gernet, *Anthropology of Ancient Greece* (Baltimore: Johns Hopkins University Press, 1981), p. 83. Gernet makes this point by analyzing the passage from *Agamemnon*, the episode which immediately precedes Agamemnon's death: 'Agamemnon accomplishes his own destruction by likening himself to the gods and by accepting the sinister consecration that contact with the purple cloth brings with it. And if, before admitting defeat, Agamemnon's last word can be taken as an expression of shame over the waste of such a thing of luxury, we can find in this scene, if we desire, witness of a bourgeois form of avarice.'

intrinsic nature of this type of treasure is its ambiguity which can lead either to the owner's triumph, or to his demise, or indeed to both.

As anthropologist Zurab Kiknadze has pointed out, in Georgian folklore and mythology accidentally discovered treasure must invariably and inevitably belong to the community, that is to say, to the political community, and must be put to political use. The treasure will never cede itself to a person who does not represent the community or, as a private person, does not represent a body politic. The rarely successful encounter between the treasure and the hunter is a manifestation of the person's charisma, his mandate to rule or indeed to act as a priest. Therefore, the treasure effectively reveals the two bodies of its discoverer, the physical and the political, and only such a charismatic person can put the treasure to proper use.

While P'arnavaz's rite of passage is modelled after Zoroastrian religious and epic traditions, his adventure is also a typical example of the foundation myths spread across Caucasian oral traditions. The foundation myths of a village, a tribe, a religious community, or larger polities, known in the east Georgian highlands as the *andrezis*, often recount a hunter's unexpected discovery of hidden treasure. In most cases, however, the *andrezis* are pessimistic accounts that focus on the unsuccessful, or indeed tragic, encounters between a hunter and the treasure, which often result in forgetfulness or in extreme cases in a catastrophic resolution. Other *andrezis* recount stories of a hunter's transformation into a priest who, during a hunt, witnessed an unexpected hierophany, such as a cross or a divine dove, and as a result founded a religious or a political community on that same spot[18].

One typical account, for example, tells a story of Torghva the hunter, a pretender to the royal throne, who was an illegitimate descendant of the royal Bagrationi dynasty. Although Torghva was a historical person and lived in the fourteenth century, he was soon transposed into the realm of mythology. Torghva was entrusted to hold the Pankisi valley by the king, when he rebelled and wished to take control of the valley. One day he was chasing a wondrous deer in the forests, when he stumbled upon an ancient ruin. Inside he discovered a massive treasure. The treasure was protected by a sword-wielding giant and an eagle-like bird. Torghva escaped through the same entrance and the entrance immediately vanished. The *andrezi* draws a moral conclusion: 'For this reason it is said among us, that if the treasure does not give itself to you, neither you nor your family will profit from it'[19].

---

[18] Kiknadze, *k'art'uli mit'ologia*, II, pp. 152–53.

[19] Zurab Kiknadze, *andrezebi* (Tbilisi: Ilia University Press, 2009), p. 243. Crucially, Torghva is both a historical figure whose story is recounted in the *Life of Georgia*, and also a figure of

Another *andrezi* narrates a story of a farmer who was ploughing above the ruins of an ancient fortress, where unexpectedly a treasure revealed itself to him. On top of the treasure was a golden ram. Immediately, the farmer lost his mind and altogether forgot how he came to the place or the whereabouts of the cavity[20]. Yet another tale recounts a story of a man who discovered hidden treasure but did not dare to take it, and instead fled the place in terror. Eventually it turned out that although the treasure was indeed destined for him, the hunter had missed his chance. The second time he visited the place, both the treasure and the cave had vanished[21]. Many other anecdotes associated with foundation myths narrate stories of priests and shepherds who discover treasure but eventually lose their minds and either perish or wander off the territory in forgetfulness.

The tragic consequences of the encounter of a hunter with treasure are mostly due to a lack of charisma on the part of the discoverer, a character failing that can be revealed only at the moment of the encounter with the treasure. Thus, as great as the persons who come across the treasure may be, unless they transcend their physical bodies and acquire political roles, the consequences will be dire. Often the accidental discovery of treasure by an epic hero is not a good omen, but quite the opposite. Thus, the discovery of treasure by Siegfried is the trigger that leads to all the catastrophes and tragedies that have befallen him and nearly everyone in the *Nibelungenlied*. Although the epic heroes come across the treasure, they are not the charismatic owners of the treasure, and it may only belong to the king's political body. By contrast, in the Georgian *Knight in the Panther's Skin* (twelfth-thirteenth centuries) the protagonist of the narrative, general Tariel, the rightful heir to the throne of India, accidentally stumbles on treasure during a hunt, which eventually guarantees his success, the rescue of the princess, and their prosperous reign in the Kingdom of India.

The 'Treasure' of a Christian King

In Caucasian and eastern Anatolian folklore, in several instances the physical treasure is replaced by a mysteriously lost grave of a legendary figure. This historic person is almost invariably Queen Tamar, Georgia's twelfth-century monarch and saint. The place and circumstances of Tamar's burial have traditionally been surrounded by an aura of mystery and generated a series of folk

---

folklore. The story of his hunt is a folkloric addition to the medieval chronicle. For additional comments on this event, see Kiknadze, *P'arnavaz's Dream*, pp. 19–20.

[20] Kiknadze, *andrezebi*, p. 150.

[21] Kiknadze, *andrezebi*, p. 217.

traditions and foundation myths. In the following oral account recorded by James Oliver Wardrop in Georgia in the late nineteenth century, the grave of the queen plays an identical role as the treasure of the Caucasian *andrezis*:

> The inhabitants of Murghuli, in Artvin, claim that she [Tamar] is buried there and that anyone who steps over her grave becomes mad. One evening a shepherd fell asleep on her grave, and in the morning he was mad. He wandered in the forests and wild beasts did him no harm. The people asked him where the grave was, but he had forgotten. Once again he was led by God's command to Tamar's tomb and prayed to the King[22] to cure him. He became well, but could not remember where the tomb was[23].

The most striking analogy, which shares all the features of the above-mentioned oral and written accounts, is found in the *History of the Albanians*, in the opening of Chapter 2, in the story of Babik, prince of Siwnik'. Babik is introduced as the son of Andok, the former prince of Siwnik', who fell out of favour with the Shah Shapuh II (309–79). However, following Babik's victory in a combat with the king of Huns, Shapuh restored to Babik his father's lands and honours. Once Babik's legal rights to rule have been restored, his metaphysical legitimation followed:

> [Babik] crossed the Arax River and built a village called Akorz, that is to say 'the first of the patrimonial [territories] to be wrested away [from the Persians]'. During the first year of his reign, Babik went out hunting, roaming around and looking at his deserted country. Coming to Šałat', he climbed a hill, and a deer started up and fled towards the mound covering the church. When Babik pursued it, the stag disappeared on the hill. Then [Babik's] horse's hoofs sank into the earth. Babik dismounted and freed his horse with the greatest difficulty. Everyone was astonished, and when they dug the earth away they found the beautiful church full of divine treasure and smelling sweetly. That day was the first day in the month of Hor'i. Those assembled there performed a great service on that day, and great healing took place among those present. Unbelievers who observed this were converted. Gor and Gazan, two wealthy brothers who had followed Babik with many other troops, were baptized. Then Babik drew lots [to reward them]. Gor received the village of Xot, while the younger Gazan was allotted the desirable Šałat'[24].

---

[22] Tamar is by tradition referred to as the king, not queen.

[23] Oxford, Bodleian Libraries, MS. Wardr. c. 26.

[24] Movsēs Kałankatwac'i, *Patmowt'iwn Ałowanic 'Ašxarhi* [History of the Land of Ałuank'], ed. by M. Ēmin (Tiflis, 1912), pp. 124–25; *Movses Dasxurants'i's History of the Aghuans*, trans. Robert Bedrosian (Long Branch, NJ: Robert Bedrosian, 2010), p. 52.

Although it is never explicitly stated, by 'treasure' the author refers to the relics of the saints. This ambiguity of phrasing is retained in several translations and studies that have suggested that Babik had indeed discovered material treasure. Another curious fact is that although the miraculous healings unequivocally suggest that the reference is to the relics of saints, the saints whose relics were discovered are not identified. This is indeed atypical, as the relics of the saints are not normally mentioned in passing and anonymously, and their identity matters. It is therefore entirely possible that the original story of Babik, or the schema of the story, had indeed referred to physical treasure as a manifestation of Babik's royal investiture, and that it was later Christianized by the editors of the *History of the Albanians*.

In late antique Christian narratives, the relics of the saints often reveal affinities with the royal treasure in their political nature and their refusal to belong anywhere other than a specific political or ecclesiastic community. The relics also act as the symbols of monastic and other communal foundations. Although not in the context of the foundation of a political realm, the fourth-century Syriac *Martyrdom of Pinhas* recounts a miracle of punishment, in which the relics punish their illicit owner, because legally they belong to an ecclesiastical community. Here too, as in Babik's case, ambiguity is retained with reference to the relics, specifically the joint from a finger of Pinhas, which is consistently rendered as a pearl[25].

No other late antique narrative, however, is so strongly invested in the political theology of saints' relics as the *Life of Vač'agan*. Vač'agan's journey to kingship is indeed extraordinary in its elaborate and complex incorporation of the relics of the saints in its political rhetoric. Unlike the story of Babik, which was crystallized in different circumstances than those of the first chapter of the *History of the Albanians*, the story of Vač'agan, his quest, and the discovery of the saints' relics reveals levels of complexity unknown to other similar late antique accounts. Vač'agan's entire story is built on his discovery of the relics of the martyrs, an act which serves as the main rite of passage in Vač'agan's road to legitimate kingship.

Similarly to P'arnavaz, the Albanian Vač'agan is also credited with reforms that became fundamental to Albanian identity. He restored and fortified orthodox Christianity by expelling dissent and heresy, united Albania in Christian faith, promulgated laws, and essentially defined the essence of the Albanian body politic. Vač'agan's adventures also represent the rite of passage

---

[25] For commentary, see Adam McCollum, *The Story of Mar Pinhas*, Persian Martyr Acts in Syriac: Text and Translation 2, (Piscataway, NJ: Gorgias Press, 2013), p. 27. See also CSLA E00252 (Sergey Minov).

of a charismatic king, accompanied by dreams, visions, apparitions, and other omens. Like Pʻarnavaz's Iberia, Vačʻagan's Albania saw a transformation from the lawlessness of the forests to a Christian state[26]. The structural components of the two narratives point to a deeper shared understanding of the stages of royal investiture. The journey of Vačʻagan to kingship is, I believe, structurally identical to that of Pʻarnavaz. All the liminal stages highlighted in Pʻarnavaz's story are present in Vačʻagan's account.

Vačʻagan's story opens with his presentation as the rightful heir to the throne, as he is the brother of Vačʻē of Albania, in contrast to his immediate predecessor. This is followed by his acknowledgment as a suzerain by Albanian lords and chieftains[27]. Crucially, the right to kingship of both of these figures is confirmed by the ecumenical king — in Pʻarnavaz's case this was Antiochos, while for the author of Vačʻagan's *Life* the universal king was the Iranian Shah Yazdegerd. Indeed, both receive the appropriate mandate. Thus, by descent, by popular acclaim, and by imperial mandate, both men are rightful heirs to the throne and become kings. Pʻarnavaz's dream and the descent of *farrah* is readily replaced by the light of Vačʻagan's baptism. Having repented and confessed to his former magianism, he was baptized and thus received the divine light. It is immediately afterwards that Vačʻagan undertakes the most important quest of his life for the relics of Albania's first martyrs. This episode takes the better part of Vačʻagan's entire story. However, unlike Pʻarnavaz's discovery of the treasure, his quest for the relics of the martyrs is a much more elaborate and detailed story, involving a series of processions with relics and accompanied by dreams, visions, clues, and apparitions, all leading to the discovery of the main saints of Caucasian Albania. The processions organized by Vačʻagan serve one primary purpose, to unite and mark the limits of his realm, the new Christian Kingdom of Albania. Immediately after the quest is finished and these relics revealed, Vačʻagan promulgates church canons and establishes one 'national' religion across Albania. His initiative were very similar to Pʻarnavaz's final deeds.

Thus, the two narratives present the process of the initiation of the kings and, most importantly, the demarcation of the limits of their realms. The four major stages in initiation are legitimate descent, popular acclaim, imperial validation, and the revelation of divine *farrah* through the discovery of divine treasure by the two kings. Crucially, this treasure in both cases is used specifically and exclusively for the purpose of defining and circumscribing

---

[26] This lawlessness is highlighted by bizarre sects spread in Albania, particularly that of the 'thumbcutters' whom Vačʻagan discovered in a forest.

[27] Movses Daskhurantsi, *History*, p. 21.

the political and the religious limits of the realm. While the treasure belongs
to the kings, immediately upon discovery they relinquish it and invest it in
the body politic. In Vač'agan's case this is specifically done through the distribution of the relics of Albania's founding saints across his realm and the
majestic procession with the relics. The relics of the saints, as conceptualized
in Vač'agan's story, resemble the Christianized treasure of P'arnavaz, because
both carry metaphysical and political meaning[28]. Vač'agan's relics, however,
unlike Babik's discovery, are not just relics of unidentified saints. Here the
political relevance of the relics lies in their identity.

Theology and the Politics of Saints' Relics: Agathangelos' Model

Agathangelos' *Life of Gregory the Illuminator* provides the earliest description and theologization on the nature and function of the relics of the saints
in political and identity discourse in Caucasian writing. Because the *Life* was
written when native Arsacid kingship ceased to exist in Armenia, it was Patriarch Gregory who acts as the founder of the new Christian Armenia with
its new religious hierarchical system. Gregory himself is presented as a martyr
who survives the pagan Armenian King T'rdat's torture and through divine
intercession and miracle converts him. As in P'arnavaz's story, the story of
Gregory the Illuminator is a rite of passage of Armenia from a pagan and
barbaric people to a Christian nation and an integral part of the Christian
Oecumene.

The political theologization over the essence of the new Christian Armenian nation is manifested in two crucial episodes that immediately follow
King T'rdat's conversion. One is a sermon in which Gregory recounts and
explains the universal salvation history from Creation to Incarnation, eventually culminating in the creation of Christian nations, specifically Armenia.
In Gregory's perception, the martyrdom of the virgins Hrip'simē and Gayanē
is an act of apostolic significance which has confirmed the universal message

---

[28] Rollason, 'Relic-Cults as an Instrument of Royal Policy *c.* 900–*c.* 1040', *Anglo-Saxon England* 15 (1986), 91–103 (p. 93). See also Julia Smith, 'Rulers and Relics *c.* 750–*c.* 950: Treasure
on Earth, Treasure in Heaven', *Past & Present*, 206 (2010), Supplement 5 (*Relics and Remains*,
ed. by Alexandra Walsham), pp. 73–96: '... relics which passed through royal hands evinced
an unusual, indeed exceptional, ability to transform one kind of value into another. According to the anonymous eleventh-century author, Æthelstan had turned 'transitory treasure'
into 'everlasting treasure' by acquiring relics; in effect, he converted economic capital into
symbolic capital. In view of the various possible components of that symbolic value, royal
possession greatly enhanced the potential for a political or commemorative "charge" to over-
lay relics' inherent spiritual value; it also increased the likelihood that these mean fragments
might be enclosed in new, sumptuous wrappings and display containers. An 'inter-converta-
bility' of valencies thus marked relics as a special type of royal treasure'.

of the Gospel and marks the final stage in the history of salvation. The intercessory powers of Hrip'simē and Gayanē are provided to the king and to the political realm: 'Behold the thirty-seven Christian cups who came to serve you!'[29] Gregory thus addresses T'rdat, the king of Armenia:

> But now God has sent his Son to mankind who came and walked on earth and sent his disciples throughout the whole world. These blessed ones [Hrip'simē and Gayanē], who have come as far as you, have shown you not only mere words, but also signs of their miracles through your punishments. Although yesterday you [T'rdat] killed them, they are God's and now are living and will live forever. By their intercession you will be reconciled with God according to the instructions of the companion apostle to those apostles of yours, the great Paul, who said: 'Through us be reconciled with God by the death of his Son [II Cor. 5:18]'. For the Son of God died and lived, and likewise his beloved martyrs are alive and intercede for you[30].

The second crucial episode is an account of Gregory's vision. This vision is perhaps the most important apocalyptic episode in late antique Armenian writing and crucial for subsequent Armenian identity discourse[31]. Here Gregory theologizes on the first martyrs of the Armenian tradition, the virgins Hrip'simē and Gayanē, and elaborates on the foundation of the Armenian Church. He sees the two martyrs, along with the priesthood in general, as pillars of the Church. In his vision, Gregory sees how the Armenian nation, embedded in its Church, is based on the relics of these saints:

> And I looked up and saw three other bases: one in the place where saint Gayanē was martyred with her two companions, and one in the place where saint Hrip'simē was martyred with her thirty-two companions, and one in the place of the wine-press. And these bases were red, the colour of blood, and the columns were of clouds and the capitals of fire. And on top of the three columns were crosses of light in the likeness of the Lord's cross. And the crosses of these columns were level with the capital of the column of light, for that one was higher than they. And from the four columns, above the crosses, marvellous vaults fitted into each other. And above this I saw a canopy of cloud, wonderfully and divinely constructed in the form

---

[29] Robert W. Thomson, *The Teaching of St Gregory* (New Rochelle, NY: Saint Narsess Armenian Seminary, 2001), p. 169. Thirty-seven is the supposed number of the refugee virgins who had followed Hrip'simē and Gayanē to Armenia and were martyred by King T'rdat.
[30] Thomson, *Teaching*, p. 180.
[31] Among other studies, the vision of Gregory as an apocalyptic text is discussed in the contributions by Robert W. Thomson, Giusto Traina & Zaza Aleksidze in *The Armenian Apocalyptic Tradition, a Comparative Perspective*, ed. by Kevork Bardakjian & Sergio La Porta (Leiden: Brill, 2014).

263

of a dome. Under the canopy but above the vaults I saw these thirty-seven holy martyrs in shining light, with white garments, which I am not capable of describing[32].

After recounting his vision, Gregory and everyone present start building Armenia's first church. For this purpose, Gregory brings the relics of two martyr saints, John the Baptist and the martyr Athenogenes, who was killed during the Emperor Diocletian's persecution.[33] The choice of relics, although not explicitly explained, is yet again symbolic and serves as a material confirmation of his sermon and vision. John the Baptist acts as a mediator between the two covenants, the Old and the New, as a symbol of the transition to Christianity, and as an emblem of universal salvation history. In addition, John is the proto-martyr, the earliest witness of Christ and a martyr for the faith. Athenogenes, on the other hand, is a recent martyr and, crucially, a martyr of Caesarea in Cappadocia, where the Armenian apostolic Church traditionally takes its legitimacy and origin. Therefore the relics of the two saints underline Armenia's belonging both to universal salvation history and to the recent history of Christianity and its hierarchy. These two relics, however, are validated by the relics of the proper Armenian martyrs and virgins, Hrip'simē and Gayanē, killed by King T'rdat himself before his punishment and eventual conversion. While John and Athenogenes are saints and martyrs of the Universal Church, Hrip'simē and Gayanē are national martyrs; this combination legitimates the *raison d'être* of the Christian Armenian nation. Therefore, through the interaction of three levels of Christian history embodied in three types of relics, the essence of the Armenian Church and, *mutatis mutandis*, of the Armenian body politic are validated and constitute the basis of Armenianness and its integrity.

Vač'agan's Quest

The *Life of Vač'agan* faithfully adopts Gregory's political theology of saints' relics and adapts it to Albanian rhetoric. Vač'agan's quest and discovery of relics is one of the most elaborate and complicated narratives of the genre, and to my knowledge it has no analogy in contemporary Christendom[34]. The final goal of the processions and the quest is the discovery of the relics of Albania's founding patriarch and first martyr, Grigoris (grandson of Gregory

---

[32] Robert W. Thomson, *The Lives of Saint Gregory: The Armenian, Greek, Arabic, and Syriac Versions of the History attributed to Agathangelos* (Ann Arbor, MI: Caravan Books, 2010), pp. 213–74. See also CSLA E01134 (Nikoloz Aleksidze).
[33] See CSLA E00102 (Nikoloz Aleksidze).
[34] For a study, see Mahé, 'Vac'agan III', pp. 113–29.

the Illuminator). As with the relics of Hripʻsimē and Gayanē which Gregory presents as the pillars of the Armenian Church and the nation, Grigoris is both the instrument of Christianization and a martyr on Albania's soil. Following Agathangelos' model, the author's intention is to define the place of Albania's political body in universal salvation history by describing a ritualized procession and by including the relics in political rhetoric. Grigoris's relics can be discovered only through the intercession and physical guidance of the relics of other saints.

While Vačʻagan's ultimate purpose is to discover the national saint who founded the Albanian Church and was martyred in Albania, he achieves this through a journey with the relics of two other central saints. Mirroring Agathangelos, these are the relics of Zechariah, a New Testament martyr and father of John the Baptist, and Pantaleon, who, like Athenogenes, was martyred in Nicomedia during the persecution of Diocletian. These relics were allegedly brought to Albania by Grigoris himself when he established Christianity in the country; but since then they have been lost just like the relics of Grigoris himself.

> The venerable [Grigoris] took along with him [to Albania] the marvellous and most revered stipend [of all], the honoured blood of the great patriarch and martyr Zechariah, John's father, and the relics of Saint Pantaleon who confessed the true faith of Christ and was martyred in the city of Nicomedia. [Grigoris] brought the most holy relics of the martyrs to the great city of Cʻri in the principality of the Albanians. He constructed a small church there and with great care he placed in it a portion of Zechariah's blood and some of the remains of Saint Pantaleon[35].

After Vačʻagan's accession to the Albanian throne, the relics of Zechariah and Pantaleon began to manifest themselves in miracles as a premonition of a new era in Albania's political history, reminding us of similar miracles of healing and punishment exercised by the royal treasures:

> Numerous signs and miracles took place in the city named Cʻri in that spot where the relics of the holy martyrs in Christ lay, although no one knew precisely where the remains of the saints were. Despite the fact that the inhabitants of the land were pagans, those with fevers and illnesses went to the church where the relics lay and took earth from the place. Many of these people, though pagans, were greatly cured nonetheless. The foolish religion of the evil Persians, which was always in opposition to the Church of God, [was practiced by] a certain Persian mage who came to the place

---

[35] Movsēs Kałankatwacʻi, *Patmowtʻiwn*, p. 47; Movses Daskhurantsi, *History*, p. 15. See also CSLA E00134 (Nikoloz Aleksidze).

where these relics lay to mock them by relieving himself on them. However, when he loosened his pants, his intestines fell out upon the earth, and he died in the greatest agony[36].

Therefore, the relics of Grigoris on the one hand and of Zechariah and Pantaleon on the other validate each other and create a political and theological dialectic of the universal and the national. But the author of the *History* does not fail to add another dimension to the Albanian quest for identity. As noted by J.-P. Mahé, the author must have been an Armenophile Albanian, whose literary language was the Armenian in which he composed the narrative; association with the Armenian tradition and presenting Albanian history as an integral part of Armenian history was therefore imperative. The author makes sure to incorporate in Vač'agan's quest also the relics of the Armenian saints and martyrs, Gregory the Illuminator, Hrip'simē, and Gayanē.

> King Vač'agan's letter to all the bishops and priests asked that, through their prayers, the hidden treasure [i.e. the relics of St Grigoris] might be revealed to him... At this, all the bishops assembled the priests, deacons, and clergy under their jurisdictions, and carrying the Lord's Cross, they quickly and unitedly gathered at the king's own personal village called Diwtakan. Great punishment was stipulated for those who delayed. [At Diwtakan] they greatly celebrated the memory of the Saints for three days. Now the king had a custom of standing and paying homage to the entire clergy which had assembled there. He had located the most holy relics of Gregory and the most celebrated Hrip'simē and Gayanē at Darahoj village in the state of Arcax, which a priest named Matt'ē had brought from the Armenian katholikos Yovhannēs Mandakuni [478–90], and which had been sealed by his ring [in reliquaries]. [King Vač'agan] sent for these relics and had them brought to him. When [the relics of] great Gregory arrived at the great assembly at Diwtakan, together with his comrades in martyrdom Hrip'simē and Gayanē, the king, queen, and all the grandee lords travelled a good distance out from the village to meet them ... Thus did the king with the greatest joy greet the saints along with the crowd. The king himself solicitously attended the priest who carried the relics. Bringing them to the resting place of the saints, he placed them with [the remains of the] venerable Zechariah and Pantaleon. Then the benevolent king trusted in the firm faith and virtuousness of the people and declared: 'Now I am certain that through the intercession of the great Gregory, God will grant me the most holy relics of [Gregory's grandson], the blessed Grigoris.'... They took along with them the five holy martyrs of Christ, that is, the great Gregory, the

---

[36] Movsēs Kałankatwac'i, *Patmowt'iwn*, pp. 65–66; Movses Daskhurantsi, *History*, p. 24.

venerable Zechariah, the most blessed Pantaleon, and the most renowned and victorious combatants Hrip'simē and Gayanē to intercede with great and all-powerful God so that through them his request would be fulfilled[37].

The story of Vač'agan is an ingenious example of an attempt to restore the thread of memory between contemporary times and the earlier era of the foundation of Christianity associated with Grigoris, the legendary first patriarch and martyr of Albania[38]. The relics of Grigoris symbolize the essence of the Albanian polity and validate it as an integral part of universal salvation history, recent Christian history, and the Armenian cultural orbit.

After the discovery of the relics of Grigoris, Vač'agan, as a true monarch, distributes them across his realm and uses them to circumscribe the religious and political limits of his reborn kingdom. Therefore, immediately upon their invention, the relics acquire a political value and become symbols of the Albanian polity. This lengthy and earnest procession is the culmination of Vač'agan's quest:

> The king ordered that a portion of the relics be given to each of the bishops to distribute among their dioceses, while the largest share was to remain in Amaras. With great care he himself placed the remainder in different vessels and then sealed them with his ring... Thus did the pious King Vač'agan acquire the spiritual and otherworldly booty which is the source of permanent and unrelatable goodness. No king before him, none of his ancestors, had ever received such marvellous gifts. The Christian camp also received a portion, thereby gaining indescribable riches from the mercy of God through King Vač'agan. I do not regard him as any less worthy of praise than the Emperor Constantine who ruled in the West or the Arsacid T'rdat who found salvation for Greater Armenia, since this blessed man did the same thing for us Easterners. He was the door to the light of knowledge of God, the model of many virtues... As they departed, the king went on foot, and the whole procession walked along with quiet, slow steps, like water flowing to a calm sea. The air itself rejoiced with harmonious sounds and glittering reflections. Even the angels sang in accompaniment, and it was as if the earth had become heaven ... Thus did they reach the king's own village of Diwtakan. There they laid [the relics] to rest performing a great memorial service for them. The king ordered that the relics of the saints should be anointed with precious oil[39].

---

[37] Movsēs Kałankatwac'i, *Patmowt'iwn*, pp. 66–72; Movses Daskhurantsi, *History*, pp. 29–31. See also CSLA E00888 (N. Aleksidze).

[38] Mahé, 'Vac'agan III', p. 118.

[39] Movsēs Kałankatwac'i, *Patmowt'iwn*, pp. 90–91; Movses Daskhurantsi, *History*, pp. 38–39. See also CSLA E00861 (N. Aleksidze).

Conclusion

Early medieval Caucasian political and theological discourse is a veritable crossroads of Iranian and Christian imagery. Despite the attempts to Christianize earlier accounts, Zoroastrian strata have firmly persisted in both historical and hagiographic accounts. This, I believe, is particularly evident with regard to the idea of kingship in both Armenian and Georgian narratives. Soon after the establishment of Christianity in the region, the cult of the saints was incorporated into the ethno-political discourse of the three Caucasian peoples, and the models formulated in Late Antiquity became instrumental in later political and religious rhetoric up until the twentieth century.

Vač'agan's story is, I believe, an important addition to the study of the early cult of saints. In its political rhetoric it reveals two levels of the conceptualization of the relics of the saint. First, it adopts the Iranian models of initiation to kingship and transforms the Iranian symbolism of royal investiture into Christian imagery. This is essentially achieved by Christianizing the divinely gifted treasure. Second, the treasure-relics embody political and theological meanings upon which the perception of Albanian body politic rests. In this the relics embody universal salvation history and guarantee the rightful place to Albania's metaphysical and political body in the history of the Christian nations.

Abstracts

Robin M. Jensen, "Icons as Relics: Relics as Icons"

Although the cult of relics emerged and became established somewhat earlier than the veneration of saints' portraits, both forms of Christian devotional practice, fueled by the cult of saints, were in place by the beginning of the fifth century. This chapter considers the material objects at the center of these two practices (relics and icons), examining the links between the two and summarizing their similarities and differences in regard to several key aspects of their physical composition, their ritual function, and their devotees' regard. Both were representations, albeit of a fundamentally different nature. Both were replicable and portable although in different ways. Both were essentially objects meant to be viewed and handled, even to be kissed. Both were associated (although one later than the other) with answered prayers or miracles, and both raised issues of authentication or veracity. The chapter further explores evidence that both of these types of objects were sometimes considered to be (and condemned as) idolatrous and continued to be linked as theologically controversial through the early Middle Ages and beyond.

Maria Lidova, "Placing Martyrs in the Apse: Visual Strategies for the Promotion of Saints in Late Antiquity"

This chapter highlights the significance of the material evidence for the study of the cult of saints and focuses on a number of visual strategies applied in late antique monumental art for the promotion of Christian martyrs. One important strategy was the placement of images of martyrs within the apse decoration, thereby turning them into protagonists within the regular worship of the church. Three main categories are considered: when martyrs featured as protagonists, when they were depicted as members of the heavenly court, or when they were grouped in pairs in the decorations of lateral chapels and small martyrial shrines. Differentiating among these various modes of representations is essential for building a more nuanced understanding of the worship of saints in Late Antiquity, because each type of imagery would have had a distinctive impact on the perception of martyrs and on shaping ideas of Christian holiness.

ABSTRACTS

Julia DOROSZEWSKA, "Saintly In-betweeners: The Liminal Identity of Thekla and Artemios in their Late Antique Miracle Collections"

This chapter examines the literary portrayals of the protagonists of two late antique miracle collections: the fifth-century *Miracles of Thekla* (BHG 1718) and the seventh-century *Miracles of Artemios* (BHG 173–173c). It argues that the eponymous saints in their posthumous existence were represented as liminal beings, ontologically situated between God and ordinary humans. The aim of the chapter is to answer the question of how this saintly in-between status was negotiated, through a close analysis of the means used by hagiographers. Among these means were the ekphrastic descriptions of the saints' appearance, combining both human and divine qualities, as well as the ambiguous status of their apparitions, which were either corporeal or incorporeal visions and either dream-like or waking visions. The techniques included the use of disguises and tricks often employed by the saints during their interventions, as well as the time and place of their epiphanies which also had liminal qualities.

Arkadiy AVDOKHIN, "Resounding Martyrs: Hymns and the Veneration of Saints in Late Antique Miracle Collections"

In this chapter I look at a mostly neglected aspect of the late antique cult of saints — hymns and prayers addressed to them and/or performed at the sites of their veneration. Hymns and prayers as part of saints' cult are spectacularly absent both in the scholarship after Peter Brown and in studies of early Byzantine hymnody. As I suggest, this neglect arises out of particular methodological choices that centre academic attention on hymns as literary output by named authors, rather than on the lived experiences of late antique Christians interacting with saints. In order to regain and understand these experiences, I turn to miracle collections in Greek from various regions of the late antique Christian Mediterranean, including Egypt, Constantinople, and Seleucia (primarily the *Miracles of Kosmas and Damian*, the *Miracles of Thekla*, the *Miracles of Artemios*, but also other collections). These texts, I argue, reveal that performing hymns and addressing prayers to and in honour of saints constituted the core of the ritual experience of engaging with saints and martyrs, a *sine qua non* of establishing a mystical bond with them, and structured ritual behaviour when visiting healing martyrs' shrines and elsewhere.

Xavier LEQUEUX, "Les saints myroblytes en Orient et en Occident jusqu'à l'an mil: Prolégomènes à l'histoire d'un phénomène miraculeux"

The quality of myroblyte was granted to those saints whose remains or whose reliquaries had the property of distilling (βλύζω) a liquid, often

270

fragrant and endowed with healing qualities. The chapter considers the questions raised by this aspect of their cult: the nature of the exuded liquid, the context of the miracle, the popularity of the phenomenon, the variety of sources to be taken into consideration, and the sometimes dubious historicity of the accounts.

András HANDL, "Reinvented by Julius, Ignored by Damasus: Dynamics of the Cult of Callixtus in Late Antique Rome"

While the emerging cult of bishop Callixtus (?217–?222) reflected typical patterns of the development of martyrs' cults in Rome, some extraordinary circumstances made this story as intriguing as unique. Callixtus was not only an authentic martyr, but also bishop of Rome and the first local martyr after the apostles Peter and Paul to be included in the earliest extant liturgical Roman calendar of martyrs, the *Depositio martyrum*. Through a comprehensive examination of literary, hagiographic, and archaeological sources, this chapter reconstructs the cult's evolution from its origins to the early Middle Ages. It argues that Bishop Julius I (337–352) already experimented with the promotion of martyrs' cults and used most prominently Callixtus and his cult to contest (sub)urban space. Subsequently, Bishop Damasus (366–384) perfected these experimental efforts and turned martyrs' cults into a success story.

Stephanos EFTHYMIADIS, "The Cult of Saints in Constantinople (Sixth-Twelfth Century): Some Observations"

Known as the Virgin's city and teeming with churches and shrines hosting precious holy relics, Constantinople never developed the cult-worship of traditional saints (apostles and martyrs) on a level that marked other Christian cities. At times the promotion of a saint's cult was due to an emperor's personal devotion and resulted in relics brought into the imperial city. Yet, first and foremost, in Late Antiquity religious foundations dedicated to saints in the capital owed their construction or restoration to private benefactors and to the sponsorship and support from communities of immigrants coming especially from the eastern provinces. In terms of potential and dynamic, the cults of new saints after the end of Iconoclasm (843), whether of patriarchs, monks, or figures that never existed, could not compete with the saints of early Christianity. All in all, the plurality of holy shrines and relics that pilgrims and visitors to Constantinople recorded in their accounts from the twelfth century onwards points to the coexistence of many cultic microcosms rather than to an endeavour to impose monopolies on the urban religious landscape.

ABSTRACTS

Anna LAMPADARIDI, "The Origins and Later Development of the First Italo-Greek Hagiographies: The *Dossiers* of the Sicilian Martyrs Agatha, Lucia, and Euplus"

This chapter focuses on the early Sicilian hagiographical production dealing with local martyrs. Greek and Latin bilingualism clearly distinguished this first phase of Sicilian hagiographical production from the next period of local hagiographies that were basically written in Greek. I investigate the hagiographical dossiers of the Sicilian martyrs Agatha, Lucia, and Euplus, which can be dated roughly before the Byzantine conquest of the island by Justinian. Taking into consideration both Greek and Latin versions of these martyrdoms, I discuss the development of the cult of these three Sicilian martyrs in Byzantium as described in their liturgy and literary reception by later writers. The chapter thus aims to look into the transformations and resemantizations of the figures and the legends of Agatha, Lucia, and Euplus in the Byzantine world.

Ian WOOD, "The Lives of Episcopal Saints in Gaul: Models for a Time of Crisis, *c.* 470–550"

In the late fifth and early sixth centuries a significant number of hagiographical texts written in Gaul concerned bishops and their dealings with Roman and barbarian generals. It is possible to see these texts as setting out examples of ideal episcopal behaviour in a time of political crisis.

Michał PIETRANIK, "Saints and Sacred Objects in Eastern Roman Imperial Warfare: The Case of Maurice (582–602)"

Several sources portrayed the east Roman emperor Maurice (582–602) and his entourage as great enthusiasts of the cult of the saints, their relics, and images. Notably, during Maurice's reign the incorporation of numerous objects of Christian piety and worship into the sphere of war can be observed. This chapter examines the ancient evidence about the military use of relics, images, and invocations to the saints during the reign of Maurice in order to demonstrate how the sacred objects were increasingly perceived as sources of divine aid and protection in imperial warfare. The main question is whether Maurice's attitude towards relics and images promoted the creation of new ways of involving these objects in military activity.

Nikoloz ALEKSIDZE, "Martyrs, Hunters and Kings: The 'Political Theology' of Saints' Relics in Late Antique Caucasia"

In early medieval Caucasian historical narratives, i.e. Albanian, Armenian, and Georgian, the quest, a miraculous discovery, and processions with the saints' relics were established as components of a strategy of royal investiture. Although in the Roman Empire the discovery of holy relics had been part of the discourses of power since the fifth century, the Caucasian narratives introduced further dynamism in this phenomenon. Late antique Caucasian historical writing emphasized the typological similarities in stories about the discovery, ownership, and distribution of material treasure and the relics of the saints as signs of a monarch's divine investiture. The chapter argues that since in Late Antiquity Caucasia was an integral part of the Iranian commonwealth, the Iranian tropes of charismatic kingship and royal legitimacy on the one hand and the Christian cult of saints on the other have produced unique conceptualizations of the materiality and politics of saintly relics.

INDEX

Index of Saints, Persons, Places, and Subjects

Abgar (apocr.) 38, 43, 172
Abraham (bibl.) 21
Abu Girgegh (Egypt) 59-61
Adam (bibl.) 21
Adauctus and Felix (saints) 37-38
Adso 132
Aetius (general) 223-24
Agatha (saint) 69, 182-200, 205-10
Agathangelos 253, 262-65
Agaune (abbots of) 220-21
Agnes (saint) 24, 28, 53-5, 63, 68-9, 208
Ahura Mazda (deity) 255
Alaric II (king) 216, 218-19, 226-27
Alban (saint) 228
Albania (Caucasian) 252, 260-61, 265
Aldhelm 63, 184-85, 196
Alexander the Great 253
Ambrose of Milan 32, 39, 100
Anastasia (saint) 170, 220
Anastasius the Synaite 128, 130
Andrew of Crete 102, 175
Andrew the Apostle 24, 112
Andrew the Fool (saint) 179-80
angels 66, 238, 267
Anianus of Orléans 217, 224-25
Anicia Juliana 166
Anthony of Lérins 216
Anthony of Novgorod 161
Antiochos I Soter (king) 255
Antipas of Pergamon 132
Apamea (Syria) 235, 245
Apollinaris of Ravenna (saint) 51-53
Apollinaris of Valence (saint) 218, 220-21, 223-27
apse 24, 26, 47-47
Arax (river) 259
Aristotle 23
Armazi, see Ahura Mazda

Armenia 253, 262-8
Arsacids 262, 267
Artemios (saint) 81, 83, 89-95, 104-05, 107-08, 110-14, 175-76
Asterius of Amasea 33, 58
Athanasius of Methone 191
Athenogenes (saint) 264-65
Attila (king) 217, 219, 224-27
Audoin/Ouen of Rouen (saint) 133
Augustine 30-31, 39, 125, 222, 227
Autun (Gaul) 133, 228
Avars 232-34, 239
Azon (king) 253-55

Babik of Siwnik' 259-60
Bakchos (saint), see Sergios and Bakchos
Bahram (king) 242-43
Bari (Italy) 125, 129
Baripsabbas (saint) 174
Barsanuphios and John (monks) 9
Basil II (emperor) 190, 199, 203, 207
Basil of Caesarea 170
Basil the Younger (saint) 179
Beirut (Lebanon) 171
Bercharius/Berchaire (saint) 132
Bibian (saint) 215-17, 220, 222-23, 228
Bithynia 127, 130, 175
Blachernai (Constantinople) 164
Boukoleon (Constantinople) 172
Bullinger, Heinrich 19
Burgundians 221, 223, 225-27

C'ri (Caucasus) 265
Caecilian of Carthage 20
Caesarea Philippi (Palestine) 39
Caesarea Maritima (Palestine) 264
Caesarius of Arles 218, 220, 226, 228
calendars 110, 145, 150-51, 154, 159

INDEX OF SAINTS, PERSONS, PLACES, AND SUBJECTS

Calepodius (cemetery of) 153-56
Callixtus (saint) 141-60
Calvin, John 19
Canosa (Puglia) 133
Cappadocia 170-71, 264
Capsella Africana 38, 41
Capua (Italy) 68-69, 71
Carpocratians 23
Cassian (John) 221
Cassian of Imola (saint) 33
Cassius Dio 23
catacombs (Naples) 34, 41
catacombs (Rome) 21-22, 24-25, 34-35, 38,
    54, 57, 70, 143-48, 151-58
catacombs (Syracuse) 194
Catalaunian Plains 224
Catania (Sicily) 182-84, 186-95, 199-206, 210
Chalcedon (Bithynia) 58, 128
Chalcedonians 107, 115-16, 119-20, 231
Chalkoprateia, church 164, 243
Childeric (king) 225
Chilperic (king) 221, 226
Chlothild (queen) 225
choir 112-13
Choricius of Gaza 66
clergy 69, 113, 116, 156, 223, 226-27, 266
Clovis (king) 218-19, 225
Constantia (Constantine's sister) 30
Constantinos Akropolites 204, 210
Constantine the Jew (saint) 129
Constantine VII Porphyrogenitus (em-
    peror) 170-71, 173, 190, 209,
Constantinople 58, 89, 104-06, 113, 122, 129,
    132, 134-36, 161-80, 187, 190-94, 198-200,
    203, 207-10, 230, 237, 244-45
Constantius of Lyon 94, 215, 220-21, 228
Crispus, Crispianus, and Benedicta (saints)
    34
Cross, see True Cross
cures, see healings
Cyprian of Toulon 218
Cyprian of Carthage 33
Cyril of Alexandria 116, 119-20, 170
Cyril of Scythopolis 128
Cyrus and John (saints) 82-83, 95, 104-08,
    115-16, 119-21

Dalisandos (Cilicia) 84
Damasus 32, 149-51
Daniel (bibl.) 21, 244
Daniel the Stylite (saint) 164
Demetrios (saint) 164
demons 94-95, 116, 177
Denis (saint) 228
Dexianos 86
Diocletian (emperor) 194, 200, 264-65
Dionysius Exiguus 136
Dura Europos (Mesopotamia) 21
Dynamius of Provence 220

Edessa (Mesopotamia) 172, 239, 241
Egrisi (Georgia)
Eleutherius, Projectus, and Accolitus
    (saints) 66
Eligius (saint) 254
Elijah (bibl.) 51
Elisabeth of Constantinople (saint) 126
Elvira (Iberian Peninsula) 27, 30
Ennodius of Pavia 215-16
epiphanies 79-96
Epiphanius of Pavia 215, 218, 222, 225
Epiphanius of Salamis 30-31
Eptadius of Cervon 219, 225, 228
Etna (Sicily) 183, 191
Eucharist 18, 42, 111, 223
Eucherius of Lyon 221
Eugenios of Trebizond 131
Eugippius 218, 220, 228
eulogia 41-42
Euphemia (saint) 33, 56-58,
Euphrasius of Poreč 64, 66, 72-74
Euplus (saint) 200-05
Euric (king) 227
Eusebius of Caesarea 30-31, 39-40,
Eusebius of Thessalonica 238
Eusebius of Vercelli 75
Euthymios of Constantinople (saint) 178
Eutropius of Orange 215, 222
Evagrius Scholasticus 236-37, 241, 246
Eve (bibl.) 21

farrah 250-51, 254-55, 261
Faustus of Riez 221

278

INDEX OF SAINTS, PERSONS, PLACES, AND SUBJECTS

Febronia (saint) 82, 91, 175
Felicitas (saint) 55-57, 69
Felix II (pope) 150
Felix IV (pope) 64
Felix of Nola (saint) 124, 126, 128, 133, 137
Felix, see Adauctus and Felix
Flavian of Vercelli 75
Forerunner, see John the Baptist
Forty Martyrs of Sebaste 79, 103, 110, 134, 245
Franks 216, 225

Galla Placidia (mausoleum of) 75
Gaudentius of Brescia 68
Gaza (Palestine) 9, 66, 77
Gelasius I (pope) 183
Genovefa of Paris (saint) 217, 224-25, 228
George (saint) 113, 168
George of Pisidia 236
Georgios Maniakes 172, 193, 199-200, 205
Georgios Skylitzes 172
Germanus of Auxerre 215, 221-22, 225, 228
Gertrude of Nivelles (saint) 132
Gervasius and Protasius (saints) 39, 69
Glykeria (saint) 134-35, 233
Gregory of Antioch 237
Gregory of Nazianzos 170-71
Gregory of Nyssa 32-33, 109-10, 170
Gregory of Tours 124-26, 217-18, 239
Gregory the Great 31, 184, 195, 200
Gregory the Illuminator 253, 262-67
Grigoris of Albania 264-67
Gundobad (king) 223-25
Gundovald (usurper) 239

Hagia Eirene (Constantinople) 134
Hagia Sophia (Constantinople) 47, 166, 232
Hagia Soros (Constantinople) 164-65
healings 21, 39-41, 79-95, 103-22, 167, 175, 177, 194, 245, 259, 265-66
Hermagoras of Aquileia 73
Hierapolis (Syria) 171
Hilary of Arles 220
Hodegetria (church of) 165
Holy Apostles (church of) 163, 166-71
Holy Tile (relic) 171

Honorius I (pope) 55, 57
Hrip'simē and Gayanē (saints) 262-67
Hyacinthos of Amastris 126
hymns 97-159, 230

Iberia (Caucasian) 249-68
iconoclasm 18-19, 26-27, 77, 170, 173, 179
icons 17-46, 58, 171, 178-79, 241
incense 41, 108
incubation 79-122
Ioannes Kaminiatès 131
Ioannes Tzetzes 199, 210
Ioannes Tzimiskes 171
Irenaeus of Lyon 23-24, 41
Irene of Chrysobalanton (saint) 179-80
Isaac (bibl.) 21

Januarius (saint) 34, 36, 38, 41
John and Paul (saints) 34
John and Paul (church of), see Santi Giovanni e Paolo
John Chrysostom 32, 135, 170, 234
John of Ephesus 246
John of Epiphaneia 246
John of Jerusalem 30
John of Nikiu 246
John the Baptist 105, 136, 167-68, 170-71, 175-76, 264-65
John the Evangelist 124-25
John the Faster 178, 244
Jonah (bibl.) 21, 24
Joseph the Stoudites 179
Julia Florentina 183, 200
Julius (pope) 146-53, 159
Jura Fathers (saints) 220
Justinian (emperor) 161, 166, 168, 177-78, 182, 232-33, 238

K'uji of Egrisi 254-45
Kalvisianos 200-04
Kalykadnos (Isauria) 82
Kamouliana (Cappadocia) 43, 245
Kartli (Caucasus), see Iberia
kerōtē 108, 110
Khosrow II (king) 235, 242-44
Komentiolos (general) 237

279

INDEX OF SAINTS, PERSONS, PLACES, AND SUBJECTS

Kosmas and Damian (saints) 26, 64-65, 73-74, 82-83, 104-07, 110, 114-15, 127, 177
Kosmidion (church) 105-06, 177

Lawrence (saint) 33, 63, 69, 136, 208
Leo of Catania (saint) 191-92, 195, 202, 206
Leo I (emperor) 237
Leo VI (emperor) 169-70, 178
Lérins (Gaul) 214
Levesque de Burigny, Jean 191
Liberius (pope) 54, 146, 150
Limenius of Vercelli 75
Limousin (Gaul) 225
Litorius (general) 223, 226
liturgy 18, 20, 42, 48-50, 55, 59, 77-78, 97-122, 144-45, 150-51, 159, 179, 182, 184-85, 190, 198, 210, 223, 230, 233, 243, 246
Lucia (saint) 184, 194-200, 205-06
Lucifera 183
Lucilla of Carthage 20, 42, 45
Luke of Sicily (saint) 132
Luke of Steiris (saint) 130
Luke the Evangelist 163
Lupus of Troyes (saint) 217, 220, 224-25
Luther, Martin 18-19

Magnus Maximus (emperor) 216
Mandylion of Edessa 38, 43, 171
Manuel I Komnenos 172
Marcel the Archimandrite 136
Marcellus of Die 216-18, 220, 223-24
Martin (saint) 126, 221
Mary Pammakaristos (church of) 173
Mary, Mother of God 19, 21, 24, 26, 29, 37-38, 42, 47, 49-50, 54, 61-67, 83, 95, 164-65, 170, 173, 176, 242-43
Matrona of Perge (saint) 136
Maurice (emperor) 135, 168, 178, 229-48
Mauritius of Catania 193, 199
Maximos of Tarsus 85
Maximus of Riez 220
Maximus the Confessor 42
Mcxeta (Georgia) 254-55
Meletios of Antioch (saint) 32
Memorius of Troyes (saint) 219, 224-25
Menander Protector 232, 245-46
Menouthis (Egypt) 105, 115-16, 119

Mésaritès, Nikolaos 135
Messina (Sicily) 200
Methodius of Constantinople 127, 187, 191, 192, 199, 210
Methodius of Olympus 185-86,
Michael III (emperor) 170
Michael Psellos 193
Michael the Archangel 223
Michael the Archimandrite 131
Mirax (saint) 124, 132
Mithraism 249
Moses (bibl.) 21, 51
Movsēs Dasxuranc'i 252
Movsēs Kałankatwac'i 252
myron 123-37

Naples (Italy) 34, 36, 41, 201
Nereus and Achilleus (saints) 69
Nicolas of Myra (saint) 125, 129, 131, 137
Nikephoros of Constantinople 178
Nikephoros Phokas (emperor) 171-72
Nikephoros Sceuophylax 129
Niketas the Patrician 172
Nikolaos Mystikos 178
Nikon the Metanoeite 130
Niphon (saint) 179
Nola (Campania) 124-26, 128, 133

oil 41-2, 108, 126, 129, 134, 136-37, 187-88, 245
Optatus of Milevis 20, 42
Orientius of Auch (saint) 215-17, 220-23
Orléans (Gaul) 226
Ossettes 255
Ouen, see Audoin of Rouen (saint)
Oxeia (Constantinople) 113, 175-76

P'arnavaz 251, 262-67
Palermo (Sicily) 183-92, 205, 209-10
Palestine 66, 103, 119
Pammachius 34-35
Pancharios (saint) 174
Pancras of Taormina (saint) 200, 206
Paneas (Palestine) 39
panēgyris 109-10, 112
pannychis 109-16
Pantaleon (saint) 69, 176, 265
Pantepoptes (monastery of) 173

280

INDEX OF SAINTS, PERSONS, PLACES, AND SUBJECTS

Pantokrator (monastery of) 173
Paschasios (governor) 194, 196
Patiens of Lyon 215, 221-22
Patras (Greece) 124, 191
Paul the Apostle 9, 21, 24, 28, 33-34, 64, 72, 159, 201, 244, 263
Paul the Deacon 215
Paulinus of Nola 42, 124
Pege (Constantinople) 165, 233
Pera (Constantinople) 177
Peribleptos (monastery of) 173
Persians 92, 164, 231-35, 237, 239, 242-44, 250-55, 261, 265, 268
Peter of Argos 191
Peter of Atroa (saint) 126, 130
Peter the Apostle 9, 21, 24-25, 28, 33, 43, 51, 63-64, 69, 72, 159, 168, 182, 185, 195, 207, 233
Petronilla (saint) 34-35, 38
Pharos (church of) 172
Philippikos 236, 237, 240-41, 246
Photios of Constantinople 47-48, 178
pilgrimage 19, 33, 44, 83, 97, 104-10, 112-13, 118-22, 153, 156-57, 161, 165, 167, 176-77, 179
Pinhas (saint) 260
Plateia (island) 113
Plato 23
Polycarp of Smyrna 9, 20,
Polyeuktos (saint) 166
Polyeuktos (patriarch) 170
Poreč (Istria) 64-65, 73, 74-75
Priscus (church of) 68-69, 71
Priskos (general) 241, 246
Procla (saint) 174
Proclus of Constantinople 134
Procopius of Cesarea 233, 235, 245
Provence (Gaul) 216, 226
Prudentius 33, 100
Psellos, Michael 193, 210
Psimethos (Sicily) 187, 189, 207
Pythagoras 23

Quintinianus (governor) 182, 185-87, 189

Ravenna (Italy) 33, 51-54, 66, 73, 184
reliquaries 33-34, 38, 41, 43-44, 119, 134-35, 241, 245, 266

Remigius of Rheims (saint) 218
Révérien/Riran (saint) 133
Rimini (Italy) 75-76
Rome 22-26, 28, 33, 35, 37, 53, 55-56, 58, 61-66, 71, 141-59, 184, 195-96, 200, 208, 210
Romanos I Lekapenos (emperor) 171, 209
Romanos the Melodist 101-03, 21-22
Ta Rouphinou (Constantinople) 176

Sabas (monk in Constantinople) 126, 130
Sampson (saint) 176-77
Sant'Agnese (Rome) 54-55
Sant'Apollinare in Classe (Ravenna) 51-54
Sant'Apollinare Nuovo (Ravenna) 184
Santa Maria in Trastevere (Rome) 146, 149
Santa Maria Maggiore (Rome) 62-63
Santi Giovanni e Paolo (Rome) 34-35
Santo Stefano Rotondo (Rome) 70-71, 76
Sardinia 141-42
Sasanians 250-51
Seleukeia (Isauria) 82-88, 97, 104-06
Serenus of Marseille 31
Sergius (pope) 57
Sergios and Bakchos (saints) 66, 69, 166, 239
Severinus of Noricum 227-28
Severus of Ravenna 73
Shapuh II 259
Sicily 181-210
Sidonius Apollinaris 221, 223, 225
Sigismund (king) 225-27
Sigolène of Troclar (saint) 132
Simeto (Sicily) 187, 189
Sixtus III (pope) 62-63
Slavs 232, 234, 239
Sophronios of Jerusalem 104, 106-07, 115-22
statues 24, 39, 58, 84
Stephanus of Lyon 215, 222
Stephen the First Martyr 39, 69, 200
Stephen the Younger (saint) 179
Sulpicius Severus 215-16, 21
Suso, Henry 18
Symeon Magistros 170
Symeon Metaphrastes 208, 210
Symeon Stylites the Elder (saint) 40, 100, 236-37
Symeon Stylites the Younger (saint) 40-41, 100

281

INDEX OF SAINTS, PERSONS, PLACES, AND SUBJECTS

Symmachus (pope) 55, 183
Symphorian (saint) 223, 228
synaxarion 124-25, 132, 135, 165, 190-93, 198-99, 203, 205, 207, 209-10
Syracuse (Sicily) 127, 187, 194-95, 197, 199, 205-06, 208, 210

T'rdat (king) 262-64, 267
Tamar (queen) 258-59
Taormina (Sicily) 200, 206, 207
Tarasios of Constantinople 178
Tarsos (Cilicia) 171
Tbilisi (Georgia) 254-55, 257
Thekla (saint) 79-91, 94-95, 97-98, 104-06, 110
Theodora (empress) 167
Theodora of Thessalonica (saint) 127, 131
Theodore (pope) 70, 72, 200
Theodore of Sykeon (saint) 129, 244
Theodore the Recruit (saint) 32, 81
Theodore the Stoudite 126
Theodore Trichinas (saint) 132
Theodoric (king) 216, 223, 27
Theodosiopolis (Armenia) 242
Theodosius I (emperor) 30, 234, 240, 244
Theodosius II (emperor) 166, 235
Theodosius of Caesarea 42
Theophanes the Confessor 126, 241
Theophylact Simocatta 134-35, 178, 232-34, 240-43, 246
Theotokos of Elaia (church of) 174
Therapon (saint) 174-75
Thessalonica 60, 124, 127, 131, 169, 238-39
Thomas of Apamea 235

Thomas the Apostle 242
Thrace 234, 236
Three Brothers of Lentini 207
Three Youths (bibl.) 21
Timothy (bibl.) 69, 163
Trevico (Campania) 205
Trisagion 115
Troyes (Gaul) 219-20, 224-25
True Cross (relic) 42-43, 171, 234-36, 245, 266
Tychon (saint) 130

Ursus of Ravenna 73, 184
Ustica (island) 183

Vač'agan I 252-53, 260-68
Valentinus (saint) 147-51, 159
Venice (Italy) 200
Victricius of Rouen 68
Vigilantius of Calagurris 41
vigils 97, 108-14, 122, 223
Virgin Mary, see Mary, Mother of God
Visigoths 99, 215-16, 218-19, 223
Vouillé (battle of) 216

Walburge (saint) 126, 133, 137

Yazdegerd 261

Zechariah, father of John the Baptist 265-67
Zoroastrianism 250-51, 257, 268
Zotikos (saint) 177